CROSSING BORDERS

CROSSING BORDERS

A personal journey
engaging the heart and mind

WILL CARR

as told to Rebecca George

GLB PUBLISHERS   **San Francisco**

Published in the United States by
GLB Publishers
P.O. Box 78212, San Francisco, CA 94107
www.GLBpubs.com

Cover Design by GLB Publishers

Library of Congress Cataloguing Control Number
2007908825

ISBN   9781934203064

1-934203-06-8

First printing Jan. 2008
10 9 8 7 6 5 4 3 2 1

*This book is dedicated
to all the angels
who protect us and
four-legged creatures
who heal us.*

Will Carr and his dog, AJ, live in Marin County, across the Golden Gate Bridge from San Francisco. He became Advertising Director, North America, for Swissair upon returning to New York. Moving to San Francisco he worked as Advertising Director of Koret of California. After completing an M.A. in Counseling, he worked as a Guidance Counselor at a Marin High School. His paintings, ceramics and photographs have been shown in galleries on both coasts. Aside from travel articles in newspapers, this is his first published book.

TABLE OF CONTENTS

Chapter   Page

There are black and white photos after pages 132, 204, 288, and 344.
There is a color-picture insert at the center of the book.

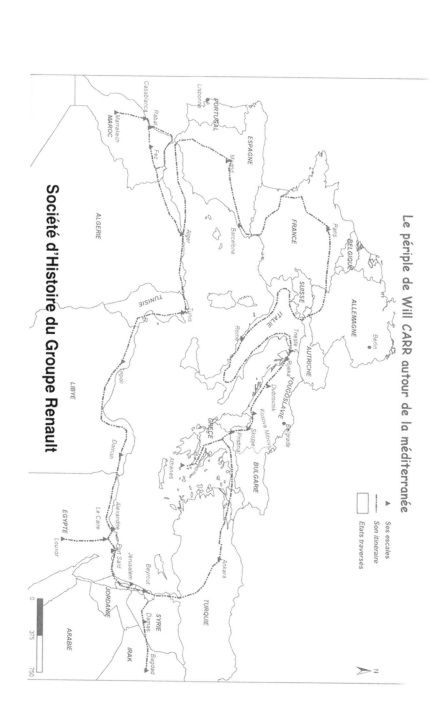

Le périple de Will CARR autour de la méditerranée

▲ Ses escales
····· Son itinéraire
☐ États traversés

Société d'Histoire du Groupe Renault

PROLOGUE

Sometimes my memories come back to me like scenes in a play: In the opening act I'm a bold young (27 years old) American man at my going-away party, primed to drive a car through eighteen countries on the other side of the world. All subsequent acts are filled with scenes of adventure, awe, friendship, discovery, and love.

Other times those memories flow as a series of vignettes, like an author's chapbook of stories. Tales of traveling from the United States to Europe, through France, Germany, Austria, Switzerland, Greece, and Italy. More adventures in Turkey, Lebanon, Jordan, and the less-welcoming land of Syria. On to Egypt, Libya, Tunisia, Algeria, Morocco, and Spain.

Usually, though, the images reel through my mind like the unbroken stream of a movie. Starting with the farewell in Greenwich Village, New York, followed by a journey across the Atlantic ocean; segue to my arrival in France where I pick up my new 1953 Renault 4CV. I drive around the Mediterranean, exploring ancient lands, cultures, and peoples, encountering thrills and dangers, and coming of age. My constant companions are my journals, camera, and sketch pads.

As I traveled long roads that were sometimes dark and lonely, my mind turned with the wheels of my car. Intimate inquiries and personal realizations were substantial facets of my journey, and I learned first hand that the very act of self-examination is a significant aspect of the answers it can reveal.

For six months, I crossed many borders, and not only on land. I sought to press through those walls that separated my sense of self and self-respect from the attitudes and prejudices of my fellow human beings. I searched the pathways that connect me to all the other people in my life, as well as studying every curve, corner, and niche of my own mind, spirit, and personality.

This style of journey can't be accidental; it must be pursued. It happened more than fifty years ago, yet to this day, I am unwilling to settle for what are merely acceptable parameters. I will always explore beyond what is expected. If I were to live any other way, my life would lose its art.

Issued July 5, 1953

1

Farewell to the Village

On a warm September night in Greenwich Village, New York, in the year 1953, my roommates threw a going-away party for me. I had been sharing a simple 2-story house on Charles Street with two other young men, neither of whom ever became more than sharers of the rent. We were all too busy creating our adult lives to get to know each other well; while my roommates followed their own dreams, I worked at a reputable advertising agency during the day, and supplemented the goals I had envisioned for myself by attending Cooper Union artist's college at night.

Why was I about to leave my home, my job, my state, my country? Because I had come to the realization that those brilliant, tunnel-ending 'goals,' those self-and-society-defining prizes, were less important than the general expansion of my life.

It came as a pleasant surprise that my busy roommates decided to celebrate my journey with a party. As our guests arrived, I regarded them with the nostalgic eye of a soon-to-be world traveler. The poets, musicians, artists, and students, male and female, wore their hip uniforms of jeans with rolled cuffs and t-shirts (no logos back then, unless you count university insignias), and the girls' t-shirts usually had collars. If sneakers were worn, they were Keds or Converse. Hairstyles for the boys were short, and many of the girls wore bangs in front with the length in back pulled into a ponytail.

My neighbor Mary was an exception in style; she showed up with a short, expensive, Audrey Hepburn-like hairdo, a cheap, simple black dress, and bold, bulky jewelry. She also brought her pet skunk, for show. Mary tried hard to be considered 'bohemian.' By coincidence, she would be boarding the same trans-Atlantic ship with me in the morning. Mary, who hailed from a wealthy family, would be traveling first class all the way. I would not be able to travel first class, because although my family was far from poor, I intended to finance my own trip. How could I otherwise test my own mettle? The sort of answers I sought were not based on the questions of my family or my social standing. Any curiosities and subsequent illuminations had to be my own. I didn't want to be a tourist, I wanted to be an explorer.

At that time in our nation's history, my generation carried a strong sense of pride. Our country had saved the world from its terrible war less than ten years before (World War II), our citizens were artistically and intellectually innovative, we were a strong, young society with a few dollars to spend. Gender roles were strictly defined by Barbie dolls for girls and Davy Crockett paraphernalia for boys. Korea was a bit of a stickler, but by late 1953, our troops had reportedly left that country.

Carried by conversation, we flowed through the kitchen to the front stoop, or out to the small park behind the house. A friend who worked as a local disc-jockey had borrowed a stack of records from the station, and spun popular show-tunes for us on a record player. Occasionally, he threw in some Nat King Cole, Louis Armstrong, maybe Glenn Miller.

In and around the music, our voices bounced from topic to topic. The New York Yankees were headed toward winning five champion-ships in a row, while on television, Lucy Arnez had broken prudish censor barriers by going to a hospital for (gasp!) childbirth. Ray Bradbury published *Fahrenheit 451* and Jack Kerouac put out *On The Road*. Barbara Stanwyck was still hot, and Marilyn Monroe was catching the attention of the world and the heart of Joe DiMaggio. A new President had been sworn in that year, too. Eisenhower.

The subject of politics did arise at that party, especially since I would be traveling to where the world war had ended not long ago, and where still more wars were being waged. One particularly loaded question was asked by Terry, a struggling poet: "Do you think Eisenhower means it? About that 'even-handedness' business in the Middle East?"

I answered, thoughtfully, "It's hard to say. I think he wants to be more 'even-handed' toward the Arabs, because they have all that oil." I expected the President's new policy, specifically the adjustment in attitude toward Arabs-versus-Jews, might have some impact on my travels since I am Jewish.

"They're battling over there, Will." This comment came from another friend, Richard, who had joined us with a glass of beer in hand. "There's a lot of guerrilla warfare going on, and here you are a Jewish man, about to travel through Syria, Palestine, and Egypt."

"That's what worries me, too," said Terry. He gestured freely as he spoke to me, dotting his words with puffs of smoke. "They're not going to want a Jewish man in Syria. How do you propose to get into that country?"

When Terry sucked on his cigarette, it drew my gaze to his mouth. Not a month before, I had french-kissed a man for the first time in my life. We had only engaged in 'necking,' which literally meant not going below the neck, but still. The lips that now held my attention had received that first kiss.

However, Terry's question was an important one. I had already heard about Syria, and had been told I would be allowed to enter that country only if I could prove I was not a Jew. I explained to Terry and Richard that a letter had been provided to me by a friend who was close to a Christian Science minister. Because the word 'Christian' stood out so boldly in the letterhead, I assumed it would be acceptable to anti-Semitic border guards.

The letter stated the following:

> William Carr, a devout Christian, wishes to visit your country. He has no political affiliations whatsoever with any of the countries of the Mediterranean or Adriatic Seas, and only wishes to see Syria as a tourist.

Even if they couldn't read English, they knew the word 'Christian' like I knew the word 'Moslem.' The lie about my faith didn't bother me because, although I had respect for my religious upbringing, it was not a driving force in my personality. In fact, what was the most profound aspect of the 27-year-old Will Carr, and the very nugget of my desire for self-expansion, was an ache of romantic absence, and a yearning for honest, potent love.

Which brings me back to Terry. He had caught my moment of sensual distraction, and he drew on his cigarette again, more seductively. Before I could respond to that gesture (unsure of how I should respond at all), Mary and her skunk interrupted us. She wore that animal like an excitable stole.

"Will? You've heard about Trieste, haven't you?"

"Yes, I have. The UN just turned it over to Italy."

"Tito—he isn't very happy about that."

"Apparently nobody in Yugoslavia is happy about it. They're about to go to war."

Terry asked, "Couldn't you have chosen a safer time to go exploring that particular area?"

All four of our well-schooled minds absorbed that question, and we laughed with sad resignation. Is there ever a safe time to explore the countries surrounding the Mediterranean?

The sound of a new arrival gave me a reason to excuse myself. Her name was Mabel, and we had met the day before in the Yugoslavia Consulate. I had been speaking with a desk clerk, trying to sell him on the idea of an art show about his native country. I wasn't getting anywhere with the proposition because the frustrations of bureaucracy don't discriminate against any nationality.

As I changed tactics and was extracting a map of Yugoslavia from the clerk, Mabel politely interrupted. She introduced herself to me and asked, in a delightful New England accent, "You're planning a trip to Yugoslavia?"

"Yes," I answered with equal politeness. Mabel was old enough to be my grandmother. She had pure white hair, compassionate eyes and a huggable vibe. I told her, "In fact, I'm planning to drive around the entire Mediterranean."

"My goodness!" Her eyes lit with interest. "I don't think that has ever been done before."

"As far as I've been able to discover, it hasn't." I examined the crude map the desk clerk had handed me. "This seems awfully outdated."

Mabel stepped closer, her eyes still bright and friendly, and looked over the map. "You won't find anything current, but I can tell you a bit about the country. My husband is a Yugoslav, the captain of a merchant ship."

What a fateful coincidence! Stepping away from the uninspiring desk clerk, I asked this kind woman, "May I buy you lunch?"

"I would like that very much."

Although Mabel could have been close to 80 years old, she walked with a spritely step, and spoke with the enthusiasm of a precocious child. That childlike sweetness was enhanced when she took my hand while we walked, and we strolled down the avenue like May-December sweethearts.

We decided to dine at the Automat, an automated diner that needed no waiters or waitresses. All the food choices could be examined through glass-fronted machines, and once the decision was made, it was a simple matter of dropping coins into a slot and sliding open the door in front of your meal. Questions arise, now; how fresh could this food have been, how nutritious? What were the standards of cleanliness? The restaurant itself fairly glowed with polish, and the food-dispensers were spotless. The meal tasted just fine, well-seasoned by the novelty of it all. Also, this was a place where presentation had been developed to a consumer level of art.

Over our auto-lunch and coffee, Mabel enthusiastically described her husband's country. "Yugoslavia is still very…rustic. You'll hardly need a map to find your way around, just follow the road in front of you. It is a lovely road, I can assure you of that. The beauty of the country is boundless. You'll be in an artist's paradise."

She continued. "Let's take a look at that old map, and I'll tell you of the prettiest areas I've seen."

Mostly, I listened as she spoke, but occasionally I asked a question. One such question was about the anger over Trieste, and she responded by saying, "It has changed hands more than a few times, and Tito is becoming quite frustrated. Their most important port is being handed over to Italy! You must be especially careful in that area."

Just as I suspected. I next asked about local customs, and Mabel gave me some tidbits of information, but reminded me I would be learning it all first hand, soon enough. (I certainly would, most notably with regard to uninvited strangers in one's hotel bed, but I'll save that for its proper place in my story.)

Mabel returned to the topic of the possible dangers. "There's so much unrest over there, and not only in Yugoslavia. The Israelis and Arabs are also at odds, and Nasser is angry about the Suez canal, while the rest of Northern Africa is upset with the French and the British. Please, be especially careful with the military everywhere you go. Always remember that if you treat them with respect, you should have no trouble."

*   *   *

At the end of my conversation with Mabel, I had invited her to my going-away party the following evening, and to my surprise, there she was, stepping out of a taxi. My friends greeted the older woman cordially, while I welcomed her with real pleasure and led her into the house. I could tell she felt awkward in the youthful group, and whispered to her, "Why don't we go to my room, where we can sit down and talk?"

With disguised relief, she nodded.

On the way up to the second story of the house, I apologized for the creaks and slants in the old floorboards, but Mabel brushed at the words with a wave of her hand. "This is a perfectly nice old place," she replied. "Are you going to live here again when you return?"

"No, I've already moved most of my possessions to my parents' home. I'll be gone quite a while."

I showed her to the desk and chair (which had come with the room), and sat myself on the bed (also included in the rent). "All I have left here," I told Mabel, continuing our conversation, "is what I'll be able to fit into my Renault."

"I can't imagine how you would pack for such an adventure. I'm still amazed that you'll be sleeping in the car."

"Would you like to have a look at my provisions?"

"I am curious. If you wouldn't mind?"

First, I showed her some of the gifts I had received during the current going-away party, including a nice mess kit and a sturdy flashlight. I then opened the large box of the traveling supplies I had gathered on my own. Using my bed for the display, I laid out a sleeping bag, air mattress, first-aid kit, map book, Coleman stove, and my gun.

The gun, of course, caught Mabel's immediate attention. "Why on *earth*," she asked, not unreasonably, "are you bringing a gun?"

"I was advised to take it for protection." I reached toward the weapon, but my hand dropped to my side before I touched it.

"Will." Mabel rose, stepped close to me, and took my arm. It wasn't exactly a clutch, but the grasp did convey a sense of earnest import. Her eyes examined my face, my mouth, my eyes, even my hair. "Look at you. You're a charming, handsome, well-intentioned young man. Nobody is going to want to kill you." Her fingers left my arm and pointed to the gun. "Unless they find you with that."

"But if I'm accosted on the road, I'll have protection against—"

"If you're searched by the military and they turn up a gun, they're going to assume the worst. Only yesterday we spoke of the troubles in half the lands you'll be visiting. There are troops everywhere, and you won't be safe if anyone considers you a threat." She took my arm again and leaned closer, pulling me in with both her serious eyes and her physical hold on me. "If you're carrying a weapon, you could be shot instantly, but if they didn't do that, imprisonment might be even worse."

Covering her hand with my own, I said, "I promise to think carefully about what you've said."

"Please, please do."

I repacked my provisions, and as we rejoined the party below, I contemplated the conflicting advice I'd been given. At the bottom of the stairs, Mabel embraced me. "I'll be off now. I only came to say farewell."

"I'm glad you did." I walked her out to the street and hailed her another taxi. Before she closed her door, she said again: "Please, whatever you do, don't bring that gun."

The intensity of her tone struck me as more powerful than that of those who had suggested I bring a weapon in the first place. Who was this woman, and what was the import of her fleeting appearance in my life? She had brought no gift but that of her warm, loving self. No—she brought more; sage advice. I could only have heard it best from her, a bystander who seemed objective, but who lost that subjectivity through the warm, brief meshing of our spirits, an angel who had one message for me that brought me safely through my trip.

I find it hard to believe I would have survived my Mediterranean adventure if I had not heeded Mabel's warning. Like a visiting angel, she came into my life for one purpose. I never saw or heard from her again.

*   *   *

The following day, my sister Anne stood with me on the dock, moments before I would board a ship called the Andrea Doria. Very few men passed us without at least two appreciative scans of my voluptuous sister. She either ignored them or didn't notice them at all—I've always wondered if she has ever been aware of the devastating effect she could have on men. Thick, dark, wavy hair, usually worn long, and smooth, olive-complected skin, combined with a finely balanced, neatly-featured face and a beautifully curved body, wow. All that, and she still radiates inner-strength and intelligence. Men can fall over themselves around her, yet that never trips her up.

With a mix of pride and shyness, she held out a package. "Here's your present."

"Ah, the secret!" She had shown up late to my party the previous evening because she had been working so hard on my parting gift. Unable to complete it in time for the festivities, she had promised to finish it before I was set to sail. I suspected she had stayed up half the night working on it, but I still had no idea what it might be.

Packages back then were covered in brown paper tied with string, which I pulled away, and a richly woven material fell into my hands. I held it up and stared, impressed. "You made this yourself?"

She let loose her full smile and told me, unnecessarily, "It's a sweater. The design is Norwegian. Do you like it?"

"I love it! It's gorgeous!" It truly was. At first glance, it could have been knit by a professional. I'm wearing it in many of the photos that were taken of me on the trip.

Anne asked me, "Are you going to try it on?"

I shed my jacket and pushed my head easily through the neck of the sweater. Perfect dimensions there. I slid my arms into the sleeves. Just the right length. The shoulders were a bit large, but I liked the broadening effect. I pulled the bottom of the sweater down toward my waist, pulled a little harder, and stopped. The length didn't quite reach my belly-button. Okay, so maybe it couldn't have been made by a professional, but that didn't mean I loved it any less.

Anne stared at me in a moment of mute concern for the fit, then we began to laugh, falling into each other's arms. Anne stepped back and said, "It won't hurt it to keep stretching it until it looks more presentable." Although she's younger than I am, she fussed like a mother trying to dress her son, giving a tug here and a yank there, until it hung with some measure of respectability.

The ship howled its final boarding blast and we embraced once more. I took a step back, then another, but she came to me and held me for a final short moment. Near my ear, she whispered, "I hope you took that lady's advice about the gun." She leaned her head back and regarded me closely, her dark, spirited eyes demanding the right answer.

I supplied it: "It's at home."

Anne's arms tightened around me, relief seeping from her very pores. "Thank God."

"Time for me to board."

She stepped back again and reached up to touch my neatly combed hair. "You be safe, and you be careful. I'd also tell you to stay out of trouble, but then how much fun would you have?"

We grinned at each other, and I gave her a gentle pinch on the arm. Just as gently, she slapped my hand away. "I thought you outgrew pinching me fifteen years ago!"

"Looks like I needed to get that final one out of my system. You take care of yourself, too, okay?"

"I will. Wear that sweater, it will bring you luck."

With a nod, I began to walk away, but Anne called out, "Remember to write to me! Oh—and tell Antonio I said 'Hi'!"

The name made me falter in my steps. More on him soon. At the moment, I stepped onto the gangplank with the light, firm steps of a twenty-seven year-old man, somewhat saddened to depart family, friends and a promising career but excited for what the future will hold.

As I stood waving from the ship's rail, next to the wanna-be bohemian Mary (who had thankfully left her skunk at home), my mind began to prepare for my journey.

What did I expect from this trip? As I've already implied, something different from Mary's apparent plans. I sought adventure rather than tourism, involvement rather than voyeurism. The places I would visit were steeped in ancient history and miracles of mankind, brewing with deeply embedded cultures, and alive with scents, scenes, and languages I had never imagined. I would not only see, but experience, something more than the comfort of First World countries.

America was an easy place to live, yet so many societies in foreign lands had been endlessly oppressed and abused. What might it be like to sit in a café surrounded by people who were willing to form revolutions against powerful, ruthless governments? How would it feel to rub elbows with those who could trace their lineages and cultural beliefs through thousands of years? There were elusive qualities in such people, qualities I had never been able to find in myself. I hoped it might be possible to absorb, perhaps through osmosis, some of their unique, admirable characteristics.

It was my intention to expand my fundamental self, and the timing was perfect. I was young, strong, healthy, courageous (perhaps to a fault), restless, and intrigued by the world around me. I hoped for more than what I had received from a relatively prosperous New York childhood, a university degree, and the start of a 'right track' advertising career. The idea of challenge attracted me, and a part of me wanted to test my own sense of self-worth. Living in a prescribed society can make it difficult to examine ourselves objectively. To never follow any call but that of convention is a slow death of self, and a drastic change in our day-to-day living is sometimes the only way to find our most honest answers. Funny, though, how simple 'drastic change' can be. Step outside your home, but instead of going to work, board a ship to another country.

Change is actually easy because it's constant. Taking control of change is where the challenge lies. Otherwise, we're nothing more than stones that are tossed and shaped by a forceful flow, a river of others' expectations.

At the time of my trip, it was also becoming increasingly important for me to investigate my sexual drive—at the relatively advanced age of twenty-seven, I was still a complete virgin. There could be any number of reasons for this anomaly, but what stands out to me now is that there existed a stalemate between what was expected of me and unanswered questions within myself.

I recalled thinking a lot when I was young, wanting a close friend, someone to share all my secret longings and mysteries of what my small world was like and the confusion I felt about why my parents seem to always make me feel on edge, as if something would trigger an emotional explosion between the two. It seemed I was always too absorbed in my own thoughts, and since we lived for my first years upstairs from my Grandparents and many uncles, there was rarely a feeling of loneliness. Our next door neighbors, a polish immigrant family, had a son my age, Eddy, and several girls. They formed part of my childhood. An old man lived in a cellar apartment next door also, and he would give Eddy and me a penny if we would show him our penises and let him feel it. It was our secret. After a few times we had enough money saved to buy treats like ice cream sodas.

In back of my Grandparent's house was a slaughterhouse where they butchered calves and cows. It was their living. I still remember the few times I saw the cow's throats being cut by a rabbi and the blood falling into the drain. I must have had nightmares about it. To this day, I can't face a vision of someone wounded with blood flowing or a surgical operation on TV. I feel drained and empty inside my body.

In September of 1953, boarding that ship was a physical manifestation of a journey I had already begun. Ignoring the call of adventure would have been an insult to my spiritual designs.

2

A Ship of Diverse Dreams

The first leg of my journey was, as I've mentioned, aboard the fated Andrea Doria. Most are aware that it now sits off Nantucket Island at the bottom of the Atlantic, but that story belongs to others.

For the journey I intended, the ocean was a far better choice of transportation than an airplane. It gave me a physical connection with the planet I was about to traverse, and how soothing it would be to float through watery currents as I approached my transformation, moving from my old life to what would be a new me. Also, it gifted me with time, time to reach the full rush of excitement about what I was about to experience, and to battle any inevitable concerns.

I began my journal on that ship, and here is an early entry:

> On my first ocean voyage, the sense of life and death is strong, yet the vast waters can hold you in a grip of pure contemplation. Everyone has, in one way or another, been moved by the ocean. For some it brings sickness, for others, love, while still others have begun to hate it for causing untrue thoughts to enter their minds. I believe many have felt real fear for the very first time while at sea.

Looking back from over five decades in the future, I can't help but wonder what I meant by the final lines of that sentimental entry. I know one great hope I harbored for this trip was that I might fall in love, as any romantic young man will hope. There was even a specific reason for me to think it might actually happen on this journey. But what could I have meant by 'others have begun to hate (the ocean) for causing untrue thoughts to enter their minds'? It also strikes me as significant that the line was immediately followed by a comment about fear.

There I was, before the Stonewall rebellion, before HIV and AIDS, before Will and Grace, Rita Mae Brown, Ellen Degeneres, and Queer Eye for the Straight Guy, wondering about my sexual orientation. I imagine there must have been fear involved, and I do remember a passing thought that I would rather not be a recipient of the harassment I'd seen perpetrated on what were called 'fags' or 'queers' in Greenwich Village. Based on the persecution I'd seen, it's possible I even felt some self-hatred for thoughts I might have preferred were 'untrue'—but then again, I think not. I clearly remember feeling, at that time in my life, "Well, even if I find other men attractive, that certainly doesn't mean I'm one of those *fags*!"

I had so few sources for information about the subject. It had been used as an insult in school; "You're a faggot (and/or) a homo!" Many of us had learned about the acceptance of homosexuality in ancient Greece, but that was worlds away and separated from my reality by many centuries of time. Once I had tried looking up the word 'homosexual' in the dictionary, but couldn't find it.

I don't remember ever hearing the word homosexual in my household. It wasn't until high school that I became curious and aware about the subject. I thought my physical attraction for my father was because I longed for his attention and love and never gave it any other meaning. But when I started to become attracted to the high school English teacher and a senior male student, and hearing the word faggot and fairy describing someone among my peers, I became frightened about my own sexuality. Was I a faggot? I tried to find books on the subject. I couldn't talk to my friends for fear of identifying myself as one and losing what few friends I had. But looking back on that time in my life, it is possible these few friends, all attracted to the same school activities I was, may have been masturbating together and keeping their secret from me.

In those days being Gay was considered a mental sickness requiring medical attention. One was considered a pervert, abnormal, sick, and not worthy of any decent society. It could destroy any future I might look forward to. The feelings I was dealing with were so acute I went out of my way to pretend I had an interest in girls. I developed friendships with several girls, but I always felt they knew something was wrong with me, that I was too different for them to encourage more than just talk. I had a hard time getting a date and felt isolated from all the fun and pleasure of being a high school student.

The homosexual men in Greenwich Village were very different from me. Effeminate clothing, heavily made-up faces, mincing walks, floppy hands, lisping tones. That was my only observable definition of what it was to be homosexual (other than the unpleasant terms such as those mentioned above), and it was something I was not. It may have been a delusion of semantics, but it was a strong delusion, nonetheless.

All I knew was that I certainly did have a desire for men, and that it overshadowed, but didn't entirely eliminate, any desire I might have had for women. My father had always been a great lover of women, and to escape becoming our parents is rarely little more than a fantasy. Could I be a man able to break away from that fate?

In retrospect, I can't help but wonder how much influence my father's personality had on my decision to take this trip, but more on that later.

The bottom line? When I seek the foundation of any general concerns I might have had on the deck of the Andrea Doria, I can say I felt real fear about the wars, and about guerilla warfare (our phrase for 'terrorism'), and I worried about the anti-semitism I was bound to encounter. In those days, it didn't occur to me that there would be a problem with anti-Americanism, and in fact there wasn't, not really. However, my largest concern was with the personal answers I hoped to find.

Who was I, really? Adventurer or homebody? Advertiser, or artist? Boy or man? Most importantly, who was I, sexually? If it were true that I was some breed of sexual deviant, what would my family think? How might it affect them?

Although I strolled the decks with these thoughts in mind, it never occurred to me to act on any physical urges during the voyage. Not that the opportunity didn't present itself—it did, at least once.

The proposition came from a deep-voiced black man who had probing, intelligent eyes, and his name was James.

When you're on an extended cruise, you often find yourself in conversations with people who are more than strangers, more than acquaintances, but less than actual friends. I had seen James a few times in the dining room and on deck, but apparently he had taken more notice of me than I had of him. He engaged me in conversations two or three times, but if he made any subtle hints or advances, I was too innocent to notice. It wasn't until near the end of the trip that he made his intentions clear.

We sat relaxing in a pair of deck chairs, and both of us had books open on our chests, but the warm, breezy, salt-scented day had drawn us away from reading. In a slow, lazy voice, I dreamed aloud about where I intended to travel.

James abruptly interrupted with a question: "When, exactly, do you expect to be in Italy?"

"Hmm, let me see. My best guess is that it could be before the end of October."

He turned to face me, sitting sideways on his deck chair, his elbows on his knees, his hands hanging down between his legs. "Listen."

My head was turned toward him, though still resting against the back of my chair. When he said 'listen' (then hesitated), I gave him my full attention with an eye-shading salute.

"I'll be in southern Italy all of October," he said, "staying with a friend. You could come for a visit. My friend has plenty of room, and I'm sure he wouldn't mind offering you a bed for a few nights."

No, that wasn't when James' flirtations became clear to me.

Polite by both nature and nurture, I murmured something tactfully dismissive about the possibility of taking him up on his offer.

James sensed my reticence, and tried to sweeten the pot: "My friend's place is a very nice villa. You'd love it."

"If I'm in the area…"

"I think you'd like my friend. His name is W.H.Auden. He's a poet—have you heard of him?"

I met James' piercing, serious eyes, and finally answered in an unsteady voice, "Yes, I have heard of him." As many know, W.H. Auden was a courageous man. He had come out of the proverbial closet at a time when being openly homosexual meant certain disapproval, probable harassment, and possible death. With no small measure of embarrassment, I said again, "If I'm in the area I'll try to look you up. It might be fun."

James nodded his acknowledgment of this weak promise, and moved off to find another diversion. I'll interject here that years later, while reading *Giovanni's Room*, I glanced at the book-jacket photo of the author. James. James Baldwin. I could only laughingly imagine how different my life might have been had I taken him up on the offer he made to me aboard the Andrea Doria.

There were two specific reasons I never went to Auden's villa. First of all, these men were decidedly homosexual, openly so, and all those previously mentioned unpleasant labels could be applied to them. 'Queer' was simply not a word I could imagine attaching to myself. Therefore, I couldn't conceive of diving right in, so to speak, with such a group. To be surrounded by worldly men who had already defined themselves and who might attempt to define me was an idea I found intimidating and frightening.

Secondly, I was saving myself for someone else, someone who happened to be in Italy.

Left alone in my deck chair, I pulled out my wallet and extracted a photograph of the most handsome man I had ever seen. This was Antonio, bearer of the name my sister had sung out as I boarded the ship, and he waited in Rome to meet me. It was possible he felt as much anticipation as I, but that was unlikely; the fantasy of our first meeting had been built and explored and re-experienced in my mind too many times to count.

Anne had given me the photo. Six months before my departure, she had been on her own vacation in Europe. Our parents had planned her trip, though, hoping she would lose interest in her sweetheart, a Catholic man. A non-Jewish fiancé was not acceptable, and in fact there were terrible scenes about the feelings and long-term intentions that she shared with David. My parents had set up a long overseas trip for her, and had encouraged her to seek out friendships with other men while traveling—Jewish men.

One trait Anne and I share is to take on the appearance of succumbing to the wishes of those who tried to control us, while following our own hearts and desires. With a mutually respectful agreement between her Catholic sweetheart and herself, she agreed to explore, fully, while overseas.

It was in Italy that Anne had met the stunningly sexy Roman named Antonio. "I found him very interesting," she'd told me, "but as things turned out, I wasn't exactly his type."

"I thought you were every man's type!"

She laughed that off, as always, either unaware of or unconcerned with her endless attributes. "Not *every* man wants a woman, Will."

Understandably, this comment gave me pause, and as I sat there (pausing), she handed me a photograph. "His name is Antonio, and he showed me the romantic side of Rome."

Something in her voice made me ask, "Were you lovers?"

"Not exactly. I let him know I wouldn't mind being kissed, but he didn't respond during the first few outings. It wasn't until the day before I had to leave that he finally did kiss me, but as we began to touch and pet, he suddenly pulled away. Will, he even started to cry."

"What happened?"

"He told me he found me beautiful, even desirable, but he couldn't be with me. He was upset because he didn't want me to think for a minute that his problem had anything to do with me, personally."

Impatient for the punch-line, I asked, "Anne, what was his problem?"

"He's homosexual."

'Pause' again. I examined the photo closely. Perhaps a few years older then me, standing with a casual elegance in a tasteful, tailored suit, classically handsome with a Roman nose and noticeable cheekbones and a charming, luscious-lipped smile. I could tell by the shading of the black-and-white picture that he had gorgeous, sun-kissed skin. "He doesn't look homosexual," I remarked, because I still assumed there was a definitive look.

With a sigh, Anne agreed. "He certainly doesn't. I had been so impressed by this gentleman who never made an improper pass at me, and it turns out the reasons were biological."

Ignoring that insightful observation, which was before its time, I continued examining the picture.

Anne asked me a rhetorical question; "Do you want to know what else he said?"

"Yes." I wanted to know everything about this man, yes indeed, but I certainly didn't expect to hear what Anne next told me.

"He said he couldn't stop thinking about the picture I had shown him of you."

"You showed him a picture of me?"

She hummed an affirmative. "I think it was the second time I saw him, we were talking about our families, and I told him I only have one brother. I showed him that picture of you, you know the one, you gave it to me before I left, to keep me company." She chuckled, and I had to join her. Anne, not able to find anyone to keep her company? Absurd.

"You were saying—" I prodded. "He couldn't stop thinking of my picture?"

"Yes. When he said that, I brought it out again and he looked at it with such affection, I gave it to him."

For a moment, I was speechless.

She casually gestured toward the photo I held in my hands. "You can keep that, too. You'll want to be able to recognize him if you meet. You'd have to find him in Rome, of course."

"Meet?" This was six months before my own trip, and at the time, the seed of traveling had only been germinating in my mind. Now, it sprouted as I asked, "He wants to meet me?"

"He does. He said he'd be delighted to show you around, and I can give you the name and number of the place where he works."

Within a week, my little sprout of a plan had flowered, and that was when I began making firm plans for my trip around the Mediterranean.

What I find interesting about that conversation with Anne is that I hadn't been with a man in any way, yet. (It would still be months before I exchanged kisses with the struggling poet named Terry.) I hadn't discussed my inclinations with anyone, not even my sister, who was also my dear friend. Throughout that conversation about Antonio, Anne never made any mention of the fact that I might be homosexual, and to this day she has always insisted it wasn't her intention to 'set me up' with him. We're the only two children of our parents, though, and we've always been close, so she might have had the same subconscious intuition about me as I did.

*　*　*

On the Andrea Doria I gazed at Antonio's photo for the thousandth time, wondering if I was sailing toward love. Again I will stress this:

Although I thought I couldn't be branded with ugly euphemisms, I did want to love a man, to make love to a man, and have him make love to me. This man in particular. Note the stress on 'love' and 'love-making,' not to be confused with blunt, one-word descriptions of my sexual personality.

My deck-chair musings were interrupted by Mary, who dropped into the seat James had recently vacated. She squinted through her stylish sunglasses at the tourist-class guests around us, wrinkling her nose but not speaking her distaste aloud. "Will, if you'd like, I can sneak you into first class for a swim." (We of the lesser-budgets didn't have a swimming pool of our own.)

I agreed, because the sun had chased the cooling breeze away. Not much later, I met Mary in my bathing suit, and she slipped me into the pool area. There I rubbed elbows with the rich-though-not-famous, mentally rolling my eyes as Mary pointed out a man here, a woman there, and told me gossipy details of their wealth.

As I've mentioned, my family wasn't poor. In fact, my father had built up a successful meat-packing business . Despite that, I was making this trip on my own, as much as possible. Before earning a fair living at the Sherman and Marquette advertising agency, I had acquired some income as a Army reserves lieutenant, and had spent about a year working in my father's business. Altogether, I had saved enough to purchase the round-trip tickets for my sea voyage, as well as the new Renault that awaited me in France. (The car cost $1,200.00, which is probably comparable to spending about $22,000.00 for a new car these days. A notable difference is that my car was made of metal, not fiberglass.)

After my swim, it was time to return to the tourist-class dining room for a meal, and I looked forward to it. These people interested me more than Mary and her first class passengers.

At dinner, I shared a table with Angelina, a nice girl who had been born in California to Italian immigrant parents. Theirs was a farming family, in California as they had been in Italy. Angelina's reason for being on the ship was as complex as many others I had encountered. The stories of these lives affected me, and it shows in a journal entry:

> …the old Italian couple returning home with nothing except the clothes they had on, cheated by their own son; a young

boy bringing his mother's lifeless body back to Italy for its final resting place; a girl traveling to meet the Italian man she was meant to marry....

Angelina's story was the last. She hadn't met the man in person yet, but he could be considered her fiancé. Sitting across from me, dressed in her polka-dotted house dress and worn, green, knitted sweater, she smiled her bashful smile. Her face was ruddy and healthy, clearly showing the effect of hard, honest work. She possessed a dignified pride, but the unusual situation her life had presented to her had left her ruffled.

As we enjoyed our dinner, she told me more about how she had first begun exchanging letters with her fiancé, who hailed from her parents' home town in Italy. They remembered him from his childhood, even before Angelina was born. He had served in WWII, but was captured and not released until after the end of the war. A few years later, Angelina's parents had introduced her to him through letters, and soon their correspondence became one of her few interests outside of farm work. In time, the man proposed that they marry by proxy, and that he would come to America, but Angelina felt she didn't know him well enough. It was far too intimate a commitment to make without first meeting him face-to-face! She had decided to travel to Italy for that meeting, and he promised to be waiting at the dock when we arrived a few days later. She brought her sister along to give her assurance that all would go well. She showed me the letters and asked me to look at the handwriting and tell her if I thought he was a good man from his handwriting. I tried to assure her he was.

After dinner, she brought me to the crew quarters of the ship, as she had a few times before. She had befriended much of the crew, and they had extended a standing invitation. It flattered and pleased me whenever she brought me along.

Picture a scene of the poor Irish in the bowels of the Titanic, singing and dancing, joyfully and thrillingly, to their self-made music. In my situation, the song, dance, food, and frivolity had an Italian bent, as most of the waiters, stewards, and deck hands were from that country (as was the ship itself). Accordions accompanied voices through love songs and ballads, sometimes bawdy lyrics, often energetic dance tunes. Each night I attended, wine flowed and a sort of pizza (quite unlike American pizza) was always available for snacking.

As the end of the voyage approached, I, along with everyone in tourist-class, began to feel a tense, uncertain, excitement. I describe it in a journal entry:

Many of my fellow travelers had as much or more purpose in making the trip than I. I could see it in their faces as they looked more and more out to sea, or watched the water, their eyes fixed on one spot. I could feel it in the dining room when meals would be more hurried, with less talk. Or in the social hall, or the crew's quarters at night, especially during the final days. There were more serious, quiet conversations, each looking into the other's eyes for help or reassurance. Everyone seemed at once afraid, happy, confused, expectant, and at times very sad when the thought of landing was with them.

Although I spoke of others, most of those words were also about my own mind and emotions. However, I was twenty-seven years old, and my concerns were less important than my happy, excited expectations.

The Andrea Doria first docked in Naples, but I and a handful of others would only spend a few hours there, then return to the ship for transport to Cannes, France. Angelina would be one of those permanently disembarking, and I stood next to her, scanning the people below for the man she was about to meet. She held the photo of his face out for both of us to see, and our eyes moved from the image to each of the men waiting on the pier.

With a gasp, Angelina pressed her hand flat to her chest; she had seen him. I touched her elbow. "Where is he?"

She turned to me, her eyes glistening with tears of pleased astonishment, her lips pressed together in a contained smile. Pointing, she said, "He's there. Right there. Do you see him? He's not standing…. He never told me…."

Angelina's betrothed sat waiting, joyfully waving, in a wheelchair.

I remember Angelina well, and fondly. Perhaps I subconsciously found parallels with my own situation. I was able to empathize with the mix of hope and uncertainty, the desire for a definitive answer, the anxiety of an answer not preferred. Yet as it turned out, at least for Angelina, this man would most likely be perfect for her. To be needed fulfilled the nurturing aspect of her personality, and that was something I could also understand. As my sister will attest, a driving aspect of my own personality is to care for others. Anne has even been known to comment that I'm most comfortable with people who have problems, issues, or needs.

Men can wish to nurture, too.

3

'Gay' Paree

During that brief port of call in Naples, those not staying in Italy were allowed to leave the Andrea Doria for a five-hour look at the town. The first thing I did from the shore was capture a nice photograph of Naples, with Mt. Vesuvius in the background, and the Andrea Doria.

I let Mary convince me to split the cost of a tour guide with her and some others from the ship, including a Japanese woman named Mitchiko. It was our first steps in Europe, and we couldn't help but walk through the town wearing that curious, awestruck tourist's stare. What we didn't expect was that we would be the recipients of equally interested stares from the local populace.

We checked our hair, our clothes, we even wondered if there was something about our way of walking that brought us so much attention. A kind stranger eventually explained; few people in this area had ever seen a Japanese woman. Mitchiko smiled, lifted her chin and squared her shoulders, proudly accepting the honor of exposing a populace to another nationality. I jokingly suggested she lift a hand as we walked, tipping it back and forth, closed-fingered, like a visiting dignitary in a parade.

That short visit only gave me a passing taste of what was to come. Soon after re-boarding, we were brought to France. Although I didn't have my Renault yet (I would be picking it up in two days), I felt that my true adventure had begun.

In Cannes, I found an inexpensive hotel, something most likely used by traveling youths or low-income locals. The proprietor was a friendly fellow who understood my school-learned French well enough, and his daughter Celeste could speak some English.

Celeste led me to my room, showing polite interest in my visit, asking questions with her delectable accent. "Is this your first vacation in France?"

"*Oui.* I can't wait to see more of Cannes."

"I think you will enjoy our city. How long will you stay?"

"Only today. Tomorrow morning, I need to leave for Paris. From there, I'll be picking up a car, and start driving across Europe."

"You will be *driving* across Europe? *C'est bonne!* Which countries will you visit?"

This was the first of many conversations that would run the same way throughout my trip, and which usually drew similar reactions: Surprise that I was driving instead of taking planes, trains, or tour buses, then astonishment when I explained that I would also be passing through communist countries, parts of the Middle East, and Northern Africa.

Eyeing me candidly, her polite attitude changed to one of piqued interest. "If you like, I can show you some of Cannes. I know where we can rent a bicycle for you, not expensive, and you can see much of our beautiful town." It sounded perfect. I felt much less like a shamefully obvious tourist once I was up on two wheels and in a pair of shorts, like so many of the locals. Although I moved more quickly than if I had been walking, my senses were still saturated by this new land. The entry from my journal brings it back to me with clarity:

> My eyes sought many things during the day: A chauffeur, waiting in a limousine, drinking from his bottle of wine every few minutes. Strong, verbal arguments about who ran his car into whose bike, motorbike, donkey cart, or other car. The color of the buildings, the clothing, the food, and the Mediterranean Sea so blue, it was all incredibly beautiful.

There were endless restaurants, and many displayed their wares freely; oysters, vegetables, bright red unshelled shrimps, pastries. The choices offered did not need a person's hunger to be appreciated.

In the main park, at the center of the town, an orchestra played outside. I wandered near the water, watching the passersby, and secreted a photo of two distinctly French women.

Having come from New York, one would expect that none of this should have been particularly surprising to me. Yet as much as Cannes had an atmosphere similar to any city, it was absolutely new to me. We didn't have such varieties of international foods available as we do today. It was unheard of to display menu items in the windows of restaurants—even the Automat had its understanding that food belonged either in a machine or on a table, but not in a front window! Finally, to the best of my knowledge, people rarely shouted at each other in the streets of American cities as conversationally they did in France.

We're all human, but we certainly live in societies that are strikingly different.

Celeste and I parted in the afternoon, and in the early evening, I went out walking again, this time heading toward the pier. Here I have a journal entry that reminded me of the changes our own language has experienced:

> The water and the boats attracted me, perhaps because I felt they and I were the only lonely things in an otherwise gay, happy, and spontaneous city.

Yes, in the early '50s, the word 'gay' was still used to express a lively feeling. Now, I find it an interesting term to describe a homosexual man, offsetting (possibly even challenging) the difficult, often frightening mix of emotions we experience.

I stood at the edge of the Mediterranean, wishing I had someone to share my first day in France. Celeste's company had been pleasant, but she had only been a passing acquaintance. Now I felt the loneliness of the water, which seemed bereft because no one was sailing, and of the boats, because their owners had laid them to rest. Off went the travelers to grand hotels or flower-covered villas high above the city, leaving their boats chained like sad, bereft dogs. A graveyard could not have been more despondently peaceful, and one 'for sale' sign read to me like an epitaph to a dead person.

The day was nearing its end, and I returned to my hotel. I know I've commented that it was a poorer establishment, but my room did have a large window with a pretty view. The sun was setting as I entered, and I threw the shutters wide open. A momentary contentment flooded me as I saw shades of color threading through the city-tones of black and white. After the sharp brightness of day, the softening light of approaching night somehow brought everything within my grasp. It was a joy to fall asleep, with my eyes slowly closing on the sky painted with dark, red-tinted clouds.

When I awoke in the morning, I found that Celeste had slipped in with breakfast while I lay sleeping. My lonely mood of the night before was set aside by the continental mix of croissants, jelly, jam, and hot steaming coffee with lots of milk—in other words, *cafe au lait.*

I left the hotel with a fond farewell to that sweet French girl. She wished me well on my trip, and I responded by telling her I was ready for anything. It tickled me to no end when she responded; *"Ooo la la!"*

My trip to Paris was via train, where I had another taste of how different the French were from Americans. The ride felt like a traveling reunion, and it seemed that most people either knew each other, or were happy to make new acquaintances. As far as I could see, the average Frenchman's luggage consisted of one bag for bread, sausage, pâtés, etc., another bag for wine, a third for fruit and candy, and a fourth for clothing. Everyone enjoyed the food, passing samples to one another, pouring wine into extended glasses. Although I wasn't included in the festivities, I thoroughly enjoyed observing it all. I must admit, it also made me hungry.

There was no dining car that I knew of, but each time the train stopped, vendors would hurry to the windows, and a purchase could be made without even climbing out of the car. I watched the flurry of exchanges, somewhat intimidated by the abbreviated speech and quickness of the movements. One man let out a shout as the train pulled away before he could grasp the bread he had paid for. I left each stop hungry, but relieved that I hadn't surrendered any of my limited funds for naught.

My third class ticket, which I had purchased without a reservation, meant I had been standing throughout this rather long trip, and I was exhausted by the time I reached my destination. That must have added to the fear that struck me once I was off the train and in the station. Although I'd had more than a few semesters of French, the training was useless amidst all the noise and confusion that surrounded me. I checked my luggage, then hurried out of the station and into the city as quickly as possible.

I knew a young man who was living here at the time, and held his address in my hand. When Michael had visited New York more than a year before, he had stayed for some months and we had developed a friendship. His father was French, and Michael had returned to live in France for a while. My first bus ride through Paris was in search of this friend.

My attention was instantly captured by the intensity of odors. Baking, perfume, aged meat, dried vegetables, old sewers…all manner of scents were blended together, titillating my senses. The sights, though, were stronger still. What an incredible experience to round a curve and look, there! again, over there! So many actual subjects of the paintings and drawings I had examined and admired while studying art at Cooper Union in New York. It came home to me that as much as I had visually studied, I had never really seen these streets, buildings, and people until that moment.

I found Michael's upper-class apartment, but unfortunately, he wasn't home. All I could do was leave a message that I had arrived, and would contact him in the morning.

I found a hotel, and returned to the train station again for my luggage. My excitement had settled, and I handled the situation with confidence. I dropped my bags in my room, freshened up, and set out to walk the streets again. My fellow students at the art school would have given much to lay their eyes on the source of so many of the scenes we had analyzed so thoroughly.

Cooper Union was the biggest reason I was here in September, rather than some months sooner; I needed to complete my final semester there before I left. Although my Bachelor of Arts is from the University of Illinois, I had continued my education on the advice of the head of the art department at Sherman and Marquette.

At that ad agency, everyone started in the mail room. That sort of thing really did happen, just like out of an old movie. If you wanted to work your way up the ladder, you had to apply yourself, find your own way. As an aspiring artist, I gave my focus to the art department, and eventually caught the attention of the department head. He encouraged me to investigate Cooper Union, and perhaps that was his own personal litmus test for young, enthusiastic employees: send them off to see if they could pass that elite school's difficult entrance exam.

Some luck certainly mixed with what youthful skill and talent I must have possessed, because I was accepted. Throughout the two years I attended CU, I was allowed to work in the art department of Sherman and Marquette, but as fate would have it, I decided to quit the agency and take this trip as soon as my final semester was completed. There's no point in looking back and second-guessing my decision, as in wondering if I might have become an advertising executive. I prefer to have no regrets. How could I despair of having seen such an exciting part of our world at so impressionable an age?

On my second day in Paris, I was able to reach my friend Michael on the phone, and he immediately retrieved me at my hotel. He greeted me warmly, and it felt good to see him, but that was a regretfully fleeting sensation. As we walked to his car, Michael said, "You need to get out of that place. We have to find you a better hotel."

I looked back at the low building, which was older and not in perfect repair, but quaint and welcoming enough. "It seems fine to me."

"No, it just won't do." It wouldn't have surprised me if he had added, 'What would the neighbors think?' Or, worse, 'What would people think if they saw me parked at this place?'

This wasn't the young man I remembered from the previous year. In New York, I had shown him the sights, and had taken him to see my sister where she was attending William Smith College in Geneva, New York. With her roommate, a Belgian from Brussels who spoke fluent French, the four of us had double-dated a few times. I thought we had formed a real friendship, but this Michael came across as a bit stuffy. Maybe he had no real need for me, now?

I should interject here that it wasn't unusual for me to date women, but as I have already admitted, I was still a virgin. While in college years before, when many men and women meet (and copulate with) their future spouses, I had watched girls being 'pinned'—something equivalent to getting a ring or varsity jacket from a steady boyfriend—and I understood it was expected I pin a girl of my own. None of the women I met inspired romance in me, though, so I never attempted to move beyond necking. Eventually, subtle pressure from my parents prompted me to find a quiet, placid girl named Leeanne. Because she was apparently content with nothing more than kisses, I dated her for nearly two years. She attended Vassar College, where she lived in the same dorm as Jackie Kennedy (I should say Jackie Lee Bouvier, at the time, and I was even able to meet that great lady). Leeanne and I were serving our own private purposes by dating each other, though, and after she graduated we parted with no further expectations.

I boarded a military bus to search for a new place to sleep. Access to military amenities were no problem, because while at the University of Illinois, I had been in the ROTC, then for two years following my graduation, I was trained as a lieutenant in the Army. No, I wasn't in World War II, although at the age of 18, I should have been drafted into the end of it. In truth, I was called up to serve, but was turned away after the physical for a suspiciously minor medical problem.

Not a month before, at a society-type party, I had met the man who eventually stamped my papers as "medically unfit." At the party, that man and my father had spent more than a little time in private conversation, and although I never heard a confirmation of it, I've always assumed my father had requested special consideration in my case. Retrospectively, I find it intriguing that my emotionally-absent father was so concerned about my welfare. At the time, I wondered if his concerns were more connected to the family name than to me.

Father had a tendency to bestow his charismatic personality on everyone but me. He charmed women, impressed men, loved my mother, petted and played with my sister, but would only acknowledge my presence when circumstances demanded it. I was rarely aware of Father noticing me, and can't attest to what he might have said about me when I wasn't around. That he found a way to keep me out of serious military duty says more about his feelings than I ever witnessed. Hence, I felt his motives were mostly connected to his social standing, which of course made me more conscious of how he would receive the possibility of my homosexuality.

Might he have already sensed my sexual leanings? Did he shudder at the idea of sending me off to a situation which, at that time, revolved exclusively around men? Or, did he constantly observe me from that lofty, fatherly, caring distance that some men acquire toward their sons? Although the term wasn't used easily back then, I tended toward pacifism. Perhaps my father had been so very aware of that aspect of my personality that he would try to manipulate the draft board.

Whatever the case, if he did know me intimately, he hid it well.

Returning to the original point: my albeit off-kilter military connection came in handy a few times during my trip, as in the free bus ride I enjoyed in Paris. During that ride, I noticed a distinguished gentleman, perhaps in his forties, sitting across from me. I could see on his face, and read in the very air surrounding him, that his excitement at discovering Paris (or re-discovering it, in his case) equaled mine. We spoke for a while, but when the bus neared the end of the line, I asked the driver if he knew of an inexpensive hotel. Before the driver could answer, my gentleman friend introduced himself as Werner, and suggested I come along with him to the hotel where he planned to stay. The place was situated on the left bank, in a student section of the city, so we left the bus and shared a cab to that area.

The rooms were suitable and affordable. With a thanks and a "see you later" to Werner, I hurriedly dropped off my bags, and set off to (finally!) retrieve my Renault 4CV. In no time I stood before her. My trusty carriage, my traveling kitchen, my miniature mobile home waited for me in shining splendor, redolent with the sweet reek of 'new car.' An economical 4-cylinder engine in the back, the trunk in the front. Four doors, which opened opposite of normal, and a sun roof that could be slid open to let in the sky. Small and squat enough that I could practically leap her in a single bound, if necessary. Actually, this little French car looked quite a bit like—should I say it?—a frog. I don't mean that as a racial slur, it's simply the best analogy.

The Renault was the French answer to the Volkswagen Beetle,

and its design was secretly conceived during the German occupation of France. The manufacturers (and Louis Renault himself) had been ordered to produce military vehicles, but Renault wanted a small, conservative car for the inevitably difficult years that would come after the war. It was believed the rear engine and rear-wheel-drive would also mean a superior ride. 4CV prototypes were built, but it wasn't officially unveiled to the public until 1946. Soon after, it gained a few nicknames, one being 'the flea,' the other 'the lump of butter.' The latter was not only for its shape, but because many of the first models were painted yellow. That color had been chosen by the Germans, with the idea that it could blend well with African sands where the car was intended for use as a military vehicle. (How so? Surely they didn't mean to chase anybody down, because the early vehicles topped out at a speed of about 57 mph. And it couldn't have hauled anything, because it only had 4 cylinders and three gears.)

My car (green, not yellow) had many of those same specifications, although my newer model would be able to move at more than 57 mph if I so desired. Modified Renault 4CVs did, after all, become winning race cars over the years. I also had that great sun-roof, and I don't know if those were supplied in the military version of the car.

At the agency, I climbed around the interior like a child investigating a strange playhouse. The sales manager stood politely outside, no doubt wondering why a young man felt the need to explore everything except the engine.

In the back seat, I immediately saw it would be difficult to find a comfortable sleeping position. I pushed at the passenger seat in front of me and asked the manager, "Is it easy to remove these?"

He raised one eyebrow in what might have been a practiced move. "The bucket seats? It is not difficult."

I climbed out and squatted on my haunches next to passenger side. Both the bottoms and backs of the seats were flat, so I didn't think they would weigh much. I found a lever, then a large wing-nut. "How does it work?"

"The car?"

"No, the removal of the seat."

A poorly concealed sigh escaped the man's throat as he hunkered down next to me. "Turn that nut, pull there, now push here, see—*voila*."

I maneuvered the passenger seat out of place, tried angling it into the back, then into the driver's side, then set it outside. Climbing in again, I tried various sleeping positions, and found that with that passenger seat removed, I would be able to curve my air mattress from the front of the passenger's side to the floor behind the driver's seat. It wouldn't be difficult for me to curl up, as I'm only about 5' 8" tall.

The Renault manager waited with long-suffering patience as I struggled to return the passenger seat properly to its place, determined to do it on my own. When I finished, I straightened and said, "I'll be sleeping in this car."

"Oh?" His enthusiasm was underwhelming.

"I'm going to take this little car," I told him, "and prove to the American public that you can drive a Renault through hundreds of pretty little towns and villages around the Mediterranean sea. I'll show them that a trip doesn't need to be limited to the regular tourist circuit of Paris and London and Madrid. With his own car, a fellow can experience all that's off the beaten path, meet the local people, and become a part of everything around him! Don't you think this would be excellent advertising?"

He looked so far down his nose at me that if his goatee had been any longer, it would have split his perspective of my image. He only shook his head and said, with a mixture of disdain, fondness, and disbelief, "Crazy American."

The purpose of my trip instantly expanded. Now I intended: 1) Exactly what I had just described to Monsieur l'agent du Renault; 2) To meet the seductively photographic Antonio, and 3) To prove to Monsieur l'agent du Renault that there's a difference between Americans who are crazy and Americans who are adventuresome.

The agent proceeded to show thoroughly un-mechanical me how to care for the car; checking the fluids, pulling the plugs, testing the battery, and so forth. I settled the information into my short-term memory, and rolled away.

My trip was on. The only thing I would have considered crazy was the idea of passing up such an experience.

Back at my hotel, I found the gentleman Werner and showed him my fetching new vehicle. He enthusiastically suggested I celebrate by joining him, along with some friends of his, at dinner that night. The exotic French food was as delicious as I had hoped! The hors d'oeuvres were artistically cut vegetables meant to be dipped in an anchovy sauce that had only an essence of salt. For my main meal I had fish, I don't remember what kind, but it melted like warm butter in my mouth. A small cloud of potatoes were more flavor than substance, and cooked baby carrots were served in a light brown, syrupy glaze.

After we ate, (and finished the obligatory, delightful bottles of wine), Werner and I followed his friends' car in my Renault for a tour of nighttime Paris. My memory of Notre Dame lit up against the night is better than any photograph I could have taken.

Late, later, later still, Werner's friends went their own way, and he and I took a ride to the Champs Elysees. We parked, and within two minutes, we were approached by two most entrancing girls. They asked, both in French and English, if we wanted to make quick love for 2,000 francs, or 5,000 francs to share the remainder of the night. The women were quite attractive, and I hadn't scratched opposite-sex love from my psyche, but still. Who would have to pay for orgasm in a city like Paris? Who would ever need to pay for it at all? It was everywhere, especially here. If I hadn't been near-obsessed with thoughts of Antonio, this was the city I would have chosen specifically to seek romance—but it certainly wouldn't have been with a prostitute!

Werner might have been the more likely choice, but he and I never made love. The idea that he might be attempting a seduction was so far from my mind that to this day, I can't be sure if that was his intention. The fact that I was saving myself for Antonio had blinded me.

Strangely, the fantasies of Rome held so little moral confusion for me, and now I remember it all with a sensation of… 'bemusement' might be the word. When I thought of being with the Roman Antonio, I imagined love rather than sex. Perhaps that was because I had no literal foundation for sexual fantasies, but on the other hand, my preference for romance over lust was probably why I hadn't yet had a sexual experience.

I never even masturbated as a youth. Why? For starters, my mother had always warned me that masturbation would cause me to go blind. Yes, we've all heard that before, but my own mother gave this admonition with such authority that I believed her. I didn't find out until much, much later in life that there's an actual precedent for Mother's certainty: In 1870, a woman named Ellen White wrote—what shall I call her writing? I'll say she put together a lot of pitiful, self-indulgent material about the horrors of masturbation. She used words like 'paying the penalty of violated laws' and that nature 'will protest against the abuse she has suffered.' White insisted that many masturbating fiends sank into an early grave, but if they had enough constitution to live and continue embarrassing themselves in front of the deity-that-be, those sinners were always afflicted with 'pains in the system' (like liver, kidney, and lung damage), also neuralgia, cancerous tumors, and yes, blindness was among the problems to fear from the dread disease of 'self-inflicted orgasm.'

If Mother was exposed to that sort of nonsense during her own formative years, I can understand why she felt it her duty to pass it on to her young son. She couldn't have expected my father to educate me with respect to sexuality, because his emotional unavailability toward me was obvious to her, too. It could have been that she overcompensated for what she knew I lacked in that relationship, and was especially tender with me, but it could also have been that my father was overcompensating for my especially affectionate mother. Never having fathered a child myself, I wouldn't be able to say what motivates parental behavior. I would like to think, though, that any child of mine would have received the utmost love and attention.

I see I've wandered from Paris again. I and my temporary companion, the kind engineer named Werner, gracefully declined the suggestions made by the ladies of the evening. Chuckling, we strolled to the L'Arc de Triomphe. The structure was unlit, (the night had long turned to a deep, dark morning), but L'Arc was huge, its shape massive against the dark sky.

Still unwilling to succumb to sleep, we headed toward Montparnesse, and once there to a nightclub, where we watched a terrific show. More prostitutes approached throughout, and I learned then what was meant by the expression that Paris was 'naughty but nice'. Werner and I proceeded to move from one nightclub to another, stopping briefly at each establishment to absorb the local, after-hours color. As dawn began to break, we searched through Montparnesse, and then Halles, the marketplace, for a bite to eat. I hadn't ever seen vegetables and fruits so large and inviting in America, so richly scented and alive with deep greens, luscious yellows, and sugary oranges. An *Ad hoc* still life.

We settled on French onion soup at 6:30 a.m., which may sound unappealing but it was more than a meal, it was an experience. They served it in huge bowls, topped with melted cheese that had been toasted to a golden brown. This treat fully addressed the senses; the simplistic presentation held a stimulating allure, the flavor was outstanding, the texture smooth and satisfying, the very smell of it was intoxicating.

After we returned to our hotel, I stole some daylight hours of sleep before finishing the paperwork on my Renault with local officials. Werner and I then spent another evening on the town. After a long meal we explored some more of late-night Paris, and here's the entry from my journal:

> …we found a cave nightclub in the student section. It looked like it had once been an old Paris sewer, now it was filled with smoke and people. The entertainment was supplied by the patrons themselves, and there was a fine group spirit as French singers and guitar players joined in.

There must be places like that still in existence, but are they still as easy to find?

There were two reasons I was able to easily leave Paris after these extraordinary experiences. One was that a long, provocative road lay ahead. The other is because I knew I would be back the following year, on the final leg of my journey.

Little did I know that I would taste a morsel of my future when I returned.

4

European Road Trip

My Renault was set to go. I was fully prepared. Maps, sleeping bag, lantern, Coleman stove; check. Wine, tea, instant coffee, and for my first meal on the road I had purchased cream puffs, French bread, chicken pate, and grapes. When I approached the French/German border, I stopped to enjoy my meal, and prepared to sleep in my car, parked next to a manicured, unfenced farm field. Nobody bothered me, which I suspect would be unusual these days.

This was my first night of transforming the car into a mini-bedroom. The trunk was full of my necessities, and much of the inside of the car was filled, too. This meant it was necessary to finagle the removed passenger seat onto the driver's seat, unless I wanted to leave it outside, which didn't seem the right idea while on the side of a well-traveled road.

Once the driver and passenger seat were occupying the same space, I rearranged my in-car belongings to a steady, secure stack on the rear seat. With wind that's unlikely to come from my lungs these days, I blew up the air mattress, fitted it into place, readied my sleeping bag and pillow, and closed the door.

Some of us have slept in odd beds, and in unusual positions, throughout our lives. This particularly rare accommodation, for me, has never been topped. It served my young self adequately, though, and before long, I would become quite adept at preparing my car for rest.

The following morning I restructured my car, drove to Strasbourg, and crossed the border into Germany. Because the Renault had no radio, I sang to myself along the way. I once got caught in a circle of the old French song 'Frere Jacques' and couldn't find the end, which had me chuckling with each refrain.

Saturday night I stayed in my car at a German camping ground outside Offenbach. There, I took some time writing in my journal by flashlight, but curious passersby from the campground made me self-conscious. I doused the light and lay looking up at the stars through the sun-roof, my body bent but comfortable.

It was strange to be in the country of a race that had brought so much recent terror to Jews. Stranger still, I felt somewhat separated from it; my ancestry was not of German Jews, and I was not Israeli. I was an American, if a label need be applied, and that I also happened to be Jewish was incidental.

My ancestors came from lands further north and east, in "The Pale" of Russia, to be exact. The Pale extended from the Baltic Sea to the Black Sea, and it had been set up as a buffer zone between Moscow and Europe. The Russian government had forced Jews to live in that place, gathering them from other areas of Russia and deporting them there.

My family had arrived in the United States from The Pale in the late 1890s. Our original name was Kartzmer, and although it's pronounced exactly the way it looks, it was changed to Carr at Ellis Island in the year 1898. 'Carr' has no definitive nationality I know of, therefore I felt I would have no reason to fear anyone discovering my Jewish roots and treating me roughly for it. (Obviously, this would become particularly important when I began traveling through countries of the Middle East.)

I traveled to the top of a mountain, then down again through forests so dark, thick and tall, the trees looked like walls. Villages were nestled among the trunks, each holding a singular enchantment for me, and my fingers itched to capture them with a paintbrush. However, I only had a minimum of supplies at the time, and in those early days of my trip it was hard to halt my forward momentum. Instead, as a nod to my creative impulse, I sang out every song that crossed through my mind as I drove.

I came to a place called Wolfbach, which was a little village I thought more likely to be found in a country like Holland. The inhabitants wore peasant costumes, small canals were everywhere, and quaint homes edged closer to the street with each succeeding floor.

Not far outside that town, a girl waved for me to stop, and I pulled over. The first thing I needed to know was whether she spoke English, and she did, quite well.

She asked me, "Would I be able to get a ride with you?"

"Where are you going?"

"Tubingen."

I cleared the passenger seat of my map and invited her in. Holding up the map, I asked her, "Can you show me where that is?"

"Certainly…. It is here." She stabbed the spot on the map and smiled engagingly, in case it wasn't the direction I was headed. Lucky for her, it was right on the way to Reutlingen, which was my day's destination. "I can take you there, no problem."

"Thank you." She settled into her seat and asked, "You are American?"

"Yes."

"You are a nice American man."

I was happy she thought so. We made our introductions as I drove, and I learned she had a delightful German name, perhaps 'Sebine' (pronounced 'Seh-bih-neh'). I said, "You speak excellent English, where did you learn?"

As Sebine answered, I listened with pleasure to every 'v' that replaced the letter 'w'. "I studied it in school," she said, "and when the war came I spoke with many Americans, and learned more. You are too young to have been in the war, is that correct?"

"That's right. This is my first time in Europe."

"I think you will find it a beautiful place. Will you be in Germany long?"

I explained the nature of my journey, and she nodded enthusiastically. When I mentioned the areas of the Middle East, she warned me, "They are having many problems in that area, now that Israel has been formed. You are lucky you are not a Jew." The word came out like 'Chew.'

"But I *am* Jewish." That was unplanned, although certainly some part of me wanted to see her reaction.

I could feel her staring at my profile. I turned to get a better look at the expression on her face, and saw her working her chin as though she thought she should speak, but couldn't find the words. I smiled. "Surprised?"

"You are Jewish?"

My smile broadened. "Yes. Did you expect I would have horns growing out of my head?"

She laughed, sweetly, openly. "It is not—you are not what I expected."

"You've never met a Jewish man before?"

"Not that I know of. In school they told us Jews had horns."

It didn't occur to me that I could really spin her brain by adding that although she was very pretty, I might be more attracted to her brother. Even if the thought had passed through my mind, I still wouldn't have spoken it aloud; it would have been a more dangerous admission. Jews weren't the only victims of Hitler's regime, and homosexuals were at the bottom of the list for a sympathetic reaction.

Sebine laughed again, shaking her head in wonder, and I hoped she had shaken free a few notions that had been banged into her skull as a child. "Will," she said, "I do not care if you are Jewish, I am more interested that you are American. Have you heard of Nat King Cole?"

"You bet." I began to sing *Unforgettable*, and she immediately joined in. We then proceeded to sing every song we could think of for more than an hour, pausing only when she would touch my arm and point out a special sight. Do drivers still sing with the hitchhikers they've picked up? Maybe not; cars these days come with radios.

The Neckar River began to run alongside our road, and Sebine told me, "There is a wonderful restaurant in Tubingen, it sits right on the river. You must have dinner with me tonight."

How could I resist? She may have been mildly flirting, but I wouldn't have noticed. When it comes to the dance of flirtation, I've never quite been in step. All I knew was that this pretty young woman had charmed me, and we pulled into the restaurant in the late afternoon.

We sat in a booth that looked out over the water, taking our time with a hearty German meal of venison and *spetzle*, which are tasty, rich noodles. We watched the sun drop lower in the sky, and the water of the river blended with the backlit woods and hills. Sebine told me of her plans for the future. Did she intend to marry and have children, or become a professional in some field? I don't remember, only that I couldn't have enjoyed her company more. No commitment, no expectations, no underlying hopes or desires.

Later we walked through her fair, irregularly built town, strolling among the jolly people, passing the quaint squares. The Hohentu bingen Castle sat majestically above us, filled with students of the University it had become.

When Sebine and I parted, it was with a smile and an innocent embrace. We didn't exchange addresses or phone numbers, and that was apparently what we both wanted; brief, simple, non-obligatory companionship.

*　*　*

A few days later found me at a military PX, purchasing supplies, and then on the road to Munich. Before long, there I was, in October, in Munich of all places. *Oktoberfest!*

I must admit I didn't feel comfortable about leaving my car parked along the streets of the city during the great celebration. For all I knew, the police would object, and I was also concerned about all those people drinking themselves senseless, then barreling around the streets in their big European cars long before drinking-and-driving laws began to be strictly enforced. The problem was that after a number of enquiries, I learned there wasn't a single available room to be found in the city.

In a flash of genius, I approached a taxi driver and gave him a wink. "Excuse me, but do you know where I can find a house with…very *pretty* women?" (Wink again.)

"Of course, I know that!" he answered, fortunately in English, although his accent was heavy enough that if he said much more he might have lost me. He opened the back door of his cab. "I will take you."

"But I have my own car."

Confident in the number of paying fares he'd find that night, he gave me simple directions. I found the place and approached the Madam. Again, I was lucky she spoke English.

I addressed her, "Madam," (what else?) and asked, "Would it

be possible to rent a room from you tonight? After the celebrations? I only want to sleep, nothing more."

She looked at me, then beyond me, then over her own shoulder, smiling as though I were trying to pull a joke on her. When she found I had no accomplices nearby, she said, "I understand. We can be discreet."

"No, I'm serious. I only want a place to sleep, that's all." It still astonished me that a person would actually pay for something as simple to obtain as sex. "What would you charge for a room that would be for me alone?"

Now a new, though still cynical, understanding lit her eye. "I am sorry, but if you would like a place to call your own for the night, you would not be able to bring a *Fraulein* in from outside."

I captured her eyes with my own and spoke very seriously. "Madam, there are no rooms available in Munich. I would sleep here, that is all. I promise you, I would never bring anyone else here to be with me." My gaze traveled across two women who sat on a couch beyond the entryway. "The Frauleins here are the most desirable in the city, and if I did want companionship, I wouldn't hesitate to come to you for it."

The Madam's cynicism faded and I saw a flickering of the woman underneath the persona. Here was a lady who accepted the nature of her existence and its oddities, she might have had a child or two in her lifetime, she had certainly loved and lost. Only human, just making a living, a woman who was now confronted with a polite young man who truly wanted nothing more (or less) than to sleep.

I said, "I have my own sleeping bag and an air mattress. If you have a corner anywhere, I could just curl up."

She took my arm with that sensual intimacy a Madam can convey with a touch, and led me inside the house. "Let me see. Of course I cannot give up one of my rooms, especially during the Oktoberfest."

I nodded my understanding. "Of course not."

We came to a door and she opened it to a large bathroom. It was scented with perfumes, and its counter-tops were filled with makeup jars, powders, lipsticks, and more womanly accoutrements I never could have identified. Pointing to a length of carpet along one wall, she said, "You could lay your mattress there, and you wouldn't be bothered."

My eyes gathered in the room again. "Wouldn't I be in everybody's way?"

"This is a fifth bathroom of the house, and it is used most often in the late mornings. Throughout the night, the Frauleins use the toilettes nearer their rooms."

With a friendly shrug of acceptance, I said, "I'll take it." I pulled my wallet from my pocket and raised the question with my eyebrows.

The Madam stroked her chin thoughtfully. "You have American money?"

"Yes, but not a lot of it."

"I will let you sleep here for two dollars and forty-five cents."

The odd amount made me laugh, but I realized it probably translated into a clean figure in German marks. Whatever the case, the Madam might have mistaken my chuckle for a response to the absurdity of paying cash money to sleep in a bathroom, so she added, "I will include breakfast in that price, of course."

"Oh," I said, "in that case, how could I refuse?"

"You will tell me if you wish to have company for the evening?"

"Of course."

"She would only be a small additional payment."

"I'll let you know." I paid for the room, the deal was made, and that was the first and last time I've ever spent money in a whorehouse.

Time to return to the streets and find the center of the celebration, which had already been underway for more than a week.

Munich at the end of 1953, on an Oktoberfest night, was free and happy, quite a place to be. Most of the cars were huge gas-guzzlers, trundling along through wide streets, dodging the merrymakers who often offered a draught from their stein to passers-by. The police were grinning more than scowling, and it could have been the largest 4th of July party I've ever seen, only colder.

For those who are curious about details: The Oktoberfest originated right there in Munich, about two hundred years ago, when the citizens of the city were invited to participate in the celebration of Crown Prince Ludwig's marriage. He married Princess Therese, which is why the area where the Oktoberfest is celebrated (for two whole weeks!) is called 'Theresienwiese' (Theresa's field), or the abbreviated "Wies'n" to the locals.

I followed the revelers through the Wies'n until I heard English being spoken, although the accent wasn't American. Not exactly British, either. I caught up with the group of party-goers, and found they were tourists from South Africa.

"Hello!" I called. "Can you direct me to the nearest beer garden?"

There must have been about six men together, but they turned as one, smiling at the clearly American tone of my voice. "You've found the right place!" one said. They spread apart, offering me a path to the opening of a giant 'tent' (more of a permanent building), and at the end of this human tunnel I could see dozens of steins had just been raised in a toast. Before I could start searching for a stein of my own, one was thrust into my hand. I joined the toast, "Skoal!" and the party, for me, was off and running.

A question: How long can a man hold a gigantic stein, filled with beer, while his arm is extended in front of him? It can be counted in minutes—the weight increases exponentially—but when a crowd of hundreds is counting with him, he can press out a few extra seconds.

Another question: How fast can a woman eat a giant pretzel (or 'brezn')? Quite quickly, if she's had practice, and again it helps if a huge crowd is cheering her on.

If you're at an Oktoberfest and you happen to land in the path of a group of people spinning through a dance, you'll be caught up in it. Hands clapping in unison, feet kicking, bodies turning with elbows linked, and very few drops of the special, incomparable German beer are spilled.

Every so often, I stopped long enough to eat a bratwurst, smothered with sauerkraut and onions, dotted with German mustard and ketchup. The ketchup, incidentally, was darker and bolder than what we're used to, and you could see specs of the spices in it. Half-chickens were served, too, with heavy breads, and "hax'n," which is pork knuckles. I also tasted pastries, and nuts that had been salted and cinnamin'd, and creamy ice creams. Despite all that sustenance, I managed to stay about as drunk as I had ever been in my life. This is why my memories are sketchy after the first few hours. I do know the band was dressed in short pants and suspenders, with adorable little caps on their heads, and I remember our waitress needed a ride home, so at the end of the night I and my South African friends brought her and her husband out for coffee, and then to their house, before daybreak.

I slept in the bathroom at the whorehouse until late morning, when a tap at the door told me there was now a need for that particular room's business, and I made myself scarce.

After Munich I headed for the Zugspitze. This is the highest mountain in Germany, and it's named for the snow-slides that often fall on the steep northern slopes. The border between Germany and Austria runs right through this range. The mountain had been climbed many times before, and I wasn't equipped for that anyway, so I rode the cable car to the top.

That was something I could add to the common book of tours, but now it was time to return to my trusty Renault and continue driving. I arrived in Innsbruck, Austria while it was still daylight, bright enough to see that the people were much like most Germans in coloring but not in the construct of their faces. Also, something about the people of this town made me think they were a basically happy lot.

Preferring to walk, I parked my car and wandered on foot, absorbing the quaint, somehow different agelessness to it. It was strangely easy to find the center of what was one of the largest cities of Austria, more like finding the hub of a small town.

In that town's center I stopped for something to eat, feasting on (of all things) whipped cream. It's one of my weaknesses, and I had heard that they make fabulous whipped cream in Austria. It's true. Absolute delight; thick and rich with none of the waxy taste that can come from an aerosol can. I must have eaten a pound of it, and would have eaten more if I didn't worry I might spoil my love of it.

I sat in the square, watching the people pass, awed by the surrounding mountains, the flower-and-vine-covered stone buildings, and the small castle-like homes. A group of American girls passed by, following a man who happily led their tour, and I said hello. They told me of a wine festival, said they were headed there, and insisted that I join them. I agreed, because although I didn't know what to expect, I assumed the experience would be enjoyable if shared with this lively group.

The festival exceeded my hopes of a pleasant evening. The singing and dancing were endless, and I do love to dance. I like to sing, too, and was able to join in the way a person might when they can guess the tune of a hymn, and enthusiastically make acceptable word-like sounds along with the choir.

A queen of the wine festival was elected, she was toasted with hearty cheers and respectful admiration, and we all feasted like royalty. I'm sure there must have been meats and carbs and such, but all I remember is the desserts, such a colorful variety! I sampled everything: chocolates and cheeses and fruits and pastries with luscious fillings and covered in light frostings. Also (of course!) mountains of whipped cream. Nobody seemed ashamed of eating like this. Not once did I see a woman shake her head demurely and say, "I must watch my waistline." I remember the people had large, healthy builds, but none of them were obese. They fully indulged in their foods and desserts, with no guilt, because it was dairy country, and the hard labor they did on their farms was better than any workout they might have achieved in a gym.

What a life. What a festival. It would have been enough fun without the wine, but of course the reds, whites, and blushes made it all the more playful. I wish I could go back again, but then, every nuance would need to be the same (including the era), and I think my memories are best left unsullied.

I woke early, clearheaded (thanks to youthful resilience), and treated myself to breakfast. I might have had whipped cream in my coffee. At the restaurant, I met a ski-boot manufacturer, which must have been some sort of cosmic fate, because I did indeed want a pair of ski-boots that had been made in Austria.

This professional took one look at my shoes and said, "You'll need a special pair, for those narrow feet." We went to his shop and he took my measurements, then promised to have the boots ready when I returned. That wouldn't be for many months yet, but neither of us saw any reason for mistrust. Those were the days.

After a final farewell to my friends from the evening before, I checked my map. Switzerland was next, then I would enter Italy. Italy, Rome, Antonio. My sexual clock was ticking, and I could barely manage my impatience.

Traveling through Austria and Switzerland on a rainy, overcast day is not something I expected to be satisfying, yet a muted radiance existed, with color bleeding through the gray. The subtle beauty snatched at my breath. The little villages were positively picturesque, and there was plenty of time to admire them as I crept carefully through them, dodging goats, chickens, and cows.

After stopping a few times for directions, I decided it was better to ask children. Adults usually began babbling an answer (or a question of their own) in a language I couldn't understand, but children would simply turn, look, and point.

Once I found the border road, I knew I would be able to make it to St. Moritz that night. I would be more than ready to rest by then. With my fatigue came another nudge of lonesome depression, despite (or perhaps because of) the beauty of the drive. The road from Austria into Switzerland was rugged and gorgeous, everything so tall, from the trees to the mountains to the waterfalls. I had heard the people would be the same. It was difficult to shake the wish that I could share it all with a lover, or a close companion of any sort. I patted the dashboard of my car, seeking comfort in the hum of her engine, and sang her a few ballads.

The change between Austria and Switzerland was surprisingly noticeable. I saw it in the land, which became more rough, and in the roads, which were hilly and less maintained than others I had traversed. Also, it seemed the amount of farm animals on the road had quadrupled. I don't think I moved faster than about ten miles per hour each time I passed through a village, for fear of harming the livelihood of these people. Yet, I began to wonder deliriously if there was some sort of cow conspiracy; they timed their road crossings to coincide perfectly with each village I approached. They all looked alike, not as individuals, but as groups. Was I driving in circles?

Obviously, I was getting too tired. By the time I arrived in St. Moritz, it was raining and dark, and that lurking depression had begun to hover around me like an aura. I found a fine hotel—not for sleep, because I could only afford my Renault accommodations—but for currency exchange. They short-changed me, which was the last thing that should be done to a travel-weary young man. I spent a few minutes blearily running figures through my mind, then made a bit of a fuss. "The exchange you've given me doesn't match the sign you have posted in your window!"

The clerk made a show of doing another tally on a sheet of paper. "Ah, yes, I see that is so."

"Please pay me the additional amount."

"That, I cannot do."

"Excuse me?"

"I cannot re-do the transaction, our paperwork does not allow it."

It seemed that he had misinterpreted my use of the word 'excuse,' and I attempted to explain. "When I say 'ex-cuze' it means, 'I beg your pardon.' I did not ask you to offer me a lame excuse."

What had been an excellent grasp of English became broken and confused. "I do not understand."

"All I need you to understand is that you must compensate me for the discrepancy. I demand the proper exchange, which means you owe me…" I needed a piece of paper of my own, but the concierge held up a hand.

"Sir, allow me to offer you a meal at our fine restaurant, by way of compensation."

"A meal?" He was a smart boy; I must have been palpitating with hunger by that time.

"Yes, we have the finest chef in St. Moritz, and you may order anything you like from the menu."

It was time to give in. "I think that would be acceptable, thank you."

"No, thank *you*, sir."

Whatever. I was able to choose a delightful meal, and considering that the amount they had underpaid me in the exchange had only been equivalent to about two dollars U.S., it was quite a bargain.

After dinner, I returned outside to the rainy night and drove to an empty parking lot at a different hotel. The place hadn't yet opened for the season, so I ignored the 'No Parking' sign and prepared my little auto-bedroom. Admittedly, dealing with the removal of the seat in the rain was uncomfortable, at best. By the time I was properly set up, dry, and snuggled into place, I was ready to drop into a deep slumber.

Before I nodded off, a car pulled up next to mine, and a couple climbed out. 'Good,' I thought, 'it looks like I'm not the only one ignoring the parking sign.' The couple glanced in at me with no more than a mild curiosity, and walked on. I fluffed my pillow and sought a more comfortable sleeping position, but the headlights of another car flashed over me. Then another. This was turning out to be quite a busy parking lot, and every second couple couldn't resist a look into the strange car parked in their lot. I propped myself up on one elbow and peered through the rain in the direction everyone was headed. A cinema. Lovely. They would all be back in a few hours to gaze in at my sleeping self before they climbed back into their cars and started their engines with a collective roar.

It crossed my mind that I should put a sign and a change box on the window: "See the American sleeping in his Renault, only ten francs a peek." Then I fell back and slept deeply until morning.

The follow day broke with a shining sun, and my depression was born away on its rays. I had rested well, and sometime that day, I would enter Italy.

5

A First In Italy

Late morning had arrived by the time I crossed into Italy, which is a country that entranced me within minutes of arriving in its sunshine and warmth, its smell and filth. Yes, even the 'filth' was entrancing, because Italian muck is different than American muck. Also, it meant the people there might be slightly less civilized than those I usually associated with, which is something I think each of us should experience at least once.

Besides, it wasn't dirty everywhere. Not by any means. That was only a first impression—the feel of a border town. Naturally, there were many modern, clean places in the country despite the poor areas that were still recovering from the war.

Before long, I passed through a small town by a lake and was caught in a thick crowd of people, pigs, chickens, vendors of fresh fruits and vegetables, stalls of clothes and shoes, and jewelry counters. The open market was in full swing. There wasn't room for my car along with the shoppers and sellers, so I enthusiastically decided to stop and explore. There were many things to see, feel, and experience there, not the least of which was the people of Northern Italy. After parking my car in a safe spot, I began to investigate this fascinating bazaar.

Everyone stared at me, and I stared back because there's no crime in curiosity. The extremes of color and noise were like a hyper-reality. We of the human race must try to feed and clothe ourselves, supply and acquire, yet how differently we do so in our various lands!

One woman in particular caught my eye. She wore a simple, tattered black dress, feet shod in what looked like cardboard sandals, and stringy hair pulled back in a tight bun. It was not only by that appearance, but also by the lines of strain and endurance on her face that I could see she was very poor. What had captured my attention was that she was standing so very still, in those sorry sandals, gazing at a display of cheap shoes. While I watched, she finally moved, turning around to face the vegetable stand behind her. The stillness came over her again as she stared at the food. After a while, she took two steps toward the food, and in those two steps, I could see how her feet hurt her. Her head swivelled on her neck back to the rows of shoes, forth to the vegetables, and back again. Once or twice, she repeated those few steps between the vendors' stalls, as though testing the pain of her feet against the ache of hunger caused by the activity of walking.

My humanist spirit berated me for not offering money to her. I didn't belong in this world, I was an aberration. No one in this town seemed inclined to beg; might it wound her pride if I bought her a pair of shoes? Would she become the subject of mocking pity, or even perilous envy? I stood a moment longer, fingering the coins in my pocket, watching as she chose a thatch of greens, paid, and hobbled slowly away without another glance at the shoes.

A break in the market activities enabled me to make my escape, and I returned to my route. Once again, I found my heart beating double-takes at the delightful still-life scenes I passed. Walled villas, sculpted trees, and strikingly smooth, blue water surrounded this well-paved road to Milan. I stopped only once, to cook coffee and make sandwiches, then arrived in Milan in time to be quite confused by the post-siesta traffic.

Eventually, I found an awesome, carved-etched cathedral wall to photograph and now that I had satisfied my inner tourist, I found the autobahn that would eventually bring me to Portofino.

Once off the autobahn, I passed through the towns along the Riviera. Somehow I knew Portofino would be a special place, although many of the villages I passed could have held anyone for a long stay. But Portofino…. Here is what I wrote in my journal about that town:

> It was at the end of the peninsula, almost on a point. The road was narrow, hugging the cliff toward the water on one side, and the mountain on the other. The color of sea, earth, and sky reached its perfection in the tiny little harbor town. Friendly locals were pleased to lend a human element to the beautiful backdrop.

Apparently, I wasn't the only one taken with this precious place; Truman Capote was there during my visit, which I knew because of small-town telegraph (gossip). Besides, the man had parked his yacht right in the harbor. Because attitudes then were slightly different than they are today, I could have found out where he was staying and made his acquaintance. Other distractions took my time, though, so I passed the opportunity.

My most amusing experience in Portofino was when I met some American tourists, two girls from Iowa, and we went swimming in a rocky cove near their hotel. The water was so inviting, so clean, and its buoyancy was remarkable. The girls decided to swim to an opposite area where they could sun themselves, but I stayed on my side of the cove to enjoy some peace.

A squeal of alarm caught my attention, and I stood to peer across the water at my friends of the present. They were speaking to a fisherman, who stood in his boat holding up an octopus. One of the girls called across to me, "Will! He says he caught that thing in this water not ten minutes ago!"

Cupping my hands around my mouth, I hollered, "You'll probably break some speed records swimming back to this side!"

More squeals as I laughed to myself, then the other girl began to speak earnestly to the fisherman. He shook his head gruffly, but looked my way, and even from the distance I could tell he was grinning, probably tossing me a wink. He began to motor away from the girls, and they danced and spun circles of desperation on their shore, begging him to return for them.

With a weary shake of his head, he spun his boat around and retrieved them. They thanked him all the way back across the water, while I sat down to watch their progress. I couldn't stop laughing, imagining an octopus-driven movie like *Jaws* some decades before that one hit the big screen.

When they were safely back to our original side of the cove, I suggested a picnic to calm their nerves. We drove to a nearby village, St. Margherita, and gathered a lunch of breads, cheeses, fruits, and wine. Back toward the water, to a stone dock in the port. There I sat, ironically in the midst of every heterosexual man's dream: Two comely young women, recently retrieved from potential tragedy, enjoying the oldest and (many say) the best meal of all. We talked about our lives and hopes and fantasies, we joked and sang songs together, even planned to share dinner later in the evening.

While we finished our picnic, a boat drew near—possibly sent by the heroic fisherman—and we allowed ourselves to be talked into a relatively inexpensive tour. I completely enjoyed the shared companionship with the girls, then and again, later, when we dined on broiled shrimp with cold, home-made mayonnaise, a fabulous treat.

That I had no designs on those women might have made for the sweetness of it all. Compatriots sharing a small segment of their own subjective adventures. No flirting, no nonsense, nothing but enjoyment and appreciation.

After the girls went back to their hotel that night, I stayed up longer, staring again at boats resting in the horseshoe that made the port. I began to realize how dangerous it was for me, a place like this, because the more I wanted to remain, the harder I would have to fight to go. But I did need to leave; an important awakening awaited me in Rome, and that was still a few stops away.

On my continued Italian travels, I passed through Pisa and continued on to Florence. There, I spent the night at a campground, on my air mattress under the stars, rather than inside my car. I was surrounded by German, British, and French tourists, but didn't hear another American accent. I lay staring up at a sky, which seemed brighter then than any I've seen in subsequent decades.

This was the first actual camping I had ever done, sleeping on the ground. Some ten years before I'd gone to a 'camp,' but that was really more of a place-away-from-home for rich kids. My father sold meat to the camps, and gave them excellent discounts in order to pay for my tuition. He must have wanted me to be exposed to the higher side of life, rubbing elbows with the wealthy, hoping I would crave it. At the moment I slept under the stars in Italy, my craving was more for real camping than for the high life.

It crossed my mind, more than a few times during my younger

years, that my father saw me more as 'offspring' than as 'son.' My idea of a father is a man who tries to guide his son not only in how to make proper choices in general, but also how to discover what choices are best for the boy as an individual. Further, the best sort of father wishes a good life for his adult son, with emphasis on what the son interprets to be that 'good life.' Under the stars in Florence, hands behind my head, comfortably extended on my air mattress, experiencing these foreign lands, it felt as though I had made an excellent choice. Not only had I separated myself from the selfish desires my father laid on me like a burden, but I could also become a case-in-point; "Submit to your own dreams." If we only ever follow the demands of those around us, we will never be able to look in the mirror and see 'self' looking back.

Father's dream, when I was a child, was that I would become a doctor. I had been mentally groomed for it, and in fact it was more than Father's dream, it was his expectation. That I had chosen to study art instead had created an even larger distance between us. We were two like-sided magnets, bouncing back from the very physics of the opposition our sameness created.

Did I say sameness? How could I possibly be like my father? Well, I've already mentioned that his charismatic personality kept him surrounded by admiring men and women, and there have been times in my life when I seemed to have the same sort of draw for people. I also believed in family, country, and friendship on a level equal to his. Most telling is that he, too, had always made his own choices, for better or worse—no matter what his parents thought of his behavior. There's little doubt in my mind that if he'd been born with a creative bent, he would have strayed from the business world with hardly another thought.

That night, I dreamed of a long but cold embrace, and awoke tangled in my sleeping bag, shivering in the dawn.

I spent another few days in Florence, visiting with another friend of Anne's, a man who was definitely a card-carrying heterosexual. Pleasant and polite, Marcello showed me (in his professional capacity) the popular Thomas Cook's Tour. It included the Medici tomb with Michelangelo's famous sculptures, the Bronzini doors of the basilica and the Medici chapel. It was perfect for my 'tourist' mode; out from behind the wheel and following an actual guide to famous sites.

The day after my tour I had lunch with a friend of Marcello's, who drove me through much of Florence, then took me to an exurb called Fiesole. I shared much friendly conversation with this young man, until later in the day, when he dropped me at a place on the coast where I wanted to continue wandering. Who should I meet within five minutes of his driving away? Mary!

Mary, who had left her pet skunk back in New York, the woman touring Europe with her duplicitous mix of first class reality and bohemian fantasies. I greeted her warmly.

"Will," she said, somehow putting a sort of Ivy League accent on my name, "how nice to see you. Have you enjoyed your slumming vacation?" She laughed with the new Italian friend who stood obsequiously beside her.

What could I say, and still remain polite? "My trip has been wonderful, so far, thanks. How about you? Getting good treatment at the hotels of Europe?"

"They're divine. So many touches you'll never find in the States." She wove her arm through the crook of her friend's elbow. "Why don't you have dinner with us tonight? You must be positively stahhved for some fine dining."

I could have said no, it would have been the most dignified response, but I do love good food. Further, I needed a ride back to Florence. Finally, what I was really 'stahhved' for was English-speaking company. (I assumed the Italian friend spoke English, but at the moment, all he had said was "Hi" when we were introduced.) In any case, I set aside my integrity and said, "Sure," then couldn't resist a subtle dig by adding, "I didn't have any other plans for the evening."

The dinner was admittedly delicious, and in the throes of companionship and wine, I agreed to get together with Mary again in the morning for some sight-seeing. At that time, I met more of the 'friends' she continually gathered around herself. I put quotes around the word 'friends' because when one lives a wealthy lifestyle, one never knows which friendships are real. For all I knew, many people might have truly enjoyed her company. In my particular case, I am easy to please in my friendships, and especially so in my acquaintanceships, but I was never thrilled to be sharing airspace with Mary.

However, as I said, I wouldn't dream of letting on to this in her presence, so she must have assumed I liked her. This became fortunate for me, because while the group of us walked through the streets of Florence, she was invited to the country for the weekend. She turned to me and said, "Will, why don't you stay in my hotel room while I'm gone?"

"Thank you, Mary! I would love that!" I would, too, because although I only planned on one more night in Florence, I'd have plenty of time to luxuriate in the surroundings she had temporarily abandoned. That night, I had my first hot bath in a long time, then stretched out on the down-filled mattress to swim in clean sheets and an eiderdown duvet.

Sure, I could have stayed the second free night, if I wanted to, but the fine room would have to be left regrettably empty. Nothing could stop me from the morning's plans: Rome. Antonio. I had some sort of cellular certainty that this would be the first man I would make love to, and he would be the first man to make love to me. In my mind, nothing could change this path of my fate.

It was time.

*   *   *

I'll start my story of Antonio by mentioning the boy I had kissed in New York, the struggling poet named Terry, who had come to say goodbye at my going-away party. He had given me the name of someone in Rome who could probably put me up for the night, an American man named Roger. I contacted that man as soon as I entered Rome, and he was more than willing to offer me his guest room.

Roger stood tall and effeminately slender, with an air of sophistication beyond his years (he couldn't have been more than about thirty-two). He was cultured and intelligent, with kind eyes set in a smooth-skinned face, and an aura that seemed lit for ambiance. He dressed impeccably, also had neatly groomed hair and nails.

I could instantly tell Roger was homosexual. He had the sort of softness I had seen in those who so proudly and openly strolled the streets of Greenwich Village. That certain vibe was with him, which I must say also meant he was very much of what I assumed I was not.

Yes, even on the verge of meeting Antonio, the man who had captivated my dreams and fantasies, I still didn't consider myself homosexual. As far as I could understand the way of my world, I was a man who would probably marry a woman and we would have a family. If before I married I experienced sex with other men, that would be acceptable. It didn't seem like a wrong sort of life, and at least in that ideology I was enlightened: Sex is not a sin. We're all sexual creatures, and it doesn't have to be dirty and ugly. That, in my opinion, is a concept which has been forced down our collective throats by entities larger than ourselves, like our churches and societies and families.

Now that I'm on the subject of the sort of sex called 'casual,' I should mention I did have one additional idea of how to finance my trip beyond savings, and possibly selling travel articles to the Renault agency. Trading sensual favors for room and board had also crossed my mind, even before I left the States. I don't know how my inexperienced self had created the concept, but it had indeed occurred to me that a nice man might provide me with a meal and a place to sleep if I exchanged kisses and touches with him. Odd that I would think in terms of what is essentially prostitution, when I find payment for sex to be a fundamentally absurd notion.

Even more strange is this: At the time I was thinking I might be willing to trade my affections for accommodations, I had never conceived of anal penetration. I'm not kidding. Is it just me, or does everyone have trouble interpreting their own twenty-seven year-old fantasies? Although I can understand my naiveté in that situation, based on an experience when I was very young. More on that later.

Back to prostitution: What a provocative word that is. I find it interesting that people have trouble with the concept of selling or trading their bodies for gain, yet we often sell our emotions, our mental health, even our very souls. For what? Gain. Advancement. Money.

As I've mentioned, my father (and in fact both my parents) had encouraged me to become a doctor, but that held no allure for me. My distaste for the occupation was kick-started when I was much younger; for those few years when we lived with my grandparents and some uncles.

At first, I did try to give in to my parents' desires. I started with pre-med at a university, but felt no academic enthusiasm. As an early course in dissection approached in my curriculum, I became more and more ill at ease, and less and less interested in schoolwork. Just before I was forced to begin cutting flesh, I gathered the strength against my parents wishes, and changed my major to the arts.

My point is yes, my parents were unhappy about my decision, but I didn't sell out on my emotions, mental health, or self-respect under their pressure. I couldn't pretend I was more interested in wealth and stature than I was compelled to follow my own passions. That I achieved a 4.0 grade average for my Bachelor of Arts was, for me, the empirical evidence that I had answered the call of my true aspirations. I don't even want to think about what my GPA would have been if I'd stayed in a field that didn't suit me!

What I'm saying is that prostitution is a many-faceted concept; demands are continually made upon us to sacrifice all sorts of aspects of ourselves. Which paths do we ultimately choose, and why, exactly? What human being in this society can judge the choices of others with a pure conscience?

* * *

All that said, the circumstances for encounters based on financial need had not yet presented themselves to me. It was still early in my trip, and I had been frugal. Besides, there was no need to struggle with any such conscience-thumping questions in Rome, because

Roger welcomed me generously, and showed me to the room in his home where I could sleep. In my newness to the ways of same-sex attractions, I had no idea of whether Roger felt any sort of sexual interest in me. As far as I could tell, we only ever spoke together as two friends who had just met.

In fact, at first it was difficult to hold a coherent conversation with Roger, because now that I was in Rome, thoughts of Antonio had permanently crowded to the surface. He was so incredibly close, now. We were on the same continent, in the same country, the same city. The handsome Roman had admitted his homosexuality to my sister, yet he stood tall and sturdy in his photograph, with a straight back and strong wrists. He wore masculine clothes, didn't use make-up or earrings. The encounter I had created in my mind could teach me how to love men without following any sort of prescribed look or attitude that might be labeled deviant. This man was bound to have a profound impact on my life.

Fate had its grip on me, even on the both of us, whether Antonio was aware of it or not. My ideas of our first interaction pinballed between love, lust, passion, sex, and romance. If the meeting didn't provide all of the above sensations, I knew it would produce at least one of them. The fates, or God, or Rome, or whatever power can be garnered by the fantasies we create in our own psyches…something made the approaching encounter irresistibly inevitable.

* * *

Roger, my kind and charming host, sat me down and placed a drink in my hands. "Tell me, Will, how has your trip been so far?"

"Incredible. I take it Terry told you about my travel plans?"

"He certainly did. You're only at the start of your adventures, aren't you?"

"Yes, I have months to go, yet, and about a dozen countries still on my agenda."

"You must get lonely, at times."

"I do. But I'm…" I wouldn't tell him how I intended to spin that problem right out of existence, as soon as possible. "I've met some wonderful people along the way. Fellow travelers, hitchhikers, other Americans who are touring Europe…" Did he expect me to mention lovers, too? I hadn't had any. Yet. More than anything, I wanted to borrow Roger's telephone and call the number my sister had given me for Antonio. However, I'd been raised better, so I said, "Roger, I'm curious. How is it that you're an American living in Rome?"

"I'm working for the United Nations."

But he was so young! "That sounds like an important job."

"It sounds like more than it is, at least thus far. For the moment, I'm a glorified secretary, but I have hopes, of course, that this will lead me to higher positions."

Such a modest man, and I liked his kind face. He was obviously intelligent, and worthy of respect. Our conversation deserved better focus from me. However, just as I determined that, Roger gave me the opening I had been seeking.

First, he said, "You'll have to let me treat you to dinner, tonight." No, that wasn't it. What he said next was what I'd been hoping for: "Unless there's anybody else in Rome you know of, somebody you've planned to contact?"

Before speaking, I took a breath to steady myself. Then, "Yes, as it happens, there is someone, he works at *Il Messaggero* newspaper. His name is Antonio Carlotti, and my sister met him while she was visiting here earlier in the year. I'd like to call him." I trailed off; my enthusiasm had slowed my perceptions, and it had taken a moment for me to notice the emotions that had played through Roger's eyes at the mention of Antonio's name.

Roger smiled widely, stood, and paced a step. He abruptly sat down again, as though he'd just caught himself acting silly, but didn't bother to disguise his delight. "Antonio! I know him, many people do. What an unbelievable coincidence that you know him too!"

"Well, I don't exactly *know* him, but my sister does, and she thought we should meet. He's aware of my plans to visit Rome, and he is sort of expecting me, but he didn't know when I'd arrive. If I can borrow your telephone?"

On his feet again, Roger said, "Oh, please, allow me. He's a lovely man, please allow me to contact him and tell him you're in town." He strode into the small den in his apartment, but returned a moment later. "Would you like him to join us for dinner tonight, if he's available?"

Nothing on earth could have changed my reply; "Absolutely!" I could only hope Roger wouldn't feel left out from the moment my eyes met the eyes of the man from the photo.

Roger returned to his den, dialed up the number of Antonio's offices, and engaged in a brief, enthusiastic conversation. He returned and told me, "I'm afraid it will only be the two of us tonight, but tomorrow, Antonio will be free in the afternoon."

"That will be fine." No, it wouldn't, but what difference could it make to wait one more day?

Roger and I enjoyed our dinner together, but when I lay down that night, it was with the image of the sensual Italian man I would be meeting the following day. I was in such a near-swoon, I couldn't have found the strength to masturbate even if I'd wanted to.

*   *   *

The phone call came at about 2:30 in the afternoon, while Roger was at work. A low voice spoke into my ear with that indescribably sexy Italian accent; "Will? I am Antonio, the friend of your sister, you know? I spoke with Roger yesterday evening, I am sorry I could not join you for dinner."

Fair wit had abandoned me, I might have stuttered something to the effect of, "You have nothing to be sorry about."

"I am now free for the afternoon, if you would like to meet?"

"Yes." A single, affirmative syllable? No problem.

"Now we must decide where to meet. There are cafes, or I could come to where you are staying."

"Come here." More single-syllabled words, which also happened to be fraught with *entendres*.

"Where are you?"

I was sitting at Roger's desk in his den, and if I hadn't been stopped by the fact that I was staring at an envelope with his address on it, I might have answered, 'Rome.' Instead, I read the street name and number to Antonio, who responded, "I will come soon."

There came that subtle, extra *entendre* again. I cradled the phone and stared at it a moment before grabbing a tissue and wiping the residue of my moist palm from the receiver.

Aside from the den, there was a living room, a kitchen, my guest room, a bathroom, and Roger's bedroom. I toured the place twice, twisting my fingers together, smoothing my hair, brushing lint from my clothes. Trying to force calm, I sat at the kitchen table and alternated between breathing and smoking. A slow, animate snapshot came to me of Antonio, in all his fleshly glory, embracing me. Advancing like a silent movie, he touched my eyebrows and my lips, kissed me, kissed my neck. Necking, all we were doing in my fantasy was necking, and my own imaginary doppelganger grasped me by the lapels and gave me a slight shake. There would be more to it than that.

When the buzzer sounded downstairs, not twenty minutes after his call, I leapt to my feet and pressed the button to let him into the building. Although it would take a moment for him to climb the stairs, I went to the door and opened it. Waiting, I shifted my weight from one foot to the other, trying on first a smile, then a serious expression, then a flirtatious grin. Fortunately, when he rounded the end of the hall, I knew my face had settled into a look that was calmly pleasant. My heart had found its healthiest rhythmic beat and my trembling had settled, because the reality of these long months had finally come to the moment of culmination.

Somehow, he was even more attractive than he had been in his photograph. His mouth was gently smiling, and he moved with the grace of a confident, professional man. Emotional balance streamed from his steps, and he wore class like a second set of clothing. Visible through this elegant, captivating persona was an aura of kindness, and just a sprinkling of a bashfulness in his curiosity that came clearer as he neared me.

We shook hands, and while the skin of our palms met for the very first time, his eyes held mine for a long, searching moment. With just that look, it felt as though he had lifted my hand, turned it, and kissed the softest part of my inner forearm. Even though he didn't do that, he surely read my feelings on my face. I stepped back and invited him in.

We sat at the small kitchen table, across from one another, and I believe we spoke. I might have offered him a drink, but if I did, he declined. The subject of Anne, the woman who had instigated this meeting, never even came up. To be honest, I don't remember that we spoke at all.

I do remember that he stared as much as I did. With his gaze, he examined my face, my hair, my ears, and the set of my shoulders. I watched his long eyelashes open and close with every blink, and when his tongue showed for an instant while he licked his lips, I swallowed like a hungry man who had glimpsed a tasty morsel of food.

Antonio stood, stepped around the table, and touched my arm. His fingers slid across mine, and he lifted my hand slowly, pulling me with a gentle invitation to my feet. He turned and walked toward the nearest doorway, which was fortunately the room Roger had so generously provided for me, and led me to the bed. He stopped there, touched the corner of my mouth with his thumb, and kissed me more slowly and sweetly than I had ever been kissed.

If a profession was established in this world specifically for the indoctrination of making love to men, Antonio could have been the CEO. Was it specifically because he was Italian? Such a violent history might be tempered by their deep appreciation of graceful art and artistic splendor, their passion for rich foods and wines, and their devotion to giving and receiving affection.

We undressed as lovers do, helping each other, sliding out of shirts and socks and shoes and underclothes as we continually touched and kissed. We pulled the covers back to the cool sheets beneath, and lay stretched out on our sides, front-to-front, more kisses, more touches, nudgings and lickings and suckings in all the right places. If there was any conversation, it was pillow talk; whispers and murmurs.

We did not have oral or anal sex; the meshing of our bodies, the deep kissing, and the closeness to his nude, male body was enough to bring me to climax. My first orgasm was something I imagined could never be matched again. His first orgasm with me titillated me enough to initiate the beginnings of my second, which outstripped the first. Did we climax again, and again after that? It's possible, even probable, because we were there for hours. More notably, I was twenty-seven at the time; young enough to be incredibly virile, but old enough to have a lot of catching up to do.

* * *

I didn't hear Roger come home. All I know is one minute, Antonio and I were feasting on each other with eyes, hands, and mouths, and the next moment, Roger was standing in the doorway of the room in a purple rage.

"What is this! Oh, my God!!! How could you??? You would use my home for this? Will, this is not acceptable! How dare you!"

While Antonio and I fussed with the covers, our clothes, and our dignity, Roger continued to rant. "You are no longer welcome in my home. You'll have to leave. Gather your things—my God, get dressed, first—then gather your things, and leave. You're going to have to leave here."

He stormed away, and I fell back on the bed for a moment, hoping to regain my senses. Every iota of fear and uncertainty and hesitation I had ever experienced, with respect to my desire for men, tried to leap to the surface of my consciousness and conscience. Those sensations were immediately driven back by the true answers I had uncovered with my gentle First, most notably that there is a beatific purity in love-making, no matter who the willing partners happen to be.

In the end, all personal reactions were replaced by the sense of decorum that had been bred into me. I had offended my host, a man I found to be generous, gracious, polite, and (present moment excluded) charming. An apology was in order.

Antonio whispered, as he pulled on his shoes, "I would invite you to stay in my home, but at this time I am living with my parents. I will find a place for you to sleep during your visit here, I promise you that."

I finished dressing, combed my fingers through my hair, and offered honestly grateful thanks. "But I'm going to speak with Roger, first."

"I understand. I will meet you below. Take as long as you need, I will wait."

We slipped from the room and I saw Antonio out of the apartment. Roger wasn't in the living room or the kitchen, so I went back to the guest room and packed my bags. After I arranged my few belongings at the door, I ventured into the den, where I found Roger. There he sat, his usually perfect hair askew, the knot of his tie yanked off-center, holding both a cigarette and a neat shot of scotch in one hand.

"Roger…"

He looked up at me with tortured eyes. "Oh, Will, I am so sorry—"

"No, I'm the one who needs to apologize!"

Brushing at the air with his free hand, he shook his head. He tried to speak, failed, drank from the glass, and sucked in a lungful of smoke before he began again. "I'm ashamed of my behavior. There was no good reason to attack you like that. You were only—" He shook his head once more, as though to clear it, and pulled at his glass and cigarette again.

I sat carefully on a chair near him and leaned forward. "Roger, please let me explain. When my sister first handed me that picture of Antonio, I knew right then I was destined to make love with him. I've never even been with a man before today."

"But Terry said the two of you had… He wasn't positive, but he strongly suspected you were…" He trailed off and narrowed his eyes, trying to remember.

"Terry and I only kissed," I told him. "We were never lovers. This is the very first time, for me, so I wasn't thinking clearly. Antonio and I should have found another place to go."

"No." Roger finished his drink, set down the glass, stubbed out the cigarette. Speaking with his head lowered, he said, "I'm so embarrassed. Everyone in Rome, all my friends, even I myself have been attracted to Antonio." He ventured a look to see if I was buying it, and in my innocence, I was. I assumed he truly was jealous that I had conquered Antonio, not that the jealousy might be directed toward Antonio seducing me.

Roger continued, "To have found the two of you there, in bed together, it was more than I could stand. It felt like something exploded inside me. I want to take back everything I said about you leaving here, you can stay as long as you want. And please, offer my most sincere apologies to Antonio, and don't hesitate to spend time with him." He took my hand in both of his and looked sincerely into my eyes. "You will stay, won't you?"

He seemed about to cry, and I've always been a pushover for tears. "Of course I'll stay, Roger. It would be my pleasure. I can assure you, nothing like this will happen again."

"Don't say that. I want you to enjoy Antonio's company while you're here. I'm happy your first experience was with him."

What a kind man, was Roger. I stood and said, "I should put my bags back in the room, and get downstairs."

With no small measure of contrition, he asked, "Antonio is waiting for you?"

"Yes, he is."

"Enjoy your evening. Remember that I'm happy for you both."

"Thank you, Roger."

I joined Antonio, and told him of Roger's regrets and his sincere apology. Antonio gallantly accepted that with an understanding nod, and we were off together for an evening on the town.

While we indulged in a romantic dinner together, we finally spoke of my sister, also shared the stories of our lives, exchanged dreams, difficulties, and all the usual topics. We were two men who had just made love and had been admonished for it, and now we were exploring what more might come of our union. Ironically, all we really shared in common was an admiration of opera and a healthy respect for loving romance.

During post-dinner snifters of brandy, our conversation slowed to a halt. Our communication, on the other hand, continued. We watched one another, even offered our own selves up for observation, looking off as though interested in something away from the table while the other completed his examination.

Talk is measured and there are basic rules to be expected. Intuition is a better guide; much as I might have wished otherwise, I couldn't deny that somehow, the chemistry of this three-dimensional Antonio didn't mesh with me. I wondered, What could it be? My first instincts were correct; he's an admirable man, polished, with a healthy self-respect untouched by arrogance. He's perfect. How can I feel that something is missing?

The nature of my thoughts supplied the answer: Yes, he was perfect. What was lacking was imperfection. Sure, he might be the type to have the occasional extra-affair, or become unreasonably angry with a lover now and then, but he had the basics of the human condition down pat. He knew himself, accepted himself, had achieved the career of his dreams, and he was a whole person all alone. He and whatever mate he chose wouldn't result in my ideal of $1+1=1$. He didn't need me to complete him.

As is true of all life's episodes, it's hard to argue the philosophy that everything is meant to be, or not. Apparently, the purpose of Antonio for my life was to open the door that was specifically sexual, and nothing more. (Not that sexuality is a small awakening!) What I had sought in my fantasies was love, but in reality, it wouldn't hold. Antonio and I had undertaken only physicality. It seemed our lusty embraces held enough of a sort of love, though, and I suppose they do for all men.

Those considerations of Antonio aside, I had lost my virginity to a man. I hadn't been consciously aware of harboring any real guilt, yet it did exist inside me. It was built on a combination of expectations and censures from my world, but when visualized, its face was that of my father. Therefore, although I couldn't have enjoyed my experience more, it still seemed beyond the realm of what was acceptable for the overall me to be called 'queer.' I preferred the idea of referring to myself as merely 'sexual,' rather than homosexual. The only thing that caused waves in that illusion was the next man I met in Rome. I'll call him Bob.

I wonder if it's true that most people end up attracted to those who have similarities to their parents. My personal preference is for men built like my father; inherently strong, heavily muscled, with more density than sculpted bulk in his body. The kind of man who can turn me on is built with a low center of gravity, and has the gait and stance of a wrestler. To this day, I can still become excited by watching wrestling matches. It wouldn't surprise me to learn that many Gay men watch it, and purchase wrestling magazines, because there are so many sexual overtones to the sport. The man in me is drawn to the measured brutality, and I'm compelled by the desire to master another for the sheer power of mastery. Wrestling is not about home or family, institution or country; it is about men facing men, about intimate grasping and pressing of strong bodies. Achievement in wrestling is based on strength, determination, and desire. Desire to win, to conquer, and to gain the respect and admiration of not only one's opponent, but of all who observe.

As it happens, my father was athletic in his school days, and was in fact a wrestler on his college team while attending Rensselaer Polytechnic Institute in Troy, New York. When I was a child, the only way I could imagine being physically close to him would be if we were to wrestle, which is something we never did. Never once do I remember that we touched or hugged, much less kissed or cuddled. Or wrestled. My first wet dreams were fantasizing wrestling with my father. He would lead me down into the basement of our home, spread a mat, undress before me, then I would undress, then he would grab me, smother me with kisses, rub his body all over mine, hold me tight with his strong arms, look into my eyes, tell me he loves me and give me the strength and know-how to be a man, guide me into becoming a full human being, all the things that Fathers are suppose to give to their sons. To this day my favorite means of masturbating is to watch wrestling, preferring hunky men, even fat men like sumo wrestlers, each wearing only skimpy jockey shorts. As I watch them, I visualize each of them getting their cocks harder and harder, just as mine is doing now as I write this. Unlike most Gay men who place much value on whether a penis is circumcised or uncircumcised or whether it is large or small, the size of one's cock seems to make little impression on me since I am mainly a top, but I do know through experience that the bottom man enjoys a large uncircumcised penis more. Since I am now 81 years old and HIV

Positive, two factors which greatly limit my finding partners, this form of sexual release of visualizing wrestling is easy to come by. More than treasure or fond memories of my Father, I believe this is the best gift he left me.

His non-demonstrative attitude toward me felt, at times, like a conscious determination on his part. Some shrink or another might like to speculate that my father could have had latent tendencies, and feared getting physical with his soft-spirited son. If I'd heard that hypothesis, I would have responded, "What about all the women he seduced throughout his life?" The shrink could come back with the idea that sexual *conquistadors* are especially passionate people, therefore capable of all types of love. At that point (in this supposed therapy session), I would stroke my chin and say, "Hmm. Mother mentioned that he did once room with an actor in college, and she had implied; 'You know how those *creative* people can be....'"

Who knows. A therapist would probably have more fun with the knowledge that as a pubescent child, my favorite erotic fantasy was that never-to-be-had wrestling match with my father. There were times when it was necessary for me to share a bed with my father, perhaps when visiting friends or relatives with limited sleeping accommodations. During those long nights, I would lay awake, but shift as though in sleep in such a way as to find contact with him. I wanted to feel his skin. Because I had some fear of him (more on that later), it could only be on those rare occasions of forced sleeping arrangements that I could investigate my curiosity about the touch of my father's love. It was a curiosity of pure, innocent youth.

Now, all psychological rationalizations aside, I identify my father's behavior as bare selfishness. Perhaps it was that very selfishness that implanted a demand in my young heart, a demand that insisted on being heard. I *would* receive love and affection from a man!

*   *   *

Which brings me back to Bob, the man I met on my third night in Rome: He was built quite like my father. Bob was also a painter, something I was only aspiring to at the time. To top it all off, he was a fellow American, in Rome for a show of his work.

Here's how it happened: The night I returned home from my

evening with the delectable (though decidedly not wrestler-like) Antonio, my heartbroken host Roger presented a peace-offering.

As we sat with nightcaps, he ventured, "Did Antonio offer to take you sight-seeing tomorrow?"

"He has to work, but I do plan to absorb everything I can about this city on my own. I want to see ruins and museums and churches and art galleries—"

"I've heard an American painter has been showing his work at a local gallery, and tomorrow is his last day in Rome. Would you like to come with me and meet him?"

"Yes, I'd like that very much."

A pause, then Roger added: "I've heard he prefers men."

There went that trip of my heart again. Odd, that sitting there speaking with Roger, who I knew 'preferred men' himself, did nothing for me. Yet fantasy men, like the photogenic Antonio or an American painter in Rome, those men made me feel like someone had stuck a chattering card of fate in the spokes of my destiny. That both fantasies had a turn of truth astonishes me.

*   *   *

The evening of the show, I dressed in the best set of clothes I had, which in truth was a rather nice suit. Remember: in the 1950s, respectable young men who were touring foreign countries were more likely than not to have a suit and tie in their luggage. Properly attired, Roger and I arrived at the gallery, found glasses of wine, and began examining the paintings of this American artist.

All were portraits, as far as I could see, quite well done, very professional. I looked forward to meeting the artist, but before I could, a sturdy gentleman caught my eye. He was dressed a little more casually than I was, in a suit but no tie, and the top button opened for the sake of his thick neck. He stood about my height, and although his chest was almost as deep as it was wide, his stomach was flat and firm. He had a thick head of hair styled in a curly, grizzly crew-cut, and a square face, a strong jaw. As I watched him, he wrote something on a piece of paper and handed it to the woman standing next to him. Others stood waiting to talk with him, and it struck me—I clutched Roger's shoulder and pointed. "Don't tell me *that* is the artist?"

Roger smiled. "That is the artist. Bob Levin. I take it you're looking forward to an introduction?"

I was already making my way toward him. This man could have tackled me to the floor using nothing but his arms, and I would have been swooning before I hit.

Roger slowed my steps with a touch on my elbow. "He's deaf, and doesn't speak."

"He can't talk?"

"He might have the power of speech, but I imagine it would be difficult to understand him."

This did nothing to dampen my enthusiasm. Like the sweet Angelina from the Andrea Doria, I want to care for a man as much as I want to love him.

When I first locked eyes with Bob Levin, I saw a mirror image of what I just described: Here was someone who wanted to love a man as much as he wanted that man to care for him. At the first meeting of our eyes, Bob instantly tapped whatever emotions and longings Antonio had not answered.

Roger made the introductions, and while we shook hands, I put every measure of attraction and affection I could muster into my smile. I didn't think words would work, but Bob scribbled something on his pad and handed it to me.

'I can read lips, if you'll just say something.'

My smile turned into a grin and I said the first thing a person might say to a talented artist: "Your work is excellent."

He gave a demure nod of thanks, met my eyes again, and held them a long time. A man who cannot speak draws on every other sense, including the sixth, to communicate. I might have blushed.

I said, "I hear you're from the United States. What part?"

Five quick strokes on his pad, then he showed me, 'N Y'

I couldn't stop grinning. "New York? That's where I'm from!"

More people were beginning to crowd around us, and a sense of urgency quickened my heart, but what could I do? I said, "We'll have to exchange numbers, and we can meet for coffee when we're both back in the States."

Bob's full lips stretched back in a smile that suggested seduction, and he nodded his head. Ignoring the others waiting for his attention, he pointed to me and began to write again. His note said, 'Why're you in Rome?'

"I'm traveling, driving a Renault through all the countries around the Mediterranean."

He raised his eyebrows and thrust out his lower lip, nodding; an expression of admiration. Writing again, then: 'What's your work?'

The heat tried to rise in my face, because I wanted to tell this man I shared his passion. "I was working for an advertising agency, but what I really want to do is paint. I plan to do a collection of Yugoslavia, focusing more on places than people."

Again the approving nod. An older gentleman tapped Bob's shoulder. Bob held up a hand to the man, then furiously scribbled for a long moment, tore out the page, and handed it to me. At the top of the paper it said, 'Off to London tomorrow, commissioned to do portrait.' In the middle of the page was his full name, phone number, and address in New York. At the bottom of the note he had drawn an arrow pointing to his address, and had written, 'Back there next year.'

Nodding my head, I said, "Me too." For both of us, that could have meant anything from a few months (it was now late-October), to an actual year's worth of time.

Bob pocketed his notebook, grabbed my right hand with his left, and gave a gentle squeeze. A second later he slid his right in, now holding on with both hands, and squeezed again. His eyes never left mine. It felt as though he had passed a vibration of promise through our clutch.

I squeezed back. The people around us turned him away, drew him into their group, but he continued glancing over his shoulder at me.

Roger joined me as I backed away. "Will," he said, "that man is obviously quite attracted to you."

"Did you think so? I sort of felt that."

"You felt it? I was beginning to wonder if you were capable of realizing it at all, when a person is attracted to you."

At the time, I looked at him stupidly, because his words didn't make any sense. Now, after years of gradually acquired wisdom, I can say Roger may well have been more jealous of Antonio than he had been of me. Some men can find my style of naive innocence alluring, while others may think it's boring, even frustrating.

Bob, in the meantime, seemed to like the package he'd just been introduced to, and as I reached the door, I heard him call out to me in a loud, heavy gutteral voice: "Bye."

We'd meet again.

REPUBBLICA DI S.MARINO
ENTE GOVERNATIVO TURISMO

27 OTT. 953 D F R 1653

VISTO DI PASSAGGIO

REPUBBLICA DI S. MARINO

10

MARCA DA BOLLO

ΤΕΛΩΝΕΙΟΝ

Εἰσήγαγε σήμερον ... οι ὑπ' ἀριθ.
707069 πολυπτύχου λήξεως
20-9-54 Ἐν αὐτοκίνητον ἐπ Renault
βατικὸν ἡρίας
μὲ ἀριθμ. πλαισίου 193472
μηχανῆς 296

12

6

More Italy, More Men

I did dutifully explore Rome, but didn't see or experience anything that could be considered special or unusual. Correction: The entire place is special, but I have the feeling most people have a sense of that, so I don't think it's necessary to expand here. Other than to show a photo....

After I left, I drove a bit further south for a brief overnight stay in Naples. After the places I had already seen in Italy, Naples made no serious impression upon me. Pompeii, on the other hand, struck me with a magical sensation of true, historic Roman energy.

Many are probably aware, on some level, of the Mt. Vesuvius eruption in 79 AD that caused the devastation of Pompeii. There is more history to the place than that, of course! The municipality was founded by central Italians sometime in the 6th century B.C., and became allied with the Greeks, who were in control of the Bay of Naples. About a hundred years later a group called the Samnites conquered the municipality, and over the following centuries, blended some of their own architecture with that of the town. Time marched on, in that backwards way it will when referring to the times of B.C., until the people of Pompeii tried to take arms against Rome in 89 B.C. They fussed around with fruitless battles until 80 B.C., at which time it became a Roman colony.

As the decades rolled into the first century AD, Pompeii became fully and appreciatively Romanized. Its location made it a popular point for passage of goods, and it became a prosperous city of some 20,000 souls. Writers lived there, and artists, and of course merchants. People loved and made love, families grew and thrived there, many visited the restaurants, bars, and bathhouses, and they attended events in the Colosseum.

Is it possible that some true, mystic energy remains, because this bustling community was captured so suddenly and absolutely? At the time of my visit, the casts had already been made, long ago, of the victims. Those quick-formed shapes of crouching, terrified forms, hard-ash-husks which had once held the remains of human beings, they had been injected with plaster, and still remain today as ghastly monuments to Mother Nature's wrath.

The heat, the shock, the wave of astonishment of the volcano was felt around the Mediterranean Sea, and so much emotion might have literally captured an essence of the people who lived and died there in the first century. It seemed I could feel the Romans moving through the streets of Pompeii, I could sense the breathing, loving, civilized lives they were leading before that eruption halted them in their very steps.

The most eerie, perhaps lesser-known fact about the devastation of Pompeii is about the date the volcano erupted and smothered the sun in a darkness of smoke and ashes. The date was that of the Vulcanalia, which was the festival of the Roman god of fire.

As I departed Pompeii, I left a few prayerful vibrations of my own behind, in the form of awed respect for the place.

The next length of road brought me to a little fishing village called Positano. People of my generation may have read about it back in the fifties, in an amusing article written by John Steinbeck. That article can surely still be found, in libraries or on the Internet, and it's worth a read.

Italy is indeed an extraordinary country, and in that country, Positano might be the most awesome place of all. It is the single Italian town I couldn't resist returning to more than once in my life.

Now, I can only say that the specific time I was there was when I should have experimented with actually lingering for a while. It truly has changed. Yes, there are still stairs to navigate whenever one wants to go anywhere, because the town is built very much up the side of a mountain. Those walkways are still covered with wondrous climbing flowers and plants, too. It's a small Italian paradise. Unfortunately, it's impossible to keep a paradise hidden from the wandering tourists of our world, and the wisest of those people know when to land and set the anchor in stone.

Yet at the end of 1953, when I stumbled across this small site of heavenly coastal Italian life, I found myself among a very small handful of foreigners. There were probably no more than a dozen of us, and I'm sure I met most of those dozen, because there was one central place where we all gathered. Buca di Bacco, it was called; located on the beach at the base of town. It was a sort of Italian bar and grill for us foreigners, and we would sit there under the grass roof, sipping drinks, exchanging conversation, and watching the Mediterranean (or more correctly, the Bay of Naples). I remember meeting a blind Canadian there, also a German poet, an aloof Russian, and an American named Mark. There was an Englishman, too, who obviously had plenty of money, because I could see his mansion-like house perched high up the mountain.

I was introduced to the Buca di Bacco by a man named Vincente, who I'd met via remote introduction by Roger from Rome. Roger had known I would be visiting this town, and had given me Vincente's name, certain his friend would offer me a place to sleep. Vincente was another homosexual.

It may seem that I had suddenly tapped into an exclusive network, but that's a false impression. True, Vincente was literally a man's man, and as I merrily sailed into town, I wondered if he and I might enjoy each other physically. In truth, when we did meet, I found him handsome in that deliciously Italian way, with thick dark hair, bright white teeth, long eyelashes, and beautifully carved features, both facially and physically. Yet a fundamental attraction was, sadly, not there. I imagine Vincente must have thought I was crazy. I don't imagine he had been, or ever would be, refused by many Gay men in his lifetime. Certainly, those swarthy good looks and his tantalizing nationality rarely left him wanting.

Although I had no interest, I believe Vincente did, and this made me somewhat uncomfortable. Fortunately (for the situation) he had unbreakable plans on my first evening in town, so I whiled away the time at the Buca di Bacco, wondering how I could get out of staying with him. That is where I met the American named Mark, who although I don't remember how he made his living, I did know he was a very intelligent man, a Princeton graduate. We struck up a conversation, and before long, he asked where I would be staying while in town.

Because Vincente wasn't with me (he'd told me he would find me later in the evening), I was able to look Mark in the eye and say,

"I haven't decided, yet."

"Well, then you must stay with me! I have a comfortable little home, with a nice Italian lady who takes care of things."

"I wouldn't want to put you out of your way—"

"Not a bit of it! I insist you stay with me. Please allow me to make your stay as comfortable as possible."

Once again, many Gay men might look at me askance, because Mark wasn't my type either, although he was attractive in a smart, wiry, worldly sort-of-way. I'm not even sure if men were *his* type, at all, and never attempted to find out. Our comradely companionship was all that interested me.

What interested me even more was another of the foreigners, the German poet, whose name was Stephan. If the word had come to me in 1953, I could have been the one to coin 'hunk.' Before Mark and I left the Buca di Bacco that night, I had taken notice of the short, stocky man with the heavy mass of unkempt hair, the strong, thick thighs, and bright, piercing blue eyes that I occasionally caught flickering my way. He was speaking to someone else, and I was busy in my conversation with the engaging Mark, but yes, I noticed Stephan. However, this time, the fates knocking against my groin were of the more playful variety.

Here is the closest I ever come to taking the initiative: When Mark and I passed Stephan on the way out, I said, "We'll have to come back here tomorrow." Stephan heard me, of course; I had aimed the remark in his direction.

When Mark and I arrived at his home-away-from-home, we were greeted by the mouth-watering smell of a pot lightly bubbling on the stove. Mark went to it and said, "It's my main household duty to remember and take this off the heat." He opened the lid and tipped it toward me, offering me a deeper breath of it.

"What is it?" I peered into the large cast-iron pot, becoming instantly submerged in the steam of its exotic, distinctively Italian scents.

"Pasta sauce. Sophia keeps it going all day long, but I'm supposed to let it cool each night. If you're hungry, I can boil up some pasta."

I was tempted, but not at all hungry.

Mark said, "Don't worry about missing out, because it'll be on the stove the whole time you're here."

With a smile, I said, "Thanks, I'll wait, then. But how wonderful, that you have your own cook!" He couldn't have been more than a year or two older than me, yet there he was, living this amazing life.

Mark grinned. "She costs me the equivalent of about five dollars per month." He recovered the pot and said, "She's supposed to keep the place clean, too, but her heart isn't in it the way it is with the food." He grabbed a cloth and wiped at the drippings he'd left on the marble countertop next to the stove.

I squinted into the dimly lit room beyond the kitchen, and had a sense the place was neatly kept but not polished. Mark saw me looking and asked, "Ready for a tour?"

We passed through a wide, arched entryway between the kitchen (which we had entered first from outside) and the living room. He switched on a lamp that sat on a tall table just inside the entryway, then crossed to a tall floor lamp and lit its brighter bulb. In the wash of the two lights, I saw the floors were all tiled, and the walls were of a dark, rich, wood paneling. To my left was a large fireplace with cooling ashes. Close to it was an armchair of a natural fiber that matched the couch across the room. "Don't worry, you won't have to sleep on this old couch, I have another bedroom. You'll have your own WC."

For those young Americans who are unfamiliar with the term, a WC is a water closet or a bathroom that has an old, pull-chain style of toilet but no bath.

My host began to step through a curtained doorway, but I had moved toward the couch to admire the window behind it. Yes, the window, not what was outside, because I could only have seen my own reflection and the lights of the room behind me.

This window was about three feet high and seven feet long, with three separate panes of glass, and only the two outer panes could be opened. What I found architecturally brilliant was the fact that the center window was arched into the wall above, but on either side of it—the paneling above the panes that were openable—had been curved down to frame the edges, too. The effect was positively artistic.

I turned to Mark, who still stood next to the curtained doorway, which I realized was also an arch. Mark was grinning again. "Nice, isn't it?"

"Incredible."

He pulled the curtain aside to reveal his bedroom. When he switched on the lamp, I saw the smooth pattern of brown tiles had continued in from the living room, but two thick area rugs would keep his feet from the cold. All that tiling might be the reason the fireplace had been lit during what had been a warm-ish day. His two big bedroom windows were heavily curtained, but I wouldn't know the reason for that until morning. A huge dresser and wardrobe might have been made from the same oak tree as the tables in the living room.

We stepped to another doorway in his room, and he showed me the toilet, sink, and clawfoot tub that made up his bathroom. "Needless to say," he said, "you can use the bath whenever you like. Unless I'm in it, of course."

I laughed and thanked him, delighted that I would be happily soaking again not so long after my indulgence in Mary's luxurious hotel. Have I mentioned that while I was growing up, showers weren't so commonplace as they are now?

We backtracked through to the kitchen again, past the stove (and cooling pasta sauce), past the kitchen door we had entered from the patio. We passed beneath another wide, arched entryway into a nice-sized dining area, which had another carved-wood table, this one for meals. The left wall of the dining room also opened into the patio, via a sliding glass door, built in the spirit of the window in the living room. Obviously, the door itself wasn't arched, but the header over it was, filled with stained glass. Two long side windows ran up to the top corners of the slider, but their upper edges were also curved.

The curtained (and yes, arched) doorway on my right led to the room I would be using. It was only slightly smaller than Mark's, but the windows were as big as his. The curtains weren't as thick, which again would become significant in the morning. A smaller version of his dresser and wardrobe were there, mismatched, but of natural wood and nicely kept. A small open doorway led to the WC, which housed only the toilet, a stand that held a pitcher and bowl, and a fair-sized shaving mirror. Mark picked up the pitcher and said, "We'll fill this up for you now, then we can have a nightcap."

I was almost in a daze, lusting after a home like this, in a town like this, in these enchanting lands. The idea that I could ever afford such a life was beyond me. It wasn't until we were back in the kitchen that I was able to stutter out, "A cleaning lady is one thing, but it must cost a small fortune to rent this place."

"It's fairly expensive for Positano, but it came fully furnished. And the view is going to knock you out, once it's daytime."

He paused, his eyes merry, but I would never be so crude as to come right out and ask the price.

* * *

The first morning in my favorite Italian town hit my sleeping eyelids in a blaze of light. The curtains in my room, just basic, average curtains, might as well have been sheer as stretched gauze. Remember; this is on the western coast of southern Italy, on the side of a mountain that poured the town down into the sea. The sun wasn't even coming directly at us. Yet the light was so big, pure and insistent, it lifted me from the bed. The only thing about my awakening that was stronger than the light was the rich, meaty, garlicky, herb-heavy smell of food in the house.

I stumbled out to the dining room where the brightness filled every corner, spreading through the passway into the kitchen and beyond into the living room. A fleshy, grinning Italian woman, possibly a few years younger than my mother, called out to me from the kitchen; "*Bon journo!*" She waved me toward the patio table outside and bustled back to the stove.

The stained glass above the dining room's sliding door sent soothing colors throughout the room, and the door itself was fully opened to let in the fresh morning air. Mark sat at the table outside that door, gazing at the Sea of Naples. He held a cigarette in one hand and a cup of real coffee in the other, with a pot and a spare cup next to him. When he saw me, he said, "Will, good morning! Come see the view!"

I was way ahead of him; the view had already captured me in its dizzying panorama. We were about two-thirds up the mountain, and because Portofino is built at such a steep angle, I could look over the top of the town straight down to the strip of gravelly beach below. The Amalfi Coast, wild and unspoiled, wove into the north and south horizons, and pinnacles of rock thrust up from the sea in front of us.

It was fairly early, not quite eight in the morning, and all I could hear was the sound of sea birds and the rustle of leaves. I sat next to Mark at the patio table, drawing in the pure, clear air, absorbing the tranquility.

Mark poured coffee for me. "Breathtaking, isn't it?"

"It is."

The short, full-figured Italian woman emerged from the kitchen with a large plate, and Mark introduced her as Sophia. He said to me, with a smile, "I hope you're hungry."

"Famished, and the smells from the kitchen are an appetite aphrodisiac."

Sophia set the heaping plate in front of me, and me alone. I stared dumbly, assuming it was simply what it appeared to be: pasta. She laid down a napkin, a fork, and a spoon, then straightened up and pressed her palms together waist high, watching me.

"Thank you." From the corner of my mouth, I said to Mark, "Pasta, for breakfast?"

"Taste it."

Sophia was still waiting, like a chef from the kitchen of a great restaurant standing before a famous food critic.

I spun some of the pasta into the spoon, picking up bits and chunks of the melange on the plate, and pushed it into my mouth. I sat back in my chair and chewed slowly, eyes closed, trying to catch every curious, delightful, startling, and subtle flavor. After I swallowed, I opened my eyes, but Sophia had returned inside the house.

Mark saw me looking toward the kitchen and said, "She could tell how you felt by the look of rapture on your face."

"She's a genius. This is unbelievable." I touched the platter front of me. "But shouldn't we be sharing this?"

"I've already eaten. A little earlier than usual this morning, but I didn't want my guest to wake up alone."

Swallowing the new bite I'd taken, I said, "Please, don't let me put you out of your usual routine."

"Not at all. Now that you've met Sophia, you'll be on your own in the mornings."

Another bite had already made it into my mouth. This time I detected a delectable chunk of sausage, and moaned with bliss. After I had swallowed again, I asked, "What exactly are the ingredients of this meal?"

"Let's see. There's the famous sauce, which is like a sourdough starter recipe. You know, always the same base, and each time you use a little, you simply add more flour. In this case, it's more tomatoes, along with who knows what other little vegetables and seasonings, that are added. For breakfast, she makes a separate skillet of bacon and sausage, scrambles some eggs into it, and have you noticed the beans in there? Only a few."

I examined my plate more closely, and yes, there were a few baked beans in there.

"When the skillet mix is ready, Sophia ladles in some of the sauce, then pours it over the pasta."

"I could never pull this off at home."

"You enjoy cooking?"

"Sometimes I think it's a prerequisite for people who love food as much as I do. I'm an amateur, though."

"Then you might have trouble preparing this dish. I tried it once while I was back in the States, and it was ridiculous."

It might have been right then that I became determined to return to Positano someday, because I knew I would be craving this crazy breakfast in the years to come.

While I surprised myself by finishing every scrap on my plate, we talked more about our lives, shared personal vignettes, and built a friendship that would oddly only last during my three-day stay at Mark's *casa buena*.

After Sophia cleared the table and brought a fresh pot of coffee, Mark said, "I need to run some errands this morning, but I'll be back here for lunch. What are your plans for the day?"

"I'm not sure, but I could definitely schedule in lunch a-la-Sophia."

"In that case I'll meet you back here, and after, we can head for the Buca di Bacco."

"You won't mind if I use your place to catch up on some rest while you're gone?"

"Please do, relax, enjoy yourself."

I spent the remainder of the morning like a wealthy man, lounging in the sun on the patio, writing in my journal, making notes for an article I was putting together for the Renault Agency. (I wouldn't know if they'd care to buy it until I asked, because they still seemed to be balking, but it was fun to hope.) Near eleven o'clock, I soaked in Mark's bathtub, sipping juice, smoking cigarettes, reading a magazine. I had planned to be out of the tub within fifteen minutes or so, but that's where he found me when he returned at 11:30.

Standing in the doorway of his bathroom, hands on his hips, he said, "You really know how to relax."

"I hope you don't mind—"

"Are you kidding? Everything's jake. Lunch will be served in about a half-hour; I'll meet you on the patio."

I climbed out and toweled off, wishing on the one hand that this could be my daily life, yet knowing the fact that it *wasn't* my regular life is what made it a particularly special experience for me.

The afternoon of my first full day there, Mark and I returned to the Buca di Bacco. We sipped cocktails for no more than an hour before Stephan arrived, and I couldn't even feign surprise as the stocky German approached our table.

He spoke English fairly well, greeting Mark with a pleasant familiarity. His eyes fell to me when Mark introduced us, and I don't think he looked away again for another half hour.

After a while of friendly conversation, someone from a group a few tables away called to Mark, and he excused himself to join them.

Stephan and I stared at each other a long moment before I broke the silence. "Stephan…you're a poet." We had learned only a few things during the first thirty minutes of talk.

"Ya. And you are a painter."

"Aspiring."

He raised his eyebrows in question, and I clarified. "I was working at an advertising agency up until I started on this trip. So what I really am is an ad man who is hoping to become a painter."

"Maybe vhat you really are is a painter, who has been taken away from it by *vork* as an ad man." Stephan smiled what I came to learn was his normal, disarmingly succulent smile.

I told him, "I like your interpretation better than mine."

"Ya, das is goot."

What else could I say? "Ya."

Stephan laughed and stood. "Come vahk mit me."

It was my turn to raise my own eyebrows in a question. Again with his smile, then he used two sturdy fingers to mimic walking across the table. "Vahk. Vahk mit me." He flung his hand against his chest, then his arm toward the beach.

"Oh, I get it." I stood and wobbled a bit; I might have had a few too many cocktails. Stephan caught my elbow and guided me out from under the grass roof to the rough sand beyond it. As we approached the edge of the water, his fingers slid down my forearm to my hand, which he squeezed once before releasing. I turned my head partly toward him, smiling, and he winked. That simple drop of an eyelid slid down to my groin.

We 'vahked' along the coast for what might have been about a half-mile, enjoying the day and the view with a pleasant, comfortable silence between us. When Stephan stopped and turned toward me, my body and face relaxed, preparing for a kiss. But he gave a single, regretful shake of his head, then tipped his chin toward the buildings that flowed down the mountain above us.

He must have seen the hopeful desire collapsing in my face, because with a sudden bark of a laugh, he sprinted away from the water, toward the base of the mountain. I followed, running behind him with my longer stride, yet unable to catch up. When he reached a small outjutting of rock he halted abruptly, turned, and I ran into his arms like something out of a movie.

I know he fell to the ground on purpose, but immediately rolled me over on my back and propped himself up to gaze affectionately down on me. While he was staring into my eyes, I couldn't resist admiring his heavy arms on either side of me. My fingers stroked the downy blond hairs of his biceps, and his lips kissed me on the temple. With a sudden movement, I turned my head to catch his mouth with my own, but he made the kiss gentle on my lips. Then on my eyebrows, cheeks, chin, and the tip of my nose. Is it possible to swoon while lying down?

He kissed my lips again, and we touched tongues this time, slowly, sensually, and lingeringly. Our erections pressed together, with only the material of our light trousers between us.

A shout from somewhere—it might have come from down the beach or from above us—rocketed us apart. One moment, he lay on top of me, the next, we sat casually side-by-side, looking out at the sea. The shout came again, closer this time, and it was the sound of my name. I stood and peered out from the outcropping to see Mark striding jauntily down the beach, shading his eyes against the lowering sun. Before I could complete the thought of slipping back into the half-hiding place, Mark saw me, and called, "There you are!"

I sat down again and rested my hands carefully in my lap. Stephan was sitting sideways, with one leg extended, the other knee up and hiding his crotch, his arm casually resting across the raised knee.

Mark flopped to the sand in front of us and offered his pack of cigarettes. While we both accepted, he said, "Stephan, you should join us for dinner tonight."

"I can never say no to Sophia's pasta!" His adam's apple bobbed as he tried to swallow his salivation, but when he rubbed his thick fingers against the corners of his mouth, we all laughed. Sophia could have been a wealthy restauranteur in any city. I had a private laugh of my own, too: Stephan acted well, pretending his salivation was only about food.

The three of us sat smoking, exchanging stories of favorite dishes, while the sun fell closer to the water's most distant edge. A light haze of clouds gathered on the horizon, drawing heady hues from the sunset, and our conversation drifted into an admiring silence.

As the sun dropped, pastel blazes of red and orange lifted higher and higher in the open sky above. I quietly commented that if it continued this way, the entire sky would be covered with color. Mark said, "From many angles, that's exactly what happens."

We were quiet again, until the last sliver of solar yellow disappeared under the indigo-blue water. When it disappeared, Stephan leapt to his feet. "A race, back to Buca di Bacco!"

We three young men charged down the beach, laughing, gaining and losing ground on one another, for a few more pre-dinner cocktails.

Sophia outdid herself again, using meatballs with her sauce this time, including a long loaf of bread with the meal, and individual bowls of olive oil and balsamic for dipping the warm bread. We had stopped at Stephan's for two bottles of red wine, and Mark had supplied one more. The three of us sat on the patio again, because although the night was cooler than it had been when I first arrived, the food, wine, and easy talk kept us warm.

What sheer pleasure, sharing space with these new people, including the jolly Italian cook refilling our plates and glasses as quickly as we could empty them. Again, the specialness was due to the moment, rather than the regularity of such a life.

By the end of the meal we were as satisfied as men could be without having had sex, although that was still pending, at least between Stephan and myself.

Mark excused himself and staggered inside, leaving me alone with Stephan for the first time since our kisses on the beach. The poet stared at me, lightly tapping the lip of his wine glass against his chin, his cigarette smoldering away in his other hand. We waited without speaking for at least fifteen minutes, until Sophia came out and asked in her broken English if we were hungry for anything else. Both of us burst out laughing, and shook our heads at her patient smile.

"Then I go," she said, and left with a friendly wave of her plump fingers.

We waited another ten minutes before I went inside to see what had happened to Mark. He lay half-sprawled on the couch, softly snoring through his partly open mouth. It looked as though he had lost his balance near the couch and once he landed, it hadn't occurred to him to stand up again.

When I stepped back outside to tell Stephan the status of our host, he grinned mischievously (and seductively). With no further ado he stood and held out his hand for mine. "We go."

"Where?" In my mind, I chanted, 'Say your bedroom, say your bedroom…'

Stephan said, "Back to the beach."

"Oh. Okay."

We followed the stairs of the town down and down, moving through the covered walkways, which in the 11 o'clock night, were only faintly navigable by a few lit houses along the way. The patio bar of the Buca di Bacco still had a few foreign guests, but we crept silently by.

When we reached the water's edge, Stephan took my hand again, and led me along the light surf, away from the dimming lights of the town. Aside from the occasional drift of drink-inspired laughter from the Buca di Bacco, the only sounds were our breathing and the hushed push of water against the shore.

Stephan stopped and looked around as if setting his bearings, then began unbuttoning his shirt. Despite the obvious, I asked, "What are you doing?"

He only stopped long enough to begin unbuttoning the shirt I was wearing, then returned to his own, smiling lasciviously. By the time my shirt and shoes were off, he was naked, and prancing over the waveless edges of the sea into deeper water. Now that I had caught on, I yanked off my trousers and undershorts and joined him.

The water was not exactly warm, but warmer than I expected, and we floated easily, side-by-side. The stars above us were magnified by the sea, by the wine we'd been drinking, and by the sweet, transitional love I felt in my heart for the man next to me.

Our hands brushed, then he grasped my fingers, and pulled me into his arms like I was a young boy. I hadn't been aware that we'd floated close enough to shore again that he could stand, but he easily held me cradled against his wide chest, his feet planted firmly in the gravel beneath us. He kissed me while he held me that way, and as I kissed him back, I slid down to stand against him. We kissed and touched and I held him in my hand while he held me. We stroked and manipulated each other, in that sea, under those stars, until we were both satisfied—for the moment. We spread our mixing seeds through the water with kicks of our feet and waves of our hands, rebuilding the energy we had expended, tackling (and wrestling) and kissing some more, then gently holding each other while submerged to our necks. We experimented until we could reach orgasm simultaneously, and believe me, it was trouble well taken. I felt I was being baptized into gay sex.

If the most romantic afternoon of my life had been spent with Antonio in Rome, then the most romantic night of my life had been spent with Stephan in the Mediterranean Sea. So Far.

* * *

Although I continued to stay at Mark's, feeding on the indefatigable pasta and occasionally enjoying his company, I spent most of the rest of my days there with Stephan. We made love a few more times, but we were having as much fun with anticipation as we were with the act itself.

It wasn't easy to leave that place, and when I returned years later, it was impossible to recapture the essence of my first experience there.

After fond farewells to Positano, I was back in my Renault, driving northward again. I stopped in Rome for another quick visit; coffee with Antonio and lunch with Roger. They pressed me for stories of my time in Positano, but I could only gaze off and smile dreamily in response. They seemed to understand.

After that second brief stop in Rome, I chose to stay the night in a little place called Pesaro, where I found a quiet spot on a beach to camp. There wasn't another soul to be seen. With my Coleman stove, I heated the bowl of pasta Sophia had sent with me, and sipped wine from a bottle of wine I had purchased along the way. Watching the water ebb and flow, I mused on the state of my travels.

I had experienced same-sex sex, twice, now. As an odd sort of spot-check, I ran my hands along my arms; still felt the same. My mind stretched and fingered its way into dark corners and niches of curiosity about *me.* Had I changed? Or was it the world around me that had become different?

No. It was me; I had changed, and that's why the world seemed different. The man who determined to take this trip became an historical self with every passing moment. The man emerging was shedding old skins and beliefs, and learning new truths, the most significant of which is that homosexual human beings are as varied as heterosexuals. Some were more effeminate, others dressed or spoke outside norms, others still were downright indefinable, impossible to force into a given category. My maturing self guessed that I might be one of the latter. Perhaps (I told myself) I was even a 'temporary' homosexual.

Here's how I saw it in my 1950s, 27 year-old naiveté: I just happened to be traveling as a single man. Would I have engaged in any of those assignations if I had already found a wife, and she was at home with our children? Absolutely not—I've never been the type for extra-marital affairs. Would I still desire men after I found a woman I wanted to marry? Probably. Nevertheless, the same reasoning could be true if I were heterosexual, and married; I was bound to find other women attractive. It never had to mean that I would be unfaithful to my spouse.

Ultimately, what I'd experienced was based on the fact that I did not yet have a wife and family. (The fact of my not having married by my age, and that I was continually battling a recurring sense of loneliness, somehow didn't make enough of an impression on me.) Maybe I imagined at some point I would get over it, not desire men anymore. Worse, I might have told myself I could sublimate it, that I had the power to ignore it. Or, perhaps some whispering part of me said, 'You'll live a regular man's life every day, but once in a great while, you'll reach a breaking point. At that time, you'll find a fleeting love-affair, and return back home.'

Ha. We try to manipulate reality, but it won't budge, will it? No amount of desire to follow proscribed norms change that. A homosexual man cannot emotionally thrive in a marriage to a woman. I speak from experience gained later in life.

Later, I'll explain that last remark. I promise.

Fifty years in my past, I blithely, and in retrospect, rather bravely, continued my travels across those unknown lands, by road and by thought. When I left Pesaro, I found myself in the little republic of San Marino, which is an independent nation, and at the time had a population of 12,000 people. I looked it up; in fifty years, that number has only barely doubled. Remember, that's the population of the entire *nation*. Quite a tiny place. My first impressions from my journal read this way:

> Its charm is unforgettable, the people are friendly and warm. With its isolated position, San Marino has been able to maintain its freedom throughout the centuries, perched high on a mountain overlooking what might have been the largest panorama I have yet encountered in Europe. This little country's belief in its own democratic attitude, plus its advantageous ways, has allowed it to remain an example of the fight and struggle against oppression and tyranny for centuries. One could easily imagine walking through its streets hundreds of years ago. The ancient fortresses and towers remain intact, as well as the original houses and streets themselves.

*   *   *

Here's what I came to understand: San Marino is an enclave—a nation completely surrounded by another country—Italy. Of course it follows Italy's lead in most ways, with one notable diversion: it declared neutrality in WWII. The government of San Marino was confident it could get away with that, because even Napoleon had respected San Marino's independence when he invaded Italy in 1796. That recognition was confirmed by the Congress of Vienna in 1815. Then, in the mid-1800s, Giuseppe Garibaldi, of Italian Unification fame, took refuge there. The government of San Marino helped him toward his goals, and by way of thanks, Garibaldi guaranteed that

San Marino would always be an independent sovereign state. It held.

The thing is, the Second World War had as harsh an effect on San Marino as it did on Italy. Unemployment and inflation grew out of control, and the political class at the time wasn't up to the challenge of getting the nation back on its financial feet. In fact, the politics of this little country changed too easily, because the parties in the beginning of the 20th century were so disorganized.

A fascist party was developed in 1922, and in 1923, the High and General Councils were dissolved, and transformed into a Principal and Sovereign Council. A new election was held, but the candidates were mostly fascists, with a few catholic representatives. Fascism continued to dribble in from Italy, and it held until the early 1940s, when socialists elbowed their way in and took over in 1943. This might have been why San Marino was able to become a refuge for the victims of WWII, including saving a group of Jewish people from concentration camps.

Yet, at the time I was there (or, historically, between 1945 and 1957) the socialist republic was ruling with a moderate communist party. It was the first communist country I had entered, but none of this effected me. As might be clear in my journal entry above, I was more impressed by the personality of the place.

As easily as a person would drive from New York to Pennsylvania, I returned to Italy, and made my second-to-last stop in that country.

Venice! These days, most of us Americans have heard of this astounding city, so I'll sum it up with the journal entry I made at the time:

> Truly it is best to see Venice first at night, for it is so soft and surreal. I had dinner in a rotisseria, where everything looked so delicious displayed in the window. Then I walked and walked until I arrived at St. Marco Square, which looked to me like the setting of many striking dreams I've had. St. Marco square is huge, and a beautiful thing to behold. The size, grandeur, and the repetition of the facade all made their effect instantaneously.

After Venice, I entered a city which not long before had belonged to Yugoslavia. Trieste. It's a pretty port town, with gorgeous architecture and a Neapolitan air about it.

But.

Picture the location of this city: Just at the top of the 'boot' of Italy, on the eastern edge, the port straddles Italy and Yugoslavia. It is also tucked in beneath Austria, and in fact, it was under Austrian rule in the 1800s. As far as I learned, the Italians were quite unhappy with those rulers, and the previously mentioned Giuseppe Garibaldi wasn't thrilled, either; he included it in his attempts at the unification of his country. After the First World War, the city was granted to Italy, and all seemed settled. Yet, only a few days before the end of WWII, it was the Yugoslavs who liberated the occupied Trieste, and made claim on the place. When Yugoslavia signed a peace treaty with Italy in 1947, the best the two countries could agree upon was to call it the 'Free Territory of Trieste.' That didn't work very well.

The Territory had been put under U.S. and British military administration, but when they saw how the frustrations continued to grow between Italy and Yugoslavia, they attempted to give it back to Italy in 1948. This was not acceptable to Yugoslavia, so in 1953 they tried to divide it into zones that would give the city and northern lands to Italy, while Yugoslavia would only receive the southern area. This arrangement felt like an insult to Yugoslavia, but they became downright infuriated by early 1954. At that time, it was called a 'finished deal' when the Yugoslavs were awarded a larger amount of land, but the city itself still went to Italy.

Confusing? I suppose it is, but hopefully it will suffice to say that while I was there at the end of '53, the tension was taut. Yugoslavia was already of a highly 'insulted' disposition, and they were closing in on the feelings of fury.

What a mess. Yugoslavia was ready to fight for what they thought rightfully belonged to them; their troops were gathered on their border and training. And of course, their country was the next place I would be visiting, after Italy. More specifically, I would be entering Yugoslavia via Trieste, of all places. The tight pressure in the air was a bitter liquor brewing under a dangerously ill-fitted cap.

7

Peaceful Man in a Military Land

The road above Trieste was draped in the sort of weighted quiet one would find at the start of a life-or-death chess match. There didn't seem to be another soul around, nor did it seem anyone wanted to be there, in that land between two angry countries.

To put it bluntly, I was scared. I couldn't even indulge in my usual form of self-entertainment by singing through my repertoire of songs as I drove.

When I reached the border, the road was barred, and three guards came out into the cold to tell me I could not enter Yugoslavia. After this abrupt order, two of them ran back to the warmth of their hut, while I sat staring straight ahead, undecided, knowing I couldn't simply delete this country from my list. Of all the lands I would visit, this one held the most mystery for me.

One of the border guards had remained behind, clutching his gloved hands together, lightly stomping his feet, slitting his eyes against the brisk wind. I turned to him, wondering if he meant to watch me until I was gone. But he smiled at me.

"You like my country, see my country?"

I glanced toward the quiet guard shack, then back to the man who continued smiling through his young, foreign handsomeness. I smiled back. "Yes, I do."

"It is nice country. I tell you, how come in, where come in."

Shouldn't I have asked whether it was actually legal to cross at another place? I didn't. "I would really appreciate that." He looked at me with confusion, and I simplified my English: "Yes, please, thank you."

His grin might have been at all my politeness, or he may have been having fun conversing in a foreign tongue. He pulled a scrap of paper and stub of pencil from his pocket and began scrawling a map. "Here, you drive. When you here, you drive…up."

"I turn there?"

A vigorous nod. "Turn, yes." A stab at the paper. "You drive now here, and here…" More scratched lines, then, "Drive here, you in my country. You tourist, you okay." He made the 'okay' circle with his thumb and index finger. That was such a useful signal, I don't know how it fell out of practice. Maybe the 'thumbs up' replaced it.

I thanked the helpful guard, swung my car around, and within about a half hour, I was thoroughly lost.

Fortunately, I was still lost on the Italian side of the border, and therefore didn't hesitate to ask the first person I saw on the road if he could speak English.

This small Italian farmer, with a worn, pleasant face, said, "I speak English, yes."

There went the first hurdle, now came the next: "I don't suppose you can tell me where I'd be able to enter Yugoslavia?"

Leaning companionably against my door, he asked, "Why would you want to enter that country? They are ready to declare war on us. They have amassed 25,000 troops very near here."

Would I need to answer him before he would answer me? He might have been bored, lonely, and looking for conversation, so I decided to tell him something interesting. "Have you heard of Life Magazine?"

"Yes, I have."

So far, so good. "Well, I know Yugoslavia is ready to go to war over the Trieste issue, and I'm writing an article about it for Life Magazine." Why not? Maybe I would try to write a story about it someday and submit it to Life. I kept my expression sober, and I hoped, literary.

The farmer pushed off from my door and said, "I will come with you, and show you where you will be able to cross." He rounded the front of the car and climbed into the passenger seat. "Can you return me here after I show you?"

"Absolutely. No problem." I was going to find a way in!

As I followed the farmer's simple directions, he told me how he had acquired such a firm grasp of English: His family was emigrating, one-by-one, to the United States, and their parents had made sure that all of them understood the language quite well. Two of his brothers were already in America, he would go next, then his sister, then their parents would arrive when everything was prepared for them.

This is one aspect I learned to admire about the people who lived across the Atlantic. For the life of me, I can't think of a single situation where an American family emigrated to a new land together, like that. Thoughtful preparation, then the adult children heading off first, and setting up a home for the parents. Who knows; maybe I haven't heard of it because so few people can find a reason to leave the States. So far.

In any case my farming friend and I traveled about seven kilometers over rough terrain, until we came to a small road that led through some trees. He had me stop the car, and pointed. "Follow that road for less than a kilometer, and you will be in Yugoslavia. It crosses a larger road, and there you will turn right. It is the only road you can travel, the rest are closed by the military. That larger road will bring you into town."

Silly me, I didn't bother to ask which town I would be in, and to this day, I don't know where I stayed my first night in that country.

I returned the farmer to where I had found him, retraced my rolling steps, and crept through the woods. It felt like soldiers were hiding behind every tree, and as it turns out, that was probably true. Who knows what they made of the frog-like car and the decidedly un-Italian-looking man driving it? Surprisingly, I wasn't stopped by a military road-block until I was on the main road, near the town.

The soldier approached me warily, frowning, slinging his awkward-looking rifle further back on his shoulder. He rested his hand against my half-open window and spoke, but I have no idea what he said. All I could do was tip my head and shrug. He then spoke in what I knew to be clumsy Italian, and the phrase *Carte de passage* broke through the mist of my language barriers. He wanted to see my passport. With an expression and attitude no less serious than his, I showed him my papers, and said, "Tourist." Fortunately, that's a fairly universal word.

After accepting the documents, the soldier readjusted his rifle and stepped back to his companions. For a long while, they examined my passport, wrote things down in their notepads, and muttered together. Had I been the type to easily break into a nervous sweat,

I would have been drenched. If I hadn't taken the angelic advice about leaving my gun behind in New York, they certainly would have been able to read it on my face, they would have searched the car, and I doubt I'd be writing about this here and now.

All the soldier did when he returned was hand my papers back to me and wave me on. I couldn't believe it, because although I hadn't been sure what to expect, simple passage had been low on the list of possibilities.

As the farmer promised, the road led me right into a town. The place was filled with more soldiers, on the sidewalks, streets, and in buildings, looking equal parts busy, bored, and ready for action. I was pleased to find a hotel with an available room, because although the building looked poor and dismal, it would be better than freezing in the cold night. Besides, I had no intention of sleeping in the car. I wanted to be inside, safe, and looking as much like an average tourist as possible. In the morning, I would beat it out of that area to what would hopefully be calmer locales of the country.

The only thing I needed before sleep was a meal. The hotel had a large dining room, and if it had been earlier in the evening, I'm sure it would have been filled with hungry troops. As it was, I saw only one other table occupied; two men sitting together, who watched me curiously as I took a table near the center of the room.

A waitress hesitantly approached me, nervous about speaking to me and taking my order. She dropped a menu on the table, which I opened, but of course I couldn't read the thing. The hopeless, helpless expression on my face must have transmitted across the room, because one of the gentlemen at the other table walked over. "Excuse me, do you have trouble to read the menu?"

"Oh, thank God, you speak English. I would really appreciate some help with this."

"Of course!" He leaned over my shoulder as he described my options, and I settled on the goulash, bread, and wine. He told the waitress, who informed me (through my helper) of the price. The man saw me trying to calculate the exchange in my mind, and said, "You have question about the cost in American dollars?"

"Yes, as a matter of fact I do."

"It will translate to possibly twenty cents for your meal."

I grinned. "That's about right for my budget." When this kind stranger readily and affably returned my smile, I asked him, "Would you and your companion like to join me?"

"Thank you, yes." He waved his friend over, and translated back and forth between us as I enjoyed my meal. I shared my wine with them, and they shared their harsh but oddly tasteful cigarettes with me.

By the time we had finished another bottle of wine, my English-speaking friend said, in a low voice, "If your—what is the word, 'budget?'—if your budget is small, possibly you would want to change some American things for Yugoslav money?"

Why, as a matter of fact, I would.

Now we come to another idea that had entered my mind, with respect to financing my trip: some under-the-table commerce. As I traveled through Europe, I had begun collecting some tradable items from the various U.S. military posts I had visited along the way. Remember; my military reserve status gave me full access to such establishments, and their fairer prices.

Although it was unnecessary in the empty, late-night Yugoslav dining room, I whispered. "What are you looking for?"

"Blue jeans?"

Too bulky. "No denim, but I do have three pairs of American knit pants."

"Possibly. American cigarettes?"

Not enough to make it worth the trade.

"Nylons?"

"Yes, I have nylons, actually silk stockings. I also have lipstick." Those items were light, easy to transport, and explainable as gifts for attractive women.

"You have room here at hotel?"

"I do."

We retired to the room I had rented for the night, which wasn't bad size-wise, but only had a single queen mattress on a box-spring, an old chipped dresser, and a basin for shaving and washing. My companions commented on the warmth, and the English speaking man told me he'd heard that only one room had heat in the hotel. Apparently, I been the lucky recipient of that room.

They proceeded to buy most of my nylons, all the lipstick I had in stock, and all three pairs of pants. I also made an excellent trade on some American currency for Yugoslav dinars, about twice the market rate. That little visit would cover the entire cost of my visit to Yugoslavia.

Before long, the gentlemen left me with a congenial shaking of hands, and I fell into the bed feeling satisfied, savvy, and relatively wealthy. It might have been near midnight.

This vignette might beg the question: Why would a predominately lawful man engage so readily in such an unlawful activity? Well, I might have been influenced by my father.

I believe I've already mentioned he had a successful meat-packing business. One can imagine that in WWII, during the days of rationing, this gave him a special sort of power. (Not unlike the kind that would be gained from a liquor dealer during prohibition, but that was the short-lived market of a different family member.) My father's tight-rope walk on the less-than-legal side of the law came in the form of dealing in black market meat. I must say that is tastier than it sounds.

For those who weren't alive during WWII, and who haven't learned of life in America during those days: there was indeed a lot of rationing going on. Not only did individuals need coupons for staples like meat, milk, butter, but restaurants were restricted, too. The wealthier factions of our society still wanted to enjoy the occasional meal out, though, and the restauranteurs wanted to supply it. They turned to the black market for extra meat, and the black market turned to my father.

He got caught.

Yes, Father was caught red-handed by the Feds, and sent to jail. It certainly wasn't 'hard time,' in fact it was the very jail where Martha Stewart was incarcerated. It seems they tried to make it look rougher than it really is during the Martha debacle, or at least rougher than it once was, because when my father returned home after his six-month sentence, he referred to it convincingly as the 'Country Club.'

Needless to say, I would have been much, much worse off than he'd been, if I'd been caught selling my black market goods in war-ready Yugoslavia.

Two hours after I fell asleep in that hotel, I woke to the sound of my door slowly opening with a long, eerie creak. My eyes opened so wide the whites could have glowed in the dark. I slammed them shut when steps—the sound of two people carefully walking—approached my bed.

For a long, drawn-out moment, I visualized the lights coming on with a shocking blast, and soldiers standing over my bed holding the goods I had sold, the silk nylons skewered on a bayonet. I couldn't imagine the friendly men I'd interacted with had come back to rob me, it just wasn't possible. Even if they had returned with the idea of thievery, one shout would have brought dozens of uniformed men running.

My covers were slowly drawn back, and a pressure dipped down the side of my bed. One of the intruders had sat next to me! I pretended to sleepily, unconsciously turn over, but I was trying to edge away. I stopped moving when the mattress sank down again, but on my other side.

Two men were climbing into bed with me.

Now, I have no idea of what other Gay men in my situation would have done. Reach out? Giggle? Sit up in indignant protest? I lay there, staring blankly toward the dark ceiling. I heard the soft sound of, "Ahhh," then a single word, which I didn't understand, but memorized for a later translation.

On either side of me, the covers were drawn up, and within seconds, I could hear the heavy breath of sleep in both my ears.

Unbelievable.

More unbelievable is that I was asleep moments later, and only dimly remember the quiet, early-morning departure of the two men who had shared my bed. Incidentally, I later found out the meaning of the word I heard, and put it together with the sound the man had made. It translates like this: "Ahhh, warmth."

When I said it had been a very cold night, and that I'd been given the only heated hotel room, I hadn't been exaggerating.

* * *

I can't help but laugh as I look back on that, but I remember what my friend Mabel had said. She's the elderly lady I'd met in New York, remember, the one who had advised me to leave without my gun. Mabel had said I would learn the local customs soon enough. How could I know whether bed-sharing was a common practice? I certainly didn't want to cause any trouble in this strange, tense country. With all that military presence, one doesn't ask unnecessary questions.

The other thing to bear in mind is that America in the fifties, or more specifically, Senator McCarthy, had been spreading all sorts of bizarre rumors about communists. They were capable of anything. There I was in an essentially communist country and, much like my German hitchhiker who had never knowingly shared airspace with a Jew, I had no idea of what to expect from these people.

This could be the reason I never suffered any truly dire situations throughout my trip: I took it all in stride. Actually, that statement includes a fact which I see I have failed to mention until this point: I can't help but wonder if a member of the McCarthy tribe was extremely interested in my trip around the Mediterranean, especially my visit to Yugoslavia.

A man—I'll call him Jon— had first approached me back in New York. I believe it was right after I finished my coffee with Mabel, not long after I had been in the Yugoslav consulate. How to describe Jon… Picture Joe Friday at about 30 years old, same government-issue suit, same haircut, same no-nonsense affect. I don't quite remember how we met; he might have approached me and referred to a supposedly mutual friend. He said he'd heard about my trip, and was intending the same sort of adventure himself. "If you like," he'd said, "we could travel together, and share expenses."

I remember warily eyeing this complete stranger, and although I'm basically a sociable man, I was put off by the idea of him as a traveling companion. Most likely I thanked him politely, but I'm sure I gave him a firm 'no.'

"Perhaps," he countered, "we'll meet along the way. If you're strapped for cash at the time, we could share a room."

Knowing me, I might've responded, "Perhaps," and left it at that.

Did he show up at my going-away party? Maybe, but if he did, it left no impression on me. Did he watch the Andrea Doria motor away from the dock? I have no idea. Did I meet him along the way, while on the roads around the Med? Yes. And the first time happened to be in Yugoslavia.

However, I first needed to get out of the odd, threatening little border town I was in, and there were a few more adventures to be had before Jon's path would coincidentally cross mine.

* * *

The soldiers were still present along the roads, in the woods and the villages, marching, singing, and maneuvering. I didn't dare to stop along the way, and made the entire trip in about 6 hours, despite the terrible condition of the roads. The military presence didn't diminish as I came closer to Rijeka, but only changed by the look of their uniforms which became more naval.

Once in Rijeka proper, I went to what's called *Putnik*, a tourist bureau. A man there spoke English, and was more than happy to escape his desk to show me his small city. He even took me on a short trip to Opatia, a delightful resort a short distance outside of town. He was quite a pleasant companion, and here it comes up again: Was he always that helpful with tourists, or did he have a particular fondness for young men traveling alone? Was I obtuse, picky, uninterested, or handicapped with regard to the come-on? I suppose the next question is: would a woman traveling alone assume that every man who showed friendliness and generosity wanted to sleep with her? That isn't a rhetorical question, I honestly don't know the answer. How about a heterosexual man, would he have taken every opportunity to try to have sex with any woman who showed the slightest interest in him?

None of that is exactly fair, though, because I don't know if every Gay man who has recently come out will desire sex with every other man who wants it. Yet it would be understandable if it were true, because after my first experiences, I did notice that sensation of a child's first taste of candy: more, please. However, if the first taste had been chocolate, and the next piece offered had been licorice—still sweet but not quite the flavor he was expecting—one never knows what an innocent would say next.

Speaking of tastes, I haven't gone into great detail, but I should probably say that while on this Mediterranean trip, not only did I never have anal sex, I had no sort of activity beyond the sort of intense kisses and caresses that result in orgasm. Unless you include Hettie, but I don't know how that figures in because she was a woman. That astounding experience didn't occur until the end of the trip, though, so I'll save it for its proper place.

I suppose my point is that I was simply guileless back then. It may have been the way I was raised by Mother, and her sexual admonitions, and by Father, with his blank lack of affection toward me. It may have been the era, but I'm not so innocent these days as to think sexual drives, desires, and proclivities are any different now than they were fifty (or a thousand) years ago. I guess it was just me, and I suppose I should feel some pride in being what might be considered an unusual Gay man. I'm quite particular in my sexual choices, and I move gradually as I learn. If anything, that makes sexuality all the more special to me.

*　*　*

Back to Yugoslavia.

Now that I was in a less-frightening town than the one I'd left, I intended to follow through on my desire to capture various areas artistically, hoping for a gallery show of this country so unknown to average Americans. I attempted to buy some supplies in Rijeka, which might have been my first mistake. Film for the camera, nope, too much red tape in a country poised for war. A drawing pen, yes, but no holder for the point. Paper, yes, but much like the sort of heavy, rough, wood-chipped paper one might find in a kindergarten classroom.

Fortunately, I did already have watercolors in the car, and I decided the funky paper might give my art an original slant.

By the time I felt prepared to start, it was too late, meaning the light wouldn't be right. There was nothing left to do but observe the people and cast about for ideas for the next morning.

Here's how I described my first night in Rijeka, from my journal:

> Like any Saturday night, it was a time for having fun. I saw the local hangout and sat nearby on a park bench. The women had no makeup and no style. They weren't too original even with what they did have for color. The boys would stop by the windows to see who the girls were inside, and the girls looked coquettishly out at the boys.

I returned to my hotel, determined to rise early and begin to paint. The following morning I went back to the square with my paints and paper. A few people were passing, the early light was superb, and the square had a quaint, other-worldly feel. I attached my paper to a board, set out my watercolors, and laid down some initial strokes.

A sensation behind me caught my attention, and I looked over my shoulder to find an older man idling there, smiling shyly. He gestured that I continue, and I returned my attention to the paper. A few more strokes of the brush, and I heard whispers. Behind me, two women had joined the man to watch. When I faced forward again, I saw three children curiously approaching. I think I managed about one-fourth of the watercolor before the crowd became too embarrassing, and I packed my things away. To this day, I'm not entirely comfortable being observed while I paint, but back then, I was far too self-conscious.

I brought my supplies back to my room, retrieved my camera, and hurried back to the square for some photos. It was my intention to capture my original artist's vision on film, and finish the painting in privacy. After two clicks of my lens, a group of children gathered, wanting their pictures taken, and I couldn't refuse their bright, playfully pleading faces.

When I was finished with them, I turned back to my intended subject, wondering if my first two shots of the square would be enough for my painting. I found myself facing not the vision of my interest, but a man in a brown uniform with a red star patch. Not only the police, the *communist* police! He crooked his finger for me to follow, and walked away. What choice did I have but to obey?

When we entered the police station, he politely offered me a seat, then held out his hand, palm-up, as though I should give something to him. My first instinct was to turn over my camera, which he accepted, but held out his hand again. This time, he clarified by saying, "*Carte de passage.*" Ah. Passport time again.

He took it and my camera away with him, smiling blandly over his shoulder at my attempts to speak with him. Fifteen minutes later, he returned with another man, someone who had probably bragged to his friends that he knew English. That man blushed furiously while no coherent words were exchanged, but I was made to understand that I must wait some more.

I waited, and waited. Occasionally someone would look in on me and gesture that I remain seated and continue waiting. Everyone knows how time can flex and flux, as in the speed of a half-hour airplane flight as opposed to thirty long minutes stuck in a holding pattern. What astounds me is how many thoughts can be pushed into those elongated seconds, especially while sitting in the police station of a communist country where you're unable to speak a syllable of their language.

Very few people were aware of the actual dates that I expected to be in Yugoslavia. Nobody at all knew exactly where to find me in that country. What if I were thrown in jail for some strange reason? Had someone found out about my transactions from the night before? Had I accidentally groped one of my innocent bed-partners in my sleep? Wasn't homosexuality illegal in communist countries? (If the latter were true, might that have been one of McCarthy's hidden reasons for despising them?)

My internal questions were endless, and they covered everything from fear of being secreted away to a cold, distant, rock-splitting quarry, to what sort of gruel would be served in even the best Yugoslav prison.

All told, it was an hour and a half before a person who honestly did speak English arrived. Fortunately, my mind was immediately put at ease by that person; he was a soft-spoken, small-boned, gentle man. He explained that the concern had been with my camera. "You are not allowed to take photographs of the harbor," he told me. "They would be of value to our adversaries."

"But I didn't take any photographs of the harbor. None at all."

"That has been ascertained," my translator replied. "While you've been sitting here, one of the officers spoke with the children in the square. He was told you are a painter, and when the crowd grew too large for you to see what you wanted to paint, you left, and returned to capture your painting with a photograph."

"That's exactly right. I took some pictures of the children, too. Is that okay?" It seemed like a good idea to show my willingness to cooperate, even if the information was surely already known.

"You are in no trouble at all. Please accept the return of your camera and passport, and enjoy your visit to our country."

I was ready to leave Rijeka, post-haste. New children gathered to watch me loading my car, and indicated that their friends told them they, too, could have their picture taken. After a quick glance around to ensure there were no uniformed observers, I gamely lifted my camera for one last photo. The click came as a dead, empty sound. I didn't even need to look to find that my film had been confiscated from the camera. Had I, in fact, taken some innocent pictures of the harbor? I can't remember, but if so, they were probably ruined when the officials removed the film. I reloaded with a fresh roll, took a fast shot of the children of Rijeka, and climbed into my car.

In the '50s, it didn't much matter if the police of one town had somehow developed my film and found that I had taken photos I wasn't supposed to. I also had no worries about whether they had copied every scrap of information from my passport. All data they gathered about me probably wouldn't leave that town until computers came along.

The silly thing is, I hadn't done anything that could have landed me in a prison. No, wait, that isn't quite right: There was that uncommonly strict policy about lipstick and nylons to consider.

It seems I haven't commented yet on the visual beauty of Yugoslavia. Strong mountains met the soft sea, and along the coast as I drove, islands dotted the Adriatic. Every shade of every color I could imagine poured through the skies, lands, and waters. Great terrain, but I could do without the politics.

At the time, I believe the country was called 'The Federal People's Republic of Yugoslavia,' and was composed of various republics: Serbia, Croatia, Bosnia, Herzegovina, Macedonia, Slovenia and Montenegro, as well as two provinces, Kosovo and Vojvodina. Those who keep close track of the news are familiar with how everything has been rearranged in that area, by now.

As I headed toward the city of Sibenik, I was moving down the coast of Croatia, nearing the southern-most tip of Yugoslavia. Along the way, it grew dark, and I came across an incredible scene, which I describe in my journal:

> I was driving along, singing quietly to myself, when I rounded a curve and my lights revealed a group of about twenty girls gathered in what had been total darkness. They were perched on the white rocks, singing in a deep, sad tone. Their dress was quite colorful, of that I am sure. My instinct was to stop, and when I did, they spread and scattered like the sheep I had passed before. I wished they would have remained.

I stopped in the next village to eat and sleep. Because I had my trader's money jingling in my pocket, I treated myself to another dinner at a hotel, where the owner's wife served me black bread, eggs, salami, and wine. She brought hot water for my instant coffee, and in response to her great curiosity, I offered her a cup. Like all instant-coffee drinkers, she lied perfectly, telling me (and herself) that it was as tasty as if it had been freshly brewed.

I could tell it would be safe to sleep in my car that night, so I parked under a tree near the hotel and made my bed. A slightly different, but equally mystic song floated through the quiet to me, and I'll insert the journal entry about it:

> While falling asleep, I heard more singing, this time men's voices, coming from the hotel. I am sure few American tourists have had an opportunity to hear this; it was like a church chant, the same tune, all right, with one particularly

impressive tenor voice, while the rest were deep and resonant. At times, it sounded like there would be tears in the singers' eyes if I could see them?

I woke the next day with the decision to make another attempt at public painting. This time, I was slightly less inhibited (the minimal military presence may have helped), and I was more able to work with a few observers behind me. Somehow, I got it across that I preferred people not to stand too close, and they cooperatively gave me more space. Occasionally I would take a break, and we would communicate through smiles and gestures. I felt that this was the first time I was able to reach these Yugoslavs, but still wished we could communicate more deeply. To feel that I knew something of them was nice, but to truly understand them would have been so much more satisfying.

It came time for me to continue southward toward Sibenik. Before I hit the road, a man asked me (using our simple communication techniques) if he could ride with me part of the way, and I agreed. He climbed into my Renault with a battered briefcase, which was apparently a sort of man-purse for him.

As we headed down the road, I learned that he had lost his right eye during the big war, and gathered he had become an extremely poor person. Yet at the end of the ride, he opened his briefcase and insisted that I take three wormy apples, at which point I offered him some chocolate. Without further hesitation, he offered me money, in return. This was too much for me, as I could see he was trying to surrender a large chunk of his meager means of survival. I gently refused his money, and we parted with a mutually respectful handshake.

Soon I turned inland and began to climb into mountain country where the land became rocky. The peoples' dress was different, colorful and ethnic, the women in scarves and long skirts that appeared to be more like costumes than clothing. Although the roads were rough, the animals and people were the worst obstacles. My approach was always ignored, but if I blew my horn, it caused confusion and fear, and both folk and livestock would scatter with no organization. Twice I had to slam on the brakes within inches of a goat or chicken. Everything spilled; my water, food, all aspects of my luggage, and most frustratingly, the wine.

Although Mabel from New York had told me I would only need to follow the road in front of me, there were more forks and crossroads than I would have imagined. Too many times, I simply guessed at which road to take, and too often, I was sure I had become lost in a wilderness of rocks, sage pine, and water—the water being a strong, steady rain that had begun to fall.

During one particularly confusing stretch of road, I found a shepherd walking alone in the rain, and I ventured a request for directions from him. Much to my amazement, he spoke perfect English; when he was much younger, he had lived in Gary, Indiana. In celebration, I opened a bottle of wine that had not spilled, and we sipped, smoked, and exchanged stories while the rain beat against my tightly closed sunroof. After it let up, he gave me clear directions to Sibenik, and we parted. This short-lived friendship brought lightness and warmth to what had started as a rather dreary day.

An entire shipload of Americans had been out to sea as I sat enjoying wine on the roadside, but by the time I arrived in Sibenik, they had docked in port. The only reason I was aware of it was because I had wandered down to the dock (drawn as always to the water and the boats) and I heard English being spoken with clearly American accents.

I've never been much of a man to use foul language, but I could only laugh as I heard the cussing and rough voices beside me. I stepped closer and said, "It sounds like I could be standing on a dock in New York!"

This brought friendly greetings from the group, and before long, we were talking like old friends reunited. These men were part of a crew from a coal ship, fresh from the States, making a delivery in Sibenik. Companionably, we watched the local reactions to arriving and departing passengers, and compared the public displays to that of our own towns and cities. Here, little emotion was shown, and only a few kisses. Mostly the people interacted with words alone, and when the distance began to stretch between them, silent, solemn waves.

My new friends, particularly a man named Pete, invited me to lunch on their ship the following day. I enthusiastically accepted, and watched them board the small boat that would bring them out to their floating home for the night. My own little sleeper, parked next to a hotel, was ready for me to curl up and rest, and before long I was in a comfortable slumber.

The next day I was brought aboard the ship, and was instantly surrounded by sailors who treated me as one of their own. A Gay man's dream? For me, it felt more like a brotherhood. Brothers who fed me well; our lunch was, of all the delightfully American meals, corned beef and cabbage. I felt right at home.

The man named Pete became my host and sponsor, of sorts. He was the picture of a sea-faring man, with rough, weather-burnt skin, hair that was a dark, longish, messy thatch, and a guttural voice one expected would say 'Yar!' at any moment. His build was solid but his skin was loose, as though he had once been much heavier. Although I guessed he was around thirty-five at the time, his face seemed lined and scarred beyond his years.

Pete introduced me to an endless score of his shipmates, cluing me in on all their nicknames. (Oddly, he didn't have one, unless 'Pete' wasn't his given name?) Before we left the ship that afternoon, he and some of his accomplices loaded me with gifts of smooth American soap and cigarettes. I felt rich, and agreed when Pete asked if I'd share expenses for a room with him at the hotel where I had parked my car.

What I didn't share was his interest in locating a pimp, but I gamely accompanied him on his quest. As we roamed the town, stopping in bars, I took only one drink to each of his three. The man could really toss them back, but he didn't hold his liquor as well as he imbibed it, if that makes any sense. He was a slurrer and a staggerer, but in a friendly way; the sort who would smile and lose the strength of only one eyelid, giving him an awkward, loopy expression. Any minute, I expected him to toss a loose embrace of friendship around my shoulders and declare, "I love you, man."

Before that could happen, he found himself an available lady, and I wandered off to see what sort of deals I could find in the local marketplace. I still had one precious pair of nylons to exchange, and my best purchase was a gorgeous cigarette case for the cost of those nylons, plus a thousand dinars. (Total price for what was a classy, elaborate, sterling cigarette case might have been about three dollars.) I also stumbled across the amusement of a movie being filmed right there in Sibenik, but I'd like to save the details on that for a bit later.

After dinner, Pete found me and talked me into joining him for (more) drinks at a local establishment called 'Sharifs.' He had discovered it a few nights before; a fascinating place on the outskirts of town, up a dirt road, through a stable, into a cave. The decor was wine barrels, dirt, rows of glasses, and Yugoslav farmers who had faces that just begged to be sketched. The men played a gambling game with their fingers, loudly shouting out a number to confuse their opponent, and the point was that the total figure finally displayed must add up to the amount called. Decades later, I learned that the sort of bar we were in was called by various names, and I'm going to see how close I can come to the spelling: They were known as a *krcma*, or an *ostarija*, or a *konoba*. Apparently there aren't a lot of such places left today. The game is still played along the coastal Adriatic Sea, though, and I've heard it called *ora* or *sije-sete*. Just some trivia, there.

At our own little *krcma* that night, we sang songs and shared each other's drinks. I sang the Illinois Alma Mater as a Yugoslav song, and the crowd loved it. Pete's affection for me must have increased when he saw I could have as much fun in a bar as he could, but then again, he might have blacked out the entire experience.

The next day we had more rain, and I was invited back to the ship for another lunch. Roast beef this time; I was in heaven. Pete hid a 5-pound can of coffee under his belt and convinced me to conceal a blanket around my waist, also a few boxes of Rinso for my laundry. I had visions of snuggling in a warm, dry, clean blanket with a hot cup of fresh-ground coffee, but Pete canceled that fantasy when he sold the booty for 3000 dinars. He needed plenty of money for drinking. Drink he did, all the way until dinnertime.

Back to the ship for another good ole American meal, but by this time Pete was really feeling it. He announced that the drinks would be on him back at our hotel, and we trooped back there in a large group. I ended up in a room full of about twenty bored, sex-hungry, excitement-craving seamen. Did I mention Pete wasn't the only one who was drunk? Every last one of them, as we said back then, was pretty tight.

If I were another sort, I might have been experiencing a different sort of tension. These men had warm hearts toward me, as though I was some sort of mascot. They wanted to do everything they could for me, and insisted they would stow me away on board the ship and I could go back to the States for nothing. They couldn't imagine that I would want to continue traveling through a country that was girded for war, and said once the captain met me and knew my situation, he would offer to bring me back. My situation? I was taking a very long trip on an extremely low budget through exciting places and interesting times. There wasn't anything about that I wanted to change. I couldn't help but bask in their attentions, though.

While these sweet men drank and drank, I discovered they suffered from an inferiority complex about being sailors. 'Why,' they asked me, 'does everyone consider a seaman a bum?'

I answered as best as I could; "People see you as drifters, and you can imagine why, since you do drift across the oceans of the earth. The thing is, a bum or drifter on land can go days, months, even years without lifting a finger to work. In my opinion, you can be proud of yourselves, because you work hard. The way you live takes a certain courage and a definite self-motivation."

This satisfied them for a few more rounds of alcohol, until another maudlin question came; "But why don't we ever get any respect?"

Yes, I'd been drinking too, but could never have begun to match their pace, so I was sober enough to try some philosophy: "If a person doesn't experience something himself, he can't understand what sort of respect you deserve."

One of the young men couldn't shake his despondency, and asked the fellow next to him, "Exactly what sort of respect do we deserve?"

"Less than most," came the dour reply.

"For you, maybe. Myself, I'm a gentleman who's only been

temporarily put out of his place."

General laughter did nothing for the displaced gentleman. He leapt to his feet and grasped the shirt-front of the man nearest him. "I'll show you what's funny!"

When the fists began to fly, Pete guided me out of the room with an expert touch. "Sharif's," he mumbled.

It sounded better than the brawl in the room, and I followed him into the hall. Rather, I walked with him while he leaned on me, slurring on about his travels, his desires, his dreams.

We were approached by a man I recognized as the dishwasher from the ship (nickname 'Scrubs'), who I hadn't once seen take a drink. He had a room of his own in the hotel, and probably spent the evenings curled up with Melville, or possibly the Bible. I propped the semi-conscious Pete against a wall and held him braced there with my forearm, while Scrubs greeted me warmly. "Having fun tonight, Will?"

"Fun enough, I guess." We both winced as a loud thump came from the room I had been sharing with Pete. "A few of the boys from your ship are enjoying themselves in my room, though."

Without hesitation, Scrubs held out a key. "I've got an extra bed in my room. You can sleep there, if you like."

I gratefully accepted the offer, because it wouldn't have surprised me in the least to eventually discover, in my own accommodations, a pile of bloodied bodies.

I peeled Pete off the wall and considered heading him right back into the fray, and leaving him there for the night. But he straightened and called out, "Sharif's! Where is my favorite speakeasy? Are we there, yet?"

"Why don't we wait until tomorrow night? I'm starting to feel a little sleepy—"

"Cock and bull!" he growled, lurching down the hall and into the street. Because it seemed my duty to watch out for him (or at least watch him), I followed.

He made it up the dirt road and through the stable, but at the cave, he lay on the cold rocks and winked out like a light. I pushed and tugged at him, but he refused to move. All that was left for me to do was return to the hotel for help. Since I couldn't find Scrubs, I established which two of the shipmates were closest to sober, and returned with them. We half-dragged Pete back to the hotel, deposited him in the room, and left a note to return to the ship after he had sobered up.

What influence can a mere note have on a man determined to drink himself into oblivion? Hours later, he found me asleep in Scrubs' room, and woke me to tell me how much of an insult it was that he had not found me in the room we'd taken together.

I squinted at my watch. "I thought you were already out cold for the night. How did you find me?"

"I know where Scrubs is staying. Where is he!? Scrubs, show yerself!"

The wise dishwasher muttered and turned over in his sleep.

Pete sat on the edge of my bed. "It got too quiet in our room, and it woke me up. So then, all I did was take a little walk to the park, and the coppers picked me up, took me down to the station!"

I sat up. "You were arrested?"

"Naw, they only kept me there long enough to piss away a few beers."

"Why didn't you just go back to your room?"

"Because I was looking for you!"

I collapsed back on the bed. "Pete, I'm sleeping."

"Okay, let's sleep." He pulled back the covers and climbed in next to me.

This irritated me, but I suppose I was too polite (and too tired) to kick him out. He stank of liquor, and his face had aged an extra few years from his latest night of excess. No matter. Scrubs woke the next morning at 5a.m. and gathered Pete out of bed. He told his drowsy mate, "We're headed back to the ship, we've got work to do," then whispered to me, "Try to get some rest. You don't have to be out of here for another three hours."

I rolled over and closed my eyes against the last sight of the irksome Pete. Funny thing is, I've always remembered him fondly.

8

The Mysterious Man Called 'Jon'

I drove away from Sibenik through a bright, clear day, feeling fabulous and in full voice again, serenading my trusty chariot. My destination was a town called Split. This is an ancient city where the Diocletian's Palace is located, and I found both the town and the palace to be exceptionally fine diversions.

The town itself was a thriving seaport, with ship-building facilities, a cellulose plant and a mining center. About twenty American tanks were scattered in disarray on an embankment near the port, and a group of soldiers were working on them. I passed them with the pride of citizen from the country that had ended the world war less than ten years before.

Soon I was at the *Putnik*, which is not only the best source to find information on hotels, but also a place for messages to be sent or received by travelers. What did I find but a note waiting for me from Jon, the mysterious stranger who had offered to join me on my trip. He had already passed through Split, but would be in Dubrovnik in a few days. If I liked, I could ask for him at the *Putnik* in that city, and we could spend some time together.

I thoughtfully folded the note and slid it into my wallet. What did Jon want from me? Here came that strange, oblivious reaction of mine again: It never occurred to me that he might have a sexual interest. I'll admit with no further ado that to this day, I don't know if that was his true motivation. He usually acted businesslike, and always looked so typically federal, I couldn't help but focus on the possibility that he was one of McCarthy's lackeys.

Of note: 1953 is the year the Rosenberg husband and wife were executed for being communist spies. The concern about (and threat from) communists was serious stuff. More relevant to myself: Early in the year, while I was still back in the States, it had become known that McCarthy wanted to investigate colleges and universities. He had been gripped by the idea that schools had become riddled with 'communist thinkers.' At the time that was going on, I was attending Cooper Union Art School, and everyone knows creative types were at the top of McCarthy's list. Incidentally, it wouldn't surprise me to learn McCarthyism was an influence on James Baldwin (and probably W.H. Auden) choosing to live outside of the U.S.

While I'm on the topic, and because I'm presenting my story in book form, I should also add that another of McCarthy's targets were 'anti-American' books in libraries. His minions looked into the Overseas Library Program and supposedly found 30,000 books by "communists, pro-communists, and former communists." After the publication of this list, these books were removed from the library shelves.

Back to the original point, which is why would I be a suspect? Well, I was also in the military, although it was only reserves, and another aspect of McCarthy's paranoia in 1953 was the idea that communists were infiltrating the military. I'm sure I could have been loaded with potential to be one of the 'bad guys,' and the fact that my lineage began in The Pale of Russia didn't help my case at all.

In the spirit of The Land Of The Free, I will state here and now that I was not, nor have I ever been, a communist. Yet see how easily I might have been wrongly condemned? When a certain sort of maniacal man is given too much power, we're all at risk, each and every one of us. (Was that a subtle hint about my views on the state of our government in 2007? I'll leave the question unanswered.)

Back in 1954, not many months after the time I was in Yugoslavia, Eisenhower about had his fill of McCarthy's antics. The man had tried to discredit the President's Secretary of the Army! Journalists who had been suppressed until then were intellectually released, and within a year's time, McCarthy was exposed as a lunatic who had finally been given enough rope to hang himself. Still, one can imagine that throughout that final year (during half of which I was still traveling), McCarthy was desperately scrambling for true-blue-Reds. Was Jon one of his scouts? Was I a potential victim of McCarthyism? Were communists considered the terrorists of the 1950s?

My curiosity began to rumble, and I decided I would look for Jon once I arrived in Dubrovnik. Little did I know he would attach himself to me (metaphorically, of course) for quite a while after that.

Until then, I had some time on my hands and some sights to see in Split. My first meal in that town was at the Hotel Bellevue; it was a tasty rice dish with tender chunks of veal. I wrote in my journal, watched the people, and attempted a few conversations. Somehow or another, I learned an American woman was staying at another nearby hotel, and went to introduce myself. She turned out to be a dietitian from Norfolk, and as friendly as I'd hoped. It was late, time for me to make up my bed in the Renault, so we made plans for breakfast the next day.

After our breakfast, I suggested to the woman—I'll call her Virginia because that was where she was from—that we take a day trip to a village called Solin. I brought my camera, and before long, I became surrounded by locals who wanted their pictures taken. I gave in and took a shot of a small family and their cow. I also found an ancient Roman ruin, complete with an old wine cask, and I seated myself there for Virginia to take a photograph.

Back in Split, I wanted to see the Emperor Diocletian's Palace, but Virginia had already taken the tour, and retired to her room. I carried on contentedly alone.

At the entry of the palace, I stopped to take more photos. Of particular interest was a group of children dancing in front of a small Sphinx, which had been gifted to the Diocletian Emperor by Cleopatra. However, before I actually entered the palace itself, an English-speaking Yugoslav man approached me and began a friendly conversation. What did I think of him? That he was attractive, or desirable, or that he might want to know me in an intimate way? None of the above. I probably thought something like, "Now, here's a pleasant fellow." When he invited me for a meal at his home, my next thought must have been, "And generous, too!"

This man—I'll call him Bogdan—served a delightful, simple meal of wine, cheese, and bread. The bread was drizzled with extra-virgin olive oil, and the wine, from an island off Split, was a local delight.

Our conversation flowed, relaxed and enjoyable. Bogdan, who always wore a gentle, open, almost marveling expression on his face, was impressed by the tales of my adventures to date. I also told him of the charming company I had been sharing while in his marvelous town, and his first reaction was to invite Virginia to join us for the evening, insisting he could show her a better tour of the Diocletian's Palace than she probably first experienced. (See? Maybe he really was only kind and generous!)

We retrieved Virginia from her hotel, and Bogdan was true to his word. The Diocletian's Palace is awesome, and for a bit of history, I'll write here what I learned of it:

Diocletian was a Roman Emperor, and after abdicating in the third century, he spent the last years of his life in Split. Enchanted, I presume, by the astounding beauty of the town of Split; the historic inner-city which surrounds the palace, is built on a wonderfully landscaped terrain that slopes gently to the Adriatic Sea.

The palace complex was divided into two halves, and the half that held the more luxurious structures (such as the emperor's public and private living areas) was along the sea-front. The other half of the complex was most likely for housing soldiers and servants. Although the structure was built from the local white limestone, other materials were imported, including fine marble, Egyptian granite columns, and that Sphinx, the gift from Cleopatra.

Last point of note: Both the inner-city of Split and the Diocletian's Palace are so special that I heard UNESCO adopted a proposal to include them in the register of the World Cultural Heritage. Wait, one final point of note: Both the city and the palace were fed water from the Jadro river near Salona, via aqueduct, and its remains can still be seen (to this day) along the road from Split to Salona.

Enough vicarious sight-seeing for the moment.

After our tour, Virginia and I treated Bogdan to a fine dinner—royally, I must say, because we'd just left the palace. We had two of the national dishes, one a skewered mix of liver and onions, while the other was something that was shaped like hot dogs, but tasted disconcertingly like hamburger.

After we had squeezed all the companionship from the shared day together, the three of us took our leave for the night. The next day I was ready to head south, toward Dubrovnik.

Along the way I came to a town called Makarska, and instead of passing through, I decided to stay the night. Such a gently pretty village; it covered the waterfront and was surrounded by pines and mountains. As I rolled into town, I saw a huge wedding, attended by what must have been 500 people. As I watched the festivities, the sun dropped in the sky, setting off night colors on mountains that glowed with a deep, rusty hue. Darkness deepened, and the lights of the little communities on the mountain were so high they looked like stars. The sparks of brightness in the early night was as aesthetically pleasing as the sunset's blush had been.

Although all this was fulfilling enough to enjoy alone, I couldn't resist the sounds of a dance in town. I found the source, in a hotel, where a large group of young people were dancing to familiar American songs. It was exactly what I was looking for. Even better; when I scanned the crowed, I saw some people I knew!

I've mentioned that in Sibenik, while I was for the most part enjoying (and sometimes avoiding) Pete-the-drinker's company, a film was being shot in town. I had watched for a while, and during one break, a handsome young actor approached me. We shared a brief but friendly conversation until we were interrupted by the directors. The actor took a moment to introduce me to the directors, then we parted ways.

Now, in the town of Makarska, at the big dance, the young actor and two directors remembered me. We all stayed for hours, and both myself and the actor (I'll call him Frederick) danced (with women) often, even though there were several couples of men dancing with men and women with women. Between dances, we sat sharing wine, cigarettes, and conversation with the directors. As it turned out, the film location had moved to this town, and they would be continuing the shoot in the morning.

Near the end of the evening, Frederick clicked his fingers and said to the directors, "I think Will would be perfect for the part of an extra."

"Non-speaking," I interjected, "of course." The film, a story about WWII, was entirely in German.

While the directors considered this, Frederick added, "I'm thinking of the scene where the Yugoslav partisans need to escort the Allied POWs through the woods."

"Yes!" said one of the directors, and the other agreed; "He does have the right sort of face for it, doesn't he? And a nice way of moving."

The idea of being in a movie appealed to me, but before I could respond, the first director sweetened the pot: "We can pay you. Not much, only the equivalent of about $25.00USD."

So it would be fun, and I'd also be paid for it! I signed on.

The day after the dance, we all met at the set. They dressed me in some out-of-date Yugoslav fatigues and sat me in a make-up chair. Being 'made-up' was an interesting experience, and actually rather enjoyable. Once I looked the part, I joined the other extras for the scene. When the directors finished explaining things to the German actors, they turned to me and spoke in English: "You and your comrades are moving through enemy territory. You are escorting two men, escaped prisoners of war, who must safely reach the edge of the water. A rowboat will be waiting there for them. After they board, you and your comrades will push the boat into the water, then watch as they row out to sea. A submarine is waiting out there to bring them to safety."

"So, I need to creep through the woods, leading these men, and act as though I'm looking out for the enemy?"

"Correct. You are a courageous Yugoslav who is risking his life to help these prisoners of war, because you believe in the Allied cause. You are a caring man, and the concern for your charges must be apparent in your face, and in the way you move. After you and your compatriots push the rowboat off the shore, watch them for a short time with hope and determination, then return to the forest."

I must have done well; at the end of the day, the directors invited me to a small after-party to celebrate the shoot. One of the directors even said I could keep the clothes I'd worn for the part. The actor Frederick and I spent a few more hours enjoying one another's company, and all told, it was a delightful experience. Sadly, I don't remember the name of the film, and never saw it, so I don't know how I looked in my acting debut. I have always remembered Frederick, though, and our momentary friendship.

After I left Makarska I passed through Metkovic. What a dirty, dreary town—at least it was so, at the time. No disrespect is intended if it has improved over the decades.

I picked up a hitchhiker there, a middle-aged man headed to his own small village about ten kilometers south. We could barely communicate, yet we enjoyed each other's company. I say that because when we arrived at his home, he wouldn't let me leave until I'd had some beer, then shared a bottle of wine with him. While I walked unsteadily back to my car, he pressed another bottle into my hands, begging me to accept it as a gift. It was meant as an exchange for the transportation I had provided, I was sure, but I felt obliged to offer something else in return: I took pictures of the man and his family, or they might have been his friends, or both. I only remember pointing and clicking, and smiling as someone else took a few shots.

After I left, I drove about a half hour, then rolled to a stop on the side of the road. I needed to eat, and hopefully clear my woozy head. I squinted through the bright day and realized I was on the edge of a high pasture overlooking a fiord. Perfect for a picnic.

While I cooked myself lunch, the bright, warm afternoon was quiet but for the occasional song of a passing bird, and perhaps the earth-breath sound of shifting breezes. When those soft winds dropped away, and the birds had either settled or flown, the ensuing soundlessness (combined with my meal) worked a somnolent magic on me. I dozed, bathing in the sun, but when I opened my eyes, I discovered myself surrounded by three ladies, a road repair man, and a younger girl.

Fortunately I had only removed my shirt for the sunbathing. I greeted the group politely, smilingly, while I gathered my belongings with careful, non-threatening moves. They watched me warily, but when I lifted my camera and gestured the question of a picture, they smiled. Photography was really taking off at that time.

We spent an hour attempting to communicate, and what most clearly came through to me was that the old women were shepherds. One of those women was particularly touched by the knowledge that I was from America; apparently Americans had treated her quite well in the past. The very mention of my country brought tears to her eyes. Could that happen in today's world? Probably, but not as likely. When I parted from those people, and our passing of lives, it was with great warmth.

*   *   *

Before long I was in Dubrovnik, where a quick stop at the *Putnik* told me the curious man named Jon was indeed in town, staying at the Imperial Hotel. Waiting for me.

How interesting.

First, though, I wanted my own view of the area. I parked my car, and as though they were part of a beehive community that had spread the news about my camera, Yugoslav children gathered to have their picture taken. I obliged, then gently shooed them away, and walked over the drawbridge into the enchanted walled city of Dubrovnik. Here was a place that belonged in another century, and in fact the walls had taken centuries to build. Well, the original sections were thrown up in a hurry at a time when the town was officially called Ragusa (but still also known as Dubrovnik) because the Barbarians were invading like madmen.

The highest walls are somewhere around 75 feet tall, and thousands of feet long. Inside them is the old city, including a huge fortress, fortifications, towers, even a moat. There was also what was once a canal, which is now used as a street, and is lined with buildings. As I explored, walking along the tops of the walls, an awesome view spread out beneath me; not only of the stunning Adriatic Coast, but also the narrow streets and red roofs of the entire town.

The coast is steep and rocky, with deep coves and beckoning beaches. The mountains are high and wooded, and many of the trees are oak, which I believe is where the name 'Dubrovnik' came from. Those mountains drop right down to the sea, and in the amazingly clean sea are islands. Supposedly, one of those islands is where Richard the Lionhearted was shipwrecked on his way to the crusades.

The roofs are uniformly red, but I don't know (or remember) why. I believe the original tiles were called 'Roman tiles,' which were reportedly light and not the best for waterproofing. However, even when those tiles are replaced with something newer, they always remain red, to this very day.

A fascinating city.

After I finished my solo tour, I found Jon's hotel. I called him from the lobby, and on the telephone he said, as though we had known each other for years, "Will, I'm happy you called. I'll be down in a moment."

I ambled idly through the lobby, wondering what more I would learn about this strangely persistent man. As soon as he stepped from the elevators, I remembered why I had suspected that he might be connected to the government in some way. What a drab man, in his boring black shoes and gartered black socks and dark suit with its plain white shirt and bland, narrow tie.

He wore a noncommittal smile as he shook my hand. "Wonderful to see you, Will. Can I treat you to dinner?"

"Sure." He recommended the restaurant next to his hotel, and soon we were seated, sipping wine.

"Tell me," said Jon. "Have you been enjoying your trip so far?"

"Very much so." It felt like we were speaking from a script. "And you?"

"It certainly has been interesting." He then asked, "Have you made any new friends?"

Aha. Perhaps here is where I would find that no, he wasn't a federal agent, but was a Gay man (in desperate need of a new wardrobe) who wanted to know me better.—No, wait, maybe his question was a probe about who I'd been interacting with in this communist country!

It didn't matter. Fully confident of my non-communist status, I told him much of what I've written in this book to this point, and as I felt no attraction to him whatsoever, I excluded only the details of my sexual explorations.

"But you're still traveling by yourself," was his only eventual response.

"This is true."

"You sure must get lonesome."

"Occasionally. My Renault is pretty good company." I was only half-joking. By that time, I'd grown very attached to the little car. She'd been reliable, ever-ready, accommodating, and never had any critical reactions to all my singing.

Jon reached into the inner pocket of his suit and pulled out a small, bound atlas. Flipping one page at a time, he found our location, and ran his finger along the route I had described. "Where are you going next, Greece?"

"After I've finished seeing Yugoslavia, yes. How about you? What's your agenda?"

"I'd like to see more of this country before Greece, too. It would be nice if I didn't have to blow through it on a train. I wish I could catch a ride with you."

"Jon, if you'd like to ride with me a while, I'll be fine with that." The wine I'd been drinking brought me close to adding, 'If Senator McCarthy wants proof I'm not a communist, he can have it.'

Jon asked, with what might have been a tinge of insecurity, "Are you sure you won't mind?"

"Sure." Another wine-induced thought—As long as you keep your hands to yourself.

Just what *was* this man up to? That his response to my question about his agenda had been somewhat dismissive didn't escape me, but he wasn't the only one who could be enigmatic. Throughout the rest of the meal I did most of the talking, which isn't always my way, and my monologue was intentionally banal. Jon didn't seem to mind. He had so little to say. Hiding something, maybe? Or was he just a dull man? I guessed he wouldn't be a cumbersome traveling companion, although at one point he certainly did get in my way. That story will come later.

In Dubrovnik, I stayed in my car while he stayed in his hotel, but we toured the town together the next day. It didn't bother me a bit to retrace my first steps across the stunning walls of the inner-city of Dubrovnik.

By the following morning, I had already learned that spending large sections of time with Jon wouldn't illuminate anything about his personality. His mid-line smile and barely competent conversational abilities were becoming a real bore. The only initiative he showed was when he spotted a movie theatre and suggested we see what was playing.

An American movie was featured: "The Secret of Prisoner Lake."

Why was a contemporary American movie showing in this ancient city? Evidently, it was their only form of entertainment, which could also explain why there was such a thing as a morning matinee in the middle of the week. In any case, I heard the people of Dubrovnik would see the same movie over and over and over again, which I realize is commonplace these days but at the time, I found it bizarre.

First and foremost, I should mention that the Republic of Dubrovnik was, I heard, the very first republic to recognize the United States of America as a sovereignty. What foresight! In fact, speaking of foresight (in more of a moralistic vein), Dubrovnik abolished slave trade in the 15th century. Sure, they had a class system, but liberty was of the utmost importance. Oh, the vision, outward and in-looking, of these people.

This remarkable little city was quite prosperous and peaceful for almost five hundred years. It was first established in the 7th century, back (as I said earlier) when the Barbarians were doing their barbaric marauding. Throughout the following four or five centuries, the people built their wealth and influence by trading on the Mediterra-nean. Much of that time they were under Byzantine protection, until Venice took over in the early 1200s and kept control for about 150 years. Eventually, Dubrovnik became a sovereign state again, and all was well until a devastating earthquake hit in 1667. So much of this incredibly historic place was destroyed but rebuilt (thank goodness) with its renewed sense of appeal.

News-hounds are probably aware that Dubrovnik was destroyed again in 1991/92, senselessly and mercilessly bombed, which broke my heart. Although I've heard a number of international organiza-tions have rebuilt the marble streets and sculptures since the bombing, I value the memories from my visit in the '50s.

To finish up with what happened to Dubrovnik after its terrible natural disaster in the 1600s: Napoleon conquered it in the early 1800s, and it was annexed to Austria for a while, then in the early 1900s it became a part of Yugoslavia (or, as the country was known as at the time, The Kingdom of Serbs, Croats and Slovenes). When WWII started, Dubrovnik was connected specifically to Croatia but was under Italian and then German occupation for most of the rest of the war. It was liberated in 1945, and became a part of Tito's Yugoslavia.

The life of this city is something like a human life, to me—those struggles through good times and hard times, while always maintaining a sense of self. And the resplendence of it! Lord Byron, Agatha Christie, and George Bernard Shaw are a few who agree with me. Shaw even wrote, "If you want to see heaven on earth, come to Dubrovnik."

Early the next morning, Jon walked casually up to my car at the moment I had completed its re-conversion from bed to carriage. "I've found a nice place to swim," he said.

His unusual initiative surprised me into immediately responding, "I'll get my trunks."

The beach was pretty, and the sun was warm enough to keep us from being too chilled by the water. A group of children edged closer and closer to us, curious, but darted away when I lifted my camera. Laughing, I pointed it at something and clicked it, then said, "Picture! Photos! Photography!" They understood the terms from the movies, I supposed, because they gathered back around me. I showed them the camera, turning it carefully, allowing them to touch it. It's possible to make the same fleeting friendships with children as we do with adults, and I spent the rest of my day at the beach enjoying their company.

Jon and I returned to town, and I brought the car in for greasing and an oil-change. The mechanic had no grease gun, but I'd bought one somewhere along the way for the equivalent of about 2,000 dinars. When I let the mechanic use it, he handled it with such loving, sweetly envious care that I offered to sell it to him.

"No," he said in his thickly-accented English, "too much."

"Is 100 dinars too much? You could afford that, couldn't you?"

If his eyes had gotten any bigger they would have tumbled out of his head. "100 dinars? For this?"

"Yes. That's a fair deal, don't you think?" It meant the man's livelihood, and he'd done such a fine job on my car. With my negligible mechanical abilities, I'd be better off finding others to grease my engine, anyway.

He scrambled to get the money, and I could tell after we made the exchange he wanted to embrace me, but was too shy. I squeezed his shoulder and thanked him for the work he'd done.

The morning after was as fair and lovely as the day before, with blue skies and a strong sun. Once I had Jon and his belongings loaded into the car, we left with the intention of reaching Cetinje, the old capital of Montenegro. Along the way we stopped at Kotor, which was another interesting walled city, then proceeded up a steep, serpentine drive. I have to admit it was nice to have a companion on some of those rough roads.

A gorgeous fiord dropped away below us as we climbed, higher and higher. At each curve we thought we had reached the top, but the rugged, intimidating road continued on.

I don't remember how long it took us to reach Cetinje. Once there, we found the one new grand hotel for Jon, but to his dismay, it was like a big, cold, barn. All the other people staying there seemed alone and unhappy. It was bitterly cold, yet for reasons I couldn't understand, everyone had their doors standing wide open.

As there was no advantage in staying in the drafty hotel, I readied my car in advance for sleep. Once Jon was checked in and settled, we had a meager, unimpressive dinner in the hotel's restaurant. I don't think there was a fresh vegetable in the entire town. After dinner Jon spotted yet another theater, but this one was showing a series of films on Yugoslavia. There were six shorts that I found interesting enough, telling of the history and beauty of the country. A lot of it was propaganda (what else), but with much truth about the beauty.

Before long, we were on our way to what I spelled in my journal as *Andre Jeuika*. It was a very pretty mountain village, but the hotel was worse than the one in Citenje; drafty, no heat, and paper-thin walls. The people of that village must have seen us as passing benefactors; their prices were easily tripled, including at the hotel, where they charged 80 dinars for additional blankets. (It was much too cold for me to sleep in the car.)

The one decent fellow I met there was a jack-of-all-trades who advised me to let the water out of the car so it wouldn't freeze overnight. He surely saved my radiator, and God only knows what I would have been charged for a new one in that town! It probably would have taken a week for a new radiator to arrive, and the funds for my trip would have been chipped away to pennies. Thanks to that man, Jon and I were able to start out in the morning with no difficulty. Some angels flit in and out of our lives quite quickly.

We continued on, with the idea of finding a place with the daunting name of Kosovkra Mitrovica. As we drove, the headgear of the people changed to turbans, and by the time we passed through a minaret-filled town called Pec, I knew we had reached the part of Yugoslavia where the Turkish influence was strong.

As we rolled into Kosovkra Mitrovica, the country was much flatter, and the town quite exotic. Firstly there were more minarets, which are sort of hard for me to describe, so I'll show here how the dictionary does it: "a slender turret connected with a mosque and having a balcony from which the muezzin calls at hours of prayer." There were also hordes of people, animals, and mud. We followed a line of drawn carriages full of wood, hay, and who knew what else, all heading down the main (mud-filled) street. Eventually, we found ourselves at a river, which we needed to cross to get to the other side of town, but there was no bridge.

The horse-drawn carriages didn't have much difficulty with the water, but there was no way I was about to take my deceivingly amphibian-looking car for a swim. We parked, and apparently our looks of defeat touched the hearts of the natives, because they offered to help.

This is when I christened my Renault, as it were, with a name, and here is how it happened: I, along with Jon and approximately ten other men, lifted the car and carried her across the river. Once we were on the other side, I thanked the men who had helped, and one of them patted the fender and said, "She good."

Jon didn't see the gesture, only heard the words, and turned, looking for a woman. He asked, "Who's 'she'?"

I answered, also patting the car's fender, "Why, Dolly, of course!"

It really was an adorable little Renault. As I've said, she was more than my transportation, she had become my cocoon-like home-away-from-home, and she had treated my dependency on her with gentle respect. I had developed an attachment like one would to a helpful friend or even a beloved dog. Dolly had the personality of it all: home, friend, pet. And, of course, faithful traveling companion.

All said and done, Kosovkra Mitrovica didn't feel like the right night-stop, although the new construction on the far side of the river did show potential for future travelers. Of course, the bridge situation would have to be taken care of before it could become a tourist mecca.

Jon and I continued on to a town called Pristina, which seemed much more accommodating for an over-nighter. We parked and settled, then wandered around the town. Soon we noticed a group of people entering a small building, and discovered a play was being given by a drama group. I said to Jon it sounded like it would be—I believe the term I used back then was, 'a gas.' As it turned out, the acting was terrible, it was as though the performers took it as a lark. They might have been simply reading lines from a memorized text in their minds, and compensating by over-exaggerating their movements. All that said, I thoroughly enjoyed the enthusiasm of the audience.

The next morning, Dolly gave me trouble starting, and I figured a few mouthfuls of murky river-water must have entered the lines while we carried her across. "Dolly," I moaned, "I've just given you a name, how could you now let me down!" See what happens when you start getting too close to a woman? I'm kidding.

We were stalled on the road, but locals surrounded us again, offering to help. There must have been about 20 people there. Between them, they somehow purged some of the water from the car's lines, and got her started, but wouldn't accept any dinars. It was incredibly kind of them, and I hope their behavior toward foreigners has never changed.

Dolly, Jon and I limped into Skopje, and here is my journal entry about that town:

Skopje, the capital of Macedonia, was a disappointment. It had an empty, sad feeling, more so than I had felt in any other city. The hotels were poor, for such a large city, and so many of the people were barefoot in this freezing weather. We decided we would leave the cold, depressing city first thing in the morning.

We almost didn't get out of there, because Dolly gave me more trouble. Go figure. I was tempted to start calling her 'the frog' again. Yes, I recently referred to my attachment to her as one I could have for a beloved dog, and in fact, she sometimes purred like a cat. Yet this mechanical animal was hard to train, and when she chose a moment to misbehave, no amount of loving coaxing or frustrated admonitions could get her moving again.

Here came more local men, though, ready and willing to help, refusing all offers of payment. I don't know how I would have gotten through Yugoslavia without the generosity of the general populace. To think, I had been so concerned about being harmed in this country!

Of course, that fear was based on the behavior of the government, and had nothing to do with the actual people. We can't truly know other cultures until we've met the individuals who live in those different countries. Governments are not realistic representatives of our nations! (Okay, that's another less-than-subtle comment about our current U.S. society; a message for those who are misjudging Americans these days.)

Back to our narrow escape from the depressing Skopje. I heard their population was over 100,000, but when I stopped at a filling station at the edge of town, I learned there wasn't a drop of gasoline anywhere to be found. Unbelievable. We had no choice but to keep moving forward, with our fingers crossed, and fortunately found a Yugoslavian Army post that sold us some benzine (an old fashioned gas replacement). It would have to do.

We were as gassed up as we were going to get, and I was about to set Yugoslavia behind me. Next: Greece.

Proud to wear the sweater my sister knitted for me

Antonio in Rome

Friends along the Adriatic Highway, Yugoslavia

Along the Adriatic coast, Yugoslavia

A picture-perfect scene, Dubrovnic

Να χρεωθή να φερη μας εδωσι

Δρχ 125 (εκατον εικοσι πεντε)

Προ Τουρμις αρ. 35

(δεκα) δολλαρια

Η παρούσα ισχύει διά 15 ημέρας

Εν Θεσ/νίκη τη 28.11.53

ΤΡΑΠΕΖΑ ΤΗΣ ΕΛΛΑΔΟΣ

ΥΠΟΚ/ΜΑ ΘΕΣ/ΝΙΚΗΣ

Ο ΔΙΕΥΘΥΝΤΗΣ

177584

T.C.
EDİRNE KARAAĞAÇ İSTASYON
PASAPORT KONTROL KOMİSERLİĞİ
29.11.957
GELİŞİ GÖRÜLMÜŞTÜR

=15= Dolar
=20= yirmi T.
girişinde görülmüştür.
çıkışı giriniş,
29-11-957

9

Athens, The Acropolis, Delphi, and a Touch of Love

What a joy it was to see Salonika, with its neon lights, happy people, full shops, and heated hotels! Jon and I stayed there two days, resting, sightseeing, and loafing while Dolly was given a thorough check-up by a mechanic.

Throughout our time together, I had been paying attention with half-an-ear to Jon's attempts at conversation, but it was always small talk, never interesting. Also, to admit to my own possible paranoia, he never once asked about my political affiliations. And, while I'm addressing my general curiosity about his motivations, I should note I don't remember him ever asking me whether I had met any women during my travels. We didn't talk about women at all throughout the time we spent together, which (and this is a blind guess) I would imagine heterosexual men might talk about quite a bit. Yet, in all fairness, he never spoke of men, either. If I were asked today, 'Was Jon gay or straight?' my instinctive answer would be, 'Unknown.'

I know I once asked him the basics; "What do you do for a living, are you married," etc., but his replies barely took hold in my memory. They were either devoid of interest, or he had tucked his words into the back of his cheek in such a way that they only bounced off my attention. The best I can say is that I don't think he was married, and he might have claimed to work in some capacity as a lawyer.

As far as his travel plans, he never did share his itinerary with me. He could have been simply wandering, for all I knew. It was that those wanderings put him in my path as often as they did that was suspicious to me, but the quiet, usually unobtrusive companionship was welcome enough.

After I felt completely assured that Dolly would behave, we traveled on toward Athens. The country was divided by one range to reach a village or town nestled in a valley, only to begin another ascent. The mountain villages were quiet, with little activity as compared to Yugoslavia, and I rarely saw children. I wrote something about that in my journal, but because it's unconfirmed, I'll only show the entry here:

We learned that the communists had kidnaped whole villages of Greek children, and are educating them behind the Iron Curtain. The idea is that they'll come back to Greece someday as ideal communists. We noticed fortifications along the way in the mountain paths, and signs were posted prohibiting photographs.

Because my comment about the fortifications and photos was written right after my observation about the children, I assume I thought there was a correlation between the two.

If the communists really were kidnapping children, I can certainly understand why the villages were so quiet. Not only would the lack of young, fresh voices subdue a town, but the parents would have been bereft. It seems there should have been a public outcry, if not at the time of my visit, then at some later time when the horror of the abductions was uncovered. I wish I could remember how we 'learned' about the situation, but since I cannot, I'm only left with my disquieting curiosity.

As we continued along the road, we were followed, like the eyes in a painting, by the snow covered peak of Mt. Olympus. The 'home of the gods' certainly had a heavenly quality; it looked capable of reaching above the highest of clouds.

Even my boring traveling companion became excited as we approached Athens. We kept hoping, as we reached the top of each hill or rounded each curve, that there would be the Acropolis and the Parthenon before us. Yet it wasn't until late afternoon that we came down from the final mountain into a pleasant valley tucked in next to the sea, filled with olive trees and pines. Athens was before us.

What a sparkling clean city! And there, look, the Acropolis! The thrill in my stomach spun up into the back of my throat, tickled my nose, and I sneezed. I sneezed again, and again.

Drat!

Here I was in this extraordinary, ancient city, in a country I expected would be a highlight of my trip, and I had caught a cold.

My first night in Athens was slept away in sniffling, stuffy misery. That rest only marginally helped me, but at least I felt ready to function in the morning. First, I checked in at American Express, which was another version of Yugoslavia's *Putnik*; a place for travelers to receive mail from people who assumed you'd eventually show up there. There was no mail for me, but I asked the clerk about a less expensive hotel than what Jon could afford. (Jon insisted he would also move to whatever new accommodations I could find, and asked that I secure two rooms.) At American Express, they suggested the University Club and provided directions. Once I arrived at that youth-oriented facility, I met a Greek student I'll call 'Thomas Erasmus'. That lovely boy, who had an absolutely perfect, contemporary grasp of English, approached me and offered some guidance in his city.

His first suggestion was that I and my 'friend' (Jon) avoid staying at the University Club, which had too many student-minded restrictions. Thomas mentioned curfews, but it wasn't until later that I realized his larger concern was with respect to overnight guests. (I can't imagine what sort of relationship he thought I had with Jon, who he had yet to meet.) Thomas showed me a decent, inexpensive hotel, which I believe was called the Diathena. The Diathena was in the market section of Athens, where we'd be hearing the pulse of the town early every morning. I found that we even had a view of the Parthenon from our window; I stood on top of the chair on our balcony, leaned precariously forward, and there it was.

By the time we were fully settled in, it was early evening, and Jon went off in search of his own diversions. I was still battling my cold, and collapsed across my bed while Thomas took a nearby chair. After a short silence the sweet fellow said, with no preamble, "Will, can I tell you I think you're a beautiful man?"

This startled me, and I lifted my aching head to look at him. "What a lovely thing to say, Thomas."

"Then you don't mind my telling you?"

"Not at all." I examined him with a new eye. He seemed so young, although he couldn't have been less than twenty-one, and I was only twenty-seven. I didn't say it at the time, but he struck me as rather handsome, himself, though not the type of man I'm typically drawn to. Thomas had a full, masculine face but a soft build. His thick hair sometimes had a tendency to thrust spikes out around his forehead, which I found charming in an urchin sort-of-way.

He scooted his chair closer to my bed and gazed at me with what I could only describe as adoration. "Can I come with you to the places you visit in Athens?"

"You must have schoolwork, and I remember how rough college can be." How does a man respond to an agreeable, sensitive boy who appeared stricken by love at first sight?

"There's nothing in my schedule," Thomas rejoined, "that would keep me from accompanying you. I've had a light load all semester, and I'm ahead of things, just now."

Tired, but respectful of his feelings, I pushed myself up into a seated position. "I realize you're a grown man, but you've told me you're staying with your mother. What would she think of you spending so much time with an American stranger?"

"I think she would like you very much. In fact, I want to introduce you to her."

This boy wasted no time! "That might be nice. Unfortunately, a terrible cold has me in its grip, and I should spend the rest of the evening at a slow pace. I need to try to nap for a few hours, then grab a quick bite, but after that I'd like to sleep the rest of the night."

Tears sprung up in Thomas' eyes, and he said, "Do you mean I have to go?"

The tears touched me, but I was determined to defeat my cold. "Only for tonight. Will you meet me here at eight in the morning?"

He stood, assumed a gallant pose, and squared his shoulders. "I'll be here exactly at that time."

I rolled over and closed my eyes, but felt his gaze on my back for long minutes before the door quietly closed.

When I woke in the morning, I felt more myself again, and was ready and waiting when Thomas appeared at 8 a.m. (exactly). Jon asked to join us on the tour I had planned: The Stadium, the Temple of Zeus, and the Theater of Dionysus.

I have the feeling many are familiar with the larger aspects of Greek history, but I can't resist sharing some of what I learned while there.

When I say 'The Stadium,' I'm talking about the Panathenaic Stadium near the Acropolis in Athens. In Greek it's called the *Panathinaiko stadiq* which means 'Stadium of all the Athenians,' and it's also commonly known as *Kallimarmaro*, which means 'made of fine marble.' Indeed. This is not a countertop, not a column, not a building, but an entire stadium built of marble.

The most notable aspect of The Stadium's modern history is that this is the place where, in 1896, the first Olympics of our time were hosted.

The 'Temple of Zeus' I refer to is more correctly known as the *Temple of Olympian Zeus*. Of course there are many temples of Zeus, who's a god, after all, but the Olympian Temple (or I should say, what remains of it) is in the center of Athens. Hundreds of years passed between its inception and completion, but then it held a long-standing record as the largest temple in Greece. Here's a bit of dry wit: Aristotle once used this temple as an example of how tyrannies would engage the populace in great works for the state in order to leave them with no time, energy, or means to rebel.

The temple originally sported 104 massive columns which were each over 50 feet high. Sadly, only fifteen of these columns remain standing today, and another lies on the ground, dropped by what must have been one *hell* of a gale in 1852. (Imagine the sound it must have made when it tumbled!) Considering how awesome the site is in its diminished state, I can't begin to visualize its appearance so many centuries ago, while in full, gleaming splendor.

The Theater of Dionysus is a place any serious student of theater will know of; this is where, in the 5th century BC, the plays of Sophocles, Aeschylus, and Euripides were performed. It's on the slope of the Acropolis, because the Greeks preferred their theaters to be built into hills. The audience would sit on the ascending rows of wooden benches and watch the play unfolding in front of and below them. I could be wrong on this, but I believe the first time we contained performances in a theater was in ancient Greece, and as far as I know, this is the first structure built specifically for shows. It's hard to describe the sensation of standing in a place where you know the origins of the modern play began.

Everywhere we went that day, the Acropolis was hovering there above it all. I enjoyed the anticipation of stepping on its ground as much as the actual visit. (This strikes me as a possible theme of my life; the thrill of anticipation!) Thomas asked when I planned to see that most popular of sites, and I told him it would be the day after next, because there were more places I preferred to see first.

"What about later tonight?" he asked. "What are your plans?"

"Dinner leaps to mind."

"Good. You are invited to dine with my mother and myself, at our home."

The invitation hadn't been extended to Jon, which was fine with me, and apparently Jon didn't mind, either. "Will," he said, "I'm going to do some sightseeing on my own for the rest of the day, and have dinner on my own. I'll catch up to you in the morning."

"Fine." When he was gone, I told Thomas, "Now, I need to find your local Renault agency, and see if I can interest them in a story."

Thomas tagged along, and waited while I spoke to the manager of the local dealership. That man, who I'll call Dimitri, was the first truly enthusiastic employee of that business I met. He listened to my story with full attention, then sat back in his chair and steepled his fingers.

"I agree that this would be excellent advertising. I'd like to contact the local newspaper and see if they'll do a story on this. We can't pay you much, but we will pay you."

Eureka! Within an hour the reporter had arrived, and Dimitri had used the time to have my car washed and readied for a photo. The interview went well, the article looked great, and I have a copy of it to this day. I was only paid the equivalent of about $50.00USD, but to me, that money was gold.

That night, in greatly lifted spirits (success seemed to have cured my cold), I drove Thomas and myself out to the little country home he shared with Mrs. Erasmus.

While I drove, I felt his adoring eyes on my face, my chest, my legs, even on my hands as they steered the car. I asked him, "Do you still think your mother will like me?"

"I know she will. I told her about you last night, and she said,

'Be sure to invite him to dinner.' That was already something I wanted to do, anyway. I think you'll like our food."

"I don't doubt it. But, Thomas…" I wanted to ask him if she knew of his sexual leanings, but realized he might not know it himself. What if he saw things the way I saw them? It was possible he also believed there were men who could be called 'queer,' and others called 'homosexual' or 'heterosexual,' but then there were certain men-loving men who planned to have a wife and children. (Note that I didn't include the word 'bisexual.' I didn't even know such a way of life existed in 1953. I don't think the concept had been fully absorbed and accepted by our society yet.)

In my opinion, in retrospect, 'Gay' was the most appropriate term for Thomas, but I had no way of knowing if he would have agreed. In any case, nothing could cause me to insult my dear young friend, such a kind and gentle boy, who I also like to think had good taste in men. I rearranged the question I had begun, and asked, "Did you tell your mother you think I'm a beautiful man?"

"You bet."

Hmm. "What did she think of that?"

"She said, 'Now I *really* must meet him! and asked, 'Will he be in Athens long?'" Thomas rested his fingers on the dashboard in front of him, but I imagined he would have preferred to put them on my wrist. Or somewhere else. He asked me, "How long will you be staying, anyway?"

"Only a few days."

"How many days is that?"

"Not quite a week."

"I'm going to cry when you leave."

I slowed enough to look at him. Tears, real tears were starting in his eyes! "Thomas, that's the sweetest thing anyone has ever said to me."

Now the tears did come. Touched, I pulled to the side of the road. "Please don't cry."

"I can't help myself." He sniffed, steepled his fingers over his nose, and peered at me. "I'm in love with you."

I'm not making this up. Back then, people really made such

spontaneous admissions. In fact, the terminology from those days meant I could now refer to Thomas as my 'lover,' based solely on the fact that he loved me and sought my love in return. I think it was a charming way to use the term, and I'm a little sorry the meaning has changed.

After Thomas' confession, I scrambled around inside my own gut, trying to identify my own feelings, but only discovered affection. No real love, no attraction, no romance. I lightly touched his arm. "I don't feel that I'm in love with you. I do care about you very much…" I stopped there; it was enough. In many cases, honesty is best even if it hurts.

Thomas dropped his hands and lifted his chin toward the road. "We should keep going, Mother is waiting."

"Are you going to be okay?"

"Only if you promise we can spend all of your time here together. That's all I ask; that you give me these few days."

"How about 'most' of my time? Will that do?"

He offered me a sad smile. "I guess it will have to be enough."

If I wasn't careful, this young lover might have worked his way into my heart, but my mind (and gut) knew it wasn't meant to be.

What I now find most endearing about my interactions with Thomas is that he made his interest in me unquestionably clear. I believe it is he who first initiated a few sparks in my Gay-man-radar ('gaydar'), which until then was practically non-functional. The only time I ever knew a man might be interested in me was when he made it extremely obvious, and I admit that to this very day, I must receive some very strong clues before I'm certain. That Thomas was so open about his feelings was a courageous gift he gave to me, and for that, I'll always be grateful.

At his house, his mother greeted me with enthusiasm, and drew me into pleasant conversation while a cook prepared a tasty Greek meal that started with eggs, cheese, and bean soup with vegetables. Next we were served meatballs, then more cheese, wine, and fruit. It was easy to enjoy the company of Thomas' mother, who was an engaging, amicable woman, and she treated me (rather disconcertingly) like a suitor for her son.

After we finished eating, she said, "We were thinking of going to a dance party tonight, you should come with us."

I do love to dance. Of course, there would be no way I could dance with Thomas, but I assume Mrs. Erasmus only wanted to find a way to keep me a few more hours of the evening for the sake of her son.

Now, here's what my journal entry says about that dance:

At the party I was hit in the face by a jealous Greek lover for asking his girl for a second dance, after receiving a very obvious come-on signal from her. I later discovered she was a married woman cheating on her husband, who was away.

Ah, the tribulations of heterosexuals. The married woman was flirting with me, the young American visitor, while her boy-on-the-side was audacious enough to think he had full claim on her. It seems absurd.

More absurd is the idea that in the above-described mix, the 'young American visitor' was homosexual. Yet, as I said: I love to dance, and the 'come-on signal' was for me only an offer for more of that. If she meant anything further, only she and her jealous boyfriend were concerned by it.

After I had been slugged, everyone who knew the players apologized over and over, telling me the man was drunk. He would have to be! I mean, the nerve!

On the way back to the Erasmus home, Thomas said, "Mother, I think Will would enjoy a visit to one of our villages."

Mrs. Erasmus smiled serenely. "I think so, too. Will, would you like to join us, day after tomorrow? We have plans to go to Spata; it's a very pretty place."

'Day after tomorrow' was when I had planned to visit the Acropolis, but I replied, "That sounds delightful, I'd like to come." In the morning I would make my planned trip to Sounion, to see the sanctuary there, and could go to the Acropolis the day after my visit to the village. I was determined to save the best for last.

Mrs. Erasmus made herself scarce when we got to their house, while Thomas and I sat in my car saying our goodbyes.

Thomas said, "If I could kiss you, I would."

I wasn't about to ask, 'Why can't you?' Instead I said, "I appreciate that."

My comment confused the poor boy enough that he only smiled crookedly and climbed out of the car. "I'll meet you in the morning at your hotel," he said through the window, "and we can leave for Sounion."

"I'll wait for you."

Sounion (like Athens) was once a part of Attica, a region of ancient Greece. Here's what I wrote about my visit there, in my journal:

> I saw the Temple of Poseidon, with its remaining columns rising from a sheer cliff above the sea, at the tip of Greece. In Sounion, Lord Byron's initials are among the many who have written their names where all eyes will be sure to look. The pillars are almost pure white and wind-marked from centuries of standing in this place, which is drenched with an elegant beauty. All views from Sounion add to that enchantment, which is marked forever by God's hand. The sunset perfected the evening.

When I spoke of Lord Byron's initials, I was referring to the fact that he carved them on one of the pillars. Apparently he took time out to etch that graffiti while fighting the Greek War of Independence.

After re-reading the above journal entry, I do remember my pleasure at sharing that perfect sunset with Thomas and even with the drab, mysterious Jon, who had joined us on the excursion.

The long day ended in an early sleep, and the next morning, I was ready for a visit to a typical Greek village with the Erasmus mother and son.

Spata. What a darling place! It couldn't have been a more delightful trip. Well, strike that: It might have been nicer if a young woman named Diana hadn't come along. Here's what I said about that unfortunate girl in my journal:

> We drove to Spata with a young, unattached and gruesome-looking girl. She had nothing but alluring smiles for me. She fancied herself a singer, unfortunately for us, because she screamed louder than Helen Troubel sang. The only thing that made it bearable was the fact that her presentation of the Greek folk songs was amusing.

For those who aren't familiar with Helen Troubel, she was an opera singer. That's the music I most prefer. Imagine how Diana's screeching must have grated on my ears!

Diana was from Spata, which was why she happened to be in the car with us. Once we arrived, she tried to lead the tour for me, but it was obvious Mrs. Erasmus had been there many times before. She veered away from Diana's intended path and stopped to speak with a group of women seated at weaving machines. It was obvious the locals loved and respected Mrs. Erasmus, and one of them gave her some of the precious material they were using to create their intricately woven designs.

The material was passed to me for my inspection, and Thomas proudly whispered, "Mother has been very kind to this lady's family, and to many of the others here."

"Your mother is a special person."

"I know that. She's smart, too, because she really likes you."

"I like her, too."

Thomas beamed. Who knew what extended-family fantasies might have been tumbling through his head?

Mrs. Erasmus next led us to the most tranquil, idyllic setting I could have imagined, and spread out a large blanket. We sat in an olive grove while sheep, lamb, goats, and donkeys wandered in the fields nearby. Our picnic was made up of cold lamb, meatballs, cheeses, fried potatoes, pickled peppers, bread, cabbage, salad, and wine. What a heavenly feast. The food, the surroundings, the company, even the gruesome Diana…all of it was forever memorable.

All the girls were solicitous and gave me special attention, carrying my cameras and cases, vying for a position next to me as we walked. Somebody—it might have been me—had the bright idea of a drive in Dolly, and we all piled in to head for the nearby beach. Everyone fought to sit in the front with me for a chance to drive the car, all except gentleman Thomas, who already held the honor of discovering this playful American. Besides, he must have intuited that of everyone gathered that day, he was the one who had the best chance of winning my affections.

I should clarify that when I said everyone wanted to drive the car, it was actually only to lean against me and steer it while I applied the gas and brakes. Because I didn't want to unnecessarily encourage any of the girls, Mrs. Erasmus won the fun. She aimed us to a spot on a hill overlooking the sea.

Everybody piled out, and we laughingly slid and stumbled down the embankment to the water. After running and splashing for a while, I fell to the sand and absorbed the bliss of the moment. Unfortunately, my relaxation was truncated when I saw a group of children running toward me, battering my senses with garbled shouts. I sat up and tried to calm them, asking them to slowly explain their excitement. It was something to do with the car! I leapt to my feet and peered up through the bright day toward where we had parked, but even if Dolly was still there, she wouldn't be visible from where I stood.

Thomas, Mrs. Erasmus, and the others joined me as I started back up the slope. I asked Mrs. Erasmus if she could tell me exactly what the babbling children were telling me, and she translated as best as she could: "They say your car is moving."

"On the hill? *Off* the hill?" I sprinted upward, my heart thumping. Insurance laws are not the same as they are today. If that car had taken a tumble, I would have been, to put it in today's parlance, screwed. Reselling all the silk stockings in all the European PX's combined wouldn't be enough for me to fund a new car.

I didn't even feel winded, and before I reached the last mound before I would have sight of the road, I said, "I *know* I put the emergency brake on!"

There she was. Dolly hadn't budged. And now, she couldn't have moved if she'd wanted to; pieces of broken stone, serving as chocks, had been placed in front of and behind each tire.

Now my breath came gasping as I trudged up to stand next to my little Renault. The children gathered around me, laughing, nudging each other and falling against one another, silly American! What, is our language all Greek to you? We said it looked like it was moving a little, so we stopped the tires with bricks!

I could have throttled the little dears, God bless them. Thomas removed the blocks, and after we all laughed a little more, it was time to return to Athens proper.

* * *

What, some less-traveled people might ask, is the Acropolis, exactly? The word itself means 'upper city' or more literally, 'the highest point of the town,' which is set above everything else for safety. Therefore, the Athens Acropolis is built on the highest hill and has views toward land and sea, which made it an easy look-out. The people could gather there and huddle inside their sacred buildings whenever invaders threatened to swarm into the city.

Because of its lofty position, the Athens Acropolis started as a military fortress, then became a religious center (again the position was handy), and was even a residential area for a while. The last was changed when a Delphic Oracle decreed it only fit for gods, or something to that effect. A few hundred years later (moving forward on the calendar from B.C. times), the Parthenon was built, and it sits in the center of the Acropolis. At around the same time the temple of Nike and the Erecthion were constructed, too. (The Erecthion sits on the place where Poseidon and Athena had a contest to see who would be the Patron of the city, and is a combination of sacred precincts filled with temples.)

Most of this building happened in the 5th century B.C., and was instigated by Pericles, the Athens politician who evidently believed the Acropolis should be a small city of temples. It's the ruins of all that which we see today. The Acropolis was, for me, a symbol of the living and dead of Athens' politicians. Pride, history, triumph, and sorrow, heartily displayed.

As Thomas, Jon and I walked up the hill, I tried to tick off some of what I could expect to see at the top: the entrance, called the Propylaea; also the Pinacotheca; the various temples; the Erecthion and Parthenon. Ruins and relics and walls and gates and columns and pedestals, I would see it all. To put it mildly, I was trembling with expectation.

I expected to see some sign of the immense Parthenon as we approached, the way one might see the tops of buildings when nearing a large city. Yet no part of it showed until suddenly the entire structure was in front of us, and it stopped me in my tracks. What a tremendous visual effect! It brought strong emotion from me; the best I could describe it, in my journal, was that it left me 'feeling funny.' The Parthenon derives its remarkable beauty from its form, composition and design, also the openness of the structure against the sky. I remember at the time, I said to myself, 'I've seen the Parthenon, what more is there to see in the world?'

Ultimately, it can be described and photographed all day long, but nothing can truly prepare a person for the up-close experience. I wanted to sit and stare for hours, but the weather was too cold, with a bitter wind blowing over the entire Acropolis. That gave us the advantage of having the place to ourselves, but unfortunately, we couldn't stay long against such elements.

I left the Acropolis, and the following morning, I would also be leaving Athens. To this day, when I hear the name of that city, the Parthenon's soaring, weather-etched columns spring skyward in my mind's eye.

Thomas couldn't quite let me go. Jon and I packed Dolly, stepped toward the hotel for breakfast before the trip, and Thomas appeared with a suitcase of his own. I couldn't help but grin at him, and ask, "Taking a trip somewhere?"

"Not far," Thomas replied, eyeing the stuffed Renault. "I can only go to Delphi, then I should take a bus back here tonight."

I glanced at Jon, who watched me expressionlessly. He had only planned to go as far as Delphi with me, too, which would mean there would be no time for us alone. Not that I had any idea of what he might've intended to do with any such time. There had been plenty of opportunities, before Greece, for him to grill me or seduce me, but he had attempted neither.

It might not have been very kosher of me, but I asked the 21-year-old Thomas, "What does your mother think of this?"

He opened the cloth case he carried and without comment, held it toward my nose. The scent of food that was inimitably Greek wafted over me.

I laughed. "She packed us a lunch?"

"Enough for three." A respectful glance at blank-faced Jon.

"Well, we're going to have to rearrange a few things to fit you in."

"I can take care of that. You two go ahead and have breakfast, and I'll have everything ready by the time you get back."

I left him to it, and returned to happily discover Thomas had not only rearranged things, but had also polished the car, including all glass, metal, and upholstery. Never had an unplanned hitchhiker better earned his ride.

We departed later in the morning than I had hoped, but it was only 40 kilometers to the abode of the Oracle. I didn't expect there would be any problems until I began to notice snow flurries. As we climbed higher and higher in altitude, the snow became thicker and deeper. I drove more cautiously, and as the afternoon grew longer, I started to worry.

My concerns were swept away when we reached a summit, and began to descend from the snow-covered mountains into a green valley. It was like driving the little Renault into Hilton's *Shangri La*. With quiet enjoyment, we passed through the lush scenery, but unfortunately, it was a limited stretch. We were in a snowy cold again by the time we reached the quaint little village of Arahova, which is perched on a steep mountainside. I slowed, wondering if we should stop, but Thomas urged me on; "Delphi is right around the next bend!"

Close enough. Within a half hour we came to the magnificence of the ruins, on the Mt. Parnassas side. It was slightly sheltered from the regathering wind, cold, and snow, and the Delphi ruins were a vision of splendor, strength and power. And, to use an appropriate word from my journal: the area possessed a Godliness. The white flurries of snow falling on the velvet greenery and disappearing into the warm ground can best be described as 'the icing on the cake.'

By then the day was growing dark and heavy with clouds, so I couldn't take any photos. The picture lives in my mind, though, of walking through Delphi. Deep valleys, little brooks, tall cypresses, and all other spreading trees surrounded us in a living embrace. The Oracle had chosen her spot wisely. In legend, it's said that when she spoke, the Gods answered, and in my journal I commented that it wasn't unlikely, as the place had the most miraculous echo quality I have ever heard.

The remaining ruins had held up nicely, as ruins go. The Oracle's bath, so well-preserved, was fascinating. It had been built into the rocks, and natural steps led down to it. The system used, back in the days, was one of allowing clean water to run in, and old water to run out. I found the design to be quite intelligent and unique, especially considering the time it had been built.

We lingered in our explorations until it became too stormy to drive back to Arahova, so we went a short distance forward, into the little town of Delphi. As soon as we arrived, we were told it would be impossible to leave again, at least for a day or two. The snow had deepened to a point where no buses were able to come through. Thomas didn't seem upset by the news at all.

We had no choice but to wait, and Jon talked us into choosing the leading hotel, which was a small, clean, well-heated place. The restaurant looked nice, and as I sat down, I thought of some little fish I'd seen served in other restaurants. I had wondered if I could find them anywhere, and I really wanted to try them. Had the Oracle heard my thoughts, or influenced them, somehow? As it turned out, those little smelt-like fish were the one course available in our hotel's restaurant.

The following morning, Thomas, Jon and I were cautioned again not to try the roads, but we were ready to roll. Thomas said if we could make it back a short way past Arahova, he and Jon could catch their buses in a town we had passed through on our way in, called

Lavadia.

Driving through a storm is interesting, at best, but we made it back to little Arahova. There, a truck driver shook his head at our insistence to continue on, but told us, "Maybe, just maybe, if you follow me through, you might make it." He and his colleague filled their truck bed with sand and chains, and our two-vehicle-convey was on its way.

Arahova had been built with intelligent consideration for the annual winds and snow, and by that I mean that as soon as we left its shelter, we were hit by the storm's full force. The winds were gales, the drifts were high. When our two vehicles crested a hill, we found the way blocked by two trucks in the middle of the road. The poor fellows had been stuck there all night.

Everybody piled out and began the work of freeing the trucks. It crossed my mind that when a friend at home asked, "What did you do in Greece, besides looking at ruins?" I could answer, "I shoveled snow." It was better than the other option, which would be freezing to death.

It took hours to clear the pass, and once we were able to move forward, we made our way cautiously down the mountain. Little by little, the effect of the snow lessened until we were able to wave goodbye to our trucker-friends and enter Lavadia. From there, Thomas and Jon would be able to catch buses to their different destinations, and we even had more than an hour to spare.

I have just realized I've been neglecting to mention the dates of my travels. I'll say this; driving through a storm from Delphi to Lavadia was an interesting way to spend the day before Thanksgiving.

In honor of the American holiday, and due to the fact that by Thanksgiving day itself, I would be alone, we found our way to the only restaurant in the little town. Only Thomas had the language to speak to the waitress, and he ordered a meal before Jon and I could express our opinions.

The choice Thomas made was unfortunate. The fish that came looked horrible and was as inedible as it looked. Jon and I pushed our plates away in disgust, and Jon left to search the restaurant's kitchen for more palatable fare.

Poor Thomas sat staring at me with his wet, puppy-dog eyes. "I am so sorry. I thought you would like it. From what I've learned about American Thanksgiving, I thought if the pilgrims didn't have any turkey, they would have eaten fish."

His dejected air had already brought forth my forgiveness. "Don't worry about it. The smell is off, that's all."

However, his sorrow wasn't really about the fish. He wiped at his face roughly, almost childishly, pushing the heels of his hands against his sadness in his eyes. "Tonight I'll be on a bus home, while you'll be driving further and further away from me. I can't stand it!"

I didn't know what to say, but Jon took care of that by returning with a large plate of what appeared to be meatballs. These were at least stomachable, but I sincerely hoped I would be able to find a better meal the following day.

After our early dinner, Jon boarded his bus and was away, but he would reappear later in my trip. Thomas and I stood waiting the few more minutes for the bus that would bring him back to Athens, and his crying touched my heart. I held him in my arms, rocking him, while he said, "I'm in love with you. There's nothing I can do about it. It isn't fair!"

All the words I thought to say in reply would have sounded cliché, but only because they were true. I settled with, "I have strong feelings for you, too, Thomas, but we live worlds apart." (See what I mean? An applicable cliché.)

The air brakes sounded from the bus Thomas would be boarding, and I disengaged myself from his arms. "You'd better climb on."

Thomas grasped both my arms and stared hard into my eyes. "I will never forget you, and you will never forget me."

I couldn't argue with that.

"I am going to see you again," he added. "I promise you." It wasn't impossible, because I had given him my address in New York. He continued, "One way or another, somehow, I will get to America, and find you."

"I'd like that."

He took a step back. "You don't believe me."

"Sure I do. I'm looking forward to it."

"I can't live with the idea that I will never see you again, so you have to believe it's true."

"I believe it, Thomas." I believed it as much as I could, and with a grain of salt. My trip wouldn't be finished for months, yet, and he needed to complete college. Time could create more distance than 'worlds apart.'

But Thomas insisted. "I tell you, I'll be in New York someday, knocking on your door. Be sure of that."

As I say; only time could tell if he would make true on his promise. We parted with a final quick embrace, and once again, I was on my journey alone.

Funny how strongly I missed Thomas, once he was gone. There is much to be said for being adored. I wouldn't even have minded Jon's company, especially at that particular time of the year.

Before the close of that night I was in a small town called Lamia, pointed northward again, finding my way (ironically) to the land of Turkey. I ate a late supper (much better than my early dinner), but when I woke in the morning, my craving for overlarge poultry was stronger than before.

It was Thanksgiving Day. I had every intention of driving bravely on, but I was slow-moving. By noon, I found myself still wandering through Lamia, huddled into my army coat against the frosty cold, feeling very alone. For the first time on my trip, I even wished that I was home. Sitting with family and friends, playfully and happily preparing for our holiday repast. Impossible for that to happen here, of course.

Unless the fates are with you.

At the end of a hopeless hour of walking, I turned back toward my hotel with the intention of climbing into my car and heading along my way. A restaurant I had missed on the first pass caught my eye, and it occurred to me that just because I couldn't enjoy a turkey dinner, it didn't mean I had to skip eating entirely. I was hungry, and it was past time for lunch. I stepped inside and stomped the snow off my boots, waiting for my eyes to adjust to the dim, candlelit interior.

The room was long and narrow, and filled with tables, mostly empty. A man sat alone in one corner, and a couple sat together a few tables away from him. I took a step forward, then squinted at the next thing I saw. Was it a vision? How could it have not been the very *first* thing I saw?

At the far end of the room was a long table, loaded with plates and dishes, lit by candles. Potatoes, stuffing, gravy, salads and greens, and was that a can-shaped blob of cranberry sauce? Most astounding was the center of the table, in its place of honor: A huge turkey.

The familiar odor was seductive, and the men sitting around the table were friendly and obviously American. As I approached, I imagine I couldn't have looked more like an orphaned waif. The idea of this dinner actually sitting in front of me froze my thoughts for a minute; how to open a conversation?

Of course! I said, "Hello, you must be fellow Americans!"

Their warmth and camaraderie engulfed me; few seconds passed before they were inviting me to sit down, pouring wine, calling for an extra plate. They explained that they were working for the Marshall Plan, building new roads in Lamia, and they'd been provided with this Thanksgiving dinner by their employer.

I'm happy to finally have the opportunity to officially thank the Marshall Plan for the most memorable Thanksgiving I've ever had.

It was still early afternoon by the time we finished our meal, and I said my goodbyes in infinitely better humor than when I'd arrived. Last stop before Turkey: Alexandroupolis. There, I made the exchange for Turkish money, which isn't to say I gave up all my Greek drachma, because I wasn't quite out of that country yet. (Soon that will be pertinent.)

Alexandroupolis was a city noisier than any I had been in before. It possessed a different excitement than I had found in any other Greek city, which might have been the flush of newness; this had been a Turkish city a short time before. I checked in at a hotel room, and that night, I had for a late supper—of all things—pigeon. Would I eat pigeon today? Absolutely not. Nevertheless, at the time, that was the dish I ordered and was served, and it came with an excellent sauce. It was scrumptious, I kid you not. For dessert, I bought rich pastries and enjoyed them with tea. It was a pleasant final evening in Greece.

In the morning, I would start out for the border of Turkey.

Visas

VIZE

No. **4498** Vize : Giris,
2287   Visa : D'entrée

İta tarihi : 20 Kasım 1953

Délivré le : 20-11-1953

Müddeti : Bir sene
        une année

Maksat : Bir seyahat
            için

Nombre : Pour un,
        seul voyage

İkamet :

Beria du séjour : Ziyaret
Hususi kayıt ve şartlar : Visite

Remarques :
Fr: 22.000   Atina - Pire
               Baş konsolosu

14

10

Bazaars and Riches

It was still early when I arrived at the Greek side of the border crossing. The border guard asked about my funds, and I confessed to my remaining 57,000 drachma. It sounds like a lot but it wasn't all that much, yet he still told me it was not acceptable to bring drachma into Turkey. "Besides, it would be worthless, you cannot spend it there," he added. "You should use it to make a purchase here, while you are still in Greece."

He grandly escorted me to one of the little nearby shops, and waited outside while I purchased two bottles of a liquor called Metaxa for my 57k, a price that was a kindness of the shopkeeper, because they were worth closer to 60,000. It was just as well that the guard had waited outside, rather than entering with me, because little did I know, it was illegal to transport Metaxa across the border.

When I emerged with my innocent-looking bag, my friendly escort asked if I could take him along with me to the Turkish border, where he needed to deliver a radio for the customs officer there. It seemed the two men knew each other well, because they became engaged in a conversation that made me feel like an interloper. I politely interrupted and asked, "Am I clear to pass through?"

They both smilingly waved me on, and I entered Turkey with my Metaxa intact. This would become more of a boon than I could have expected.

The ease of border-crossing gave my attitude and energy a boost, so I decided to drive on to Istanbul, about 200 kilometers further. At first, I happily sang away the kilometers, but as the road rolled and rolled beneath my tires, and my time alone stretched into hours, that peculiar loneliness crept up on me again. There are those who prefer their own company, and those who prefer companions, and I am definitely one of the latter.

I've never really understood a preference for solitude. Human beings are, if one were to get down to the bare genetic basics, pack-animals. We like to group together, and one possible reason for that is to see what we can recognize of ourselves in others. If in another we see something we like, we either shamelessly admire it as one of our own traits, or strive to keep that person's company in hopes of improving ourselves. If we see something that repels us, we're tempted to run or lash out. In some cases, that's understandable, because there are people who are simply horrid to know. However, in subtler situations, we might be reacting—again—to what we've seen as an aspect of our own personality. I know there are those who see homophobia as an example of that. Which makes me wonder about my Father?

The topic of homosexuality never came up, but it could have.Let's say an uncle commented to my father, "Have you heard the rumors that the man who lives next door is queer?" Father's reply to my uncle's comment, if he didn't just storm out of the room in embarrassment or disgust—would probably have been, "That better not be true! I'll drag him right to the slaughterhouse." "You bet!" my uncle would rejoin. "If a faggot ever so much as looks at me, I'll slit his throat!"

Yes, the men in my family would 'protesteth too much,' especially Father. Which is a shame, because if he had been born about 70 years later, such an attractive, charismatic, sensual man surely would have made openly Gay acquaintances. He might have even experimented a bit. That, in turn, caused me to lie to him, and by extension, to myself. What a waste of truth!

I could never have told him about my same-sex preference. To imagine his reaction on that one is downright painful. Again, I can see him leaving the room, and this time it would be with anger and frustration. Terror probably would have been involved, a fear that I might have somehow contracted the condition from a subliminal aspect of his own personality. And horror, that he had spawned a deviant. The next step of my vision is that he would suffer denial and confront dear Mother, probably with balled fists, and insist that she had caused it by showing me too much affection. I can almost hear him, shouting at her, "You never wanted my son to grow up like me, so you've turned him into something else!" Then would come the blows—lashing out at everything that frightened him, mother having been on the receiving end of his impotent rage. Mother, covering up against the rain of his fists, hiding her expression of agreement—yes, she most decidedly did not want her son to grow up abusive, even if it meant he had to be Gay. (Of course, thinking people realize such ideals would have had little or nothing to do with a Gay man's preferences.)

In any case, I repeat that I never came out to Father. Sometimes, with certain people, perhaps it's best to keep certain spoken truths out of the conversation.

On the lonely road to Istanbul, I turned again to the company of my trusty, now-beloved chariot, explaining to Dolly the importance of staying in top form on this leg of the journey. I also begged her to give me fair warning if she had any pains or disorders, and I would immediately find a professional to care for her.

The reason for my increased concern? At every bend in the road, I wondered if I had become lost. When I gave in to the uncertainty and stopped to ask directions, I was immediately asked to strike a bargain of information for transportation. The man I first spoke to happened to be trying to get to Istanbul, and would only show me the way if I would take him. If he only knew how much I had been hungering for company!

Istanbul showed in the distance as a line of lights that stretched for miles across the flat plain. At last we passed through an old, impressive gate, and we had arrived.

My friendly Turkish companion seemed to have been energized by the day's adventure, and insisted that I spend the night in his hotel. No, not to share his room (or his bed), although in retrospect, I suppose that might have been an option. In any case, as I checked in, he asked if I had been thinking of dinner, but I told him I was much, much too tired.

"Then you will share my dinner," (he somehow expressed to me), "and sleep well tonight."

We dropped my bags in my room, I followed him to his, and I ate part of his cold chicken so groggily that he soon released me, and I staggered to bed.

I awoke fresh and ready to explore. First order of business was to find a more suitable hotel, and the place I settled on was still inexpensive but considered 'first class.' What they lacked in running water they made up for in sheer space. People live comfortably in apartments smaller than that room. I spent all of two minutes dropping off my bags, then returned to the streets.

So many people, so much movement and sound. Talk and shouts in more than a few languages, horns and motors and everywhere, commerce. Odors, too, the mix as befuddling and exciting as the languages. An extraordinary place, is Istanbul.

Let's see how far back I can go, when telling what I learned of it: It was first a Greek city called Byzantium (a name many will recognize), but in the early 100s B.C. it was remade into the eastern Roman capitol, modeled on Rome itself, on and around seven hills. It kept the name Byzantium until Constantine the Great was honored in the early 4th century, and the great city's name was changed to Constantinople. It remained the capitol of Christendom for a thousand years, but in the 1200s it became the focus of an attack during the 4th Crusades. Yes, it sounds odd that the Crusaders would attack the seat of Christendom. The inspiration for the invasion was based on something to do with the church of Constantinople being Orthodox (which the Pope had deemed a heresy), and that the city could be restored to Rome only if the Crusaders would take it over. In reality, the whole attack was about money. Some things never change.

Throughout the war against Constantinople, a horrifying amount of precious art and jewels were stolen and destroyed. If anything survived it was carried away, spared for material value alone, with no thought for artistic or historical impact. I'll have more comments about that sort of ideal while I'm visiting a Turkish palace, but for now, I'll get to the immediate point: It was eventually the Turks who conclusively conquered Constantinople, but it helped that the Crusaders had been at it for a while. Besides, before the Crusaders there were Persians, Arabs, and other nomadic peoples having a go at Constantinople throughout the millennium of its existence.

But it wasn't until the Moslem Turks got hold of it that the name changed to what we know it as today: Istanbul. The city then became the seat of the Moslem world, with a spiritual authority that was downright frightening. Educated rumor has it that Martin Luther once prayed for God's deliverance from 'the world, the flesh, the Turk and the Devil.'

I would soon be seeing what sort of art had replaced that of the Christians, but first, I wanted to visit the famous bazaar. A streetcar stopped next to me, and seeing it was headed in the right direction, I jumped on and was away.

What a labyrinth of small streets, and on each of them, every imaginable type of goods could be purchased. For a short while I thought my surroundings were something like what one might find in New York, but no, it was too different. The tempo was too fast, too crowded, too incredibly noisy! The smells and faces and talk and goods surrounding me belonged to another world. The sound of the Moslems being called to prayer, which I soon found would happen five times each day, added to the cacophonic music of it all.

The original two structures of the bazaar were covered with domes, and those, along with the remains of 15th century walls, had become the original shopping (and trading) area. Over the following centuries, it had spread to the surrounding streets and continued to expand, most likely to this very day.

The most valuable wares were sold in the old central area because it was more secure. Many of the streets were laid out from that center, and each area was devoted to a particular trade: gold, jewelry, leather, textiles, carpets, clothes, shoes, and so on. As the Grand Bazaar stretched and grew, so did the trades, spilling out onto the surrounding streets. There were also little workshops where craftsmen applied skilled trades that had been handed down through the generations. Hookah cafes, restaurants, and money-changing booths were interspersed throughout, too. Every imaginable need and desire were covered there.

What a frenetic way to live! After hours of ogling, I found a streetcar that would take me away back toward my hotel, and took it. Once in my room, it took another few hours just to catch my breath. In the morning, I would enjoy a more relaxed site of the city: the Topaki Palace.

Here's where I'll say more about how riches can appear wasted, or perhaps 'disrespected' is a better word. From my journal:

> I spent much time in the treasury room of the palace, where all the jewels and wealth of the past sultans were kept. Never have I seen precious stones of great wealth used for such insignificant purposes: big emeralds on egg cups, rubies on toothpicks, etc. The throne of gold and emerald was gaudy, as was most of the rest of the displays. Much of it I felt would have been more splendid if the concentration had been on not how many jewels you could place per square inch, but on the basic shape of the jewels themselves. It was a shame to use precious stones, each with so much life and beauty in themselves, for nothing but a display of lusty wealth.

After my tour I left hungry for something more modest, like a nice, simple meal. What I found was delicious, but simple? Not quite. Turkish seasonings always gave such an exotic spirit to everything I ate, and this was at a time when regular Americans didn't have such ready access to foreign foods.

I had never had a shish kabob before (probably hadn't even heard of them), but they were common in Istanbul. The variety I had for lunch were skewers of lamb, onion, and a third element I couldn't identify. For a dinner I would bring back to my hotel, I bought a treat of rice and pine nuts stuffed in grape leaves, called *dolmas*, and a roast chicken that was interesting but…well, I couldn't say, "Tasted just like chicken."

I woke the next day to the call of Moslems to worship. It struck me as what it would sound like if people were being called to a funeral; bewitching, mournful, impossible to ignore. While I wandered the streets, I watched the Moslems as much as I gazed into the endless rows of shops, until a particular item in a window caught my eye. For a few long moments before entering the store, I could only stand and stare. It was just a belt, but it had obviously been fashioned completely from silver. The filigreed workmanship was outstanding, all the way to the exquisite, finely crafted buckle that would fasten it around a most fortunate waist.

I entered the shop, which was empty of customers, and a short, dark-complected, middle-aged man hurried to my side. "Can I help you with anything, sir?"

Pointing toward his window, I replied, "I'm curious about the belt you have there. There's no way I could afford such a thing, but I can't help but wonder what it would cost."

The owner's blunt fingers delicately tapped his small mustache. "It has been a slow day for me, but I am sorry to say the belt is not for sale. It is a—a 'memory' from my family."

"Well, at least my question has been answered; it's priceless." I turned to leave, but the owner stepped with me to the door.

"Thank you for coming in. If there's anything else I can do for you, please come back another day."

"I'm only passing through Istanbul, probably won't be here much longer, but thanks."

"You are from America?"

We were standing at the door, and my hand was about to push it open, but he seemed to want to talk. I faced him and said, "Yes, I'm driving through the countries that surround the Mediterranean."

"You're *driving*? Do you mean, you are taking trains, or buses?"

"No, I have a car, a Renault."

"How interesting! Such a young man, on such a long journey. Have you just come from Greece?"

"Yes, I crossed the border a few days ago."

His eyes took on a dreamy distance. "I am Greek, myself." He extended his hand and said, "My name is Xenos."

"I'm Will." We shook hands, but before he let go, Xenos pulled me a bit further from the door.

"Did you enjoy the country of my birth?"

"Very, very much so. You must be proud of your nationality."

"As you must be, too. But yes, Greece is an ancient, highly respected culture. Did you find our people to be kind? What did you think of our food?"

"Both were a delight. I made some good friends there, and was treated to some Greek meals that were quite delicious."

The look in Xenos' eyes deepened to something sweeter as he said, "We have a liqueur in Greece, it is called 'Metaxa.' Were you able to taste a sample of that?"

Chuckling, I told him, "Not yet, but by coincidence, I happen to have a bottle of it in my room." Yes, I had two bottles, but one doesn't offer such details in Istanbul.

"You do!" If he had been a child, he would have begun a dance of glee. "Yet you haven't tasted it? How did you bring it across the border?"

"The only reason I have it is because of a border guard, who told me to use the last of my drachmas to make a purchase before entering Turkey."

"And he allowed you to buy Metaxa?"

"He didn't pay attention to what I purchased. After that, I was waved through to this country with no problem."

With some effort, Xenos calmed himself. "This is a special meeting, between the two of us. That you have never tasted Metaxa, and here before you is a man who can describe every essence of its allure."

Laughing again, I said, "If you like, I can bring the bottle over after you've closed for the day, and we can share a drink or two together."

"I will provide the delicacies!" Now he did do a dancing little quick-step toward the door. "We will feast on Turkish sweets, and I will forever honor the memory of our meeting for a taste of my dear Metaxa!" He opened the door and as I passed through, he said, "If you return at three o'clock, I will draw the curtains, and we can enjoy much pleasant conversation without interruption."

Three o'clock on the dot, I stepped into Xenos' little store. He made a great show of drawing the curtains over the window and locking the door, then brought me to a back room where a table had been spread with Turkish treats. A woman stood pouring cups of rich-colored coffee, and Xenos introduced her as his wife. An older woman sat next to a younger man at the table, and I learned these were his mother and brother. The family had been gathered for the grand re-experience of their beloved liqueur.

At the first toast, Xenos said, "We thank you for this gift, because it brings more than exquisite flavor. You have also brought us memories of our home."

We all drank, and although I was not a connoisseur, the Metaxa tasted great to me. All of us then began snacking and exchanging stories, but after their first shots of the Metaxa, the women changed over to coffee. Xenos, his brother, and I continued, albeit sparingly, with the liqueur.

After a while, Xenos left the back room, and returned with the silver belt in his hands. "You asked about this belt, and I will now tell you why I cannot sell it. Not so many years ago, it was very difficult for a man who lived outside the cities to care for his money. There were no banks nearby, and we could not safely hide our money in our homes. What we *could* hide was strands of silver thread. Each strand we purchased, year by year, was woven into a link, and with the links we created a larger and larger belt. After many years, we would achieve a finished product such as this." He held up the belt, and it glowed in the softer lighting of the back room.

"Are you saying belts were used as currency?"

"In a way. This was not so long ago. When the belts were completed, they were brought to the cities where they could be sold for money. This money could be used for retirement when a man grows old, or for a lady who has lost her husband." He handed the belt to me so I could admire the workmanship.

"Amazing." I held a piece of living history in my hands. "As I said, it is priceless."

Xenos said, "I might consider selling it to you, my young friend."

"But you couldn't!"

"I can!" He laughed, poured himself another shot of the brandy, and held up the bottle, now more than a third empty. "With twenty-five of your American dollars, and the remainder of this Metaxa, you may own the belt."

I looked at the brother, the mother, and the wife. All of them were smiling. Shuffling through my pockets, I counted out the equivalent of $25.00, (thank you, Athens Renault Agency!) and passed it over to him. He could have done better; I had planned to leave the Metaxa with him, anyway.

After such an extravagant purchase, I checked in at the American Express offices, hoping some magical replenishment of my funds had been sent from home. There was no money, but I did find a new note from Jon telling me he would be sailing in to Istanbul the following day. What a peculiar man! Yet, although his company wasn't exactly sparkling, it was company nevertheless, and I had found nothing to stop me from meeting his ship.

He greeted me with a surprisingly warm handshake, and we settled him into a hotel. It was early still, and I asked if he felt like a quick trip to St. Sophia, which is considered to be as much of a highlight of Istanbul as the palace or the Grand Bazaar.

The St. Sophia church had been around since Constantinople days, and in fact some emperors were crowned there. Before being converted to a mosque, it had been damaged by both earthquakes and invasions, and rebuilt a few times. Sadly, during all the sacking that was perpetually perpetrated in Istanbul, St. Sophia was hit as hard as anyplace else. Again, it was ransacked for the basic worth of the jewels and metals. There was once a magnificent bronze statue of Hercules there, built by Alexander the Great's court sculptor, but it was melted down for its bronze. What a shame!

Eventually it became a museum, which apparently left me so little moved that I didn't even mention that in my journal. In all fairness, I've heard the museum is incredible, these days.

We continued on that afternoon to the Blue Mosque, which made up for the depressing state of the St. Sophia. The mosque was a place of awe, and I'll insert here my journal entry about it:

How immense! Also very old and damp, and on the outside it bore a kind of faded glory. Upon the request of a man at the door, I put slippers over my shoes before entering. Inside, this religious edifice had all the splendor, color, and eye appeal that St. Sophia lacked. The floor was covered with lovely oriental rugs, while Moslems knelt, kissing their own rugs, and bowing toward Mecca in deep prayer. It was as though they were in a trance, unconcerned about any tourists that might be watching them.

The light and dark blue designs along the walls and in the high dome unified the huge room with the earth-colored designs on the rugs.

Anybody who wants to see the beauty of blue exemplified should visit the Blue Mosque.

We left for Ankara the next day. Ankara had been elected as the capital of Turkey during the Republican period, but I think anybody can understand why Istanbul regained that honor. There were sights to see, though, and Jon and I behaved like proper tourists, inspecting the Mausoleum of Ataturk and the Temple of Augustus in the Hittite Museum.

First, the Mausoleum was gigantic, and not unlike another Mausoleum that was one of the original Seven Wonders of the world (Halicarnassus). The actual body of Ataturk was moved to his Mausoleum, from his previous grave, only a few weeks before I arrived. Incidentally, Ataturk was the Turkish Republic's founder and leader.

I know I also enjoyed the Temple of Augustus and its museum, but I became distracted when I discovered a little U.S. library. That's where my touring of the city ended. I spent the rest of the evening and most of the next day reading back-issues of the New York Times, Life, and Holiday magazines. Jon spent time on his own while I was occupied, but wait, that isn't entirely true. During those hours without me, he met a friendly Turkish man. Jon (in his rather feeble, passive manner) tore me away from my reading, told me of his new friend, and said we had both been invited to have drinks at the man's club.

I consider myself a thinking man, but back in those days, I might not have been so astute. Do bona fide straight men who are traveling often 'pick up' each other for mere conversation and friendship? No trolling for girls together, simply enjoying masculine company? I'm guessing the answer is 'yes,' because many of the men I met and spent time with on my trip were heterosexual. At least, I think they were.

As must be true for many Gay men, my father was my prime example of heterosexual male behavior. Father was the quintessential macho man, usually striding through a wake of female flirtations and male admiration. Sure, he would spend time with his buddies, but it's my guess they often talked of women. My father was a seductive man, but as I've said, he never touched me. Well, that's not entirely true. I do remember one time when he touched me.

It wasn't outside the realm of possibility for a strong husband of the early 1900s to occasionally strike his wife, and as I've recently implied, that happened to be true of my father. Once in a while, my mother's chattering jabs, taunts, and verbal confrontations would result in Father raising his hand to her. My sister Anne and I were terrified by it, as children are, but knew best to stay out of the way. Besides, in my youthful wisdom, I sensed a passion in their arguments that often carried into their bedroom. I could only guess my mother found all of it combined to be acceptable threads in the weave of their marriage.

My father's outward affections toward my mother were only marginally more apparent than they were toward me. (I specify 'apparent' because they exchanged loving and sensual physicality only while alone. I know this is true because Anne and I occasionally awoke to the sounds of their lovemaking.) My point is, because Father was decidedly*not* the type to snuggle or hold hands with my mother, Mother turned to me for those displays of love, which made me feel like 'the little man.'

From that perspective of self-importance, there came a time when I could no longer watch my mother get hurt by Father, and I reacted. I was much too young to be effective, and in fact I might have been at exactly the wrong age, about ten. That's old enough to try to step in, but young enough to be forever afraid of trying it again.

We were in the car, the four of us, on the way home from a visit to some family in Albany, New York. It was dark out, and Mother and Father had begun arguing. There might have been drinks involved. It was also possible that my mother's tendency to relentlessly belabor an issue, to metaphorically tug at my father's trouser leg, contributed to the problem at hand.

At the peak of the fight, Mother grew upset and demanded that Father pull the car over. "I want OUT," she shouted. "NOW. Pull this car over or I'll—"

"You're not going to walk all the way to Glens Falls from here!"

"Anything would be better than staying in this car with you!"

Anne and I made ourselves as tiny as possible in the back seat. If Mother climbed out of the car, would she take us with her? The idea of that was frightening, but Father's increasing anger was as much of a concern.

When Father refused to stop, Mother grabbed the steering wheel and jerked the car. Now, we children were twice as afraid. A crash? Or, if Father did pull over, would he begin to hit Mother? The tension in that small, enclosed space was so concentrated it became hard to breathe.

Father must have shoved Mother's hands away, pushed at her, possibly he took an awkward swing in the confines of the car. She pulled at the handle of her door and said, "If you don't stop this thing, I'm going to get out anyway!"

We were cruising at about 60 miles per hour. Attempting to calm both himself and the situation, Father tried a reasonable tone. "You'd die."

"That's fine with me! It would be better than being stuck in here with you!" She yanked at the door handle, but either the wind or her lack of true conviction kept the door from opening.

Father reached across her, trying to snatch at her hand or make sure the door was closed, I don't know what. Anne clutched me, and my terrified little sister whispered the question, "Is Mother going to die?"

I had to do something. From my seat behind Father, I balled up both my fists and banged them against his back. Maybe I even boxed his ears…. The memory is painful and it's hard to dig for details. I do know that in order to strike him, I had to call on a quality that had been as yet undiscovered inside myself: a monumental courage.

Now my Father, enraged, astonished at my audacity, did stop the car. He braked hard and jerked over to the side of the road, put the car in park and grabbed the handle to his door. Before he could climb out I was off and running. I ran as fast as I could, but I was such a little guy and he was a big strong man. He caught me, dragged me back to the car by the scruff of the neck. That was touch number-one. Touch number two was when he whacked me across the side of the head, hard, it stung and hurt enough to give me a headache. He opened my door, whacked me again, and shoved me in.

All of us were effectively silenced throughout the rest of the ride home.

What does it do to a family when a small boy tries to interfere with his father's abuse of his mother? I'm no psychiatrist, but I imagine it can either cause the children to become part of the abuse, or galvanize the mother into some sort of action. Leave, call the cops, something. Or, it can result in what happened that night: Give the adults enough of a pause to actually *think* before continuing the harmful behavior. Ultimately, I'm sure whatever happens has everything to do with the inherent nature of the family.

During the years following that, I might have received a final spanking or two for getting into trouble, but he never struck me in such a way again. Never once did he ever, ever hit my sister.

He loved Anne, I have no doubt of that, and he certainly loved my mother, but I've never thought he loved me. Yes, he kept me out of WWII through a friendship with the medical examiner at the draft board, but as I've said, his behavior throughout my life led me to think that might have been more about fear for his progeny than for my personal skin. Or, if he was aware of my overall delicate nature, and knew I would mentally and emotionally crumble under the stress of war, perhaps that indicates he did feel some sort of compassion toward me. But love? I've never believed it.

My imaginary shrink from some chapters back might be fascinated by that admission. How does it make me feel? Over the years I've passed through phases of: pain (of course); irritation; confusion; uncertainty; and finally, a sense of strength. I found myself growing into my own self-awareness, despite the lack of affection from the main man in my childhood. Or did that growth   *result* from his coldness?

It's time to return to my trip. Where was I? Ah yes, I and my strange (but not entirely unwelcome) companion, Jon, were about to leave Ankara.

From that city we continued south, toward the lower coast of Turkey. The longer I drove, the colder it became. We reached a high plateau, frigid and barren, and could see that the villages were hovels of clay huts and minarets, offering little color against the pale and frozen earth. It was a picture of misery and sadness, and I found myself hoping the hidden interior of these huts presented a happier viewpoint of Turkish family life. As we received no invitation from locals to enter their homes, we continued on to Konya.

It was early evening by the time we arrived, cold and hungry, ready for food and rest. We had met the brother of Konya's Chief of Police at the American Embassy in Ankara, and that man had insisted we look up the Chief when we arrived in Konya. "He is my brother," he'd said. "I will call him and let him know you're coming. He will find you the best hotel."

We had no trouble locating the police station, but everyone there claimed to be the Chief. Eventually we found the one whose name matched the name we'd written down, but he said he never received any call, and in fact knew nothing of such a brother. Imagine our surprise! Which man might have been lying, and why would either of them find it necessary? One can never tell in foreign countries what various behaviors are considered normal.

The real Chief of Police could see how baffled we were (not to mention cold and hungry), and ordered his assistant to help us find a room. That assistant brought us to the leading hotel in town, but they said they were full.

The assistant leaned smilingly across the counter and said, in a firm but commanding voice, "These are personal friends of the Chief of Police," (what do you know!), "and he expects you will give them a place to sleep."

The clerk found the owner, who returned and said, "I swear to you, we have no rooms available."

"This is a town filled with rooms," responded the policeman, still smiling ominously. "Certainly you can find a place for these men to rest their heads!"

"Of course," the owner replied. He turned to us and said, "Please accept my offer to sleep in my home."

In the morning we packed and left to explore the Konya ruins before continuing our trip. Many believe Konya is one of the first settlement areas in the world, where actual communities of people began to live together. Like the villages we passed along the way there, the ruins-homes were made of mud and clay, and I learned that in the oldest of days they were entered through holes in the roof. Jon and I had a real sense of the people who had lived there so very, very long ago. Relics of those times and people still remain in Konya.

It wasn't until we squeezed through a final narrow mountain pass that we were able to welcome the sight of the sea. Before long our feet began to thaw out, and natural warmth began to creep in through Dolly's vents.

We indulged in only a few, uneventful stops before we began the long drive to Syria. As we tiredly neared the border, we had to pass through more mountains, and while time ticked on through those slow curves, it grew darker and darker. The situation worsened when my high-beams began to flicker. At about the time I was wondering if we should try to find a place to camp, we arrived at the border town. It surprised us to find we had arrived there, because no lights had welcomed us. The electricity in the entire town had gone out.

That didn't bother me as much as it might have, because all I wanted by that time was sleep. I crept up to the border, idled at the post, and asked the guard, "Can you recommend a hotel where we can sleep tonight, before we cross into Syria?"

His answer? "I wouldn't sleep here, if I were you."

Too tired to ask why he'd made that comment, I simply said, "I don't know where else we could stay. We didn't see another town for a long time before we arrived here."

"Cross over," came the helpful reply, "and stay in Syria."

Interesting, that the place where Jews were particularly unwelcome would be somehow safer for me. I was too tired to let it matter, and I did have my letter claiming that I was a perfectly respectable Christian. Jon and I exchanged exhausted shrugs, and entered the dark country.

Visas

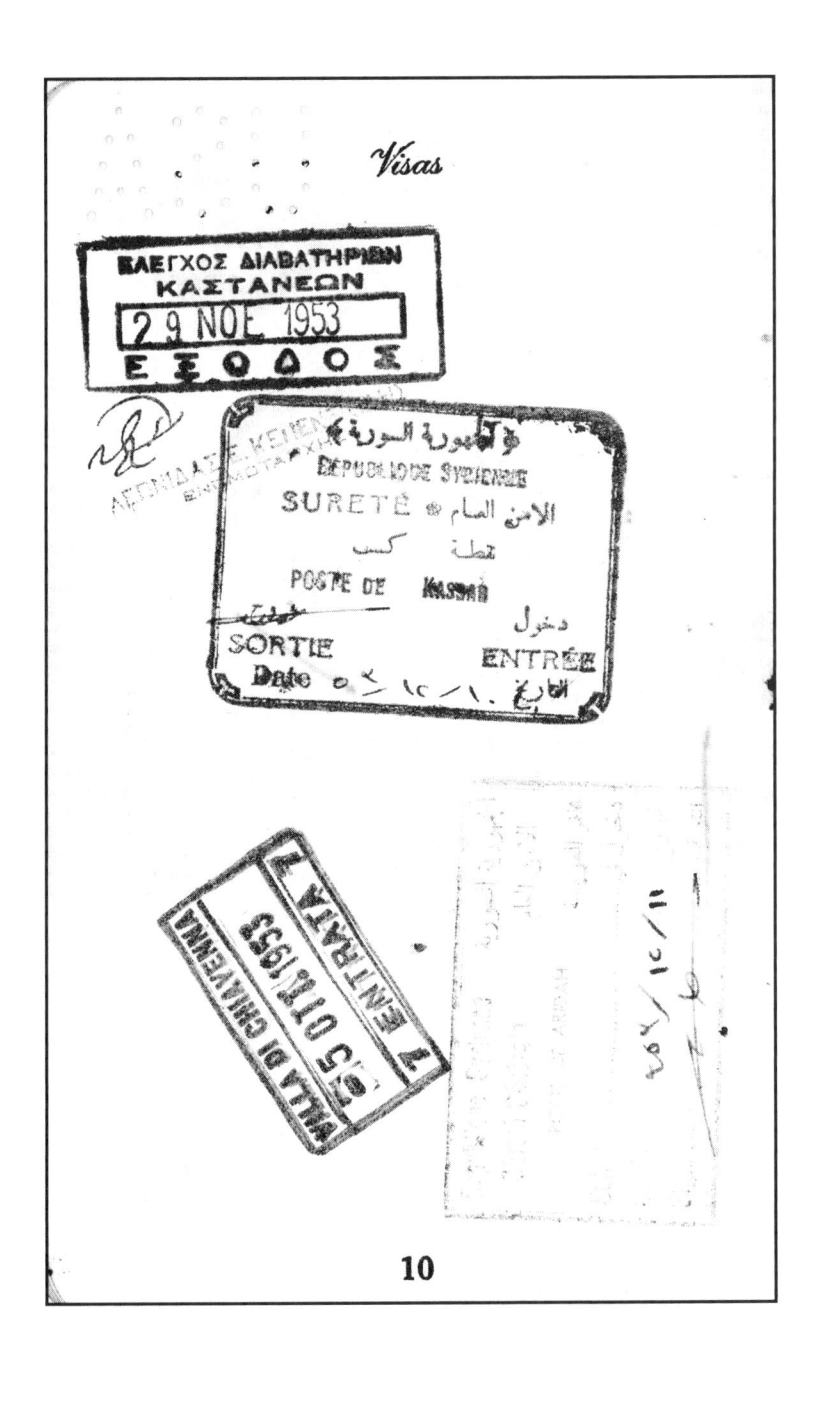

ΕΛΕΓΧΟΣ ΔΙΑΒΑΤΗΡΙΩΝ
ΚΑΣΤΑΝΕΩΝ
2 9 ΝΟΕ 1953
Ε Ξ Ο Δ Ο Σ

‹الجمهورية السورية›
RÉPUBLIQUE SYRIENNE
SÛRETÉ ٭ الأمن العام
نقطة كسب
POSTE DE Kasab
دخول
SORTIE ENTRÉE
Date

7 ENTRATA
MALTA DI CHIAVENNA
05 OTT 1953

11

Edging the Middle East

Moving from one nation to the next by pressing an automobile accelerator does nothing toward illuminating a black night. It wasn't that I expected any change; if Syria had been electrically lit, the glow of it would have spilled into Turkey. Only my strobing headlights showed us an old, sturdily attractive stone building, which could only have been the border post. I parked, shut Dolly down, and we were plunged into absolute night. It was tempting to leave the headlights on, but with all that flickering they'd been doing, it was too risky. There was no way I would chance draining all the juice from my battery.

Jon and I climbed out of the car and stood wondering if it would make sense to try knocking at the door. First, we would have to feel our way to it, because our eyes were still trying to adjust. Secondly, if anybody was inside, they were bound to be in a dead sleep.

The silence around us only added to the weight of the darkness. Jon, whose mere presence such a moment had lifted him to the heights of valued friend, whispered to me: "Somebody is bound to show up."

"Should I honk the horn?"

"That might be offensive."

I tried to lighten the moment, so to speak; "Maybe with my own electrical problems, pressing the horn will jump-start the entire town."

Jon made no sound, and I couldn't even see whether he had smiled.

The light of a lantern, which looked more like a match flame, approached us from across the road. We were greeted with a grunt and the jangle of keys. The meager illumination led us through the door of the building and to a long counter, where the carrier of the lantern lifted it to show our faces. "Tourist?"

Jon and I nodded.

"American?"

Good guess; we nodded again.

The man shook his head with what I hoped was only mild irritation, and held up his hand for us to wait.

He began to walk away, but I called, out, "Sir?"

The light stopped moving. "No English."

Not true! He had clearly said 'Tourist' and 'American.' "But you're taking the lantern."

"No English." The light was gone.

I don't know how long Jon and I stood there in our shared blindness. Some night, try climbing into a solid wooden box, closing the lid, and covering your eyes with a sleeping mask. That's how dark it was.

How often did I check my pocket for the letter about my alleged non-Jewishness? Six, eight, ten times?

When at last the lantern reappeared, I could tell by the way it moved that a different man was approaching. The new voice said, "You wish to enter Syria, yes?"

"Yes, and we need to find a hotel."

"That is your car outside?"

"Yes."

"You drive me, the village up the mountain has electricity. You talk to policeman there to enter Syria."

I could have cheered, but it would have been premature. We drove the man up the mountain, and as we rounded curve after curve, we began to see a few glowing bits of evidence of civilization. However, the 'town' was little more than an official-looking building and a few homes scattered over the mountainside. There was no hotel at all.

We were brought to the small police building, where a handful of soldiers sat spiking their coffees with something from a small flask. They cried out greetings when we entered, obviously pleased by the diversion.

Our guide rapidly explained our presence in their language, and left us. One of the soldiers spoke haltingly, "Policeman, he home." He pointed in a direction that meant nothing to me. "I call." Not only did these people have light (which seemed unnecessarily bright to me), they also had working telephones. The young soldier called the policeman whose job it was to grant access to his country, and they spoke at some length. The soldier hung up and smiled.

"He tell me. I pass you." He held out his hand, and Jon and I surrendered our passports. This boy in military clothing—he couldn't have been more than 19—paged through our booklets and squinted with false authority at all the stamps, notes, and markings. "How many day?"

"Do you mean how long will we visit?"

"Yes, how many long?"

"We're just passing through, on our way to Beirut."

The guard made a quick press of his own inking, and returned our passports to us. With a guileless smile, he said, "Welcome in Syria."

That was it. (I should note, though, that I didn't dispose of my Christian letter until after I had left not only Syria, but all of North Africa, too. Just in case.)

Jon ventured a question: "Where can we find a hotel?"

"Hotel?"

Jon and I exchanged a glance. I said, "Sleep?" and mimicked it, including a gentle snore. Jon, my straight-man, busily outlined a building with mime gestures. The soldiers broke up laughing.

Our young English-speaking friend said, "Kilometers," then held up five fingers on one hand, dropped it, and held up his other hand with two fingers extended. "Drive. Hotel. Latakia."

I asked, "Seven kilometers?"

"No. Five, seven." He extended all ten fingers and began blinking them, counting up to fifty…

"Fifty-seven kilometers!" I counted, dismayed.

The soldier nodded solemnly. *"Bon voyage."*

Ah. The talented youth was multi-lingual.

Jon and I climbed wearily back into Dolly, and drove 57 more dark, bumpy, steep, flickering kilometers to Latakia. I believe the trip took about three hours. I stopped at the first hotel I saw, and approximately a micro-second passed between the time my head hit the pillow and I was in a deep slumber.

When I woke, I opened my eyes in a completely Arab world.

My first meal in Syria was horrid. Fortunately my breakfast had been supplied by Jon, who had rustled up some pastries, but for lunch

I forced down some kind of ground lamb dish mixed with rice and (yuck) okra. My decision to add soy sauce, in an attempt to improve the flavor, was unfortunate. Until that moment, it had never occurred to me that soy sauce, an oriental version of salt, could actually go bad.

The meal quite literally made me sick. All I could do was move slowly through the day, hoping to recover my constitution. By ironic coincidence, my pace matched a situation I encountered while trying to exchange currency.

To backtrack a bit: After my pastry breakfast, I went to the bank to cash some traveler's checks. The (rather unprofessional) clerk didn't have any idea what I meant by that request, and asked me to return after lunch when the bank president would be available. When I took myself and my queasy stomach back in the afternoon, the president was thankfully familiar with the concept of traveler's checks, but they had no provisions for cashing them. Have I mentioned that bureaucratic nonsense is a universally irritating condition of all institutions?

While I waited for the bank president to sort things out, I made a few trips to the bathroom in an attempt to relieve myself, by whatever means necessary, of my ghastly lunch. At last, the decision about my financial plight came when the president told his red-faced clerk to cash a check for me (the green-faced man), "From your own account!"

The red of the clerk's face was not from embarrassment, but anger. Throughout our transaction, he muttered harsh-sounding words in Arabic, and when he slammed the currency down on the counter, I'm sure he didn't wish me a pleasant visit.

Despite what had already seemed a long day, it was barely one-thirty in the afternoon. Searching for Jon, I peered into dirty, smelly restaurants and coffee houses filled with Arabs smoking water-pipes. When I found my companion (sipping coffee in our hotel), I asked, "Are you in the mood to leave for Beirut?"

He responded, simply and agreeably, "Yes."

Anything to take my mind off my stomach.

Twice, we were stopped by military barricades and made to show our passports, but as I said, it was never necessary to show my affidavit of Christianity.

The Lebanese side of the border was grand compared to the Syrian side. Also professional; our luggage was checked and looked into quite thoroughly, and I'll say again it's lucky I didn't have a gun stashed away. We were passed through with no problem.

Now the countryside became radiant. The snow-covered mountains of Lebanon were on our left, and the Mediterranean sparkled away on our right. Pine trees spread up the mountain which were streaked with little brooks that twinkled in the sunshine. The weather was warm, oh-so-happily warm.

After more south-bound miles, we passed an Arab refugee camp. We could see, through the barbed-wire fences, people covered with the sad dirt that comes from absolute poverty. Stories about Arab refugees had trickled into the U.S., but it wasn't until later that I heard more about those camps: As the accounts tell it, the Arab leaders are the ones who convinced their civilians to evacuate their homes. "Get out of the way," they'd said. "We're going to invade, and throw the evil Zionist Gangs into the Mediterranean!" Jewish factions insist the Arab families were asked to please remain, and told their rights as non-combatants would be respected. The Jews, of course, were intimately familiar with—and horrified by—the concept of creating refugees.

Listening to their own leaders, the local Arabs left their homes and in many cases, their homelands. They migrated to other Arab nations, where they were not well-received, and many were even considered unwelcome immigrants who could not be trusted.

I heard the biggest problem was that Arab leaders were infuriated by the UN decisions first to partition Palestine, then to reconstitute the State of Israel. Reportedly, the Arab League thought Jews were on this earth to be exterminated despite the fact that many had long lived peacefully side-by-side with Arabs. It's said refugee camps exactly like the one I drove past were set up as showplaces by the Arabs, as in, "See how we're forced to suffer because of those terrible Jews?" This plan succeeded by creating pity and assistance, in the form of relief agencies that offered aid when the host country couldn't, or wouldn't, do all they could for these destitute people.

Eventually (also 'reportedly'), the camps were turned into training grounds for terrorist youths, and the target of their hatred was the newly formed State of Israel. For instance: A country like, say, Syria, would throw immigrants into the camps, then provide military training, various weapons, and whatever brainwashing was necessary to create their anti-semitic fighters. The educated rumor (and many say the fact) is that they worked hardest on the children, because a miserable, well-manipulated youngster makes for a strong, determined, angry soldier. What a sorry state of affairs.

As a Jewish man, it might seem I'm not speaking with as much force as might be called for when describing such a fiery situation. However I believe I've already made clear that rather than seeing myself as a religious Jew, I have always felt more connected to other aspects of myself. I'm an artist, a teacher and a student of life. I'm a man who loves men. I'm even more 'American' than I am Jewish. I never was Orthodox or Zionist, and we had drifted away from following our traditions while I was very young.

I did have a Bar Mitzvah, and I do have memories of Hannuka, yarmulkes, and Menorahs, and I called my orthodox grandmother 'Bubbie.' We even lived with Bubbie for a while, when my father and mother were starting our family.

My mother, who was also laxly Jewish at best, would obliviously cook a pork roast on a Friday night, and Bubbie would come into the kitchen and say, "What a nice roast veal you have there!" Bubbie certainly knew the difference, but though she honored and respected her religion, she also honored and respected our right to live as we chose.

In her way, Bubbie taught me well.

I viewed Arabs, Europeans, Middle Easterners, Northern Africans, even the communists simply as human beings who held different beliefs than mine. They lived in other countries, and had their own cultures. I was no authority on the human condition, and my being Jewish or American didn't make me right and them wrong about how lives should be lived.

At the moment, while driving past that Arab refugee camp, what I found *wrong* was the sight of innocent human beings being forced to live in sub-human conditions.

If Jon knew I was Jewish, he never spoke of it. Neither of us commented on the refugees as we passed them by, and in fact for a long while, neither of us commented on anything at all.

The next, much more pleasant sight on the road was of all the windmills. Little cement pools of water were near each of them, and we learned these were one mechanism of the salt industry in Lebanon. I once heard a rumor that civilization began along the edges of the desert because of its natural surface deposits of salt. Some also say the very first war ever was fought near the ancient city of Essalt, on the Jordan River, and salt might have even been the reason for that war.

It was still relatively early when we reached Beirut. We had hardly been there an hour when we found a club that offered the performance of two acrobats, of all things. We entered to find an incredibly attractive Swedish couple dancing and leaping and rolling around like a circus act.

I used the word 'couple' when I should have said 'pair.' These two were not married, and they were not going steady. The reason I know this is because the luscious spectacle of a man who flipped the woman around like she was a weightless manikin propositioned me.

Oh, my, my. Greek men can have that certain, classically handsome look, and there's a definitive, passionate quality in Italians, and Germans can be so ruggedly gorgeous, but the Swedes? Oh my. Yves was built like a brawler with muscles that wouldn't stop, but had the grace of a swan. Deeply tanned, a chiseled face under a heavy head of thick blond hair, and a jaw that seemed iron when he clenched it. Dreamy eyes that reminded me of my visit to the Blue Mosque. Yves, the champion of any reasonable Gay man's fantasies.

After his show, he sat at the bar for drinks, and while admirers gathered to compliment him, his eyes caught mine. He smiled and nodded in response to others while he stared at me, never looking away.

His partner, co-worker, girl/friend—whatever I should call her—knew or intuited his designs on me. She drew the group at the bar away from him, and he came to the table where I sat with Jon. We introduced ourselves, and Yves looked at Jon's near-empty glass. He swallowed off his own drink, then said to Jon, "If you would like to visit the bar, I would like to pay?" He held out some bills.

"Sure, why not."

As soon as Jon was away, Yves slid his hand under the table and grasped my knee. I almost shot out of my chair. The sexy Swede said, "You are American visitors, are you not?"

"Yes. We just arrived today. My name is Will."

"I am Yves. Have you found a place to sleep in Beirut tonight?"

I could have told him I use my car, but decided against it. "Not exactly."

"The room at my hotel is comfortable, but there is only one bed. Still, there is room enough for two very close…friends." He added flavor to that final word with another squeeze of my knee.

Okay. There it was. Clear as could be. This ravishing man wanted S.E.X. I asked, "Do you mean we would have to sleep together?" (Why take any chances at misunderstanding?)

"We will lie in the bed, and sleep when we are ready, no?"

Confirmation. Jon was approaching with his dutifully retrieved cocktails, and I had to think fast. No, I mean I had to *act* fast—my thinking wasn't much involved by that point. Yves' hand hadn't left my leg and it hadn't stopped moving. "Which hotel are you staying in? What room?"

Jon had arrived, and Yves sat back to answer in a companionable tone. He spoke the name and room number of the place where he was staying, and finished with, "I visit with others, now, is part of my job. You have questions about Beirut? Find me, ask me. I will be home after eight o'clock this evening." He stood, and with his back to Jon, gave me a wink.

While Jon and I finished our drinks, Yves finished his own at the bar, then went back to work. Jon wanted to find a meal, and I agreed, knowing I would need to wait until eight to meet Yves. Throughout dinner I managed to remain calm. We found a hotel for Jon quickly.

I settled with a parking spot in the *Place de Cannons*, which was the main square. Forcing out a yawn, trying to sound tired, I asked my co-traveler what he planned for the evening.

Without meeting my eyes, he said, "I thought I might be able to find a decent theater, find out which movies are playing."

Who'd have guessed? "Myself," I said, "I think I'll turn in early."

Another hopefully convincing yawn, I even opened the passenger door and hunkered down, as though to begin removing the seat for the bedroom transformation.

Jon asked, "Is your stomach still bothering you?"

My stomach? Oh, right. The bad food from Syria had long passed, but I said, "Maybe, don't want to push it."

"Okay, then. I guess I'll see you in the morning."

"Enjoy your movie."

Before the back of the federal-issue-suit turned the nearest corner, I was creeping into Dolly's driver's seat, and headed toward Yves' hotel.

The stunning acrobat was waiting for me with a chilled bottle of champagne in a bucket near the bed. I fell into his arms after he closed the door—literally; I had stumbled on the carpet. He caught me expertly (was it really the carpet that caused me to stumble?), and led me to a chair. "Carefully," he said, "carefully, now. I have champagne for you."

He moved with his athletic rhythm to the bottle, and while he uncorked it like a professional, his eyes wandered over my body. I removed my coat. He came back with a glass for each of us, and we toasted. Silly us, we linked arms to drink. As had happened with Antonio, Yves and I barely conversed (or if we did, I have no memory of it).

We finished our champagne, Yves took my glass from me and set it next to his on the table. He stood, and with an effortless touch of his hand to mine, he lifted me from my chair. As he drew me against his body, readying his mouth for a kiss, flash-scenes of what he would delectably do to me scurried through my brain.

That kiss. Oh, my goodness. That body, it could be against the law, but I preferred it against my chest. Those lips, that tongue, and the long minutes, all of it belonged to me; they were bliss. What was next, I knew not, but curiosity be dammed, I was ripe for the picking.

A knock fell on the door.

Yves whispered, with hot breath close to my ear, "It is nothing."

A voice called, "Yves? Have you seen Will?"

I was so stunned that I fell back into the chair. Yves lifted a blond eyebrow and asked, "It is your…friend?"

The combined nodding and shaking of my head must have made me look possessed by a demon. Before I could explain, before I could say yes it was Jon but he was barely my friend, Jon called out again.

"Am I disturbing you? I can come back later."

Yves folded his muscled arms and contemplated me for a moment, then strode to the door. I dropped my face into my hands and pulled them down, distorting my own *visage*, unwilling to let Jon see the emotions that were raging through me.

"Hi, Yves," I heard, then opened my eyes and smiled weakly as it was followed by, "Will, there you are! Glad you're feeling better. Listen, they have that new movie here, "Gentlemen Prefer Blonds." Didn't you read a review of it at the library in Ankara? You said you'd love to see it. I hurried back and looked for your car, but it wasn't there." A polite glance in Yves' direction. "We could all go. What do you say?"

What a time for Jon to string that many words together! Before I could reply, Yves said, "I am sorry, but I am tired. Work. It is hard work, and now I am tired."

I came to my feet and said, "But a movie wouldn't be tiring!" No! That is most decidedly *not* what I meant to say! I've never really been one who could think fast on his feet. I sank back into my chair. "I mean, if Jon goes to his movie, you and I could finish our conversation, and then you can rest and—"

"No, no, I sleep early tonight. I am sorry."

What strength it took, for me to swallow my groan of frustration! Apparently, Yves had decided my slip was Freudian, and that I didn't want to upset Jon. Yves must have decided he was more than just a traveling companion. My confused head-twirling after his question 'It is friend?' probably started his suspicions. I stood again and walked to him. I'm not short, but I had to tip my head back to look into his eyes. "Yves, we were enjoying our talk, and I hate to have it interrupted by a simple invitation—"

"Oh," Jon interrupted. "I didn't mean to interrupt. What were you talking about?"

Yves gave him a flat smile and said, "Sleep. Goodnight to you," he turned to me, "and to you."

I felt like stomping out of the room in a childish pout. I felt like whining, shouting, pushing Jon in the back as I followed him, shoving his spine up against his breastbone. Even the most gentle of people must have a momentary homicidal thought flit through their minds, at least once in their lives, and that was my moment.

Outside, Jon paid the taxi he'd taken to find me, and we climbed into Dolly. He then chose the journey between Yves' hotel and the theater to continue his loquacious binge, and I let him talk, not caring what he said. He babbled on as we bought our tickets, kept chatting until the lights came down, and Marilyn Monroe's name appeared on the screen.

The movie was great. But I could have killed Jon.

In the morning I opened my eyes to a busy, hustling community swirling around my car. I crawled out and stretched beneath a stand of palm trees, watching the crowded, congested and confused main square of Beirut, surprised that I had slept quite well.

By the time I had returned Dolly to her drivable form, Jon showed up with warm bread and hot coffee. His apology, intentional or not, was accepted (if I don't say so myself) graciously.

My plan for the day was to find the American University of Beirut (AUB), where I meant to look up a friend of a friend. (Do regular people still have friends, and friends of friends, all over the world? Was it more prevalent, back then?) This once-removed friend was named Kevin, and he was an English professor. Jon wanted to come along, and I figured as long as we were in the same country, I would have trouble shaking him, so I agreed.

Even before we clasped hands in greeting, I sensed Kevin was homosexual, which I've already noted was unusual for me at the time. (It has taken decades for my gaydar to develop.) Kevin certainly perceived my predilection, and he might have assumed the same to be true for Jon. I guess I wasn't surprised, because I had witnessed that very same assumption the night before. In any case, the three of us had hardly spoken for five minutes before Kevin invited us both to his on-campus apartment for drinks later that afternoon.

By the time Kevin finished with his final class of the day, Jon and I were waiting at his apartment. He ushered us inside, and soon we were roasting in the warm sun on the terrace, drinking martinis,

Portofino, Italy

Leaving the Andrea Doria at Cannes (she is now at the bottom of the ocean)

Bay of Naples with Andrea Doria and Mt. Vesuvius

Truman Capote's yacht

Andrea Doria First Class swimming pool
Thanks to Marilyn

Landing in Cannes, France with Sleeping bag and stove

Marilyn and I on the Andrea Doria

The ancient walled city of Dubrovnic, Croatia

The Acropilis (in far background) from my hotel window

Solin, Yugoslavia, sitting in an ancient
Roman wine cask

Yugoslavian Shepherd making yarn from
her sheep. She cried when I mentioned America.
She received a CARE package from the US
during World War II which kept her alive.

Queen Hatshepsut's Temple near the Valley of the kings

**Ghosts of ancient Romans walking on the
main street in Leptis Magna, Libya**

Akron and Other Uncle and relatives

AJ 12 weeks old. "Thanks for looking."

AJ, ready and willing to play ball with
anyone. He is my best medicine.

learning about each other. One thing the intelligent Kevin soon realized is if I was indeed homosexual, I had never spoken of it in front of Jon.

When our drinks were finished, Kevin insisted on treating us to a fabulous dinner on the town, refusing any contributions to the bill. After the meal, he begged us to accompany him to another friend's apartment, and I'll call that man Rudy.

Rudy, Rudy, Rudy. After the introductions, the first thing that pretty boy asked was, "Do you both play bridge?"

I said, "Yes, I do." Jon shook his head.

He tossed a significant glance at Kevin, which I didn't understand until later. We set up the table, dealt the cards, and began to play.

If Rudy had been seen on the streets of Greenwich Village, a distasteful epithet might have been mentioned in his presence. Fine features, a slender, boyish, stylishly-dressed body, soft speech, graceful gestures. He had bright eyes and a generous mouth that pouted playfully more often than it alluringly smiled. He took great advantage of his fresh appearance, to the degree that I first thought he might have been only a bit over twenty years of age, but he was probably closer to thirty.

Whenever Jon's attention was diverted, Rudy would stare or flare his eyes at me, or with a feigned unconsciousness, he would tuck his tongue flirtingly against his bottom lip. Kevin made subtle overtures, too, but Rudy was pulling all the stops. What were these two doing? I learned, eventually, that a contest had arisen between the two, and I would be the prize.

It was weeks later that I heard the story: Between classes that day, Kevin had called Rudy and told him of the attractive traveling visitor and his bland, hard-to-read companion. "I'm not sure," Kevin had told Rudy, "but if Will and Jon are sleeping together, they're hiding it well. I could care less, because I'm sure Will would be happier with me!"

"You'll have to wait," Rudy had retorted, "because I haven't had a look at him yet."

"Don't even try it."

"What, are you afraid of the competition?"

"Of course not. You wouldn't be his type."

"Then you'd have nothing to worry about, would you?"

The gauntlet had been thrown, and now the gentlemen would lay out the ground rules.

"We don't want to scare him off," said the experienced Rudy. "If we both leap at him like wolves, we might shut him down completely."

"Or," Kevin conceitedly conceded, "if we're both successful in capturing his interest, we might lose him to indecision."

After more thought, Rudy suggested, "What if we were to allow a completely different talent to decide?"

Kevin was instantly aware of Rudy's meaning. The two of them had been playing bridge, together and separately, for years, and both of them fancied themselves brilliant competitors in the game. "So you think," said Kevin, "bridge is the contest, and the victor wins Will."

"I'm not saying we shouldn't test the waters throughout the game, but we won't ruthlessly jump him. We can each let him know we're interested, but the man who wins the tournament will be the man who takes him home."

Kevin couldn't resist. If they had kept a running score of all the matches they had played together, they probably would have been at a dead tie. "You're on."

Rudy had teasingly concluded their conversation by saying, "Don't worry. I might not even think he's cute."

"Oh, you'll think he's cute. I can guarantee you that."

These two knew each other well.

As I have already implied, Rudy did find me attractive, and surprisingly, the feelings were mutual. There was some small quality he possessed that was lacking in Kevin, although I couldn't name it. They were both effeminate and almost too-stylishly dressed, but both were also good-looking, charming, and clever. Perhaps Rudy's determination to seduce me was that extra element.

Or, I was still throbbing from my previous, foiled evening.

Rudy and I won the tournament (I was no slouch at the game, myself). By 3 a.m., Jon threw in the towel, leaving Kevin without a partner, and before long, Kevin left me alone with the winner of his private contest with Rudy.

The love-making was sweet (and in retrospect, innocent), and afterwards Rudy and I talked a long while before sleeping. During our conversation, he told me he would be taking a vacation in a few weeks from his job as a purser for an airline.

"Maybe," he said, as he nuzzled against my neck, "you can replace your companion with me, when my vacation starts. It'll be soon, at Christmastime."

I spoke from experience; "It might not be easy to shake Jon loose."

Rudy dropped his head back to his own pillow and I could feel his eyes examining my profile. He said, "I know you told us you're both from New York, and that he's only hitching a ride with you for a while, but how else do you know that man?"

"To tell you the truth, I don't know him at all." My head was propped up against the headboard, and I admired the shape of the slender, almost hairless arm laying across my chest. "He hardly talks, and when he does, it's so blase that it's hard to pay attention to what he's saying."

"I can agree with that." Rudy rubbed my stomach in slow, soothing, contemplative circles. "Have you been lovers?"

Before I knew it was coming, a laugh popped out of me. "No."

"If you're not really friends, and definitely not lovers, why can't you tell him I'm going to replace his seat in your car?"

"I'll try." This time, my laugh was forced. "I should be careful with him, though. For all I know, he's working for McCarthy, suspecting me of being a Communist. I wouldn't want to make him suspicious."

Rudy sat up. "What? You think—he thinks—What are you talking about?"

"I did attend an artist's college in New York, and McCarthy has been looking into students and professors."

Rudy giggled. He had an adorable giggle, which might have been the one quality he possessed beyond Kevin's attributes. The giggle that came from Rudy sounded fresh and guileless, but when he wouldn't stop, I began to feel offended. I said, "It could happen. My lineage is Russian and I've been traveling through communist countries…."

Falling back on the bed alongside me, Rudy regained control of himself and stared up at the ceiling. "I'm sorry, but it sounds ridiculous. Either Jon is totally blind, or I am. Or, maybe it's you who's blind."

"What do you mean?"

"I can't believe Jon would mistake you for a Commie. Or that I would mistake a Commie for nothing more than a nice, sexy American man."

"But what do you mean that I'm the one who's blind?"

"It could be that he has a crush on you."

"Not possible!"

Here came the giggles again. I could have pinched him. He said, "Don't worry. If Jon does have feelings for you, he's probably lying to himself about it. I don't think you'd ever need to wear a chastity belt around him."

"I should hope not."

When Rudy's boyish chuckling subsided again, he asked, "So tell me, do you like to ski?"

"Do I! It's a passion of mine."

"You and I should go skiing at The Cedars of Lebanon before you leave this part of the world."

"I couldn't agree more!" I realize now that I've never commented on one hope I had always had for this trip: Skiing in Europe. I had only heard vague references to 'The Cedars' at that time, but the way Rudy had tossed out the name, it sounded like someone in the States saying, 'Lake Tahoe.' Incidentally, The Cedars is a ski resort at the summit of Mt. Lebanon.

Although we would still have another 24 hours to spend together, we made firm plans to go skiing when I was back in Beirut on Christmas day, and after that, Rudy would accompany me through parts of Northern Africa. Once it was all settled, we fell into a long, refreshing sleep.

Rudy spoiled me that night with dinner in his swank (and roomy) apartment. He was well established in Beirut, he even had servants. While we sat in his living room he gave a tidy little woman instructions for our meal, including candles and fine wine. We enjoyed drinks while the table was set and served, then cook and maid were politely dismissed, and I basked in the luxury of high living.

After our meal, Rudy turned on his hi-fi and played his new record, Prokofieff's 7th. We snuggled on the couch with brandies, listening to the candlelit music, stroking each other to orgasms. There are times in life when everything is just so, just right, and that was one of those times.

Now, I've mentioned that I had considered exchanging sexual interactions for a place to sleep, possibly even food. I've also said that Rudy possessed 'something more' than the English professor Kevin. Might that extra something have been money? Rudy certainly did treat me well. However, I've already discussed how I feel about our skewed concepts of prostitution, and in this case I enjoyed myself as much as my benefactor. I believe our pleasures were simply a lovely exchange of what we had to offer.

The implication of the above is fact: I was broke during the time I spent in Beirut. In contrast to Rudy's way of life, I had been checking in at American Express for some funds to continue my trip. My Mother had strongly hinted, in her last letter to me, that she wanted to send me some money, and I could expect it to arrive while I was in Beirut. I had checked during each of the days I spent there, and it never showed. When Rudy announced that he would be returning to work on December 17th, I told Jon I wanted to leave on the same day. My agreeable, enigmatic traveling companion said that would be fine.

Rudy left, but Jon and I were stuck in Beirut for two more days. Visas. What frustration we endured! During the oxymoron of free hours spent waiting, I explored the city some more, and even found a newspaper willing to write an article about my adventure. I couldn't convince them to pay me for the article, but assumed everything published about my trip would further my goal of interesting the Renault advertising department.

With more time to kill, I attended a lecture in the Art Department of the AUB. I also discovered some mouth-watering though peculiar sandwiches that cost the equivalent of about five cents; beans, a green leafy vegetable, tomatoes, radishes, and mayonnaise were fried into a slab, and wrapped in round bread. I could have lived on them, and considering my budget, that's exactly what I did for a while.

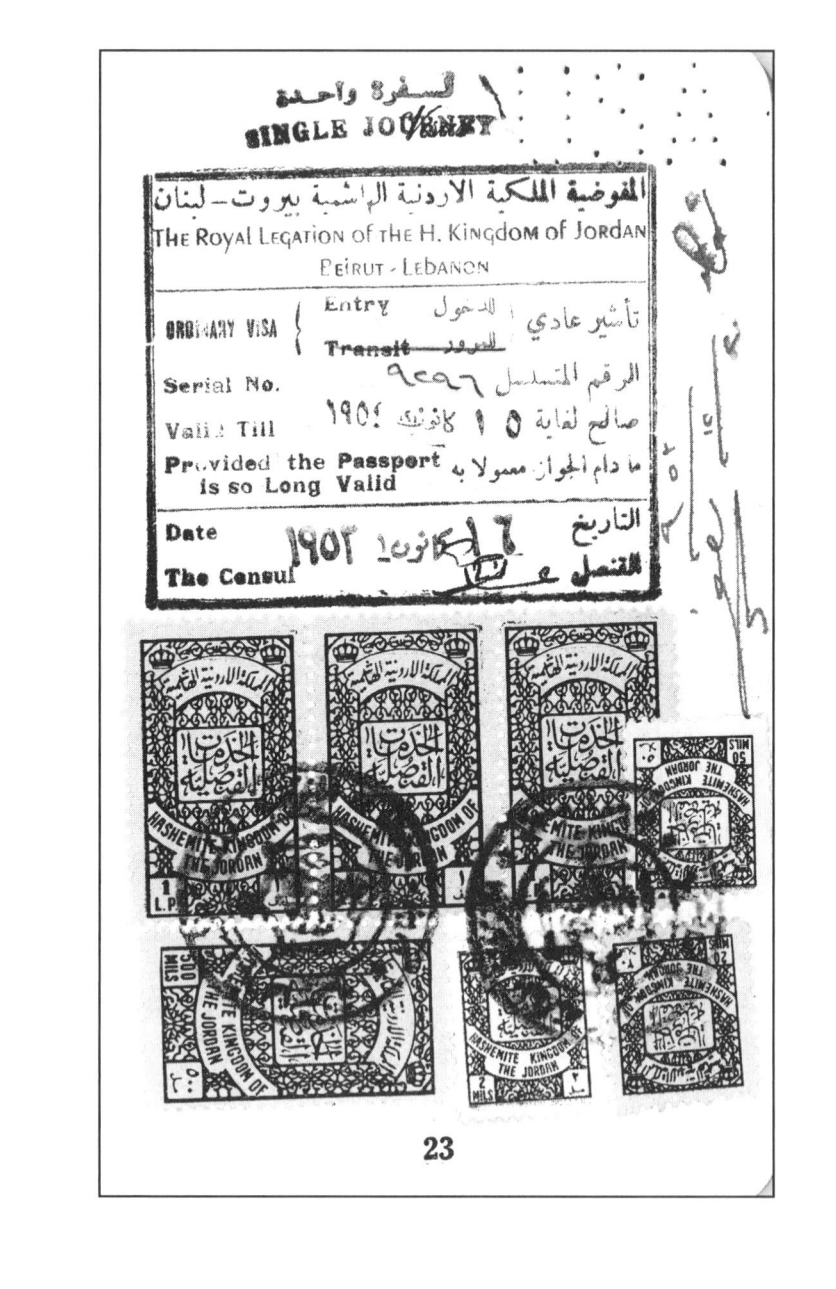

لسفرة واحـدة
SINGLE JOURNEY

المفوضية الملكية الاردنية الهاشمية بيروت ـ لبنان
The Royal Legation of the H. Kingdom of Jordan
BEIRUT - LEBANON

ORDINARY VISA { Entry للدخول تأشيرعادي
Transit للسفر

Serial No. الرقم المتسلسل ٩٥٨٧

Valid Till صالح لغاية ١ ٥ كانون ١٩٥٤

Provided the Passport ما دام الجواز معمولا به
is so Long Valid

Date ٦ كانون ١٩٥٢ التاريخ

The Consul القنصل

23

12

Christmas Eve in the Holy Land

Jon and I left Beirut on a wonderfully sunny day. Once outside the city, we began a long climb into mountains, passing the inevitable (and inevitably pretty) villages. Fast-flowing brooks wove in and out of sight along the mountainsides until we reached the snowy area near the summit. Our subsequent descent brought us into a green valley, then the road branched off to Baalbek, the ancient city of Romans.

With each mile we drove, more and more clouds covered the sun until rain began to pour down. It came hard and steady on a strong wind, which seemed to blow in every direction at once. I began to worry it would be like Delphi or the Acropolis, another highlight of my trip that would be subdued by miserable weather. There was no way I could take photographs in such a storm.

Fortunately, the magnificence of Baalbek was still easy to admire. Jon and I parked to explore, if only for a little while. While the rain turned to sleet, then to wet snow, our spirits were kept aloft by the visual thrill. Here's the entry from my journal, but afterwards, I'll elaborate further:

> The remaining 8 columns of the temple in Baalbek gave evidence to its once impressive grandeur and size. There was so much to see—the eye could never be at rest, nor could it be satisfied. These are amazing ruins. We stayed too short a time to have gotten enough out of the trip, but too long, considering the weather.

For those who are unfamiliar with Baalbek, I'll tell more here of what I learned: These ruins are the result of one of those situations where existing foundations and materials were used by conquerors to build new structures. What I mean is, one can assume there were 'ruins' in this place not only before the Romans came along, but even before the Phoenicians built there. Among other constructions by those two factions, the Phoenicians erected a temple to their god Baal, then the Romans later put up an enormous Temple of Jupiter.

As I say, though, somebody else was there before either of those cultures. I've heard many archaeologists believe the history of Baalbek goes back as far as 5,000 years, which I find stunning. Apparently, this information has been gleaned from excavations beneath the Great Court of the Temple of Jupiter, where the signs of different levels of civilizations have been uncovered.

Interestingly, it's thought that Jupiter, who was such an important deity for the Romans, actually took over the role of the Greeks' Zeus, and probably also replaced Baal, who wasn't all that dissimilar to Zeus, either. Is there a trend here for theologians to dissect and discuss? Perhaps many people have touched upon this in the past, but I openly admit that I am not any sort of theologian.

At the ruins, the 'small' Temple of Bacchus is larger than the Parthenon in Athens. Enormous fallen columns and sculptures around the rest of the place seem scattered by angry gods, and it is true that mother nature had a hand in it with some earthquakes, but it's people who have wreaked most of the destruction. We human beings sure can be fickle in our beliefs, and so angrily destructive with the beliefs of others!

A great mystery of Baalbek is that it's nearly impossible to imagine the stone foundations beneath the Temple of Jupiter had been quarried, transported, crafted, and positioned by mere humans. (Could it be 'the gods buildeth, and man taketh away'?)

The largest single piece of crafted stonework in the world is at Baalbek; the dimensions are 69' x 16' x 13', and the guess is that it weighs 1200 tons. It's called the Stone of the South or the Stone of the Pregnant Woman, depending on who you ask. Still attached to its original quarry rock at the base, it looks as if it was just about to be cut free and moved. The mystery isn't only about that single piece, though. It includes all the huge, ancient stoneworks in this area.

Modern builders have trouble understanding how the manipulation of such heavy, unwieldy hunks of rock might have been accomplished thousands of years ago. They don't even have any suggestions of how it could be achieved *today*, given the various factors of the location. Sure, when speaking of such puzzles like the

Pyramids of Giza, there has been discussion, and even evidence, of legions of laborers and animals muscling the stone around with ropes and wooden rollers. Those pyramid stones were much smaller than the stones of Baalbek, though. Maybe 1/10th the size? Also, Baalbek doesn't have the smooth surfaces and wide paths that can be found in the desert, and in fact it's up on a big hill. Even if the stones were somehow dragged there, how could they have then been lifted for such precise placement? Some sort of ancient scaffolding, plus more legions of men and animals? Rumor has it, there simply would not have been enough space to set all that up. Well, maybe one or two of the obelisks could have been lifted, but dozens of them, standing side-by-side? I'm actually a bit of an architect—I once designed a house—and I certainly can't see how it could happen. It would be hard to imagine even with the technology we have today, much less with what was available back then.

I think I've gone on about all that long enough, other than to say I hope I wasn't remiss in expressing my absolute awe at this incomparable site.

Jon and I tucked back into the dry, relative warmth of Dolly, and continued on to Damascus.

The surroundings changed drastically, and quickly. Here's what I said about it in my journal:

> Water began to flow on the sides of the road, trees appeared, and beautiful homes appeared on the high banks. A magnificent wide boulevard led us into the city, where I was surprised by what we saw.

It was the cleanliness of the city that surprised me. The accommodations were quite nice, too; Jon found a room for himself at the best hotel I had yet seen in my travels. It was very warm, comfortable, and well-kept, and I believe it was called the "Swiss Palmyra." As usual, I transformed Dolly into my sleeping space, but I took all my meals at the hotel, and the food was excellent.

We left that orderly world behind when we started out for Amman. There were more refugee camps along the way, where the shacks, streets, people, donkeys and camels…absolutely everything was saturated with filth. Once, while stopped for a moment, I accidentally met the eyes of a young male refugee standing close by. Rather than the despair I had expected to find, I saw only impotent anger. I fixed my eyes on the road in front of me, and accelerated on into the desert.

We weren't aware of passing a security check-point, and when we were stopped at the border, I was told to drive back a few miles to go through the formalities. More than anything, it was a bother. Like any sane man, I prefer irritable red tape over terrifying confrontations.

When we reached Jordan, we found ourselves on a high piece of ground looking down into the city. It was a grand entrance into the country, fitting for the Holy Lands. We entered Amman that afternoon and witnessed the spectacle of a culture that was trying to build a new modern capital out of an ancient city. Some Roman ruins remain, too, complete with an amphitheater.

We found a hotel with a cozy fireplace in the lobby, where many Palestinian refugees huddled for warmth. The topic: Israel. I listened with great interest.

The phrase 'pure hatred' has always sounded like an oxymoron to me until I learned how the Arab refugees felt toward Israel. They considered the Israelis to be horrid, evil, deranged marauders and land-thieves. While we sat there, tale after tale was told of the extensive loss experienced by these cold, hungry, hardened people. I didn't have the nerve to suggest that the Israelis couldn't have taken all that land without at least some help from the outside world, but someone else brought up the subject.

One man, whose face was a deeply-lined etching of desert life, seemed to play the part of an off-kilter Socrates for the group. He said, "We would defeat the Jews if only the rest of the world would stay out of it."

"Yes!" came the general reply. One young man, who had intimidating eyes and black hair that hung in greasy clumps, stood and raised a fist. "England. America. The United Nations. Most of the rest of the world has formed a league with the Jews. It is an unfair fight."

More agreement, until Socrates held up one hand. "America is not the worst of them. The Americans have helped supply us with arms. They have one face they must show the world, but another that furthers our cause."

"But President Roosevelt was a scoundrel!"

"He is no longer the President of that country, is he?"

I glanced at Jon, but he only sat with his cup of tea, idly smoking a cigarette, listening without any real show of attention. Deciding to follow his lead, I lit a cigarette of my own and gazed between the hunched bodies at the flames of the fire.

"It is best," Socrates continued, "to defeat one enemy at a time. After we have wrestled our land back from the Jews, only then should we begin to consider how to address each new adversary. With patience, we will always come to see their true faces."

Another man spoke up; "Personally, I'll take on whoever gets in our way, I don't care where he comes from."

"You'd be distracted from your better purpose," Socrates replied. "First, eliminate the Jews. They are the most cunning, and it is they who have possession of our land at this time. When they are gone, we can rebuild our homes, our families, and our armies."

This was met with a murmur of approval, and the talk looped back to the start of its circle: "The Jews are vile thieves!"

I snuffed out my cigarette and went to prepare my car for sleep. As disturbing as the conversation had been, that hour of hot tea by a warm fire was the only thing that saved me from freezing in the cold of the night.

The following morning, Jon and I set out for Jericho. Of all expectations I might have had about the place, the one hope that stood out in my mind was of a warmer climate. It was so, but marginally, and not pleasant enough to offset the horror of hundreds upon hundreds of beggars. What a disappointment to have all sights and sensations drowned under a sea of needy hands. How could anybody ever choose which hand to fill? It would have been impossible to give something to all of them.

Jon found a hotel called the Winter Palace, which we found was aptly named. There was no heat, it was large and drafty and frigid inside. They kept the beggars out, though, which was a relief for Jon. I, on the other hand, took my accommodations in Dolly once again, and when I tried to climb in and out of the car, the desperate throngs pressed so close that I could barely open the door. It was unnerving, much like being mobbed. The only way I could think to disperse them was to turn out my pockets, showing them my distinct lack of coin.

I don't know how regular tourists fared in Jericho, because there wasn't a single restaurant. As had happened more than a few times on my trip, I was thankful to have brought my Coleman stove. Jon and I were able to brew coffee in my car, and no one minded when we brought our full cups back inside the hotel for a place to relax. While there, we found ourselves sitting near a bright-faced gentleman who immediately turned and asked if we were tourists. We confirmed his guess, albeit with some trepidation, but our concerns were unfounded. This soft-spoken fellow was the former Minister of Education of Palestine, and was delighted to have found two young men who were college graduates. He told us in great detail about Arab literature, and I was surprised to learn how many Arab tales we Americans have gathered into our own culture.

When I wandered back to my car, I could see a small group of beggars were washing dear Dolly with the sacred water of the river Jordan. I tried to stop them, but they only smiled and nodded until the bath was finished, then held out their hands for the tips I felt obligated to give.

My impressions of the town weren't all bad, though. From my journal:

> In all fairness to Jericho, I must say the oranges were nothing like I have ever seen or tasted before. And the palm trees, fruit trees, and thin cone trees, colored by the bright sun, were awesome to behold.

Back to the reality of a common traveler; all in all, we were happy to leave. We drove down to the Dead Sea, which is (paradoxically) 1,200 ft below sea level. The beaches were covered with magnificent rocks, and the sun was warm on our skin, but it was strange to swim in that water. The salt of the Dead Sea is so heavy, it feels like a coating that can only be scraped off. When I accidentally ducked my head under the water, my eyes burned as if doused with acid. So much salt makes a body light, though, and it's as easy to float as it would be to lay on a pillow-top mattress.

Most water has a lifelike quality, through colors, movement or what have you, but the Dead Sea gave me a feeling of quiet, muddy lifelessness. It was the same color as the land around it, which was bland and empty but for a few scattered shacks. When Jon and I left, it felt as through we were creeping away, unwilling to disturb the disquieting peace of the place.

Gorgeous weather accompanied us to Jerusalem on hilly, barren roads. Our first sight of the town was from below; in a distance high above us were towers and buildings, peppered across a range of mountains that appeared to grow down from the sky. It was a few days before Christmas Eve, and I imagined the only thing that could add to the beatific scene would have been a covering of snow.

As we came closer, we saw the Wailing Wall, then the old city behind it. I had to stop at the wall, and as had happened at the walls of Jericho, Jon and I were the only people there. Odd, and again, so unlike what I had expected.

After the Wall, we found an American Colony and enjoyed an excellent lunch there, which made up for the lack of restaurant fare in Jericho. The only thing that tossed my stomach a bit was when I saw a sign advertising insurance of all kinds, including (among the basics) coverage for earthquakes. Having come from the East Coast of the States, with no experience of earthquakes, that's what made me most nervous.

When we stepped out of the American Colony we were approached by a man who offered us cleaning services of various types. We listened to his lively patter as we approached Dolly, where the three of us stopped. Staring, the cleaning man said, "You drive a Renault!"

"Yes," I said. "She has brought me quite a ways, so far. It's a good car."

"I know! I, too, have a Renault." His smile showed brown teeth and a sense of unexpected camaraderie. "Come along," he said. "I can see you have no need for my cleaning services, but I will show you some of the sights, here."

This kind acquaintance oriented us in the city, showing us the Jewish sections and also the Mandelbaum Gate, which separated two nations. This guide was filled with interesting tidbits I never would have uncovered on my own.

His last bit of advice was with regard to where I should park to sleep for the night. "Stay in the parking lot outside the American Colony. You'll be safe and protected there."

He was right, and in fact it turned out better than either of us could have imagined. The night watchman approached me as I began to transform Dolly, and asked, "What are you doing?"

"I'm going to sleep in my car, here. Is that alright? I am American." In case he had any doubts, I pulled my passport from my pocket, but he didn't need to see it.

"It would be fine with me if you want to sleep here, but why don't you take a room somewhere, instead?"

"I'm traveling on a low budget." Honesty is almost always the best policy.

"I'll tell you what," said the night watchman. "I lock up the colony at ten o'clock, and if at that time no one is staying in the Grand Salon, the room is yours."

"As I say, I'm on a very, very low budget."

"Free of charge."

How could I say no? True to his word, he appeared a few minutes before ten, and ushered me in through the gates. After all was locked and secured, he led me through the same building where Jon and I had eaten a meal. There were various rooms in this central meeting building, but at the moment, all was dark.

The guard led me into the Grand Salon and showed me the bed, a sleeper-sofa, which turned out to be surprisingly comfortable. The room had a private bath, too. "I'll be back at seven in the morning," he said. "Sleep well."

That was it. No expectations of any sort of payment from me, just a generous offer from a fellow American. I slept cozily, and woke refreshed and ready for my first entire day in Jerusalem.

A new guide cornered us, and when he said a tour of the old city would only cost $2.00 for the whole morning, we took him up on it. The price was about right for such a depressing tour, as can be seen in my journal entry:

What we saw of the old city was extremely disappointing, grimy with dirt, urine, garbage, beggars, rags, foul odors, mud, water, and dampness. Sunshine could barely brighten the place. The holy sepulcher had been destroyed of all its meaning, for it was covered with pagan materials of gold and marble.

Jon was inclined to next visit the Greek Orthodox church, where the priest in charge invited us in for a Christmas drink of wine. Throughout the church were numerous receptacles for 'offering' money, to which we dutifully contributed. That holiday wine was pretty expensive.

Also that morning we saw Christ's 13 steps (where he dragged the cross), His Stations, the place of Ascension, and the Dome of the Rock. All in all, I found no beauty in the Holy City itself, but a panorama of the Holy Land in the distance gave the eye some relief.

That afternoon, we drove to the Mount of Olives. Here another impressive view unfolded; I could see all the way into the Israeli part of Jerusalem, including Mount Zion, the King David Hotel, and the YMCA. I also was able to look into the Garden of Gethsemane and the mosque-like church on the Mount of Olives.

By the time we returned to Jon's hotel and had dinner, it was too late for me to sleep in the Grand Salon again, but I had become accustomed to Dolly's relative comforts. Before I fell asleep, it began to rain, which I knew meant it would be too warm for snow the next day, Christmas Eve.

The following morning I saw something that moved me deeply: A temporary religious amnesty.

The Mandelbaum Gate, which divided the nations, would be held open for 72 hours. What this meant is that families cleaved by borders could only see one another once a year, at Christmastime. While separated, they weren't even able to write to each other. The only way they knew how to hope would show up was a list of names, released by Israel and published the day before. Some people had been waiting five hours, and for at least a sad, pitiful few, that wait turned out to be in vain. I stared at everyone, all of whom needed only a glance to know my face was not that of the loved one they sought.

The emotions expressed by the people, as they clung to one another around the Mandelbaum Gate, is an image I will never forget. Only those on the Israeli side were well-clothed and cheerful, but it was an otherwise tense scene. What struck me was that it was all carried on beneath an American flag, because the American Consulate was a few feet away.

Next on the agenda was to retrieve someone from the airport. While with Rudy in Beirut, I had met a few of his friends, and one was a young man named Saal. Saal, who had only been visiting Beirut, lived in Jerusalem. Before I left, he had given me information about a flight he planned to take on Christmas Eve for his return home. I had assured him I would pick him up at the airport, and after witnessing the amnesty, that's where Jon and I headed.

As we drove toward the arrivals gate, I was surprised to see a blinking red light and a long, striped arm lowering in front of my car. I stopped, knowing there couldn't be a train, and watched as a few moments later, a plane rolled serenely past. Strange. The setup for plane-crossings surely must be different, these days.

Saal's flight was late, and we had plenty of time to watch the endless 'Christmas Eve in Jerusalem' tours arriving. Most of the tourists were American. When Saal did arrive, he directed us to his home, where we spent a pleasant afternoon of food, coffee, and conversation. He asked if he could join us on our drive to Bethlehem, and I readily agreed. His company would be a welcome addition to Jon's socially-challenged presence.

As we traveled on the road Saal had instructed me to use, he asked, with pride in his voice, "What do you think?"

"Of what?" I was stalling. I preferred not to say exactly what my impression of Jerusalem had been.

That wasn't what he'd meant, though. He said, "The road. What do you think of the road?"

"Quite nice." It was, too; smoothly, freshly paved. "A bit curvy, though."

"It's new," said Saal. "My brother was the chief engineer. We had to build a new road because the old one went through Israeli territory."

How odd. Imagine you've often driven from California to Nevada, and suddenly one day there's a big blockade in the road. A sign directs you to take the new road around a different mountain, because the old one would lead you through, say, Russian territory. How very odd it would be.

It grew dark before we reached Bethlehem, and lights began to blink on in the mountains ahead of us. Those lights were clustered together in numerous clumps, and I asked Saal about them.

"They're from Israeli villages. They know the tourists are coming in droves, so they purposely light up the mountains to show how prosperous they are."

Night had fully fallen when we reached Shepherd's Field, where the YMCA service had already begun. The entire program was quite simple; the choir and leader of the service were in a sort of pit, while the guests stood on top looking down into it. The singing of the choir was in Arabic.

We parked, and I climbed onto a stone wall for a better look. The service was in front of me, and beggars were behind me, pulling at my feet for money. My skin had momentarily thickened against them; nothing could distract me from the distant, softly-lit hills around the Holy Land, a reverent stage under more gleaming stars than the eye could gather in. It couldn't have been much different than the times of Christ, as nothing seemed to have truly changed, especially not the people.

Christmas songs were being sung in different languages, now. Looking out beyond where the hills and the sky met, I began to feel for the first time a sensation I had hoped for: peace on earth, good will toward men. Corny, but true. It's a sublime sensation.

When the service was over, we entered a cave hidden behind the performance pit and found a small group of shepherds eating Shepherd's Pie. They offered us some, and I found the round Arab pocket of bread, stuffed with chunks of lamb, thoroughly delicious and satisfying. Once again, I was infused with a sense of sacred love, a religious feeling toward an entity that can be named God. I knew Shepherd's Field would be a memory to cherish, but we had two more services to attend.

First, we drove back to the church of the Nativity, where I received the same impressions I'd had at the holy sepulcher in Jerusalem. Garish, and sapped of spiritual meaning. There are two places where Christ was supposed to have been born, each religion believing in a different spot. That really bothered me. I wasn't impressed by the one location we observed, either, which was covered with more gaudy baubles. In contrast, the simple Protestant service held in the courtyard, under the stars, was quite pleasant. The fine service was led by a British Bishop and an English singing choir.

Standing on another ledge, I had a perfect view of this mixed group of people, singing together, their kind faces showing love for one another and all who observed. The sense of good will washed over me again, and it was simultaneously brightened and dulled by the thought, 'If only the world could always be like this.' (How could something seem so possible and impossible at the same time?)

That the service was so simple gave it more meaning than if it had been elaborate. The twinkle in the eyes of the people was as bright and enchanting as glow of the stars above.

The final service for the night would be the Catholic High Mass. Saal was determined to secure tickets for Jon and myself to witness the event, saying, "This is really the thing to see. It's broadcast all over the world!"

To his dismay, tickets were not available. After foraging around for a while, he found us again, quite discouraged. "It's no use. Maybe you should pretend you're writing a story for a magazine about the service."

I said, agreeably, "Sure, why not?" After all, I had tried the ploy once before, and it hadn't bothered anybody.

Saal brought me to the priest in charge, and I tried out my lie. Should I have felt extra guilt for lying so blatantly to a priest? Especially since my aim was to enter the holiest of his holy services? Naw. First of all, I did intend to try selling stories of my trip to Renault, so there was at least one grain of truth. Secondly, guilt is such a harmful, unhelpful emotion. Finally, my insignificant lie didn't work. The priest apologized and said there were simply no tickets to be had.

Throughout all this maneuvering, I had been taking note of those who were entering the church. Overweight, over-dressed people with hands, wrists, and necks covered in expensive jewels, ignoring the desperate beggars almost to a point of blindness. Did I really want to sit alongside those contradictory worshipers?

Saal burst from the crowd with two squares of paper fluttering in his fingers. "I've found some, I've found tickets for you!" He pressed one into my hand and gave the other to Jon. "An usher here is a friend of mine, and he said these will get you through the door, even if you won't be able to find a seat."

I showed as much enthusiasm as I could muster, and under Saal's proudly watching eye, entered the church.

'Stifling,' was the first word that came to mind. Another word might have been 'endless.' For an endless amount of time, I stood stifled inside that mass of combed and preening society.

Maybe it will be easier to simply insert here what I had written in my journal:

> The service was, sadly, all in Latin. I couldn't understand a word of it. There was nothing to make me feel that it was a gathering specifically for Christmas, even though everyone was dressed as if for the coronation of Christ himself. Such dull pomp and ceremony. Each person within my line of sight looked to be bored, tired, and annoyed at standing—I'm talking about the Catholics themselves. I gave up, and squeezed my way through the crowd out to the Cloisters, where I sat for the first time in an hour and half. I listened to the service over the speakers, and looked up toward the Lord's domain, rather than at all the fancily dressed people. It was much more pleasant outside.

While I sat outside, the sound of retching reached my ears, and I saw a woman vomiting into some plants in the middle of the courtyard. Another blunt, unpleasant word about the service came to me: 'Disgusting.' How could the people inside strut about in gold, ermine, and velvet costumes, when so few feet away were starving, naked children? Some of those urchins were even living in the church itself, under extreme poverty. I don't know if Jesus would have been particularly impressed by his worshipers.

Jon stumbled out through the doors and found me on my bench.

I asked him, "Weren't you enjoying the service?"

He made a non-committal noise and used a handkerchief to wipe at his neck and forehead. "How about you, what did you think of it?"

Tipping my head toward the woman who was still huddled over the bushes, I said, "That describes my feelings pretty well." She was now being attended by a friend, who stood holding the well-coiffed hair back from the continuing spray of vomit.

Jon nodded sagely, and we wandered away, in search of Saal.

Saal, Jon, and I arrived back at Saal's home in the early hours of the morning. Before I could wonder too much about ridding myself of Jon's company, (I intended to soon be skiing, alone, with Rudy), he (Jon) informed me that he would be flying out from Bethlehem that day.

"Goodbye, Will."

"Goodbye, Jon."

"Maybe we'll see each other again along the road?"

"Maybe." Wouldn't bother me one way or the other.

We shook hands, and away he went to his hotel for a few hours of sleep before his flight. I only saw him one final time in my life, and at the end of this book, I'll tell what happened. For now, I'm about to retrace my steps to Beirut, and before the close of Christmas day, I would be in Rudy's arms again.

ΣΤΑΘΜΟΣ ... ΔΙΑΒΑΤΗΡΙΩΝ

ΕΥΖΩΝΩΝ

1 6 1 1 5 3

ΕΙΣΟΔΟΣ

PERMITTED
THEIR RESIDENCE IN GREECE
WITHOUT DECLARATION
FOR TWO MONTHS

الجمهورية السورية
RÉPUBLIQUE SYRIENNE
SÛRETÉ GÉNÉRALE الامن العام
DERAA 20/12/5

الجمهورية اللبنانية
RÉPUBLIQUE LIBANAISE
Sûreté Générale الامن العام
مركز وادي الحرير
POSTE de WADI L-HARIR
Entrée 25-XII-53

صرح لحامله الاقامة في لبنان لغاية
وعليه ان يتقدم الى مديرية الامن العام ٤٨ ساعة قبل انها
هذا الموعد

Le titulaire est autorisé à résider au Liban
jusqu'au 24-1-54
Il est tenu de se présenter à la Direction de la
Sûreté Générale 48 heures avant l'expiration de
ce délai

13

Thomas and I, Athens, Greece

Thomas visiting a temple of his ancestors, Athens

The Acropolis, Athens. A bitter cold day.

**Roman Amphitheater, Amman, Jordan
Notice the sweater**

**Sounion, Greece visited by Lord Byron
who left his carved initials**

This passport is not valid for travel to or in any foreign state for the purpose of entering or serving in the armed forces of such a state.

> THIS PASSPORT IS NOT VALID FOR TRAVEL TO ALBANIA, BULGARIA, CHINA, CZECHOSLOVAKIA, HUNGARY, POLAND, RUMANIA OR THE UNION OF SOVIET SOCIALIST REPUBLICS UNLESS SPECIFICALLY ENDORSED UNDER AUTHORITY OF THE DEPARTMENT OF STATE AS BEING VALID FOR SUCH TRAVEL.

13

Eventually to Africa

There's a part of each and every one of us that desires to be held by someone who feels love for us. It's human nature. What Rudy and I felt for each other did possess most of the requirements of love: We cared for one another; we were curious to know more; we shared interests and felt the sexual attraction. The particular time in our lives, and where we were emotionally and geographically, made our relationship just right. I could hardly wait to see him again.

The trip from Jerusalem straight through to Beirut would be a long one, and I started off before 7:00 a.m. The roads reflected British diligence during their mandate period in Jordan, in the form of a large military air field and personnel presence. I also passed many Arab Legion outposts, but the country was otherwise dry and empty.

It was necessary to drive through Syria again, and they wanted me to purchase another visa. I knew the cost of a tourist visa was only $3.00, and that was the amount I was prepared to pay, but they tried to pull a fast one on me. "What you need," the border guard said, "is an entrance visa." He held out his hand. "That will be $10.00."

"I don't need an entrance visa, I'm supposed to get a tourist visa."

The guard proceeded to wind his way through a complicated explanation of why he was right and I was wrong, his hand extended for payment the entire time.

I said, "You know, I don't think it's even a tourist visa that I need. I'm actually a student. I definitely can't afford to pay $10.00 to enter your country!" Whatever it took to get past this golddigger, I would say it.

"Where are you a student?"

"AUB," I immediately replied. If asked for evidence, I would produce a book Kevin had loaned me from his school, which had the university's name stamped inside the front cover.

The guard lowered his hand and eyed me for a moment. If I was telling the truth, he would have to give me a student visa, which wouldn't cost me a cent. Or, he could try the lower rate, make at least a few bucks, and be done with me.

He handed me a tourist visa, and I gave him the $3.00. It wasn't until I drove away that I realized; if he had known I was Jewish, he wouldn't have let me in at all. No matter. That was the last time I would ever try to enter Syria.

What a wonderful Christmas dinner! I was back with my lover, and among friends, too; Rudy had invited a group over, including Kevin. We all ate and joked and smoked and drank and played cards half the night. For the other half of the night, Rudy and I made love.

We left early the next morning for The Cedars of Lebanon to ski. Rudy wanted to take his Hillman, which although it was a new car, it already seemed classic. As we ascended Mt. Lebanon, I could see the spring-like day on the coast falling away behind us, and snow began to show on the sides of the road. Now that I was the passenger, I couldn't take my eyes away from the deep canyons, rushing waterfalls, and startling, sweeping vistas. Occasionally we drove through little villages, too, which had (of all things) a distinctly Italian air about them.

A few hours from the top of the mountain, Rudy and I stopped to enjoy sandwiches, fruits, cheeses, wine, and kisses. It was turning out to be one of those perfect days that skitter through our lives too quickly.

The Cedars ski resort, situated on the summit, included a large, comfortable old hotel. The room Rudy and I took was more lavish than what I had become accustomed to, which suited me fine. Little did I know, it wouldn't be so easy for my boyfriend to make such lifestyle adjustments, but I'd learn about that soon enough.

It was too late to ski on the afternoon we arrived, so we settled in for drinks and dinner. Most of the other guests at the hotel were French, teachers from the French University of Beirut. This was fortunate for me, because I needed more practice with the language. French North Africa was still on my agenda, and I certainly couldn't speak Arabic.

That delightful evening was spent sharing conversation with new faces and learning about the best slopes to ski. Skiing has been my favorite sport throughout my life, but throughout that particular winter, I hadn't yet had a chance. I had been craving it like a drug.

When I woke up next to my snuggling bed-partner, the first thing I said was, "Why don't we take a walk to the ski tow, rather than drive?"

Rudy rolled over and stretched, squinting at me through sleep-heavy lids. "Good morning to you, too!"

"Good morning!" I jumped out of bed and went to the window, where I gazed adoringly at the clean, white snow. "It isn't far, is it? To the tow?"

"I guess not. Still, I'd rather drive." Rudy tried to sit up, but fell back against the pillows. "In a little while. Don't you want breakfast, first?"

"Excellent idea." I pulled on my heavy pants, the sweater from Anne, and over the top of it, my army coat. When I turned to Rudy, expecting he would at least have his feet on the floor, I found him still under the covers, watching me with amusement.

"How about this," he said, "why don't I just meet you at the tow in about an hour?"

"Do you think it will take that long for me to walk there?" I asked, pulling on my army boots.

"I couldn't even guess." Rudy stretched again, taking up the entire bed with limbs and fingers and toes and tousled hair. "But I know an hour is going to pass before *I'm* there. And I can bring your rented equipment in the car."

"I don't think it will be more than a half-hour walk along the trails, but I can wait for you there." I bounced out and down to the dining room, where I swallowed a cup of coffee and some pastries. To be skiing again, I could barely contain my impatience! After confirming the directions to the tow with a busboy, I was off.

Close to an hour and a half had passed by the time I dragged my tired feet to the tow. Those army boots were heavy, and what had looked like little hills had become as intimidating as vast mountains.

Nevertheless, my mood was still high. The walk had been awesome; the few cedars that remained were magnificent and my imagination had soared with fantasies of immense forests which, in ancient times, had totally covered Mount Lebanon.

Astoundingly, cedars can live up to two-thousand years, and the very trees I passed had supposedly been planted at the time of Solomon. They've gained much respect throughout the centuries, these trees. Their wood has been used for everything from houses to palaces, from temples to sarcophagi, from ship masts to entire vessels. Also, I heard the pitch of cedars was used for dental pain, and it was always considered safe to sleep beneath a cedar because snakes can't bear their sawdust. There are some who say cedar was also used in Egypt to preserve corpses. The very look of these trees, and the smell of them… it had been divine to walk beneath them.

Rudy was waiting for me at the tow, though I had the feeling he'd been there less than ten minutes. My rental equipment was waiting for me, too, but when I snatched it up and examined it with my experienced eye, all I could think was "Hmm."

The boots wouldn't do; they had a look of wear and inefficiency to them that was downright Dickensian. The skis were two simple sheets of wood barely coated with wax, but at least the clamps looked functional. I set them to the size of my army boots and took a few experimental steps. It was hard to say for sure, because I never found evidence of it, but I could have sworn I heard a splintering sound from the skis.

Rudy waited under the empty rope-tows that were passing us by. "What do you think?" he asked, and I could tell his patience was wearing thin. "Is that stuff going to work for you, or not?"

By now I had begun inspecting the ski-poles. Two relatively straight sticks, roughly carved to a point at one end, while the other end had a length of twine pushed through a hand-drilled hole. "I'm guessing the answer to that is 'not'." Two more tows were approaching, so I added, "But I'll give it a try."

My first guess had been correct. After watching me stumbling and struggling down the mountain one time, Rudy said, "You can share my skis, we can switch off."

What a guy. I kept it to a minimum, giving him most of the time to slide down the mountain, and it was a joy to see him having so much fun. During my turn, I thoroughly relished the excellent paths, clear but for moguls, and the perfect pitch of the slope. For a ski-junkie, sometimes even a short-lived fix will do.

By the time we were finished for the day, I felt invigorated, healthy and happy. We stayed one more night, spoiled by the upper-class hotel, then returned to Beirut.

The drive back down the mountain was long and tiring after our athletic adventure, and by the time we were back at Rudy's house, the first thing he called out to the servants was, "Hello, we're hungry!"

He was answered by a maid who sagged with fever and fatigue. "I'm sorry, so sorry. We're sick, all of us, sick." She looked it, too, in the light of the candle she was carrying.

Rudy gestured to the candle. "What's this?"

"We have no electricity."

He scowled, but I stepped in. To the maid I said, "Don't bother yourselves," and to Rudy, "I can stir us up something to eat."

"There's no water," said the despondent maid.

"No water?" Rudy headed toward the kitchen to check for himself, automatically flicking at the light switch. He stopped, lowered his hand, and his head, and spoke toward the floor. "I'm too tired for this. Will, why don't we just hit the hay?"

I grabbed a candle from the table. "You go, I'll find some bread and cheese or something and bring it to you."

Ten minutes later, Rudy and I were dining by candlelight again, this time at the small table in his bedroom. The situation was romantically acceptable to me, but Rudy was grumpy. I could understand; it was his home, after all, that had suddenly been stripped of water, electricity, and hired help.

It isn't easy to remember how Rudy's schedule worked, but I know he needed to return to work the day after I planned to leave Beirut. He would only have to fly around for a week, then somehow, he would have another week off. At that time, he would join me during part of my drive across Northern Africa, and I was grateful for it. Those were lands where I didn't want to travel alone, because I had so little idea of what to expect from that reportedly wild country.

I made arrangements to leave Beirut by having both myself and my car shipped across the Mediterranean to Port Said, Egypt, since I could not enter Egypt through Israel. On the day of departure, the boat was scheduled to leave at five o'clock in the afternoon, so I enjoyed a leisurely breakfast before organizing my belongings in the car. I brought Dolly to the pier, then stopped by the agency to pick up my ticket.

Before I turned away from the ticket counter, the clerk said, "You'll be boarding in about an hour. Have you cleared customs, yet?"

I looked at my watch; twelve-thirty. "Why in the world would we have to board so early?"

"The crew needs about a half-hour to make sure everyone is settled, and—"

"What half-hour? We don't leave until five o'clock!"

"No, you leave at two o'clock." He checked his watch. "If you haven't cleared customs, you'd better get to it now."

Yes, it was tempting to argue, but instead I examined my ticket more closely, and discovered that the departure time had indeed been changed to 2:00. This meant the 'See you later' I had tossed off to Rudy a few hours before should have included a kiss. We wouldn't see each other again for more than a week. Rudy's friends—who had become friends of mine, too—wouldn't get any sort of goodbye from me at all!

I found a phone and called Rudy to explain everything to him, and when he choked up, I felt a thickness in my own throat.

"I'll see you in Egypt," Rudy said.

"Don't be late," I answered, sort-of-jokingly.

"Ten a.m., January 9th, the Renault dealership in Cairo."

By the time I finished with the formalities at customs, Dolly was ready to be loaded onto the boat. I made my way through hectic throngs of people to the base of the crane that was about to hoist my car, but it was impossible to tell who was in charge. Everybody wanted to be involved, calling out orders, encouragements, and suggestions. It had begun to rain while I was in the customs offices, and now the day was gray and muddy. Peering through the rain and the people, I could see the boat that would carry me; an Egyptian tub that looked like a 19th century freighter. This was not how I had envisioned riding across the eastern Mediterranean.

The crane gave a mechanical creak, and Dolly was jerked against the canvas-covered hoists around her body. I called out, "Who's in charge of this operation?"

Fingers tugged my sleeve, and I looked down to see a boy smiling up at me. "Him," he said, pointing to the man operating the crane, then holding out his hand for payment. The information wasn't worth much to me (the crane operator was the man I had directed my question to), so I dropped a dime into the boy's hand. As I stepped closer to the base of the machine, calling again to the operator, a different man stopped me. "You can't bother him, he's working. He must be careful with that automobile."

"That's *my* automobile."

"One moment, please." He held out his hand. I dropped a coin into the palm, and he allowed me to pass.

The crane operator put on some sort of brake and asked me, "Are you the owner?"

"Yes, I am."

He held out his hand.

I asked, "What?"

"Ten dollars to load the Renault."

"But I already paid that, inside!"

"I have not received it."

"I'll go find the man—"

"You need to be boarding the boat in fifteen minutes. It will take me fifteen minutes to load your auto. If I do not begin now, who knows if I will be in time?"

It seemed I had little choice. No farewell kisses from Rudy, a miserable rain, and now this. I gave up the ten and was immediately surrounded by people claiming to have secured the ropes on the car, or reserving a special spot on the boat for it, or polishing bird droppings off its windows. All of them had their hands out. My frustration surely showed as I pushed through them to the loading ramp, where I stood watching until Dolly was safely aboard.

I was more than ready to leave Beirut.

Twenty minutes on the water, and I began to feel sick. I was a land-sailor, after all, and besides, the notoriously 'waveless' Mediterranean was very rough that day. There was only one other paying passenger on the boat, an Egyptian man originally from Port

Said, who I'll call 'Abdul.'

Abdul saw my distress, and said, "Come with me, I will take you to the ship's doctor."

With great hope I followed Abdul, and he introduced me to the doctor, who was scrawny and not exactly healthy-looking himself. Regardless, I privately vowed to accept his help, because he had an intelligent face, and I was desperate.

He pulled a vial of pills from his pocket, shook two of them out and said, "Take one now, and one in the morning if you need to."

"Thanks." I started to walk away, but he tapped my shoulder. When I turned, I saw his hand out, waiting. Nothing in this area, on land or at sea, was free.

The little pill knocked me out until dinnertime, which I awoke to groggily swallow before returning directly to my bunk. Both the pill and the sleep turned out to be exactly what I needed; the following morning I felt refreshed. Abdul met me for breakfast, and told me we had been invited to the captain's quarters after our meal.

The dark skin of the captain had been further burned by the sun, and this commander sat, at about 9:45 in morning, drinking a beer. He offered one to Abdul and me, and we both politely accepted. The captain lit a cigarette, and again offered them, and again we accepted.

Over morning beer and cigarettes we learned that the boat wouldn't be stopping at Cyprus as planned. It was a place I had wanted to see, but I supposed I'd be able to live without it.

The captain asked Abdul how he felt about going home, to which Abdul promptly replied, "I detest the idea."

"But why?" asked the captain. "Port Said is a lively place to live."

"It's backwards. I can't imagine living there again, now that I know what the civilized world is like." Earlier, at breakfast, I had learned Abdul had just finished four years of study abroad as a chemical engineer.

I asked him, "Where would you rather live?"

"America. You should know, you're from there. Compare it to what you've seen while you've been here. Where would *you* rather live?"

Positano leapt to mind, but to be honest, that seemed more of a place to live only for a while. The captain and I commiserated with Abdul until it was time for ship's work to be done, and Abdul and I retired to the deck. Up until the time we entered the Suez Canal and docked, Abdul begged for details of American life. Even without exaggerating, I couldn't help but make my home country sound like the most alluring place to settle down.

But my mind was elsewhere. I was about to set foot in Africa, alone, despite all the intimidating rumors I'd heard all my life.

As soon as I stepped off the boat I scanned the dock for a crane. Would they charge me double here, too, to unload my car? Not really. It turned out that the only charge would be time. When I found myself talking to the one person who knew what was going on, I was informed that because of an Egyptian law, my car wouldn't be released until the following day. I tried to explain that Dolly was more than a car, she was a faithful companion, and a bedroom, too!

My insistence caught some official's attention, and I was led by a firm grip to the customs offices. There I was questioned and intellectually examined for two hours. Over and over, around and around; "Are you French?"

"No."

"You are British, then?"

"No."

"What is your nationality?"

I had told them this enough times already, and they held my passport in their hands as evidence. "I'm American."

"But what is the nationality of the name 'Carr'?"

"American."

Over and over, around and around. Two solid hours of pointless aggravation before I was set free into Port Said.

I had no choice but to find a nearby hotel, which was fairly easy and painless. After I had settled in, I explored the docks, and discovered they only came alive when a tourist boat arrived. That could happen any time during the day or night; a ship comes in, the docks awake!

The following morning I strolled out from my hotel after breakfast, and there in a nearby cafe sat Abdul, from the boat. We shared coffee, and he offered to join me to retrieve my car. I readily agreed, because I imagine workmen respond best to those who are speaking their native language.

Back at the pier, I found that the aggravating fates of my landing in Port Said had not quite finished with me and my trusty car. The keys had been locked inside. Yes, back in Beirut, some genius had inspected the vehicle, and when he was finished, he had locked the door and closed it while the keys continued to dangle from the ignition.

Nowadays, no problem. A locksmith opens the door and bills the offending party. However, in the 1950s, automobile locksmiths were rare, especially in Port Said. If thieves had begun stealing cars back then, they probably just broke a window. To the best of my knowledge, no one had yet thought of tools like slim jims or enterprises like chop-shops.

While we sought a solution to the problem, Abdul kept me in good humor by delivering an ongoing commentary on the inefficiency of dock workers. "There," he said, pointing to an official who had appeared on the scene. "He has heard the story, and the first thing he'll do is—see? He checked to be sure both doors really are locked! Is he a fool, to think ten people haven't already tried both doors? Or is he more intelligent than most, suspecting the very real possibility that no one thought to pull the handle of the passenger side?"

Next: "Look there, the son of one of the workers. He's a small boy, surely he can squeeze his little arm up through the air vent to reach the keys!" I thought Abdul was joking, but of course he understood the language, and could hear the discussion between the workers. Sure enough, the tiny boy was hoisted onto the hood, the air vent was propped open, and he reached his little arm inside. Abdul chuckled. "If the arm is small enough for the vent, it will never be long enough to reach the keys!"

He had me laughing, too. "They need a college graduate to help them, Abdul. Won't you offer your assistance?"

The look in his eyes changed from mirth to disbelief. "You can't honestly think they would listen to me? I would have far too much information for them! My common sense would make their heads spin, and you would be waiting here for a week!"

I scratched my chin, where I had been growing a small, unintentional goatee-like beard. "Seriously, though. What do you think they need to do?"

"They must find someone who has both tools and a mechanical brain. Ah! The idea has just come to them." Sure enough, a man standing near Abdul and myself had jerked his head in our direction after Abdul's suggestion, then hurried over to pass the information on. A runner left, and within ten minutes, returned with a mechanic in tow.

It was frightening to watch him approach the door with the rusty tools of his trade, but within minutes, the keys were in my hand, and I was on my way.

The wise Abdul asked (possibly joking) if I was in the mood for a drive, but I was, if for no other reason than to get my auto-legs back. We visited Abdul's old school, a French Lycee, and he introduced me to one of the teachers. Although Abdul certainly had no idea of my religious upbringing, the woman he introduced me to was a French Jewess. While Abdul and his friend caught up on his adventures, her brother ('Uri'), entered her office. The resemblance between the two was strong; both had high cheekbones, strong noses, short, wavy, neatly combed dark hair, and liquid brown eyes that were accentuated, rather than hidden, by black-framed glasses.

After only fifteen minutes of conversation, Uri invited me to join him and both his sisters for dinner and bridge that evening. (Only bridge. I'm almost positive. Ironically, if there had been any side-bets in this situation, it would have been about a female winner.)

That female in question was the younger sister of the siblings I had met at the *lycee*. She was about my age and taught at the same school as her sister. Apparently, this girl had taken after a different member of the family, because although I'm sure she combed her hair as often as anybody, it never looked neat. It was much lighter than that of her brother and sister, too, plus she had a pointed chin and sweet little rosy cheeks.

No subterfuge would have been necessary, as this young woman (I'll call her Michelle) was quite likable. After dinner and bridge, she and I stayed up talking until 2:30 in the morning. Were our conversations about books, movies, plays? Food, friends, or travel? I don't remember, it has been more than fifty years, after all. We probably enthusiastically discussed every single thing that crossed our minds. Once in a while, one meets a person one can sit up with all night long, and that's what I had found in Michelle.

During our conversation, I learned that the mother of the family had died, but Michelle didn't go into detail. It seemed likely that it had something to do with the war between Israel and the Arab world. The father was a lawyer, and I could tell by the furnishings of the house that he had once been quite successful, but the war had affected his practice.

The outward, obvious suffering of international hostilities is so powerful that we sometimes forget all the blackened shards that strike the homes, families, and individuals who are reluctant bystanders.

After my late night, I slept in Dolly near a hotel, deeper into the town proper of Port Said. I woke later than usual, around 8:30 in the morning, and what a stunning awakening! People rushing all around me, to work or school or about their errands. It crossed my mind that only a stranger waking up in Rockefeller Plaza, downtown New York, would understand how this startled me.

I staggered out, rearranged my car's seating, and searched for a cafe that would serve coffee and juice. The place I found was filled with gossipy merchants; apparently this was their usual morning gathering spot. The topic was the British in Egypt. I would have thought no citizen would approve of foreigners wielding power in his country (even if the foreigners had saved that country from invaders), but surprisingly, many of the men in the cafe were pro-British. England was determined to improve Egyptian economy, and of course, merchants were benefitting most from the attempt.

While in that cafe, I learned more about what had been going on in Egypt, and it increased my surprise at the men who were accepting of their foreign rulers. Two years before, almost to the day, martial law had been declared in Egypt because of widespread riots against the Brits. There had been half-a-dozen more political upheavals throughout 1953, but the most significant was in the summer of that year, when the 5,000 year-old standard of Egyptian monarchy was ended and Egypt became a republic. What sort of 'republic' would allow so much foreign influence? The sort that happens to have a canal, worth billions in commerce, running through its land.

As many know, it was a French man who finally realized the vision of the Suez Canal in the 1800s. Ferdinand Lesseps also found the financing for the project, but as has often happened throughout international history, the actual work was performed by slave labor. In this case, it was the Egyptians who supplied that manpower. This valuable strip of passage became quite a point of contention between everyone in the Mediterranean neighborhood and beyond.

At the time I was in Egypt, the year 1954 had barely begun, and Nasser hadn't quite yet taken control of the government. However, he did already have a lot of power in the country, and he wanted the British—including their 80,000 troops stationed at a military base in Suez—out. More importantly, he wanted to reunite his people who, as I've shown earlier (remember the refugee camp situation), were adrift from their brothers. Nasser had grandiose ideas of creating an Arab bloc which, united against all foreign influence, could restore Arab dignity. In the society of mankind, the only way to achieve such lofty goals is with money, and Nasser knew it. He also knew the worth of the canal that ran through his country, and in 1956, he made that historical, questionable attempt at securing its resources. I can't help but think we—as in everyone outside the Middle East—are lucky that certain factions have never found any real cohesion.

After my coffee, I met my new Jewish friend Uri for lunch, his treat, bless his heart. Later he introduced me to more women; these were fellow employees at the Suez Canal office. Was the man trying to be some sort of matchmaker?

A small group of us took a walk on the beach, which was a sweet and simply pleasant diversion. We drove along the canal on the way back, and Uri warned me that at night, drivers were expected to blink their lights for the boats. I can't remember the exact reasoning behind it…. Perhaps the sailors needed to know whether they were approaching the shore, or another boat.

While I drove Uri back to his home, he invited me to dinner once again, this time mentioning it would be his family's meal for observation of the Sabbath.

I parked in front of his house. "That would be nice. I haven't celebrated the Sabbath in such a long time."

Uri had opened the car door, but now his hand dropped, and he peered closely at me. "You're Jewish!"

"Yes, I am."

He started to speak, stopped, then threw his back and laughed. "I suppose I can understand why you don't bring it up very often, around here! But why haven't you mentioned it to my family?"

"The subject never came up." It was true, too. Because I'm not a basically religious man, it really doesn't occur to me to say anything about the religion I was raised with. I've known plenty of people in my life who were raised Christian but never attended church as adults. If they entered a Christian home in some other part of the world, would they instantly start talking about their own religious upbringing? I honestly don't know.

Uri pulled off his glasses, pressed the edge of his hand against his eyes, put his glasses back on. He was all smiles. "Let me go see how much time we have. I'll be right back, I'd like to show you a club."

I sat smoking, considering all the girls he had introduced me to in a few short days. There had been suspicious thoughts roaming through my mind about our bridge game with his sisters the night before, but today, the women he had presented to me were decidedly not Jewish. It felt like a conspiracy to find me a wife, but for the fact that I didn't think Uri had a devious bone in his body.

When he rejoined me in the car, he said we had a few hours yet before sunset (the time of the meal), and directed me to Port Said. We parked in front of a small building, and he said, "This is a Jewish club."

It was a modest place, active and proud despite all the unrest that surrounded it. During the beginning of the Israeli war, the Arabs had tried to close the club but the owners were one step ahead. When the police arrived, they found the doors locked and chained, with a notice that said in Hebrew, Arabic, and English *Closed until further notice.* Once the tremulous truce was in place, the club had reopened.

There was a younger set of Jews there that Friday night, possibly because they weren't as strict about preparing for the Sabbath as others. Or maybe they didn't have wives who insisted they remembered to wash well, give charity, and be sure the candles were lit before sunset.

Two hours later, Uri and I were at his home again, sitting at a heavily laden table of food. We had returned in plenty of time to wash, and to get the candles lit, which signified the transition from secular to sacred time. (I can't help but wonder if I might have been the 'charity' the family was giving to?)

The father of the family said blessing over the *challah*, which is a sumptuous egg-twist bread, and passed the loaf around. Next was the wine blessing, and we each drank from the same cup. Then the feasting began.

For those who are curious, the Sabbath is actually a commandment. "Six days thou shalt do thy work, and on the seventh day thou shalt rest" (or some translate the last as, 'cease work'). Since the Sabbath doesn't begin until Friday night, the women of the house are able to spend the daytime working on the meal. They make plenty for leftovers, because Sabbath lasts until Saturday night, and there isn't supposed to be work going on in the kitchen on Saturday.

So what foods did we have? A roasted chicken, potatoes, carrots, and zucchini. Salad *cholent* (stew), and three loaves of bread. There were also two different types of *kugel*, which is a food that has been varied not only over the centuries, but also by different nationalities. One of the types served for my Egyptian Sabbath was a garlicky noodle casserole, the other also used noodles but a caramelized sugar was added, along with black pepper, and it was more of a noodle-custard dessert.

The father led the singing of the *Z'mirot* (Sabbath songs). I must say, it's a lot of fun to sing well-known songs with a group of people at the dining table. When we were finished eating, Uri led *Birkat Ha-mazon*, which is grace after the meal. Although I hadn't observed the Sabbath much in the States, I felt that I was in a real, honest-to-goodness home for the first time on my trip.

Drowsy, satisfied goodbyes were exchanged at about one in the morning, and I left for Dolly to sleep away the remainder of my last night in Port Said.

My rest was interrupted by the most disturbing experience.

In a pre-dawn darkness, I had a woozy sensation that I was back aboard the boat that had brought me to this port. Rocking, swaying…. By the time I came fully awake and remembered my surroundings, I found two Egyptian policemen rocking the car. They were like college boys looking for trouble; filled with alcohol, bouncing the vehicle on its springs, urging each other on, laughing at the man asleep in his car, probably inventing nefarious reasons for my presence.

I lay there clutching my sleeping bag up to my nose, peering out through slitted eyes, terrified. What were the odds that I would spend an evening with French Jews, even attend a Jewish club, then find the Arab police harassing me in my French car? All I could think was that despite the current issues with the British, the Egyptians couldn't have been very happy with the French, either. Those people had used Arabs who were reportedly slaves to build the canal, after all, which the French then controlled for 99 years.

Worse; I had the feeling that on first sight, if an Arab didn't think I was French, the next guess would be British. The truth that although I was neither, I did happen to be Jewish, didn't help matters. I'm sure I embodied, for those policemen, the three cultures they most despised.

Worst of all: These men were armed.

They staggered drunkenly to the front of the car and sat up on the hood to discuss their options, laughing meanly at each fresh idea. I couldn't understand their language, but it was easy to figure out what they were considering: One lifted both his hands as if hefting something heavy, then threw them upwards, showing the ease of flipping my little frog of a vehicle. The second man slid off the hood and stepped back to examine the situation; an inebriated engineer guessing at the logistics of his cohort's suggestion. With an uncertain shake of his head, he approached the (thankfully locked) driver's door, yanked at the handle to open it, then tried the passenger door. He attacked the handle with such violence that I made the mistake of sitting up, which alerted them to my consciousness.

The first cop leapt off the hood and excitedly swatted his

colleague's shoulder, pointing to my open eyes. They made ugly, teasing faces, leapt forth and back from the windows, and hefted their rifle butts as if they would crash through. The sweater my sister had knitted for me was sitting folded where I had left it on the driver's seat, and for some reason, I grabbed it and clutched it against my chest. This brought more laughter from the cops, then one of them flipped the rifle around and pointed it at my head. My breath stopped. He dramatically mimed pulling the trigger and the gun kicking his shoulder back, and I could hear him bellow through the glass: "Boom!"

The next sound I heard, as clearly as if it had come from outside of me, was the thump of my heart. It may as well have been the song of a finest opera, because it meant I was still alive.

Now that I was breathing again, I scanned what I could see of the town around me, craning my neck in every direction. Not another soul on the streets, and very few lights in distant windows. My only ray of hope was literal: A glimmer of the coming sun. I remembered the rush and crush of the morning crowds, and sent out a silent prayer that they would arrive soon, all at once, and save me with their distracted, disruptive presence. With eyes and spirit alone, I gathered all my focus and willed the muted, eastern horizon light to hurry.

Both policemen looked in the direction that had caught my attention, then turned back to me. They became quiet and serious, which was more frightening than any of their other antics.

A different sight appeared at that moment; headlights from a car that had just turned onto the road. All three of us stared at it, then two sets of dark and threatening eyes returned to me. The car slowed as it crept past, causing the policemen to shoulder their rifles and step away. Another car rounded the same corner; now the earliest workers of the city were awake and arriving on the scene.

After a few final gestures that I only understood to be nasty, my tormentors swaggered away. My first instinct was to curl back up into my womb-like sleeping bag, eyes clenched shut in the darkness. Lying there, I told myself it had been my decision to take this trip, to thumb my nose at my predictable society. With a renewed determination that I could deal with anything this trip threw at me,

I emerged from my sleeping bag, pulled off the unnecessary warmth of the sweater, and busily returned Dolly to her automobile status. On the road to Cairo, my new sense of purpose transformed my suffocating fear into an unpleasant memory.

It is my fervent wish that no decent, law-abiding, kind-hearted person should ever have to endure such terror at the hands of authorities. That it does happen, despite any of our wishes, breaks my heart.

* * *

As I drove through the bright day, I saw both British and Egyptian soldiers along the roads. It was obvious they were only interested in the canal and in one another, rather than a passing tourist. Besides, these men were sober and regulated by one another's presence.

The welcome sun shone on a tributary of the Nile on one side of the road, and on the other, the Suez Canal. The ships in the canal were easy to identify, and I logged them in my journal: One French, one German, one Greek, one Norwegian, and three British.

The Nile became increasingly wide as I neared Cairo, the color became more green, and the number of villages along the road multiplied dramatically. I noted in my journal that the people here obviously had a great dependency on the Nile. More from my entry that day:

> I did not feel a dominance of poverty and disease here, but only a way of life, so different from my own. This way of life was necessitated so much by its place of a river bordering a desert.

It was a life one could only truly know by living there, but it fascinated me to be driving through it.

The next place I entered was a sizable town called Ismailia, which had a park-like prettiness. While I rolled slowly through this oasis of palms, with boats in its waters, I was reminded of the pure lakes and rivers I'd often seen in upstate New York. Clear water and colorful flora, beckoning for a canoe ride or at least a quick dip. It gave me a moment of homesickness.

In Ismailia, I accidentally pulled right into the British Garrison.

It was a huge place, full of soldiers, trucks, and supplies of all kinds. I don't remember where I heard it, but in my journal I wrote that the Egyptians said the British had built themselves an entire underground city there. Or was it said the Egyptians had been the ones who built it? Whichever the case, I was never able to verify the claim.

Cairo came as a surprise, and by that I mean that I didn't see the city until I was right in it. With luck, I happened upon the principal road, which brought me to the center of that international metropolis.

I found a safe place for parking and sleeping outside the American Embassy, then wandered the streets. It was so much more modern than I had expected, with its contemporary traffic and magnificent buildings. Here is the description from my journal:

> Cairo has a sophisticated air, more so than many other cities I have visited. Its people speak a great deal of French, dress quite well, and have an air of knowing where they were going. The streets are wide and easy to drive, but heavy with traffic. There are still enough wagons and carts being drawn on the main streets to make you feel that much native color remains, and there are also plenty of beggars.

That night, I slept securely outside the American Embassy, and woke to another glorious day. I missed most of the sunshine, though, because I stopped to see the museum, and couldn't tear myself away. What a huge, well-designed, magnificent place! The Tut collection alone was enough to make the visit worthwhile. The preservation was amazing and the workmanship wondrous; mostly gold leaf covering wood, and stunning alabaster. I also enjoyed the collection of elaborate jewels mounted with very simple designs.

On my next morning in Cairo, I found my way to the Renault dealership, which also had a garage for upkeep and repairs. There, I was royally received by a young, extremely kind sales manager. I'll call him 'Salim.'

Salim was Lebanese, one of those dark, swarthy Arab men who probably had hair on most parts of his body. He carried himself with a particular grace, though, and spoke refined English. When I described the nature of my journey, he listened with enthusiastic attention, nodding agreeably at every fifth word I uttered. When I finished my thumbnail description, he warned me, "You'll need a companion with you as you continue across North Africa."

"Yes, that thought has been in my mind. I am due to meet a friend here in about a half-hour, but he can only ride with me for less than a week."

"If you'd like," Salim offered, "I'm sure I can find someone who needs to head all the way west. Someone who can probably share expenses, too."

It sounded like a blessing, and as things turned out, it was.

جمهورية مصر
القنصلية العامة ببيروت

تأشيرة ــ دخول ــ رقم 05918
مورود

اسم صاحب التأشيرة

مدة الاقامة بمصر

صلاحية التأشيرة

الرسم المحصل غ. لبناني

بيروت في

القنصل العام

الرسم المستوفى ٨٢٠ غ.ل.
Taxe Perçue 820 P.L.

21

14

From Cairo to the Back Roads of Africa

Rudy arrived at the dealership right on time, which says much for his character.

After I introduced him to Salim, Rudy asked me, "Have you found us a hotel?"

"Not yet—"

"Allow me to recommend one for you," Salim interrupted. He explained our various options, and soon we were checking in to a comfortable room nearby. As Rudy and I finished unpacking, Salim called us in the room and invited us to lunch at his home.

Before long, we were in his luxurious, terraced apartment, sipping drinks. We met his charming Lebanese mother, who spent a moment with a cocktail of her own, then went to the kitchen to instruct the servants on the preparation of our meal. Salim led us to his balcony, and needlessly, he pointed to the view. "Quite a sight, aren't they?"

There, out across the rooftops of the city, sat the immortal Pyramids of Giza.

In answer to Salim's question, I could only say, "Oh, yes." I couldn't take my eyes away from them. It was that same sensation one has when staring endlessly and mindlessly at a new baby; trying to absorb this miracle with one's eyes, when the true method of observation lay deeper than what vision can penetrate.

Rudy had seen the pyramids before, of course, because his 'overseas apartment' in Beirut wasn't so very far from them. Yet he, too, stared wordlessly for the longest time.

With a small, understanding smile, Salim said to me, "You must have already caught sight of them, Will, while you were driving through Cairo."

"I did, last night. They had been lit by moonlight, and seemed more like an artist's rendition of themselves. From here, they look so much bigger."

"Just wait until you're closer still!"

Salim's mother called that lunch was ready, and we retired to the dining room. 'Mrs. Salim' wouldn't be joining us, but she wished us *bon apetit* and left us alone. Two servants served the food, and once again, I reveled in the high life.

A typical Arab meal has strong European influences, but is flavored with their own exciting, exotic spices. In our lunch at Salim's, each dish tasted unique and different to me, yet I had the feeling a repeated variety of ingredients were simply used in different ways. Also, the presentation was as delightful as the flavors.

Two servants moved behind the three of us who were seated, arranging foods on our plates from carts behind them. Watching my raised-eyebrow interest, my host explained what was being laid before me.

"This is only the *mezze*—appetizers. First is some baked *kufta*, which is a spiced, minced meat."

The little perfect balls of *kufta* were placed so carefully on the edge of the plate that they didn't roll once.

"Next," said Salim, "is the falafel."

I was familiar with that, and explained to Rudy, "It's chick peas. They're ground and formed into patties, then deep-fried."

"Yes, I've had it before." I guess it made sense that he would have, living so near this area.

Salim tipped his chin toward the next addition. "Now there's the *jebne*, an especially delicious white cheese."

"What's this?" I held up a sprig of something I couldn't identify. "Garnish."

See? Presentation was an important aspect of this meal.

The servants expertly used a spoon to drop a creamy dab of something in the center of the now-full plate. I glanced curiously at Salim, and he said, "Yogurt."

"Ah." I had never tasted yogurt in my life. Unheard of these days, I know. Back then, American society wasn't so desperately seeking dietary dairy products.

The final touch on the hors d'oeuvres was to place a small bowl of tan-colored mash next to each plate, which Salim informed me

قنصلية الجمهورية السورية في استانبول
CONSULAT DE LA RÉPUBLIQUE SYRIENNE
ISTANBUL

VISA d'entrée ‎سمة دخول
de transit ‎مرور

رقم السمة ‎٢٥٦٨٨ رقم الجواز ‎٤٥٤٨٨

№ *9894* Date ‎٤/١١/١٩٥٧

Nom ‎الاسم وليم هنري كلي

Accompagné de ‎رفاق ‎معه

‎مدة العمل بالسمة ‎ثلاثة شهور قادمة

Durée de validité *Trois mois*

‎القنصل
LE CONSUL

was a dip for the thin bread that had been brought to the table. "The dip is called *humus*, and the bread is *marcook*."

Speaking playfully from the corner of his mouth, Rudy added, "*Humus* is also made with chick peas, but it tastes a lot different than the falafel."

Salim grinned. "Exactly correct."

The appetizers alone could have filled me, but luckily, they had been served in appropriately small portions.

Next came the main course: A chicken casserole seasoned with sumac, which was once again something I had never heard of at the time, but it's a ground powder from the cashew family. The dish was called *musakhan*, and green beans cooked in tomato sauce were served on the side. The flavor was interesting to me, and I asked Salim, "What is the name of this?"

"*Loubia*." He gestured toward the fresh dipping bowl that had replaced my humus. "And that is called *baba ghanoush*. It's made from char-grilled eggplant, olive oil, lemon juice, garlic puree, and *tahina*."

I took a taste. "Heavenly! But what's *tahina*?"

Once again, Rudy supplied the answer: "It's a sauce made from sesame seeds."

Who would have thought?

After such an extravagant meal, I expected coffee to be served next, but the servants brought out more food.

"Next," Salim said, "Is *fattoush*, our salad."

Salad after the meal? When in Cairo, do as they do, I supposed. I could see the ingredients of this salad for myself; cucumbers, tomatoes, and toasted croutons. I thought the little flecks of green might be parsley, but discovered it to be mint. I'm not sure how that sounds to the untested palate, but it tasted fabulous.

I was willing to accept a post-lunch salad, but it also came with a side of rice. Salim explained that it was a variation of *koshary*; rice with lentils, onions, chiles, and tomato paste.

Now I was thoroughly stuffed, but how could I resist dessert? It was called *kunafi*, and was made up of a long, thin pastry that had been stuffed with sweet white cheese and nuts, then coated with syrup. As I write this now, my mouth is watering, but I have no plans to return to the place where it can best be prepared and appreciated.

With pleasure and relief, we retired again to the balcony with small-but-powerful cups of coffee. I observed, "I can see why you need coffee this strong after that sort of meal. I feel like I could sleep for a week!"

"We don't always eat so richly," said Salim, "I called ahead and told Mother you were visiting. I wanted to make sure you had a true taste of Lebanese food." Although he must have seen the pyramids constantly, his eyes stayed on them, too, while he spoke. "We'll let our meal settle, and then I hope your energy will have returned enough to take a closer look at those." He gestured outward, and not one of us had to change the direction of our gaze to see what he indicated.

I could hardly wait.

The pyramids are, indeed, 'all they're cracked up to be.' True, at the time, I was seeing them after having experienced such ruins as the Parthenon, Delphi, Pompeii, and Baalbek. I might have felt a touch of the world-traveler's under-enthusiasm, but still. Awesome. And to be so close to them! The Sphinx was fascinating, too.

Once back in the city proper, I said my temporary goodbyes to Salim (I would be returning to retrieve a new passenger after Rudy's vacation time was up), and Rudy and I went off on our own.

Rudy, the airline purser, knew a lot of men around the world. As we drove away from Salim's apartment, he said, "After we freshen up at the hotel, a friend of mine is going to pick us up for dinner."

"How much time will we have before he arrives?"

"Plenty." That saucy grin. I truly enjoyed Rudy's company.

After love-making, showers, cigarettes and cocktails, it was late enough that my appetite had returned, and I was prepared for what more might come.

Rudy's friend was an older British man out of London, who retrieved us in a chauffeured limousine. I suspected he and Rudy had spent time between the sheets, in some near or distant past, but that night, the man seemed content with richly spoiling the both of us. Also, he might possibly have been showing off to some subtly observant contemporaries. He brought us to one of the finest restaurants in the city, where my taste buds were treated to more delights, this time with recognizable European cuisine.

In the morning, Rudy and I left for our trip to what was referred to as Upper Egypt. Back in the element I had become accustomed to, I drove down the Nile with my eyes wide open for sites of less usual qualities. The route didn't follow the great river very closely, which was mildly disappointing, but all the tiny villages we passed through still held my interest. Here's how I described it in my journal:

> There was dirt and dust everywhere, and we saw much poverty among the people. One wonders how they can remain healthy enough to live from day to day. They appear happy, though, and even joke with each other. It would be interesting to have the knowledge of the language, at least enough to be able to catch their sense of humor. For me to place myself in this environment would be impossible, but for them to place themselves in my environment would be likewise impossible.

Looking back, I'm proud of my younger self for recognizing that being an American didn't mean I had an 'upper hand' as much as it was a 'different hand' that had been dealt me. Yes, it is a nicer life to have plenty of food, cleanliness, and some wealth of possessions. But is it better that we send our children off to day-care and our parents to old folks' homes? That our foods are brutally packed in pens, picked unripe, packaged, preserved and genetically manipulated, rather than coaxed and nurtured from earth and animal?

I'm speaking of our present-day approach, of course, which is why it seemed especially insightful that I noted the parallels of our differences back then.

As Rudy and I drove a long, slow-moving road that day, we were stopped several times by soldiers who asked for identification and searched the car. Rudy pouted about the ongoing interruption of our forward motion, and his nerves occasionally failed him under so much scrutiny, but my spirits remained high. My artist's eye absorbed the shapes and colors of the people, their animals, the mud huts, the sky, and the palm trees. To safely follow the road in front of me was almost a frustrating distraction.

By the time we reached Asyut, my lover and traveling companion was exhausted. This was most decidedly not a mode of travel he preferred. As soon as we were settled into a hotel, Rudy pushed open the mosquito netting around the bed and gazed at the inviting mattress. Before I could speak, he fell across the bed, and mumbled something to the effect of, "Rest."

He 'rested' for the rest of the night, while I wandered around Asyut, and he wasn't out of bed until the next morning, when we were ready for the road to Luxor.

This time, we followed the Nile more closely and saw more of the life along it, which gave me a thrill. Rudy, on the other hand, was already becoming fed up with the roadway adventure. As we slowed for the first village we would pass on that leg of the trip, he grumbled, "Just wonderful. Another day of creeping through squalid villages."

The wind had been howling throughout the drive, but we preferred the windows down, or at least cracked, whenever we smoked. A few hours into this second day of the trip, Rudy lit up, but left his window closed tight. When I reached for the knob to let in air on my side, he said, "Don't you *dare*. If I have to listen to that wind one more minute, I'll start screaming myself!"

I turned my head away, as though admiring something off to my left; it sounded like his voice was becoming more feminine by the moment. If I didn't know better, I'd have thought his lisp was a natural affliction.

After smoking a while in silence, he tried cracking open Dolly's sunroof, only to irritably crank it closed again and crush out his cigarette in disgust. "I refuse to smoke dirt."

It was true; sand and dirt were trying to make their way into every single pore of our skin, and into every orifice, even when we were sealed inside the car.

By the time we arrived in Luxor, our faces, clothes, and baggage were coated with grit and grime. Rudy insisted we stay at the Savoy. In that fine hotel, we shared a long, cleansing soak, and I gently persuaded some sexual release from my bedraggled companion. Once he was satisfied (and had returned the favor), Rudy fell into bed again, but I made the following entry in my journal:

Now I know why that river is called 'Father,' for it lends its support to the entire population of Egypt. I stopped and encouraged a family to allow a photograph. From the beginning of the Nile, with those miles upon miles of vegetable gardens on the banks, to the cotton fields, sugar cane, and rock quarries, the Nile gives food, water, shelter, and industry to all who are near it. It has great width in certain parts and I never saw its color change from a deep, dark green. It had no transparency to it.

I sipped some wine and smoked a few cigarettes, then begged Rudy from the bed to accompany me on my wanderings through Luxor.

"Only," he said, "if we take the car."

The sandy wind hadn't abated much, so I agreed.

As we rolled through the streets, one thing I noticed was that although the women of the north wore only black, the further south we traveled, the more color had been adopted for clothing. There were also more shod feet, but shoes seemed the domain of men. Very few women wore them and I almost never saw them on any of the children. When I did happen across a family who all wore shoes, I asked that they allow me to take a picture with them.

The headgear varied considerably among the people of this region, and you could easily find seven men sitting in front of their mud brick huts, each with a different headdress. I suppose it had to be their answer to hairstyles. No matter how uniform a culture expects its people to be, individuality always seeps through.

The population was afraid of my car, and of cars in general, which I guessed was because they had seen it bring death to so much of their livestock. The most noticeable animals, though, were the camels. They were everywhere, and used for everything from plowing fields to carrying sugarcane, people, and even furniture.

We stopped at a cafe and I engaged an English speaking man in conversation. The first thing he said was, "You drive that car, but a camel would be better."

Who was I to argue with his reasoning? I said, "Probably less expensive, too."

"It would cost about the same."

Not literally true, but relatively so. Rudy whispered, "A camel is the Cadillac of these people."

I gave him a sideways glance, but couldn't help agreeing. In terms of economic position camels, when compared to donkeys, horses, and water buffalo, were the best of beasts. We left the cafe and I took a closer look at them as we carefully passed them by. Camels spit, and they were massive, dirty, dumb-looking animals. They fit right in with the muck that was everywhere. It crossed my mind that pigs would be in their element amid so much mud and dirt, but of course the Moslems wouldn't think of raising them for food.

The most industry we saw was a new canal being dug, with thousands of men carrying bundles of dirt, coming up over the hill, and throwing it to the side. I rolled to a stop, awed by the sight. How different could it have been from the days of the Pharaohs, when so many thousands of Jews were building the pyramids?

I said to Rudy, "I can't believe they're digging this gigantic canal all by hand!"

"I don't think they are. Didn't we pass a steam shovel a few kilometers back?"

As if on cue, a rumbling roar reached our ears, and we turned to see the giant shovel lumbering up the road behind us. It slowed, then with a number of jerks and twitches, came to a halt.

In a breathless voice, Rudy said, "Oh, lord, it's blocking our way back to the Savoy!"

I turned further in my seat to get a better appraisal of the situation. "I think we can still get by it."

Even as I spoke a car passed us, tried to edge around the monolithic machine, failed, reversed, and parked on the side of the road. The driver climbed out and lowered his head against the wind as he approached the men around the shovel, and a gesturing shouting match began.

A clutch at my shoulder spun me around. With a wild look in his eye, Rudy said, "I will simply *die* if we can't get back to the Savoy! Do you hear me? I'll *explode* with frustration! We'll be sitting here and suddenly, Kaboom! Shattered bits of me will be flung all over you, the inside of this car, and out through the air vents to the desert!"

Quickly, I turned the car around to gauge the possibility of our passage once again. "I really think we can squeak past it, Rudy." I ventured a peek back at him.

He folded his arms high on his chest, turned his head away with great drama, and refused to speak.

Slowly, I crept toward the steam shovel. The argument between the other automobile driver and the workers stopped as they watched my tiny car edge up to the side of the machine. A worker in front of me began waving me forward with both hands, watching the narrowing passway between the shovel on one side and the loose, dangerous embankment on the other.

Voila; we were clear. I patted Dolly's dashboard and thanked her kindly.

On our way back to the comfort of our hotel, Rudy's hand slid to my knee. "I could kiss you, and when the time is right, I will. I will kiss you in the most delectable places."

With a grin, I replied that I would return the favor, "Because you, my poor boy, are in need of my most rapt attentions."

That might have become the first time I would experience oral sex with a man, but it was not meant to be.

We parked in front of the Savoy—which in my journal I compared to hotels in Saratoga Springs, NY during my childhood—and Rudy stepped out of the car with an air of sexual confidence. He swept in through the doors (which were held open by doormen), striding with his head and shoulders held in such a way that there could have been a cape flowing out behind him. However, before he could pass the reception desk, the clerk called out to him. "Sir? Sir, you have a telegram."

Rudy froze, turned slowly, and together we approached the desk. Back in those years, telegrams always gave one pause, and in fact I think that might still be true today.

He opened the sheet and read aloud: "We regret to cut your vacation short, but it is requested you return to (his airline) the day after tomorrow." Not a direct quote, but that was the gist of it.

Rudy lowered the telegram. "Hell. This is just peachy." Suddenly he grasped my sleeve and pulled me toward our room. "We'd better hurry."

However, the mood had changed; I was still a 27 year-old man who had never experienced oral sex. In the room, we hurriedly rubbed one another to orgasm, then left to find a meal, and to see what more we could see in these lands with the truncated time Rudy had left.

Our first stop was the Temple to the God Amen in Karnak. In my journal, my comment that it was as spectacular as all the other ruins in Karnak, and that the size of everything was gross, like something Cecil B. DeMille would build for a set. Here is more of what I wrote about that excursion:

> There was no subtlety to these ruins. We were surrounded by columns bigger in width than anything I had ever seen, taller than anything I could remember, more numerous than I could count, and incredibly decorative. We had no guide, for reasons of economy, but what more could he have said than 'This or that is the biggest in all the world'? I am sure no temple has ever been built of equal size. The only photographs I took were of the smallest columns.

We also saw the Sacred Lake, the Granite *souks*, the broken, hollow obelisk, and the grand Entionie ports. The work on the stone was certainly plentiful. I enjoyed the design quality of the pictures covering the walls as a group. Then I wished we had a guide, after all, for the purpose of understanding the story being told by these pictures.

For me, the most interesting of the sites from my above list was the Sacred Lake. I've heard that all Egyptian temples have Sacred Lakes, but the biggest one is there in Karnak. The waters from the lake were used to perform the rituals, and images of the gods would be sent sailing across the lake on golden barges.

I eventually learned some of what a hieroglyph (possibly) said, specifically one of those in the Temple of Opet in Karnak. Reportedly, it showed a recitation by Osiris while she was in Thebes, standing over a Luxor sovereign, who was stretched out in his bed of… begetting. (That sounds so much more professional than to say 'The place where he specifically tried to make babies.') As is supposed by some translators, Osiris called the sovereign a king of powerful gods, and said he had received a god's gem. There was also some talk of protection, and something about two sisters, one of them protecting his limbs, while the other was 'invigorating his person' with two hands. I've added this information here to give an idea of the sort of things translators think were being etched in stone back then.

It began to get dark as we drove back to the hotel. During that drive, I witnessed one of the most astounding sunsets I have ever seen; the burning light dropped down over the Nile, strangely illuminating Thebes in the distance across the river. The city and the water changed colors in direct proportion to the changing of the sun's position. Most people on earth see plenty of sunsets, but only a few of those visions stay with us for the rest of our lives. For me, that was one of those times.

The following day, we visited the Queen Hatshepsut Temple, which is built right into a rock mountainside. Rudy had hired our hotel porter to arrange everything for us, including a guide, tickets, and a carriage to use all day. We took care of ourselves by making sure we brought cameras, lunch, and extra sweaters. The weather was quite cool in Luxor, especially at night.

The guide we'd been assigned was a charming man who spoke English with a decidedly British accent. He greeted us in the carriage, and we had a half-hour ride on a road leading through solid mountains of rocks. All along the way we could see dozens upon dozens of holes, which had been dug in hopes of finding more tombs.

Queen Hatshepsut's Temple is near the Valley of the Kings, and here's what I heard of that place: Over a period of about 500 years, the tombs of famous Egyptian pharaohs were buried there. Don't quote me on this, but I think there are 21 tombs altogether. The pyramids were too easy to rob, and most of us have heard the pharaohs believed the goods buried with them were imperative to their afterlife. Some creative soul decided looting would be more difficult if the tombs were built right into rock, hence the Valley of the Kings—and, of course, the one Queen and the only woman-pharaoh (she didn't quite make it into The Valley, but is nearby.)

Unfortunately, where there's a will there's a way, and the tombs were looted anyway. At least the gorgeous hieroglyphs and paintings are still there.

Before examining the tomb of the Queen, our first stop was at Seti I's death abode, which was the richest and largest of all. Here's what I wrote about it in my journal:

> As the tomb went deeper and deeper into the rock, we could see the walls covered with pictures that were still in excellent condition. The colors were quite strong and vivid. The guide explained everything to us in detail, how each drawing was part of a group that told a story about the King himself. We examined a place where thieves of bygone days had dug a hole through the rock to pilfer the tomb.

Cursed thieves! The only hope, I guess, is that they sold their booty to wealthy people who kept it intact, rather than melting down the metals and breaking the jewels out from their settings to sell for monetary value alone.

As soon as I began to wonder when we would see the Temple of Queen Hatshepsut, our guide drove us for another half-hour to the other side of the valley, facing the Nile. Here was the Queen's temple, which had been restored to a great extent by an American group working in the area. I can only imagine how much it has been improved by now, more than fifty years later.

Queen Hatshepsut was one of those women who stood up and took charge during a time when such actions by females were startling, to say the least. She was of royal blood, and married her half-brother, who I believe became Pharaoh during a normal course of events. However, when he died, her nephew was supposed to be next in line, but Queen Hatshepsut stepped in and said, to the effect of, "No, *I'm* going to be Pharaoh, now."

According to educated rumor, she announced that a god had spoken with her, and had concluded the conversation by saying, "Welcome my sweet daughter, my favorite, the King of Upper and Lower Egypt, Hatshepsut. Thou art the King, taking possession of the Two Lands."

Because she was called, at the time, 'King,' she dressed in kingly garb and even wore a false beard. Egypt prospered during her reign, which lasted twenty years. She expanded trading relations, and it's thought she's the one who found the best sources of such bounties as gold, aromatic resins, blackwood, ivory and ebony.

The ego of her nephew won out, though, in the end. Thutmose III (the nephew) did whatever was necessary to take his 'rightful' place as Pharaoh, though no one knows how. All that's known is Hatshepsut died, and the moment she was gone, Thutmose III had her name removed from all the monuments and from the King's List, too. In my opinion we, as a society, are lucky he didn't succeed in eliminating every last trace of this great, audacious queen.

One final note, which touched me: Near the entrance of her tomb there are some old stumps of trees which were reportedly planted by Queen Hatshepsut herself.

Now, I'll transcribe the remainder of our tour from my journal, because it says it all in a nutshell:

> Next we visited the tomb of Ramses II and III, which were extremely well preserved. They were grand and full of courts; one for the people, one for the priests, one for the nobles, and one for the King and Queen. In the carvings on the wall, which were all in relief, the name of Ramses was always carved deeper and heavier than the rest.
>
> Our day of touring ended with a visit to two columns that were the only remains of the temple of Amenhoteps. Two collosi were the entrance to the Temple, but they are often almost wholly covered by water during the season of the Nile floods.

The day was over, and with it, the curtain began to close on my relationship with my dear (though occasionally bitchy, in his own amusing way) Rudy. We exchanged addresses, but never did write to each other.

I re-entered the Savoy to see if I could find information about a local mechanic for my car. Standing at the reception desk, a thought struck me: Is it possible that Rudy had arranged to receive that telegram the day before we had arrived in Luxor, while I was exploring Asyut, and he was supposedly sleeping? Yes, I supposed it was possible. Yet, if that's what had truly happened, the result was acceptable to me. My feelings weren't hurt by continuing on without a cranky, complaining passenger, and he with his lofty disposition would no longer need to endure any more of my rugged adventures.

However, I still had concerns about traveling through the current unrest in Northern Africa by myself, and I began making plans to get back to Cairo. Salim had promised that by the time of my return, he would have located a perfect new traveling companion for me.

After I found out about a mechanic, I used the telephone to call Salim. "Yes," he told me, "I have just the fellow. He needs to get to Oran. When will you be here?"

"I plan to leave first thing in the morning, and should make it by nightfall."

"I'll look forward to seeing you then."

"The day after would be better. I'll probably be tired and find a place to park and sleep the night I arrive."

"Are you sure? I could easily find a comfortable bed for you."

"No, thank you. Really, I'll be fine." Salim had been so generous to me already, throughout our brief acquaintance, and I didn't want to impose. "I'll find you at the agency day after tomorrow."

"We're set, then. I can introduce you to Kassim that evening."

As things turned out, Salim might have worried about me, because I didn't make it to Cairo at all the next evening. Instead, I ended up deep in the Egyptian desert, surrounded by suspicious, weapon-toting Arabs.

I woke and left Luxor by 7 a.m. the next day. I looked forward to being back in the relative safety of Cairo that night, because the long trip back to that city made me nervous. Despite my French car and a piece of paper that said I was a Christian, my life would be in danger if my Jewish roots were somehow uncovered. It didn't help to be a traveling tourist, either, who looked so wealthy in his contemporary car, rumbling past all the impoverished villages. Also of concern was the fact that the very day before my solo trip, the aforementioned 'contemporary car' had stubbornly refused to start.

However, the largest concern was a detour. Rudy and I had been forced to take it when we left Cairo, as we were heading southward, some days before. After we had arrived at the Savoy in Luxor, and the concierge learned of the route we had taken, he had asked if the detour near Cairo was still in place. When I told him it was, he had said, "I wonder if they'll ever finish the work, it has been many months!" Shaking his head with disgust at the slowness of roadwork—it happens everywhere in the world, doesn't it?—he said, "It will probably take them another year."

I had responded, at that time, "I guess we'll be going through it again, then, because we'll be headed back the same way at the end of the week."

"Oh," the concierge had warned, "then leave early on your day of departure, or stop for the night in Asyut, and leave from there. You must be certain not to pass through the area of that detour at night. It would be very dangerous for travelers."

I made excellent time during the first leg of my trip, and was passing through Asyut again by about 1:30 p.m. I gassed up, and the garage attendant brought me coffee while he tested the pressure in my tires, rechecked the fluids in my engine, etc. As I sat on a bench outside the garage, sipping the coffee and snacking on oranges and tomatoes, a young Egyptian man sat next to me. He gestured toward the Renault and asked me a question in his own language, but I replied in English, "I'm sorry, I don't understand."

"*Francais?*" he asked.

"*En peu*," I replied; 'a little.'

"*Moi aussi* (me too)." He held his forefinger and thumb about a half-inch apart. "*En peu francais. Anglais—non.*"

We proceeded to make do with our collective smattering of French, during which he asked if the Renault inside the garage was mine, and I admitted it was. When I retrieved my book of maps and showed him my route, he smiled with interest and made it clear to me that he was intrigued and impressed. He then found ways to tell me he was on a two-week vacation, and was headed home to visit his family in Cairo.

It was obvious he wanted a ride.

I was more than happy to have a traveler with me, someone who knew the roads, because it would be dark long before I would enter Cairo. Finding one's way through the blind-like desert darkness, alone, wasn't a pleasant thought. Especially because I knew there would most likely be that detour to contend with.

My new friend, who I'll call Akron, tossed his cloth travel-bag into the back of my car, and we were off.

We both improved our French some, as the hours passed, and learned a little more of each other. Akron worked at a school in Asyut as a gym teacher.

We stopped every hour or so, either for a short rest, or because Akron wanted to find little treats for his family. He bought cigarettes, chocolate, oranges, even a dozen pieces of sugar cane. He offered me a piece of the cane, and here is how I described it in my journal:

> If not for him, I would never have known exactly how one eats sugar cane. All the natives chew on it all day long, and I think that is one reason for their excellent teeth. To me, their eyes always looked sick, but their teeth were white and strong looking. I think mine were too, after I finished with that sugar cane.

Akron's eyes did have that unwell smokiness behind their dark color, but his teeth were, indeed, gleamingly white. He smiled often, too, which accentuated the effect. That smile might have been one of the reasons my confidence in his directions grew stronger and stronger.

By the time we neared the detour that so concerned me, the sun was sinking low in the sky. I couldn't tell if Akron knew anything about the roadwork, but it had been a while since he'd visited his home. While I concentrated on every distant speck in the road for the temporary redirection sign I knew must be coming, I tried to explain the Savoy concierge's warnings about the dangers of the area at night. With each turnoff we passed, I pointed and asked Akron, "*Ici*?" ("Here?") He kept looking at me like I was off my rocker, and continued to wave us forward, toward Cairo.

For all I knew, he was completely up-to-date about the road work, and had heard it was completed during the week I'd been away. But no; we came to a barricade, and my stomach spun with nervousness as I noted that the sun had now dropped below the horizon. I looked back over my shoulder, wondering where we had missed the turnoff, and how far we would have to backtrack before driving through dangerous back roads at night.

Akron gave my arm a reassuring squeeze, and with his endless supply of confidence, he engaged in a pleasant conversation with the guards at the barricade. Soon, he passed the man a small clutch of bills, and we were passed through. A premature sense of confidence flooded me. This native hitchhiker would easily pass us through this red tape of black tarmac! In my journal, I speculated that the entire road-improvement project might have been nothing more than an Egyptian racket.

Wrong. We might have driven twenty miles before we came to the end of the line. Full darkness had descended, and my headlights showed great slabs of sandy asphalt chunks that had been pushed up from the earth, tossed and toppled like new ruins being formed, completely impassable. I slowly swung the car in an arc, looking for an alternate route. The only meager possibility was to our left, a flat path through the sand that veered off and away, looking like a long, hard washboard. Akron grinned sheepishly and pointed in that direction.

In French, I asked him, "Do you know where that goes?"

"Oh, yes, yes! You see the many…" He waved his hand to indicate the washboard effect. "This means it is used much. I have family who live this way."

"You have family down this road?" What a coincidence. " *This* particular road?"

Akron was nodding his head and waving his hands forward, exuding assurance like an odor.

"Well, okay." I began trundling over the constant, teeth-rattling ridges, driving slowly, peering into the tar-black night beyond the headlights. For obvious reasons, it wasn't necessary to check my speed, but when my eyes did glance toward my dashboard, I slowed to a stop.

Akron asked, "What is it?"

I tapped my oil gauge. "We're low on oil."

My traveling companion's brow furrowed, and he stroked his chin with some concern. For a man who I assumed had been born with 'Be-positive' blood, this struck me as a sudden attack of nail-biting fear. The smile came again, though, and he clicked his fingers. "Benzine!" He pointed forward again.

If I wasn't so worried, I would have laughed. Did he mean to tell me there would be a benzine station along what looked like a camel path?

What else could I do? I accelerated again. Sure enough, distant lights appeared, and ten minutes later, we were parked in a tiny but reassuring garage. They not only had benzine, which I used to gas up, but also oil, which saved Dolly's poor, determined engine. My faith in Akron had been restored. I can't imagine how I would have fared without him, that night.

But the night was not yet over.

The condition of the road after the benzine station improved, which further lifted my mood. I was able to increase my speed, but soon found that only hurried us to yet another detour. This one looked military, but Akron's confidence was catching, and I calmly waited while he spoke to the guards and stroked their palms with alms.

He climbed back into the car and indicated that we take another left, away from the detour. My sense of direction, which is negligible at best, had completely abandoned me. "You really think that road is going to take us to Cairo?"

My question had popped out in English; I was getting tired. I couldn't wait to find a hotel and make myself comfortable. Yes, I was so bloody bushed that I would forego the work of transforming Dolly the car to Hotel Renault, despite the increasingly worrisome state of my finances.

From my English-phrased question, the only word Akron had understood was 'Cairo,' and he shook his head. "Tonight," he said in French, "we stay with my uncle. We will then find our way to Cairo with ease, at morning's first light."

Hmm.

He hadn't done me wrong yet, so I followed his directions. Along the way, I learned that his uncle was a peasant, but respected in his small village. "*Mon oncle*," Akron insisted, would have no problem with the idea of putting up his nephew and his American tourist friend for the night. "He will provide us with dinner, too. You will see, he is a good uncle."

A good uncle, maybe, but would he be a good host to a man like me?

The thought, however, of entering into the private corners of one of these villages, of actually spending the night in one of the huts I'd been so curious about, intrigued and excited me. I decided, "Oh, what the hell, you're only here once." ('Here,' as in Africa, or 'here,' as in life—with either concept, the statement stood true.)

Although we were deep in the desert now, our new direction led to a smooth path, then to the village, and the house of Akron's uncle. The darkness was complete; when I coasted to a stop, I saw nothing but what my headlights were able to reveal.

Here are my first impressions, as I wrote them in my journal:

> Eyes seemed to glow in the darkness when this strange mechanical monster of mine broke the stillness of the village night to awaken all curious inhabitants. As if from nowhere, my friend's uncle came out and embraced him, then what was obviously a barrage of questions flowed from uncle to nephew. I could guess at the nature of the questions: What was this American like? What can he give me? What will the village think? Uncle glanced at me often, through those unhealthy eyes, which were filled with uncertainty.

The man's home looked better than most I had seen on my travels, for it was quite large, and it even had a porch. I locked up the car and was led inside, directly into the living room. The furniture I was able to see by the kerosene lamp was mostly couches, plenty of them for sitting or sleeping, lining all the walls.

Despite all those couches, I was seated on a lonely chair in the center of the room, and a lantern was placed on a table next to me. While Akron made the proper introductions, a younger man silently slipped in and stood near the door, then another man followed him, and another after that. Soon there must have been at least 20 men in the room. About half of them had guns in crude hip-holsters, or rifles slung over their shoulders, or what I found most intimidating: swords. Some of these men wore expressions of guarded hostility, but many smiled, albeit suspiciously.

Uncle occasionally tossed a word or two toward the group, in syllables that seemed reassuring, but I could tell wariness was the mood of the moment.

While Akron continued to translate the polite questions and answers between myself and his uncle, one of the men responded to a scratching at the door, and children began shyly joining us. Their presence was a relief. With my seat and the light at my elbow, I'd been feeling like I was at an inquisition disguised as a friendly exchange of cultural information.

The presence of the children had no effect on the others in the room. An older man abruptly stepped closer, peered at me, and posed a blunt question in his own language. Akron gave a slight shake of his head, but the question came again, this time with more force. Another man stepped forward with an attitude of insistence that the question be translated for me. This younger fellow was one of those with a sword sheathed at his hip, and he hovered protectively just behind the older man.

Smiling indulgently, Akron turned to me and said, "He wants to know if you would take a gun to another member of our family, who lives between here and Cairo."

Oh, no, I thought not! Aside from all the obvious reasons that I would refuse to engage in such an errand, it also struck me that of everything these impoverished people needed, how could they place a gun at the top of the list?

I returned Akron's smile as best as I could and said, in fast French, "I can't imagine that would be possible."

Akron chose his own words, and many of them, to give my response to the man who had posed the question. A deep silence fell, and during the long moment while it stretched taut, I imagined every sort of reaction. That I would be kidnapped, or tossed out the door, my keys jerked from my pocket, and my car driven away without me. That I would be brought to a back room and held down with a pillow over my face until I stopped kicking. That the men surrounding me would filet me with their long blades, or ready their weapons and shoot on a single command, firing-squad style.

The last thing I expected was that the entire group would burst into laughter.

Not only was I physically fatigued from all the driving I'd done that day, but my nerves and imagination had depleted me. I smiled weakly at the laughter and questioned Akron with my eyes.

He explained; "I told them you would be so afraid, every official who passed you would instantly know you were carrying a weapon. Three or four seconds before they began a polite interrogation, you would tell them exactly where it had come from."

At least, that's how I think his French could have been translated. If so, he had pretty much hit the nail on the head.

Fortunately, the tension had broken, and all the children, along with half the men, filed out of the room. A few of the remaining men dragged a larger table over in front of me and set more chairs around it. A veiled woman with eyes that avoided me entered, carrying a large, deep plate, more like a shallow bowl with a drain in the middle. She set it on the table and darted away, only to return with a water jug and a block of rough soap. When she was gone again, I looked at my host, who gestured toward the jug and soap. I knew I was meant to wash without wasting any of the precious water, and I did my best. The mood of humor had been set, though, and I heard constant chuckles around me as I tried to delicately bathe beneath a dozen eyes.

When I finished, Akron and Uncle also washed, along with a few of the older men in the room. When I saw their practiced techniques, I could see why my personal ministrations would have struck them as amusing. Different lands, different washing of hands.

While Uncle finished his ablutions, he asked a question of me, through Akron, in a newly polite voice. Akron translated, "He wishes to know if you will take him to America with you."

Now, how does a person answer a question like that? My first instinct was to say, 'Why, of course! Meet me in France, and we'll board my return ship together.' My second thought was, 'Who do you think I am, the ambassador of emigration?' What I said was, "I wish I could, but it isn't in my power. However, as I continue my travels, I will see what I can find out about him making the trip." Anything to move to the next topic, and the next, until they ran out, and would let me sleep! I had become weary to the point of distraction.

The older gentleman who had asked about gun-transportation, still attended by the constantly serious, glaring-eyed younger man, spoke directly to me again. What he said sounded roughly like, "Umbruk mrk lnku."

I looked at my translator, but Akron only waited, smiling.

The older man said the three words again, then held out his hand as though I should respond. Or, (my beleaguered brain lit with the glow of a weak, fluttering lantern), not respond, but repeat? I said the words back to him, and they fell about themselves with laughter again. All of them, I should say, except the guardian-type companion, who I never once caught cracking a smile. In any case, I don't know what I said, but I believe they were simply testing my ability with their language.

The frowning young man stepped up to the small bag of clothing I had brought in from my car. He grasped the hilt of his sword, but only nudged my bag with the edge of his foot. His eyes stayed carefully on mine as he tapped my property, much like a challenge. I immediately opened the bag and showed them my clothing, including a beret I had been carrying (and occasionally wearing) since France. Uncle wanted to try on the beret, and I handed it to him. The resulting dark, brooding Parisian brought forth more smiles and laughter.

The front door opened again; the woman had returned a final time with a meal. My hunger, which had until the moment been overshadowed by fatigue and fear, leapt forth. Huge, round pieces of Arab bread were placed before us at the table, along with a number of hard-boiled eggs, and a plate which appeared to be filled with hot melted butter. Before I could look foolish again, Akron broke off some bread, folded a piece of egg into it, and dipped the small Arab burrito into the hot buttery sauce. I did not—couldn't—hesitate, and followed suit.

Anybody who has ever been on a long day-trip, which also happens to end in a late night among strangers, knows how tiring those final hours before sleep can be. Then, as soon as food hits the stomach, it becomes almost impossible to keep one's eyes open. It took all my strength to stop from dozing off while everyone else who was eating finished.

Sadly, my hosts were not yet ready to turn in. For them, I was an amusing diversion from what I imagined was a difficult daily routine. Akron, who had been my comfortable passenger, and riding with me during only half the long drive, also seemed ready for a long night's party. He knew one song in English, 'Tea for Two,' and told me he loved it, couldn't hear it enough. We heard it enough times, from him, as he sat back with his full belly and launched into a repetitive, broken-record version of the song. Uncle and his compatriots excused themselves, stepped to a corner of the room, and entered into a long conversation.

The tones of their words lifted and dropped, grew charged and calmed, hardened and softened. The guardian of the elder gentleman had much to contribute to the discussion, and kept looking at me. Once, when an obvious argument broke out, that angry young man pulled his sword partway out of his hilt, then thrust it angrily back in.

I tried to keep a smile on my face as I hummed and nodded along with Akron, pretending to ignore the group in the corner. In my peripheral vision, they looked like something out of a Hollywood movie: The stage was set in the dark, Arabic hut, the rough-looking cast was clad in appropriately bedraggled clothes, and the only man who continued to carry his (rather archaic) weapon had not once lost his ferocious expression.

My brain sagged along with my body, my exhaustion was so complete. My body did remain in an acceptably seated position, though, and my brain couldn't help but feed me more frightening fantasies after the men in the corner evidently came to an agreement about me.

Uncle came back to the table and had Akron translate: "There is not enough room for us to sleep here, but another uncle, who lives only a small distance further into the desert, has a bed for us."

By sheer force of will, I did not look at the five or so couches that lined the walls of this huge room. I stood and shook hands all around, but after Uncle released my grasp, he indicated I gather my clothing bag and follow him. He stopped at the door and accepted a gun from a man who waited there, then we all stepped outside. Uncle gestured that I get into my car and drive. Before Akron could take the passenger side, the scowling guardian climbed in to share the back seat with my belongings, and his sword.

In my mind, I uttered two words I had often heard from my grandmother Bubbie: "Oy vey."

Uncle, along with several grinning men who had appeared out of the deep darkness, began to walk along what they must have known to be a road. I certainly wasn't able to make one out. Slowly, I followed them, listening half-heartedly to Akron's friendly urgings interrupting his endless, relentless rendition of 'Tea for Two.'

I don't know how long I rolled along behind the troop. More than a few times, they stopped, walked around behind us to push my struggling Dolly through the deep sand.

There was no choice: I had to completely rely on these people. Even if I wanted to, I couldn't have turned back, because if I had, I would still be wandering today, lost in that desert. If, that is, I had survived the night. It crossed my mind to ask Akron if we couldn't just turn around and keep trying for Cairo, but it struck me that the suggestion would show fear or insult, and that could have been a large mistake.

When we reached what felt to be the exact center of absolutely nowhere, my lights fell upon a mud hut with a large barn behind it. Akron said, "*Mon otre oncle*!" and leapt out to embrace his 'other uncle.'

I simply sat there idling. I was too weak, tired, and afraid to climb out of my car. 'What do they want?' I thought. 'Is it me, my car, the contents of my car, or the whole package?'

Other Uncle showed me where to park, I complied, and shut off the lights to blindness. In those dark moments, I made sure I had stuffed my pockets with my money, papers, and passport, but what could it matter whether they were taken from my car or my lifeless person?

The dim light of the lantern grew stronger as my eyes adjusted, and I stepped out with my small bag of clothes. Original Uncle said good night and left with most of his companions, then Akron and I were led into the barn. We passed farm animals I could only smell and hear, mounted some stairs, and entered a large-ish room which had some chairs, a stove, and an old mattress in the corner. Other

Uncle held the light higher, proud of his guest accommodations. Now, I could see the bed was crawling with insects, chickens, two cats, and a dog. Other Uncle shooed away all the creatures that would obey him, took my bag from my hand, and tossed it on the bed.

When he turned around, swinging the lantern with him, I could see more people stepping up into the room from the stairs. I could have cried. What could they possibly want with me, and when would they let me sleep or die? I was prepared to accept either option, and the relief that would ensue.

Perhaps the new crowd sensed my submissive weariness, because their handshakes were warmer and friendlier. I'm sure it was quite unusual for a foreigner to be brought this far into their private world, and they struck me as kindly curious.

Unfortunately, the guardian with his sword had entered the room, too. He never took his narrowed eyes off of me, and his hand twitched against the hilt of his weapon all too often. I looked for Akron, and found he was in a chair, patting the seat next to him for me. A greedy sort of glimmer had begun to shine in his eyes, and I could only think, 'Everything you take from me now will be most of what I have in this world.'

I collapsed into the chair, and strong tea was prepared on the stove in the room. By now my nervousness had blossomed into full-blown paranoia, and when a cup of the hot brew was handed to me, I immediately offered it to Akron. He accepted without hesitation and drank deeply. That convinced me they hadn't tried to slip me a mickey, and now I must drink from the next cup that was handed to me—probably about 80% caffeine. I supposed I would need it, because lively conversations were bubbling along around me. Other Uncle was especially verbose; people from the group would often interrupt, but I could tell he always shut them down with his own position on each topic. For such a poor man, he certainly seemed richly opinionated.

A good-sized mat was drug in and placed near the stove. Five men had seated themselves there, and the one nearest to me was loll-eyed, his lower lip sagged, and his expression looked empty but for a childlike happiness at my presence. He proceeded to speak to me at length, as though I could understand everything he said. Akron interrupted him a few times, obviously telling him I couldn't converse in their language, but the man babbled on. At one point, he shifted his weight and lifted his right arm to show me that it ended at the wrist. Akron translated, "A camel bit off his hand. Cousin is telling you the camel was hungry, but I think he was trying to get fresh with the beast."

At least, I think that's what Akron said, in French. My ability with that language was somewhat limited, and my mind was in a caffeine-buzzed fog of nervous exhaustion.

Other Uncle suddenly pulled the cousin up off the mat and shooed him out of the room, giving him some sort of order. I prayed he was telling him his guests needed sleep, but worried that he was sending him off for more members of the family.

It turned out to be the latter (what a groan cut loose in my gut!) although at least the babbling Cousin didn't return with them. For a long while, Akron became involved in all the conversations, and I was left alone with my thoughts.

I couldn't decide if I was more bothered by the concern that I would never see the light of day, or that the men around me would never, ever leave. It was a miserable sensation. While Akron became engaged in what sounded like an argument, I dreaded each approaching minute that would draw me closer to the night's conclusion. Would they rob me or harm me while I slept, or not let me sleep at all?

Akron suddenly concluded his discussion and turned to me with a smile. "Are you enjoying your visit?"

"Yes, thank you, but I feel like I could sleep for a week."

That greedy look flashed through Akron's eyes again. "These men need to be awake at five o'clock in the morning to work in their fields. They, too, need sleep."

"There are fields out here?"

"Yes, and it is difficult to work them. Everyone must leave us, now." With an enigmatic smile, he turned to the group and spoke to them as one. They all began pushing themselves to their feet, and each shook my hand, said a polite goodbye. All except the armed guardian, who waited until last to leave. He gave Akron a significant stare, then for me, a threatening glare. Akron made a short, friendly, dismissive comment, and the swordsman disappeared down the dark steps of the exit.

At last. I fell into the bed. The bugs could have their way with me. The men below could empty my car and strip it of every useable part. If I were killed before I awoke, I would die happy for the final rest.

Akron climbed in next to me, and slid his hand down to my groin.

In my mind, exclamation points battled with question marks. I'd had no idea! Because I was so young, and new to sex, I did feel a reaction begin, but did Akron bring me to orgasm? I have no idea. I fell asleep.

Once during the night, the sound of steps on the stairs woke me. Whoever it was curled up on the mat near the bed, and Akron left to join the person there. The thought crossed my mind that the mat might have less bedbugs, and that there was probably room enough for me, too, but before I could act on any such thoughts, I was out cold again.

I woke at dawn to an empty room. My youth had gathered a surprising amount of refreshment from what was probably five hours of sleep; three seconds might have passed between the time of my awareness and my leap up from the bed. I quickly tore off my clothes and shook them free of bugs, pulled my pants back on, and struggled into a fresh shirt before I descended the stairs.

Dolly sat patiently, full of my belongings, in the exact place I had parked her the night before. I stroked her fender as I passed her, heading toward voices coming from the mud hut.

Akron emerged with a cup of tea, saw me, and wished me a good morning. The morning did feel especially fine to me; the early desert sun was warm and promising, and my mind, body, and possessions were intact. I said, "What a beautiful day! How far are we from Cairo?"

"No more than two hours." Akron handed me the tea, and gestured that I follow him inside the hut.

A wash basin, similar to the one I had used the night before, was sitting on a table. I used it more adeptly, this time, to the admiration of Akron and the four other men in the hut.

Akron asked me to be seated, and one of the other men left. He returned soon, smiling, with a huge bowl of rice that had a whole cooked chicken balanced on top. My smile faltered. Roast chicken and rice for breakfast?

My friend dug in and gestured that I do the same. I complied, having no doubt that this was a generous offering. The sun had barely risen, these people only had cheap woodstoves for cooking, and I imagined a poor peasant woman had probably been up half the night cooking. Also, an entire chicken was probably not disposed of lightly. I did my best with the meal, then wished I had been more sparing, because they insisted I take more and wouldn't take no for an answer. I forced down a few more mouthfuls of rice, but asked Akron to tell them I had feasted well throughout the day before, and felt no more hunger.

As soon as he translated, the other four men in the hut fell on the bowl gleefully and ravenously. I was glad that I hadn't been hungrier, because it never occurred to me that those men hadn't yet had their own breakfast. My suspicions about the treat of chicken was confirmed when I watched them savor it like it was the finest cut of filet mignon.

Akron and I wandered out into the steadily increasing warmth of the day, and I saw the armed guardian from the night before leaning against the side of the barn, glowering at me. I wished I could artistically capture his face, and in fact retrieved my camera from the car, but when I turned, I saw Akron had walked away, and was approaching the man. Together they entered into the barn.

Aha! If only I could have explained to the sourpuss that I never had any designs on his lover!

The other men emerged from the hut, finished breakfasting, and by that time, Other Uncle had come back from where he must have been taking a first look at his fields. More men gathered around me, gesturing with smiling interest at the camera in my hand. While Akron and his sword-toting friend finished their business in the barn, I took as many pictures as were requested of me.

A squawk of chickens burst from the barn when the guardian strode out and quickly away. As I followed him with my eyes, I caught sight of a cluster of women peering curiously out from behind the hut. When Akron appeared, I asked if I could have a few photos of them, too. Aside from the lady who had brought us a meal the night before, these were the first women I had seen throughout my visit in that strange part of the desert. Akron convinced his extended family that photographs would be acceptable. The women were coaxed out of hiding, and lost their fear in order to properly pose for me. For reasons I may never understand, they were even allowed to lower their veils.

Finally, Akron and I were ready to leave. Other Uncle stood next to the car as I tucked my camera back into place, and when I straightened, he spoke politely to me for a minute or two. When he finished, he turned to Akron, who translated (to the best of my French), this: "We were much pleased to have you visit us here in our humble home. You have shared a bed with my nephew, and now you are brothers, and comrades. Should you ever pass this way again, you are welcome here, and we would be happy to see you."

Ah, perceptive hindsight. All the rumors and guesses that had been made in my country about these desert people had filled me with anxiety throughout a night I might have thoroughly enjoyed. I was tempted to embrace Other Uncle, but had no idea if it would be appropriate. Instead, I shook his hand and threw in a little bow, then climbed into my car.

An hour and a half later, I dropped Akron at his immediate family's home, which was right outside of Cairo. The house was clean and well-furnished, they even had a servant. My temporary friend did hug me before we parted, and we promised to write to one another.

We never did correspond, but Akron, I'm writing to you now: Thank you for sharing a day—and night—of your unique life with me.

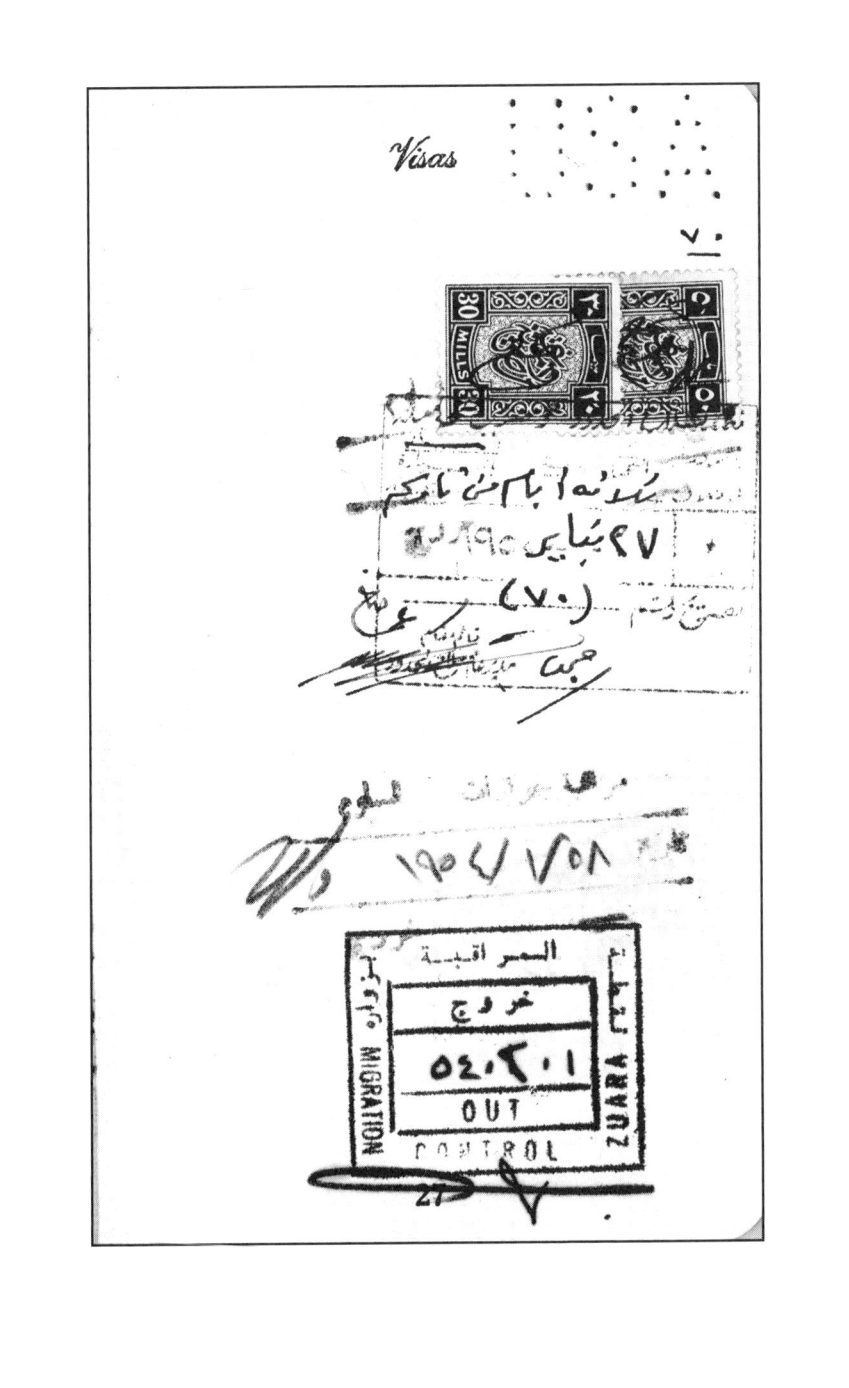

٧٠

٠ مشيرة أباظة تاركة
٢٧ يناير ١٩٥٥

(٧٠)

١٩٥٤/٧/٥٨

المراقبة
خروج
٠١٢٠٦٠
OUT
CONTROL

ZUARA

MIGRATION

27

15

Out of Egypt

Salim was happy to hear from me, and said his friend Kassim was looking forward to meeting me. I believe I've already mentioned that Kassim's home was in Oran, which is near the western edge of Algeria. As my plans of driving Dolly on this trip would end not much beyond Oran, it would be perfect.

I found Kassim to be a most attractive Arab man. His eyes reminded me of Omar Sharif's: big, finely shaped, seductive, soulful, and penetrating. Kassim had a square jaw that always seemed in need of a better shave, although I was sure he did his best each morning. He dressed well, and his mind was intriguing, too; not only did he speak impeccable English, he had also recently finished four years of study at the Cairo University where he had majored in archaeology.

There were ups and downs before we departed, though. When we first met, I outlined my plans for the drive, and Kassim said they sounded agreeable. I returned to my hotel, in high spirits because I would have a strong, handsome traveling companion for the last leg of my journey, and I stretched out on that bug-free, comfortable bed again. The physical stress of the previous night hadn't entirely left me, and I began to doze, but the phone rang and Kassim's rich voice spoke frustrating words into my ear: "I have checked my schedule once again, and I believe I cannot accompany you."

"Oh, no! Why not?"

"I must be home sooner than you will be in Oran."

"But…but maybe we can…."

"I am sorry, Will. Please, I hope you understand."

My earlier flush of positivity flopped to the earth, and I sagged back on the bed. When I opened my eyes again, it was morning.

It was a Sunday, and I called Salim to ask if he had any plans for the day.

"Yes," he said, "I mean to have lunch with my friend Mazara, he is a good fellow, perhaps you'd like to meet him?"

"I would like that, yes."

Before they arrived, I visited American Express and found that some funds had arrived from home. What a relief! It helped lift my spirits, but just a bit, because it wasn't exactly a large sum, and I was still most unhappy about Kassim's change of mind.

By the time Salim arrived at my hotel with Mazara, I was smiling, but it was rather weak. It felt improper to begin the afternoon with complaints, so I kept my concerns to myself.

As it turned out, the lunch Salim and Mazara were going to have was at a private *pension* where Mazara rented a room from a family. Mazara insisted I join them for the meal. The owner of the house was quite well educated, and spoke excellent English, but no French. Mazara only spoke Arabic and French, but Salim spoke all three languages, so the conversation was an interesting blend.

Lunch was a divinely-prepared meal of kidneys, liver, and hearts, all of which had been cooked in a tasty butter sauce. Bread and a fresh salad accompanied the meal. As we finished eating, a friend of the host appeared, and we were introduced.

This friend, like the peasant from my night in the desert, had a strong desire to move to the United States. As soon as he learned it was my home country, he asked if America happened to be in need of more civil engineers. He even leapt up, excused himself, and ran home for some paperwork. He returned with correspondence between himself and the U.N., but said he only thought of them as a stepping-stone to America. He even asked if I could help him in any way. If in fact I *had* been an ambassador of emigration, I could have brought back thousands of Mediterranean folk. This man and Akron's uncle were far from the only two instances of people expressing a strong desire to move to my country.

As Salim, Mazara and I made our way back to my hotel that evening, I told Salim about Kassim's canceling his plans to join me. Salim was surprised and indignant. "I've been wondering why your mood changed so much between yesterday and today! I'll speak with him, convince him to go with you."

"I don't know if that would work. He sounded like his final decision has been made."

"Just let me talk with him. I can call him from your room."

Mazara left us at the hotel, and in my room, I listened to Salim use his considerable powers of persuasion on his friend. Kassim agreed to come to the hotel to discuss it further.

When he arrived, we reviewed my itinerary again, and for one of the very few times on the trip, I made some firm commitments. I spoke with the voice of a man who could keep a schedule, and would take whatever steps necessary to do so.

Kassim rested one hand on my maps. His eyes, it seemed, bored into me, but he was thinking more about the timetable than about the man in front of him.

"There is a possibility," he said, lifting the sheet of paper where I had scratched out my notes, "that I can go with you after all."

"I sure could use the company." Not to mention the protection of this indigenous, hard-muscled man.

"We would have to leave tomorrow."

"No problem."

Kassim dropped the schedule and stabbed a thick forefinger on the map of Tunisia. "You see, here, I could take the bus in Tunis and make the final kilometers of my journey very quickly."

"That would be fine with me." We could iron out the details (or maybe he would change his mind) later.

He stood. "We are agreed!"

I also stood, and we shook hands.

"Now," Kassim said, in his to-the-point way of speaking, "it is too late to get our visas for Libya. We will have to wait until tomorrow to put our papers in order."

"The car needs a lubing, too."

Salim interjected, "That can be easily arranged."

Kassim nodded. "We should be driving out of Cairo before nightfall."

"I'm sure we'll have a fun trip together, Kassim."

"Of this I am also certain. Until tomorrow!" With that, he left the room.

Salim wrote a note on the back of one of his business cards and handed it to me. "Be sure to take your car to our Renault shop, and everything will be in tip-top shape for your trip."

"Thank you." I had been meaning to try and find a cheaper mechanic, and it must have shown in my voice.

Salim sensed the nature of my hesitation and waved it off. "This will be free of charge, for all the advertising you're providing for

Renault."

"Do you mean it?"

"Please, it's the least I can do."

"Salim, you've already done so much!"

With his right hand, he grasped my right to shake it, while with his left hand, he squeezed my shoulder. "You're going places, Will, and I'm happy to be a part of it."

I slept that night with a happy sense of friendship, also of security in the knowledge that I would have fine-looking, capable, native company as I drove through the rest of northern Africa.

The next morning, I arrived at the Renault agency. Dolly's tire was repaired, and she was oiled, greased, tweaked, or whatever it is those magical mechanics do. When all was ready, I walked over to Salim's office, where Kassim was waiting. We said our goodbyes to my Agency friend, and headed for the student rooming house to retrieve Kassim's belongings.

I met a young man in Kassim's room, who although we were only in the same airspace for those few minutes, left quite an impression on me. I don't remember his name, but here's what I wrote about him in my journal:

> One of the roommates looked like a starved student, with the most sympathetic pale face I have encountered. He was suffering from a cold, which added somehow to his saintliness. He was majoring in religious philosophy.

That boy's face remains in my memories to this day. What is it about certain people who pass through our lives that leaves them so emblazoned on our minds?

Something similar, though intensified, happened to me while I was still searching around for the specific college from which I wanted my degree. I had started with Rutgers, but only spent a year and a half there. During that time, WWII wasn't quite over yet, and many Army trainees (ASTP) were sent to the school to use our facilities for training. I believe those boys might have been between regular boot camp and officer training school.

Some of us students were offered the opportunity to make a little extra money by working in the gym, where the young military men would take their meals. I was paid $1.50/hour, plus dinner, for working in the serving line. On the first day, while I stood there with a giant ladle in my hand, pouring who knows what onto plates, a particular soldier caught my eye.

I would guess he must have been twenty-one or so, and I was eighteen. He was tall, big-chested, Scandinavian in looks, and this young officer-to-be had quite a presence about him. His studious countenance was topped by a military crew-cut, and fronted with black-rimmed glasses. That old-fashioned style of specs can really look fine on the right sort of face. I never spoke directly to him, but he stood out among all the others. What stays with me the most, though, was the kindly nature that seemed to exist just below the surface of his seriousness.

My younger self developed quite a crush, which is understandable, because we all experience infatuations up through high school. I'd had a few, usually on boys, but even on a beautiful girl named V. J., who was known to be sexually adventurous. But for the most part, my more youthful crushes on boys felt more like a desire for deeply loving friendship. I can understand why, because while living with my grandparents and all the uncles, I had never really made any close friends. The fault was surely mine—I had withdrawn into myself. Could that have been because of my curious feelings toward members of the same sex? Or was it a reaction to the glimmer of violence in my father's temper, and the fact that my mother seemed to encourage it? I preferred to stay quiet and unseen.

While in high school, I did eventually develop 'strong acquaintances' with boys in the drama club or on the newspaper staff (in other words, the more 'sensitive' types). I don't know if any of them were Gay, per se, but surely most of us were picked last for sports teams—I know I was. (Too bad track and skiing weren't sports where sides were chosen!) In any case, those of us who did have certain tendencies probably gravitated together naturally. Never once, I should interject, did I hear homosexual attraction spoken of in a positive way. And, more to the point, I never felt for any of those high school boys quite what I felt for the young man at Rutgers.

Each time he approached my spot in the line for food, my heart would vibrate, my skin would flush, and if forced to speak I would stutter, but I repeat, I never spoke directly to him. I did proceed to somehow learn his name (I can't remember how), and tried to find out as much as I could about him. It wasn't much; apparently he wasn't the chatty type.

This fellow became quite a motivator for me. In order to be in the same place at the same time as him, I used my ROTC position to become active as a liaison between the civilian students and these army student-visitors. But how could I bring myself to my soldier's attention? A braver boy might have simply approached and introduced himself, prepared with some banal ice-breaker like, 'So, are you ready to see the world?'

My solution was to be the first and only volunteer to organize a big dance, to which these young soldiers would be invited. At my suggestion, a sort of rally was set up for the visitors, during which I stood on the stage in the auditorium and described the dance, what fun it would be, and urged them all to attend. The closest I ever came to attempting contact with the object of my affection was to look directly at him when I concluded, "If any of you have any questions, please find me, and I'll be happy to help you."

My young man had no questions, and didn't attend the dance. I did, but this time, when I touched the women I danced with, I couldn't even pretend to myself (for my parents' sake) that they were the true focus of my affections.

I was left with nothing but ladling gruel onto the young man's plate, yet I couldn't get him out of my mind. It's likely that I began a process of fortifying my nerves to approach him, but suddenly, the training program was dropped and all the soldiers went away. More sleuthing led me to the discovery that my man had transferred to the University of Wisconsin.

The next day, I filed papers. A few months later, I was attending the University of Wisconsin, determined to make his acquaintance. This was a serious crush!

As it turned out, I will never know what might have developed had we ever spoken. Yes, I saw him at the UW campus, and in fact made myself available in his path whenever my schedule would permit, but his eyes passed across mine. Obviously, I hadn't girded my loins enough for an introduction at Rutgers, after all, and in fact never consummated my interest in any other way.

Fortunately, my attention was captured by another attraction: The University of Illinois. One weekend, I visited a chapter of my fraternity house at that university. While there, I fell in love, but this love was apparently more realistic than my feelings for the soldier. My new infatuation was for the College of Fine and Applied Arts at U of I. It seemed far and away better than what UW had to offer. The energy of my fraternity brothers was better in Illinois, more alive, and there were more of them in numbers, too. They were an active and hard-working bunch who were generally more in touch, and fitted better in the groove of what they were doing and what they were moving toward.

With a conscious effort, I pressed my mutually silent infatuation between the pages of my memory's scrapbook, and transferred to the university I would graduate from.

Back to Egypt: I guess I can count myself lucky that the meeting I had with Kassim's captivating roommate was so fleeting.

Considering that Kassim had been at the school four years, his belongings were meager, and fitted neatly into my little car. In no time, we were packed, strapped, and I thought we were ready to drive away. Unfortunately, Kassim had one last stop to make, something to do with his clearance from the Egyptian government. That took us all the way to dinnertime, and we decided to grab a quick meal before hitting the road.

It must have been 8 p.m. by the time we were driving out of Cairo. Kassim took charge as soon as we began down the highway, telling me, "I've taken this trip before, and can direct you to the fastest route."

"Fast is good, but safe is better."

"I do not see why any harm should come to either of us."

"I'm not only talking about our person, I'm talking about rough roads." Affectionately, I patted my beloved Dolly's dashboard.

Kassim looked alarmed. "There won't be any problems with your car, will there?"

Happy that I'd kept both the flat and the emptied gas tank to myself, I said, "As long as we don't have to drive over any sand-dunes."

He laughed. "There will be none of that."

We made small talk about our trip, then after a few hours, Kassim said, "We have had a late start, and should think of sleeping, soon. There is a rest house halfway to Alexandria. Here, this road approaching, turn here."

"Hold on a second. Didn't I see a turn to Alexandria a few kilometers back? It was pointing the opposite direction."

"I can assure you this will be a more efficient route."

Blithely relying on my passenger, I made the turn. It appeared to be the right choice; the road was smooth and well-maintained. It pleased me that Kassim had taken my comment about rough roads to heart.

After we had driven over an hour, Kassim made a noise like, "Huh."

"What?"

He peered at an approaching road sign, which talked about places I hadn't ever seen on my map. "Huh."

"Why do you keep making that sound?"

"What? Oh, I'm thinking there might have been a better road to take…."

I pulled to the side of the road and turned in my seat. "Oh no. Oh-ho-ho no. I am *not* going to stay in some village with any more uncles!"

"Excuse me?"

"Kassim, do you know where we are?"

"Yes, I do. It would be better if we were someplace else."

I stared at him, he stared calmly back. In a measured voice, I asked, "Where exactly should we be?"

He jerked a thumb over his shoulder, toward the road behind us. "That way."

"All the way back to where we first turned, and I said there was another sign—"

"No, not so far. Less than an hour."

It would have been better if he could have phrased that differently, as in, 'not long' or even 'a little more than a half hour.' 'Less than an hour' sounded too much like 59 minutes.

Without another word, I swung the car around, and we

backtracked. My concerns had been misjudged by nine minutes; it took 50 to get back to the turn Kassim said we should make. During that drive, Kassim produced a farmer's pastry that had been given to him by his angelic roommate before we left Cairo. It hit the spot, and improved my mood. Nevertheless, I didn't breathe easy until I saw a sign that indicated Alexandria as an eventual destination. Another hour past that sign, we arrived at the halfway rest house, a small inn, and after midnight, we were finally able to sleep.

I planned to leave early. If I was going to be traveling with a man whose sense of direction was worse than mine, I preferred it to be during daylight hours.

The following afternoon, we entered Alexandria by way of the city dump. What a smelly introduction to such a grand place! We found our way to a downtown area, where we checked in at the Acropolis Pension, which was clean and within our budget. (Kassim's finances were as tight as mine.)

Later, we enjoyed an inexpensive dinner. Sensing Kassim's urgency, I told him we would continue westward first thing in the morning, and we slept well in our surprisingly comfortable pension beds.

I woke to a bright-eyed Kassim telling me he was starving for a good breakfast. Proud to be seen with this attractive companion, I enthusiastically sat down at an outdoor cafe with him. We filled up on pita bread dipped in *labneh*, which is a rich, creamy sort of curds, also boiled eggs and cheese.

Perhaps Kassim had had bright, delightful dreams, because his spirits that morning were high. During our meal, he opened up to me more, telling me of his family and exploring the details of his personal hopes. Watching me with those warm, thought-piercing eyes, he said, "This trip with you expands my understanding of Americans, and America is one place I would like to see. Possibly, I could even work there someday." He reached across the table and affectionately squeezed my forearm. "Tell me more about your country."

His touch had meddled with my breath, but I recaptured my voice and described America's best attributes. He listened with such careful attention, it was flattering. As we neared the end of our meal, he said, "I am very happy to have met you, Will. I hope we will have a friendship for many, many years."

I hoped so, too!

We left the cafe and checked out of the pension, loaded up the car, and made only one stop to buy snacks. We were nearing Libya, along a route that fronted the sea.

On this new road, we were stopped constantly by police barricades and questioned. How many times can I thank Mabel from New York for warning me against bringing my gun? I made up for it by thanking Kassim, who explained our presence to each of the guards, and I passed through more quickly than other light-skinned men could have done. Also, I should note, my progress across that continent was made with much more ease than a Jewish man could have hoped for.

Actually, Kassim was the first to comment on that, after we passed the last roadblock before El Alamein. Gesturing toward the guards who fell into the distance behind us, he observed, "None of this would be necessary if it weren't for the dirty Jews."

It was as though this man had suddenly squeezed the heat out of the bloom of affection that had been growing inside me. Looking out my side window to hide my expression, I said, "You mean the Israelites?"

"Of course. They, along with every other Jew on this earth, are a scourge. Filth."

Wow. My eyes went to my hands on the steering wheel, and I stared at my fingers, my fingernails. Quite clean.

Noticing my silence, Kassim said, "If you have Jewish friends in America, please understand I do not mean to insult you with my disgust for them. But I will warn you to watch yourself with them. They cannot be trusted."

I tucked my lips in against my teeth before I could blurt out, 'You trust me, don't you?' Instead, I slowed and stared at a scene in the desert stretching out and away from us. "Look!"

Kassim only needed a glance. "Yes, that is the cemetery of El Alamein. Rommel was approaching from Libya, so the British moved back into Egypt and stretched their soldiers across the land. If they hadn't kept the Nazis out, Egypt would have fallen."

"Those Nazis were a pretty scary bunch, if you ask me."

Kassim didn't take the opportunity to agree. "They were pushed back through Libya, then to Tunisia. Your American troops landed in Algeria, and the Axis was driven completely out of Northern Africa." He gave my shoulder a rough, friendly squeeze. "For that, we thank you."

More grave markers were along the road, but these were Italian and German cemeteries. As we neared the Libyan border we saw other souvenirs of the war; burned tanks, gasoline vats, abandoned trucks, barbed wire, and destroyed bridges.

We were still a good distance from the border when we were forced to endure more bureaucracy, this time in the form of searching for an official to stamp our passports. If Kassim hadn't been with me, I wouldn't have known to stop at all, and it barely made sense to me. Something to do with customs, I believe. In any case, considering our location, it was like stopping in San Antonio, Texas before you could cross into Mexico.

Not that this sleepy little place was anywhere near the size of San Antonio. I asked the one young guard I found, "Will this take long? We hope to reach Salum tonight." That town, which was still on the Egyptian side of the border, was another 225 kilometers further along.

The guard narrowed his eyes and scanned me from head to toe without speaking, and I glanced at Kassim. Was it some sort of crime to be in a hurry? "Where," Kassim asked, "is the man in charge?"

"He is around town, someplace, you will find him."

Now Kassim looked back to me with a subtle shrug. We left the building and he looked up and down the road, his hand shading his eyes against the sun. "I guess we are meant to look for him."

The young guard walked out behind us and stepped up to my car. "Come along, I will help you."

Small favors.

The first stop was the official's home, but we were told he might be watching the football game at a field on the other side of town. Our guide directed us there from my passenger seat, calling out friendly greetings to his fellow townsmen. Occasionally he would point out a building or a park, and describe it like a tour guide. "And there," he said, pointing to a small, odorous restaurant, "you will find the most delicious food in all of Egypt."

I checked my watch; we had already been delayed forty-five minutes. That alone was reason enough to avoid politely patronizing any of the businesses in this town.

"There," called out our guide, "the football field!" (Or as I saw it, a soccer field.)

We pulled in and rolled down the dirt road next the field. The players and fans were strolling or driving away, all chatting cheerfully about what must have been a very amicable game.

Abruptly, I stopped the car and turned in my seat to face the guard. "He isn't here, is he?"

The guard looked sheepish. "We hardly ever have tourists, and he is never expecting to be needed."

"Nice work, if you can get it." Ignoring the confused silence, I accelerated again. "Where next?"

"We should try the marketplace. He is often there."

As luck would have it, there indeed was the official visa-stamper, lounging at the entrance to the marketplace. This man stood placidly leaning against the white-mud wall, his eyes closed, facing the sun, a small smile on his heavy lips. The picture of lax contentment.

How annoying.

I checked my watch again, and pulled up to his shins before stopping. Here is what I wrote about the meeting in my journal:

His manner was very rough at first, he must have expected trouble from me. He informed us we would have to wait until six o'clock that evening to get the certification we needed, because the official stamp was in the post office, and it didn't reopen until that time. Kassim pleaded our case, and the official said he could 'fix things' for us, but it would be a very special favor. Then he eyed my passport, which he held in his hand, and looked at me like a general to a private. He demanded, as if trying to catch me in a lie, "Are you American?" I almost laughed in his face, but was able to control myself.

The official suddenly seemed like an over-compensating actor in a play, speaking with broad vowels stretched through his heavy accent. "What is your purpose in touring?"

By now we were back at the border office (which I thought would have been a much better place to keep all official apparatuses, rather than the post office), and I explained that I wanted to see more of Northern Africa.

"What is it you want to see, in Northern Africa?"

This man was absurd. With all seriousness I stroked my little beard, which had recently reappeared, then rubbed my hand over my mouth to hide my smile. "I've seen the pyramids," I told him, "and they were remarkable. I've stopped at ruins and ancient sites, and now I hope to see how the French are living with the Arabs in the Northwest. Also, I believe Marrakesh and the Casbah would be interesting places to visit."

"Ah, yes. You are a tourist."

Stifling a giggle (and a response like 'No, actually I'm a Jewish homosexual'), I nodded solemnly. "Exactly."

The official turned my passport over in his hands once or twice more, then paged through it again. He lifted my visa close to his eyes and tilted it this way and that, although this was long before the time of holographic imagining for authenticity. At last, he lumbered over to a desk, slid open a drawer, pressed a stamp carefully onto an inkpad, then against my visa.

I politely asked, "Did you just discover that the proper stamp was in your drawer, after all?"

He looked at the evidence in his hand with some confusion, then laughed and said, "No. With this, it is now necessary for you to obtain a signature from my superior." He handed back all my documents and smiled.

I smiled back, but my eyes slid from left to right. Where was this man's superior? At the movies? Playing poker, someplace? When the stamperman simply continued to smile, I went ahead and asked: "Who is it you say needs to sign for me?"

"He is my superior."

While I struggled to unclench the frozen smile from my jaw, Kassim asked, "Where can we find him?"

The official pointed out to the road. "He will be along any time."

Kassim grasped my arm and led me outside. He said, "I will find us some water, and we can have tea while we wait."

"Fine." While Kassim found water and boiled it for tea, I played with more passing dogs, and their soothing presence prepared me for a bit more patient lingering in this place.

The original droopy-eyed official waddled out of the offices and passed us with an easy smile. "Soon, my superior will be along soon," he said, and continued on to a nearby fruit and vegetable stand.

"The oranges look good over there," said Kassim, and followed the official to the stand.

A tap fell on my shoulder, and I turned to find the official's superior. "You are the American who needs my signature?"

I wondered if these people communicated telegraphically, but didn't care. "Yes I am!" He signed my passport, and Kassim's, who had returned with a bag of oranges, the rich color of which I never see in the States anymore, and I now live in California.

While we drove away, I said, "What a bunch of malarkey."

"Malarkey?"

"Hooey. Nonsense."

"Ah. Yes. I'm sure they could tell we were determined. I believe if we had shown any hesitation, they would have kept us here for the night. The town needs some business."

"That first official, sun-bathing while we were running around looking for him! If I were a fighting man, I would have been tempted to pop him one in the kisser."

Kassim began laughing, and I thought it was because he found my euphemisms funny, but it was something else. Once he had himself under control, he said, "You would have 'popped' a man who is kindly disposed toward you; while I was buying our oranges, he told me he found you to be the most pleasant and sympathetic American he had ever met! He said, 'You are lucky to have found such a fine traveling companion!'" Kassim dissolved into more chuckling laughter.

I was flattered and embarrassed.

The sun set stunningly as we continued on toward the Libyan border. Once it was gone, the night sky became an inky felt background to a thousand handfuls of stars that had been cast upon it. From horizon to horizon, those stars against that black sky ranged from glowing spotlights to gleaming crystal chips. It was one of those times I was particularly happy about Dolly's sun-roof.

We reached Salum, the border town, which had that fascinating position of being on the sea while in the desert. The hotel we found would have only needed a sign change to become a YMCA, which was why we could afford it. Hungry, now, and ready for dinner, we searched for a restaurant that would also be within our financial constraints. As it turned out, the best place for our wallets was as native as they come. So much so that I hesitated, but Kassim looked ready to start chewing on his own forearm. He waved aside my fears and we entered the tiny, smoky establishment.

Dinner consisted of a piece of lamb cooked with beans in a tomato sauce, and after smelling it carefully (under Kassim's amused watchfulness), I took a bite. Delightful!

When we finished, I paid with a pound, but they didn't have change. Kassim entered into a pleasant, respectful conversation with the owner, then with a light touch on my back, guided me out of the restaurant.

I pulled up short and asked, "What about my change?"

"They will bring it to our hotel in the morning."

His tone was so assured, and in fact I had been impressed by the gentility of the owner, so I nodded and agreed to wait. I don't think I had much choice. Besides, despite the time-tangling lethargy I sometimes encountered, here is what I wrote in my journal about waiting overnight for my change:

> I felt no reason to distrust these natives who lived away from the big cities. It felt they wanted nothing from me, and would be only too glad to give aid if I ever needed it.

On our way back at the hotel, I watched men walking arm-in-arm with each other as they strolled past us. Some were even holding hands. I had seen that throughout Egypt (the girls were openly affectionate, too), but I suppose it struck me more at that time because the alluring Kassim walked next to me. I couldn't imagine the two of us holding hands in public, but then again, maybe I could imagine it.

I stopped in at the shared restroom of our hotel, and as I exited, an Arab man arriving with a small suitcase passed me in the hall. He tipped his chin toward the door I had just closed and asked, "Excuse me, but is that the room of politeness?"

Having no idea what such a room would be, I answered, "No, it's the bathroom or loo."

He raised his bushy eyebrows at me and sidled past.

In our tiny room, I sat on the bunk across from Kassim and asked him, "What's a 'room of politeness'?"

"It is the place where you relieve yourself."

Oops! "Why is it called that?" In our Y-hotel, I imagined it meant that we should all be considerate to one another and try to keep it fairly clean.

"They call it that because if you are a polite person, you make use of such a room rather than urinating in the street."

Before we checked out of our hotel in the morning, my change from the restaurant was brought to me, and we were on our way again.

Human beings may be interesting, but Egyptian customs are simply a pain in the ass. What an ordeal, to leave that country!

I had used up all my patience the afternoon before, in that odd little customs town. The official from that place wouldn't have recognized the man he thought was so sympathetic.

We waited endlessly for all the formalities, seated in uncomfortable wooden chairs outside an office. When I couldn't take it any longer, I stood and wandered casually toward the open office door. There, I leaned against the wall to see if I could gather some sense of the Arabic conversation I'd been hearing for nearly an hour.

A laugh. What was obviously a question, and some sort of saucy reply. More laughter. In a burst of temper I stepped fully into the doorway and glared, my hands on my hips. The official had a personal friend visiting him at work, it was obvious even to me!

The two men looked at me, and their smiles faded. The official stood behind his desk and asked, "What is it?"

"I'm still waiting for clearance *out* of this blasted country!"

"Of course you are." He stepped around the desk, tossed a word over his shoulder to his friend, then held out his hand to me. "May I see your receipts for all purchases made in 'this blasted country'?"

"What? I've shown you my receipts. Is that all we've been waiting for?"

"I have seen no receipts for food, yet surely, you ate food while in Egypt."

"I do NOT believe this! This is ridiculous! Most of the places where I've eaten don't even *give* receipts! This is a *travesty!* I refuse to be treated this way!" I actually stomped a foot in my rage, which I admit was partly fueled by the fear that I might be held back in this (blasted) country for something as stupid as receipts for food. "I'd like to speak to your superior, and then to whoever is above that man! I'm being treated disrespectfully, and I have done nothing wrong. My vehicle has been searched, my papers are in order, and I should be allowed to continue my trip!"

My reaction must have been unexpected; the guard immediately backed off, mumbling something to his friend. Without further ado, he retrieved our passports from his desk, and handed them to me and an abashed Kassim.

Voila!

When we entered Libya, we were kept all of ten minutes at their customs office. They must have known that the Egyptians had examined every detail, already. Once we made our escape from all the officialdom, Kassim and I let out a cheer of relief.

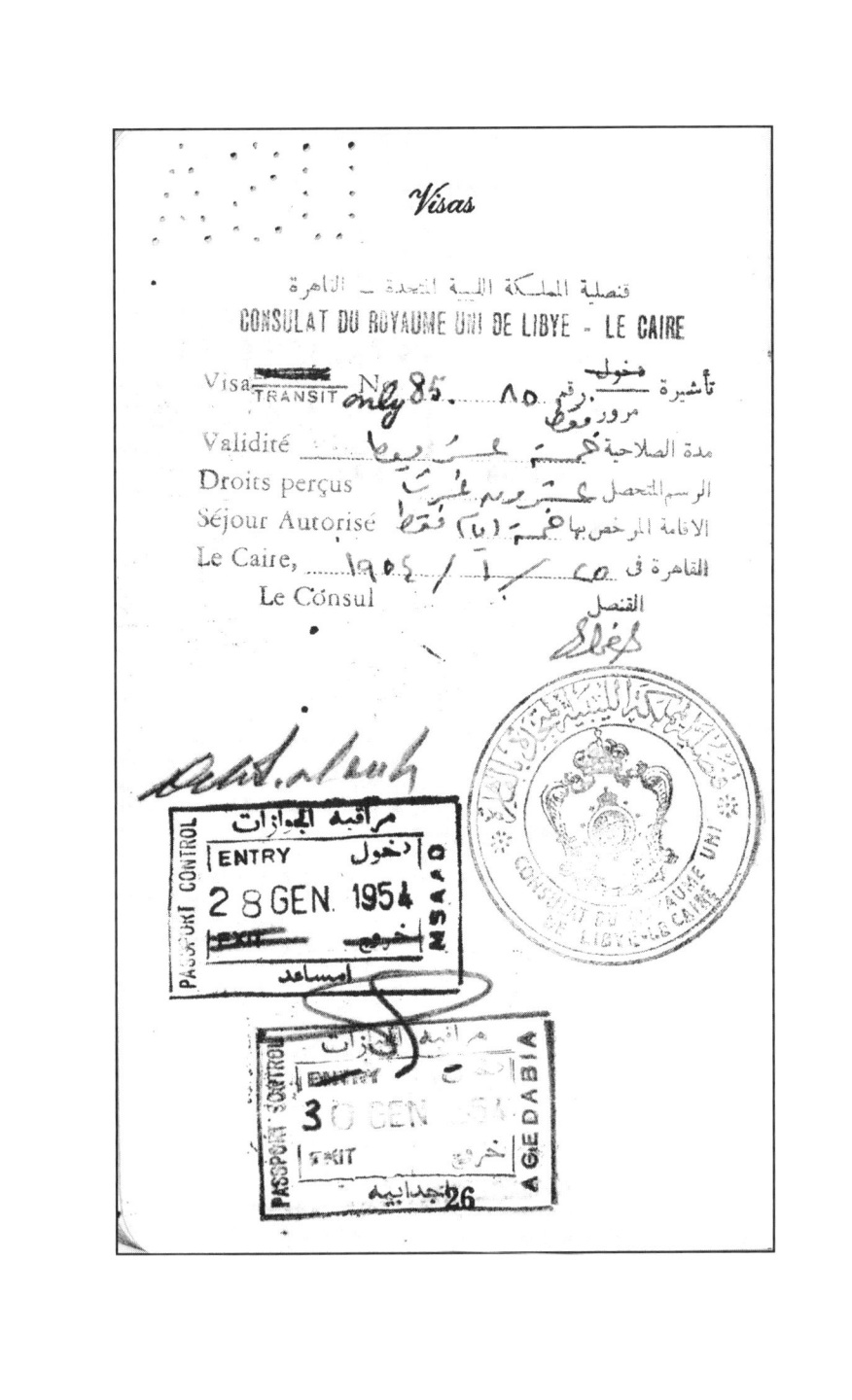

Visas

قنصلية المملكة الليبية المتحدة ــ القاهرة

CONSULAT DU ROYAUME UNI DE LIBYE - LE CAIRE

Visa ~~TRANSIT~~ only No 85. ٨٥ تأشيرة مرور فقط رقم

Validité _____ مدة الصلاحية

Droits perçus _____ الرسم المحصل

Séjour Autorisé _____ الاقامة المرخص بها

Le Caire, ١٩٥٤ / القاهرة فى

Le Consul القنصل

PASSPORT CONTROL / مراقبة الجوازات
ENTRY / دخول
2 8 GEN. 1954
EXIT / خروج
امساعد / QASRO

PASSPORT CONTROL / مراقبة الجوازات
ENTRY
3 0 GEN.
EXIT / خروج
اجدابيه / AGEDABIA 26

16

More of Africa

At the time I arrived, Libya had only been considered an independent nation for a few years. Not long before that, in the late 1930s, tens of thousands of Italians had been sent as colonists, and in 1939 Libya was officially considered a part of Italy. This is one reason it became a great battleground when Italy entered the war in 1940.

In the 1940s Australian troops were sent to Africa, and proudly helped the Allies defeat both Italian and Vichy French enemies. Their biggest challenge, though, was at Tobruk, which was the first city Kassim and I entered after leaving Egypt. In the '40s, German forces were trying to take that town and its strategically important port. Along with Allied troops, the Australians dug in, literally dug trenches and holes, and held off the Germans. The Nazis disdainfully called the defenders *rats in their holes*, and the wise Australians immediately began referring to themselves as 'The Rats of Tobruk.'

Less-mentioned is that the indigenous Sanusi family helped in that battle, too. They were an Islamic religious order that had been a powerful force in the 19th century. King Idris (named Libya's leader upon their independence) was a Sanusi descendent. His being a king might also be why the original name of Libya was 'The United Kingdom of Libya.' The Sanusis also fought Italian Colonial Rule in the early part of the 20th century, but the Italians were simply better equipped at the time.

While I was there, it was still an impoverished nation, but Tobruk was nonetheless an attractive city. Homes and businesses were spread over a beautiful, curving, constantly descending road that followed alongside the Mediterranean. I noted a single lonely ship in the harbor that had been such a strong attraction in WWII.

We passed all of that by, continuing on toward Darnah. Our visual senses were treated by the appearance of Darnah coming into view. Here's what I had to say about it in my journal:

My first view of Darnah is one I shall never forget, for it fit into its position on the sea as if put there by Rembrandt or Cezanne. We stopped for a moment, and I stood, watching as the colors, deep and vivid, played together. The sun's rays made the shades of the yellowish buildings dance against the blue sky and azure-green water. Anxious to blend with this sunshine and color, I climbed into Dolly again, and raced to the city's edge.

My muffler had abruptly surrendered. The rattling roar of my muffler-less car resounded on the main streets of Darnah, which I could see right away was another British military strong-point town. Englishmen were everywhere, in buildings and on the streets, driving big cars and, apparently, the economy. This made it easy to find a garage with a decent, ingenious mechanic who improvised a muffler until we could find a new one.

The people of Darnah were exceptionally good-natured, in my opinion; Kassim and I traded smiles with most of them as we passed. However, Kassim insisted I would enjoy the town of Benghazi even more, and we set out again early that evening.

Now we were ascending, with the gorgeous coastal sea still glimmering on our right. The road twisted and turned with the line of the country's edge until we found ourselves rolling through lovely, lively mountains.

What a contrast! To move from desert to such lush surroundings in a matter of hours brought a special charm to the beauty. As night began to fall, I watched the scenery unfolding through the twilight. Neatly tended farms were set among emerald-green fields and proud trees, while the smell of the sea always tingled at the back of my nose. When full dark came, it brought rain, and in the night we climbed up and over more mountains, sometimes crossing through narrow valleys and gorges over suspension bridges. I could have kicked myself for taking this trip during darkness.

Kassim and I were determined to reach Benghazi, although it was now nearing 8:30 p.m. We tried to find gas, but—the oil barons would be appalled—the town we were in had not a drop. That, combined with long hours of driving through what had become a continual rain, didn't help my stress-levels. Next, my windshield wipers began to act up. (Correction: All they would do was swing up, then skitter uselessly back down.) The situation grew worse still when one of my headlights began to flicker. What more could go wrong?

We drove quietly through the deepening night and together, watched the gas gauge and the half-lit road. This was another of those times that having a co-pilot was a blessing.

When Benghazi at last came into view, we spoke simultaneously: I said, "Thank God!" and Kassim said, "Allah be praised!"

Benghazi was out of the mountains, and we were back in arid country, but the rain continued incongruously to fall. It was 10:30 at night, and anyone who has taken a long road-trip can imagine my exhaustion. Extensive miles, inclement weather, the car troubles and the road had thoroughly worn me out.

Fortunately, Kassim had been in Benghazi more than a few times, and while we searched for a hotel with an available room, he met a friend of his. This young man, Ahmed, led us to a decent hotel, but could see how tired we were, and promised to look us up in the morning. I slept like the dead.

Through the night, the clouds had been swept away, but the winds were cold. When Ahmed arrived to treat us to breakfast, he warned us to bundle up, and I was happy I did. Who would have expected such weather in a desert?

Over rich coffee and pastries, Kassim told me, "Ahmed was also a student at the University of Cairo."

"How nice," I replied, wondering if the drawn, overly-thin young man was also anti-semitic. "Do you work here in Benghazi?"

"Yes, I am with the Ministry of Justice. I am a translator."

"I hope we're not keeping you from your job?" It was getting toward nine in the morning.

"No, I have the day off, and today, the two of you will be my guests." He paid the bill for our meal, refusing our offers to contribute, and said, "Save your money for the *souks*."

It was just as well. I might have spent myself down to pennies in the *souks* of Benghazi, which were elaborate and enticing. These little stores were filled with every sort of necessity and artistically crafted object imaginable. Food, medicinal herbs, clothes and other textiles, tablecloths, boxes, jewels, perfumes, goods of leather, precious metals, ceramics, and wood…. Craftsmen's shops were interspersed throughout, and one had the feeling that little of the *souk* situation had changed in hundreds of years.

Ahmed noticed that although I admired much, I wasn't buying anything. He asked, "Are you saving your purchases for another time, nearer the end of your trip?"

"Saving money, actually." Kassim and I had explained to him about my adventures, and the attempt to entice the Renault agency into buying my articles. "The last time Renault paid me for anything was in Beirut."

"Then we should go to the dealer now!"

We drove through the broad, clean, refined streets of Benghazi until we found the dealership. I gave a pleasant young man there my pitch, and he agreeably replaced, my muffler, windshield wipers, and headlight for free. Suddenly I felt less strapped for cash, because those repairs had been part of my budget, but I still didn't feel comfortable spending money on any unnecessaries.

While we waited for the work to be completed, Ahmed treated us to coffee at a cafe, and we sat next to a table filled with British nationals. When they left, they were replaced by an attractive group of Libyan boys who scowled at the departing Brits.

I, too, watched the departing foreigners, and asked Ahmed, "For some reason, I expected to see more Italians in these parts."

"They once ruled this country, and there are still many Italians here, but after they were defeated, the British moved in."

One of the young men at the next table leaned over and said, "They give us our independence, but I still feel like a child who has been granted recess at school. The teachers are still watching."

The other boys at the table agreed. "We don't want the British here any more than we did the Italians."

The third added, "Those Italians were bad enough. They moved in, took over, then told Moslems we could 'have our freedom.' Ha!"

"Some freedom that was. It was our country in the first place. Their arrogance, and now the arrogance of the British, is hard to stomach."

"A small donkey is always used."

I raised questioning eyebrows to Ahmed, and he explained, "It means, 'The weakest person is always picked to do the dirty work'."

"But we are not weak," said the first boy from the next table. "We are strong, and now that this country finally belongs to its people, we will show them all."

I suppose they did, in a way, when they struck oil in the late fifties. There has always been an inevitable strength in dollars. But no oil had yet been found at the time of my visit, and Ahmed faced the group at the next table. "How will you 'show them all'?"

One of the boys stood, his eyes agleam with pride. "We will fight, if we have to."

His friend touched his arm in a subtle plea to be seated, but seriously agreed. "Yes, if we have to, we will fight. But if that is not necessary, we still must improve our country. We are poor, but we have much of this," he tapped his head, "and this." He pressed his hand against his heart, and his compatriots followed suit. I don't know if they had a national anthem at the time, but I think not, because if they had, those boys would have started singing it right then.

Kassim, Ahmed and I finished our coffees, bade farewell to our proud acquaintances, and retrieved my freshly-pampered car. Of all the remaining options for entertainment, another cafe visit sounded best, and Ahmed led us to a place where checkers tournaments were held. We found an available board and sat down for a few games with our coffee.

Ahmed told us, "We do love our games, here."

"Just as we do in America," I countered. "Wouldn't it be nice if that was how we resolved our international differences? Only games, for wit, and sports, for strength?" It seemed like an original idea at the time.

But Kassim and Ahmed both laughed. "That isn't the way of men," Ahmed sagely observed.

Kassim, still chuckling, said, "It isn't a bad idea, if you ask me. The dirty Jews could be caught each time they cheated. All the world would see how they play."

Ahmed agreed. "Isn't that the truth!"

Neither of them noticed that I was unusually quiet for the rest of the hour we spent at the cafe. During that time I soundly, honestly, and repeatedly trounced them both at checkers.

After one last night in Benghazi, spent relaxing with an affordable repast, Kassim and I set off in the direction of Tripoli.

Tripoli was over a thousand kilometers away, and we weren't going to make the trip in a single day. Still, I had filled the car and a jerry can with gas, and felt confident that we were rich enough with fuel to reach the halfway point. That would be a town called Surt, where we could replenish the tank and gas can.

We re-entered the flat, dry desert as we drove. Along the way we passed more than a few markers with the names of towns written on them, but when we reached each of them, we found they were little more than tiny communities of four or five homes. The towns themselves had been completely destroyed by the war.

Staring at the devastation, Kassim made the comment, "Filthy Italians, dirty Krauts, damned British…" and I wondered if he was withholding his ideas about Americans only because of my presence. Or, maybe he didn't despise Americans yet, because Qadafi didn't come into the Libyan picture until 1969. (King Idris was pro-western.) In any case, I could only shake my head with wonder at his ongoing stream of hatred. It was hard to understand why this man trusted me at all, considering I was other-than-Arabian.

In truth, I had suffered some guilt about withholding from him not only my Jewishness, but my interest in men. In the case of the former, I might have harbored a hope that he would learn, by osmosis, that a person's religion did not make him any more or less a respectable human being. With regard to my blossoming love for men, it concerned me that I might add one more style of victim to his list of those to hate. Why? Because I had already lied to him up to that point, by omission. He would likely feel betrayed by that. Also, I've already commented on how some men probably do have twinges of same-sex curiosity, but it can frighten them into violence. My silence felt safest.

Near lunchtime we stopped for a picnic, choosing the shelter of one of the British first-aid stations that had been dotting our route throughout Libya. The desert winds were too strong for any other option, and I was comforted by the English-speaking military presence, figuring they were there for a reason I'd rather not confront.

When we set off on our way again, we soon passed a place I'll let my journal entry describe:

> After lunch, we came upon a huge structure striking right up out of the desert, a man-made entrance arch, built by the Italians to mark the division line between two of the three departments of Libyan colonies. This arch was between Fezzan and Tripolitania, the third department was Cyrenaica.

That night, we made it as far as a town called Misratah, which was only a few hundred kilometers outside of Tripoli. I intended to arrive in the latter, intriguing city early and refreshed from a good night's sleep.

Barely a half hour after our start the next day, we came upon a site of ruins, which I believe are called the ruins of Leptis Magna. Kassim and I couldn't resist stopping to examine what was left of an ancient town that had been settled on the Mediterranean Sea. This was exactly the sort of thing I had in mind for my off-the-beaten-path trip; anything unusual and unexpected. I hadn't thought about the fact that there would be Roman ruins in this area, especially to such a degree. They were so deserted that it gave a sensation of discovering something no other human being had seen. For a moment, I could truly understand the passion that drives archaeologists.

There were no other people, no pestering guides, only me, my companion, and souvenirs everywhere. I didn't think to pick anything up to bring home, though. Nothing was so small that it wouldn't have been a bit of a chore to carry all the way back to the States, and would I have made it through customs? (Possibly I would have, back then, and what a treasure I would have gained!)

Kassim and I walked through those ruins, awed, in a silence broken only by the subtle murmuring of the nearby sea. My imagination gave voice to whispering ghosts of all the Romans who had ever lived and died there. These people had loved, hated, played and toiled each day, they had governed and celebrated their ancient rituals, and had created incredible monuments to their Gods. When at one point Kassim and I stopped to stare at the white marble against the blue of the Mediterranean, I didn't want to speak. It felt like we were intruding into a quiet that had lasted hundreds of years.

We spent longer than we intended, wandering alone through the remains of thriving avenues. One spot had been the marketplace, over there were commemorative arches, and further along were some homes that had once been particularly grand. While we walked, I felt the same excitement as I had in Pompeii. Everything was in remarkably good condition, all things considered, and the excavating wasn't anywhere near completed yet.

There were so many extraordinary statues and, silly as it may sound, I found myself surrendering to a desire to embrace one. Pressing my body against that warm/cold marble, I imagined a merging with its resplendent grace, and for a moment, I could have been alive at the time this city had been created. When I stepped away, I offered the statue an intimate smile; to think, so much elegance was right there, right then, for no apparent reason but for lucky me to embrace it.

My indulgent companion found me a short while later, standing with my hand resting against a tall pillar, gazing inside myself and into the past at the same time. With no small effort, we pulled ourselves back to the present and returned to the car.

By the time we arrived in Tripoli it was early afternoon, and we asked a taxi driver about the best, least-expensive hotel. He sent us to the perfect place for our meager means: a house that looked more like a home for stray boys. It was run by, as I put it in my journal, 'a dolled-up Italian woman.'

After we settled in, we took a drive through colorful, modern Tripoli. Now I saw the Italian presence I had wondered about; it was in the clothing, the faces, and the predominant language of the city.

During my visit there, I noted that the people walked with a bouncing enthusiasm. The entire city was so clean, attractive, and prosperous that I thought it worthy of its status as capital of the young and promising country.

Tripolitania was one of the strongest forces toward real unity in the United Kingdom of Libya. They'd had the most interaction with foreigners because Tripoli had been, for such a long time, a terminal for caravans from the Saharan trade routes. Also, its port was once an open refuge for pirates and slave traders. If the people of this city had been forced to deal with the roughest of foreigners, it stands to reason that they would have the strongest wish to establish independence.

While touring, Kassim and I found a pretty corniche, short but wide and excellently landscaped. It followed the horseshoe-shaped harbor with such graceful charm that we parked and walked the length of it. Next we moved on through the native quarter, where there were more *souks* and more temptations. Still rationalizing that I had saved money from the free car repairs, I bought two locally made hats I thought would be perfect for skiing. I regretted that purchase later that night, but not only for my own financial reasons.

During our typically sparse dinner, Kassim told me, "Will, my finances have become desperately low. I am no longer able to share in the cost of gasoline and oil. If I do not now save every penny, I will be unable to purchase my train ticket from Tunis to Oran."

"Are you going to have enough for food?"

"Only food, and the last hotels we will need until I can catch my train."

Now, here was a frustrating development. Couldn't he have mentioned this before I spent about a half-tank's worth of gas on hats? (The hats had been cheap, but in those days, gas was cheaper.)

I wasn't about to kick him to the curb, as it were, and leave him stranded. Besides, I was making my trip with or without a co-traveler, so I only shrugged and assured him all would be well.

In the morning, I made sure my tank and jerry can were filled with gas, and we set out for Tunisia.

Pyrimid south of Cairo, Egypt

Rudy and I
On the dirt road to Luxor

In front of the Temple of Karnak, Egypt

My fellow traveler, Akron, on the road back to Cairo.

Lost in the desert south of Cairo

Lost in the desert south of Cairo with Akron.

**Tea time in the Sahara with Kassim,
a much-needed rest for us and the car.**

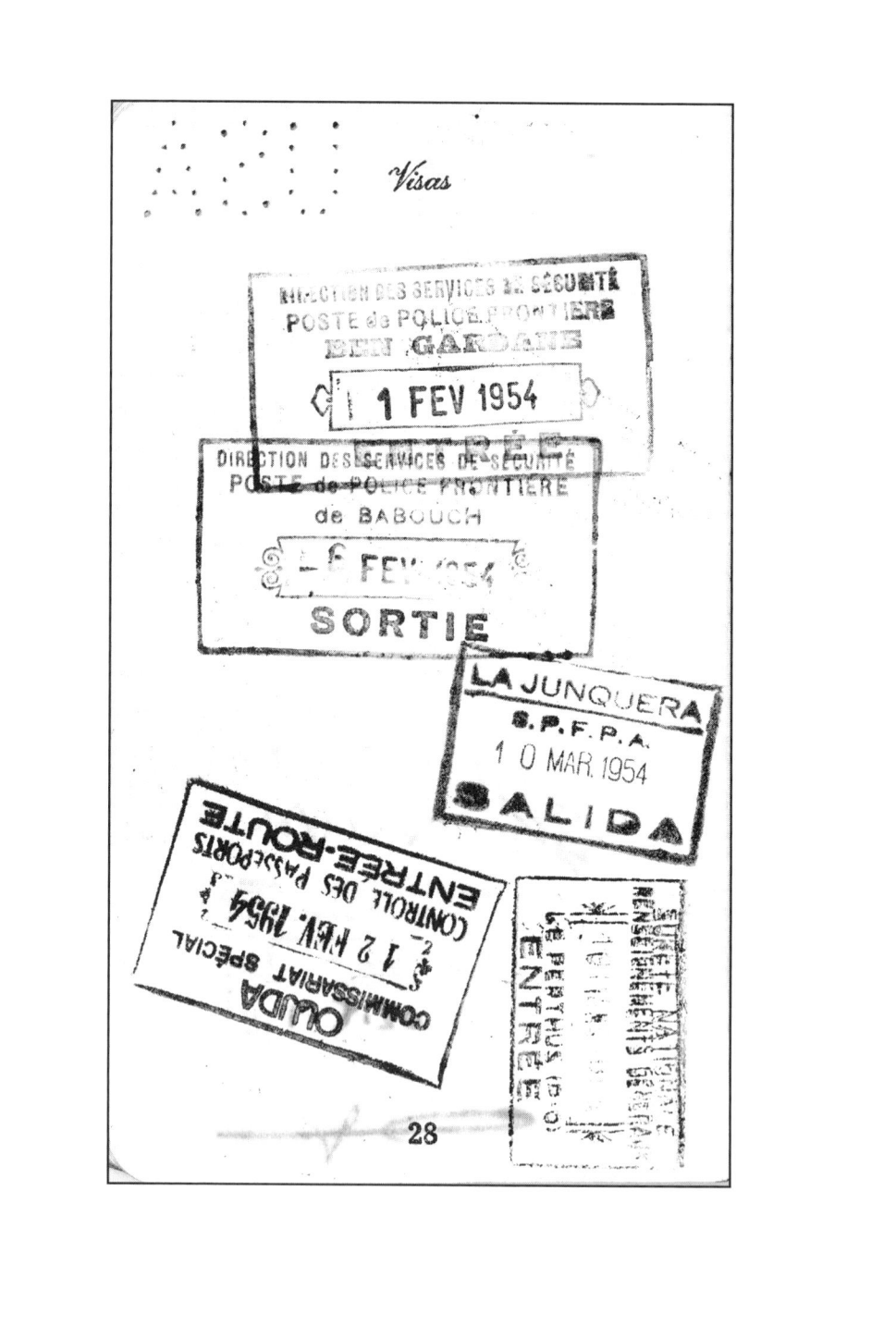

Visas

DIRECTION DES SERVICES DE SÉCURITÉ
POSTE de POLICE FRONTIERE
BEN GARDANE

1 FEV 1954

DIRECTION DES SERVICES DE SÉCURITÉ
POSTE de POLICE FRONTIERE
de BABOUCH

6 FEV 1954

SORTIE

LA JUNQUERA
S.P.F.P.A.
1 0 MAR. 1954
SALIDA

ENTREE-ROUTE
CONTROLE DES PASSEPORTS
1 2 FEV 1954
COMMISSARIAT SPÉCIAL
OUJDA

28

17

French Africa

We arrived at a time that happened to be the dinner hour for the guards, who were distracted and hurried. Somebody must have cooked up something hot for that cold, blustery day, and I imagine they'd been about to sit down to it when Kassim and I rolled up.

The guard leaned down at my window and shouted over the wind, speaking across me to the obviously Arab Kassim. Kassim translated, "There is an additional fee because we are crossing at their mealtime." The amount, in Libyan currency, could be converted to the equivalent of about $10 USD, which would be like $100 today.

"That's ridiculous," I said. "How could a traveler know to time their journey perfectly to avoid the border's dinner hour?"

Kassim translated my words to the guard, although I imagine he left out my statement, 'That's ridiculous.'

The guard simply repeated what he had first said, so definitively that a translation wasn't necessary. Before Kassim began to try, I interrupted him by asking, "Do you have any more Libyan money?"

"None at all."

"I don't, either."

Kassim gave a pragmatic nod and passed this information on to the guard, who looked impatiently over his shoulder toward the shack. He straightened, clutching his fluttering coat around his chest, still staring at the shack. Dinner was getting cold, and by now, everyone else had probably chosen the juiciest portions of the meal for their own plates. With an irritated sigh, he thrust his hand through my window, palm-up, and parked out two short words.

Kassim said, "He will accept 30 French francs."

A quick calculation told me this would be quite a bit less than $10 USD, and without further argument, I pressed the francs into his hand. We were waved through.

Just as Kassim and I finished a brief celebration of the relative ease (and discount) of our crossing, we blew a tire. I slowed, edging to the side of the road, and stopped. With a sense of 'beyond frustration,' I rested my forearm on the steering wheel, and my cheek on my forearm, gazing at Kassim. I even smiled, then laughed a little, when a particularly powerful gust of wind rocked the car. "My friend," I said to him, "please tell me you'll help me with this."

Now that we were stopped, I could roughly calculate by our swaying that the wind was perhaps ten times stronger than the springs on my car. Kassim squinted out at the blowing sand, then turned to me with a grin of his own. "No man could battle these elements alone!"

Together, we pushed open our doors, and simultaneously, they were slammed shut by the wind. This startled me, but Kassim took it in stride. "If we turn the car a bit, it may be easier. We can position ourselves to find some protection while we change the tire."

Under Kassim's direction, I moved in forward and reverse until we found the most desired angle. Now when we opened our doors, it was with careful concentration. The wind tugged at them, then held them straining open, stretching their hinges. I took in a breath, leapt out, and forced my door shut.

We darted to the trunk in the front, crouched low on bended knees, and pulled out the spare tire. It was necessary to change the tire with our eyes nearly shut against the harsh, whipping sands, and our teeth clenched against the frigid cold. At one point, Kassim's job was to steady the car as it rocked on the jack, while I rushed the old tire off and the new one on with steadily numbing hands. The change was so quick, we could have qualified for jobs on a pit-crew.

I returned the tools to the trunk, and we dove back inside Dolly. Shivering, we both wiped at our faces and clothes.

"Kassim," I said, then rolled down my window for a quick discharge of sandy spit before I tried again. "Kassim, I can barely see."

"Turn to me. Now close your eyes—not so tight. Now, I am going to brush at the sand…" He used his handkerchief to gently sweep grit from my eyelashes, eyebrows, and eyelids. I returned the favor, then we spent another five minutes trying to clear our ears, noses, and mouths. I worried that my next bowel movement might be a scratching terror.

When we were ready to push Dolly forward again, I figured the gale of a head-wind cut my mileage in half. Fortunately, within an hour we were within the protection of a fishy-smelling town called Gabes, where we were able to have the damaged tire repaired. We found a hotel that allowed us to wash our hands and faces, and also, the kind concierge exchanged some Francs for us. "No bank here will do this," he explained in French, and gave us the proper rate.

The wind was abating, but out of respect for it, we gave it another half hour by stopping at a market for bread, sausage, and cheese. We sat in the car eating, watching the steady blow change to intermittent bursts, as though Mother Nature was trying to catch her breath but was running tired. When we started out again, the weather was more manageable.

"The French influence in Tunisia sure is obvious," I remarked to Kassim. We were passing a military post topped by an old, long-waving flag of vertical blue, white, and red stripes.

"Yes. They became a French protectorate in the 1880s. Many Tunisians also fought with the Vichy French during the war."

"Wow. Going against the grain, weren't they?"

"It was the government, not necessarily the people, who supported anything Vichy French."

Something in his tone made me ask, "Kassim, were you in the war?"

He had never spoken of it, and I had never asked. It seems so impolite to press a question about what is inevitably a horrifying, life-changing experience. Yet, here the opportunity had presented itself.

Kassim played cat's cradle with his fingers for a few moments before he answered, simply, "Yes."

I waited. Before long, he added, "During the final years of the war, I was part of the underground, until I was jailed. I worked against the Vichy French in this country, and in Algeria. By the time the governments agreed with me, and joined the Allied Forces, the French who were not Vichy still felt insulted by my actions. I remained in jail sixteen months." He rubbed his neck, the muscles in his forearms jumping. "They say we are free, but we are not. The French still rule."

We were both quiet for a while, passing through village after village, until we came to an intersection where a light-skinned group of soldiers crossed the road in front of us. Kassim glared at them, his eyes taking in their clean, neat uniforms and arrogant strides. He scowled. "Damn the French."

Certainly, not all Arabs felt, or feel, as Kassim did. It wasn't necessary that all of them feel that way. Evidently it only took a handful, and that was enough for our country to wage war against them.

But that is now, and I'm speaking of then. A different war was brewing in 1954, between Algeria and the French. More about that shortly.

The town where we decided to stay the night is called Sfax, which some may be aware was the film location of the movie 'The English Patient.' It was dark when we arrived, but I could see a great deal of industry on the outskirts of the city, many smoking stacks and busy railroad tracks.

Kassim and I were both dangerously near the end of our funds, but were able to find a cheap (and terribly uncomfortable) Arab hotel. I went off in search of dinner, but Kassim claimed to feel no hunger. What I discovered to be the least expensive meal available was pastries and hot chocolate from a small shop, which suited me fine.

In the morning we left for Tunis, which is where Kassim would be taking the train to his home in Oran, Algeria.

In Tunis, a town Kassim knew well, he directed us to a restaurant owned by a friend. We had our photograph taken together, and then that friend treated us to a wonderful lunch. I enjoyed my meal, but otherwise could only sit quietly while the two of them engaged in a long, Arabic conversation. After the man left us, Kassim explained, "He is a close friend. When I first attempted to leave for the university in Egypt, I was kept in this city for two years, and we briefly lived together."

"Weren't you already out of jail when you were accepted at the university?"

"Yes. The government simply did not wish to issue me a passport. They did not trust me." While he spoke, his eyes took in each new guest that arrived. "I know many people here."

He would be boarding a train before dark, so it was too late for me to start worrying if I had been transporting a terrorist. What might the stone-faced Jon have thought?

Kassim said, "Come. You must see the local *souk*." On the way there, he had me pull into a gas station, and said, "I see now that I can fill your tank one last time."

"You won't even be with me, though."

He didn't reply, only paid the attendant. He then directed me toward the *souks*, explaining, "The entire city of Tunis was a medina—an ancient quarter—and was mostly a marketplace." He pointed to a large arch. "That is called the *Porte de France*, and was built as a medina entrance after the French expanded the city."

"It sounds like their presence here hasn't been all bad. I mean, to turn a giant market into a thriving, modern city? Seems like a positive development."

"We will never know which might have been best, because they are here now." He flapped a dismissive hand at the arch. "But I do not think their *petit Arc de Triomphe* was a necessary statement."

Well, I tried.

We parked near the entrance, and Kassim purchased a large basket. He began filling it with food and smaller items, which I assumed were gifts for his people back home. Although he never said anything about it, I suspect he had borrowed money from his restauranteur friend. If so they had been sneaky about it, because I never saw it change hands. At least Kassim had been gentleman enough to try to make good on our first-established travel arrangements.

As it turned out, part of the food he'd gathered was for the two of us, to share a final meal together *al fresco*. We seated ourselves on a blanket near the car, relived our adventures together, made plans to meet again, and I took a final picture of him.

At the train station, he faced me and rested a strong, heavy hand on my shoulder. "You won't forget to visit me in Oran, will you?" It was the third time he'd asked.

"I won't forget."

"My father and I will be waiting."

"I'll be there."

Forty-five minutes after I left the train station, I was sitting in the offices of Renault. Now that I was back among the French, it was time to work for some more financing.

The young man I spoke to was enthusiastic about my trip, and said, "I agree that it would be possible to use your story for advertising. Let me contact my superior, and the local paper, to see what we can do for you."

We made plans to meet again the following afternoon, and I left in search of a good place to park for the night. It didn't take long to establish that sleeping in my car in Tunis was not the safest idea. I asked around, and was told about a youth hostel on the edge of town which charged very reasonable rates. Because I had hopes of securing a few more francs from Renault the following day, I decided I could stay there, and even purchase a bit of food for later in the night.

I arrived at the hostel in the evening, just at dark. Not sure what to expect, I was pleasantly surprised to find the house situated right on the coastline, tucked in amongst a nest of pines. The trees blocked much of any possible view, but the subtle sound and scent of the Mediterranean carried through.

Nobody answered my knock; there was not a guest or an owner to be found. I called out, and soon saw a flashlight approaching through the trees. A neighbor had heard me, and came to explain that the 'parents' had the day off, but would return with the last train, which would arrive soon enough. "*Attendez vous*," she said, ('wait'), and left me alone.

The sound of a car on the road saved me from another sad embrace of loneliness. The hostel 'parents' had arrived! I waited for them as they rolled to a halt, but approached when they climbed out of their car with arms full of bread, wine, and flowers.

"Hello! Can I help you with that?"

Husband and wife offered friendly but curious smiles. I explained, "I'm looking for a room to stay in tonight, do you have one available?"

"*Mais oui!*" said the wife, letting me take a bag from her. As we entered the house she continued, in French, "Yes, we do have a room.

Did you wait long?"

"Not at all."

"Have a glass of wine," said the husband. Soon we were seated with wine and cigarettes, discussing my trip.

The wife asked if I would be purchasing a meal with them, but I told her I had food in the car, and would prepare it there. She left to arrange her flowers throughout the house, and her husband commented on my tenuous grip of his language. "You will be happy to learn," he said, "that the others staying here can speak some English. You might prefer to converse in your own language."

Yes, indeed, I was happy to learn it. "Are they American? Do you know if any of them are traveling toward Algeria?"

"They are French, but I know they have learned at least a little English. I believe they are searching for work, and that might bring them to Algeria. You will have to ask them."

I finished my wine and thanked him, then went out to my car to make myself dinner. It consisted of a satisfying bowl of soup, a small loaf of French bread, coffee, and pastries for dessert. When I was done with my meal I returned inside to settle into my room. I picked up a book to while away the time, but was soon interrupted by the sound of a loud motor, and through my window I saw a Volkswagon camper pulling in. Three boisterous young men, my hostel housemates, were returning from a long day in town.

All of them were under twenty-five, two of them bearded, and they were filled with laughter and camaraderie. After enthusiastically greeting me they offered me wine, cigarettes, and conversation—what more could I want? The four of us spent half the night learning about each another, communicating with their broken English and my similarly flawed French.

As the hostel husband had informed me, they were searching for work. The first bearded boy, the tallest of the three (I'll call him Jacques), said, "There is nothing to do in France, we must come to North Africa to find jobs."

"There does seem to be a lot of rebuilding going on around here."

"This is true," said the second bearded young man, who was about my size and build. (Jean.) "As you can see, even though the end of the war is less than ten years, it is not so easy to find its remains."

"Every man in France can find work here, and is taking it," added the small, prematurely-balding 'Michel.'

"There's sort of a different reaction in the States," I told them. "While the men were all overseas, their jobs had to be filled by those left at home, including women. When the men came back, they wanted their old jobs, but there had been a lot of changes. Women didn't want to give up their work. Also, many of the factories closed up, because all they had been doing was making war-related materials. Employment was strange for a while, there."

What struck my new friends as most fascinating was the concept of American women proudly earning wages at men's jobs. Michel said, "*Les femmes*, they must be relieved to be at home again, are they not?"

"Oh, I'm sure many of them are." Little did we know the feminist revolution was fast approaching!

"Tell me," said Jean, "what are your plans while in Tunis?"

"I'll be meeting with the Renault agency in the afternoon tomorrow, but otherwise I only want to see the area."

"We can show you around, if you like."

I would like!

We all spent the following morning wandering through the ruins of Carthage, which I may have found more intriguing if I'd seen them at the start of my trip.

After our touring I left my friends and returned to the Renault agency. My contact there said his superior also thought the story of my trip might be a boon for their company, and the local newspaper was interested in printing it. A reporter arrived, and like the actress being sent to a make-up professional, Dolly was brought to the shop area for a tune-up and polish.

The reporter interviewed me, we were photographed, and the representative of my reluctant sponsor paid me enough (thank goodness!) to help fund the end of my African trip.

It was late by the time this work was finished, so I only stopped to replenish my food supplies, and went directly back to the hostel. My friends were there, with food of their own, and we prepared it all together. It was a dinner shared by a temporary family of brothers, and we smoked, drank, sang, and talked the night away.

They were busy the next day in their search for jobs, so I found myself once again wandering through the amazing *souks*. Those of Tunis were remarkable. With new money in my pockets, I made one purchase, which although it was against my better financial judgement, my heart was most pleased with it.

The owner of the shop was a Jewish man, and for one of the very few times while in North Africa, I told him I had been raised Jewish, too. He brought out some of his personal work, a series of brass trays bordered with silver. The craftsmanship was brilliant, and a particular piece, which had been decorated with the 10 commandments written in Hebrew lettering, caught my eye.

The owner asked, "Would you like to purchase this?"

"Yes, but I'm on an extended trip, and my funds are running low."

"What would you pay for it?"

In my mind, I laughingly thought, 'I have nothing like Metaxa to trade for such an item at the moment.' I made him a very low offer, the most I could afford, assuming he would simply say 'no,' or counter-offer something that would draw a simple 'no' from me.

"Do you have children?" asked the shopkeeper.

"Not yet."

"So young, to be buying such a treasure."

I ran my fingers along the fine raised lettering that flowed around the perfectly formed edges of the tray. "What I mean to do with it is give it to my grandmother. She would cherish it."

He eyed me, and it seemed he could see the truth in my statement. Holding out his hand, he said, "I will accept your offer."

Unbelievable! Bubbie prized that tray until the day she died.

That night, I shared a last dinner with my French hostel-mates, because I would be leaving the next day. We had such a night of revelry that I didn't wake until late, and by the time I had eaten, prepared my car, and said my final farewells to Tunis, it was late afternoon. I knew I wouldn't be able to make it to my planned destination, which was Constantine. Instead, I found a small village that night, in the mountains of Tunisia, just before the Algerian border.

I suppose I had been pushing that little Renault to the maximum of her abilities. While climbing the last mountain before the border (and before I reached the town there), she began laboring as if she were running out of breath. "What is it, Dolly?" I asked her. "Are you okay? We don't have far to go." A sign told me I was only ten kilometers from the town, but it pointed straight uphill. Moments after seeing that, the red warning light for oil flashed on. The thought of Dolly's poor engine burning up, or melting down, or whatever it is that happens to a dry motor, it broke my heart. The light on the dashboard held my attention better than the road. I begged and beseeched Dolly to keep moving, promising I would get her some oil as soon as humanly possible. I also swore I would never again assume that a day of ministrations in a garage meant I didn't have to bring spare fluids!

She got me to the summit of the mountain, and I coasted into the village, Dolly's engine cooling while she rushed down the mountain as though a handsome lover waited at the bottom. I steered us right to a garage, where the desperate strain of the danger to my car must have shown on my face; the wicked mechanic poured the oil in, then asked me to pay twice the price. I was so incensed I climbed into the car and told him to sit in the passenger seat. As soon as he closed the door, I drove directly to the most official-looking building in town, found someone in charge, and explained that the mechanic had tried to take advantage of my dire situation by doubling the cost of oil. The official set things straight, and I returned the contrite mechanic to his garage.

I heeded Dolly's warning and stopped for the night, but left early in the cold morning, determined to make it to Constantine that day.

The transition between Tunisia and Algeria was as easy as crossing a border of one U.S. state to another. Most noticeable to my chilled self was the welcome warmth of a vigorous sun.

The mountains gave way to large green hills, rich with vegetation. I could see why the French found these lands so alluring. Tiny communities were strung along the coast, and I assumed they were Arab fishing villages, but it was hard to say. The French character of the buildings, people, and landscape was so strong. This was disconcerting to me, and here's what I wrote about it in my journal:

> There is a sadness to the mixture of the two cultures; it feels
> as though neither the French nor the Arabs can truly claim

ownership of this wonderful land. The French government had incorporated Algiers as part of France itself, and everyone in Algiers has French citizenship. It was divided with 3 departments, each represented in the assembly in Paris. Tunisia and Morocco are governed as protectorates, and although each has maintained its own nationality, it seems there's no such thing as an 'Algerian.'

The Arabs, who make up the largest part of the population, want the French out, claiming the land as their own. Of course the Arabs are the real natives of the land, like our own Indians. They say the material good which the French have performed has only been for the benefit of the French themselves, and they have otherwise altogether forgotten to build spiritual and mental respect between the peoples of this country. There is deep emotional hatred among the two groups and many French people express fear of the natives.

Still making my way toward Constantine, I stopped in a town called Bone because I needed to exchange some currency. Poor timing; it was a Saturday, and all the banks were closed to the public. I did see a few weekend workers through the glass doors, and once or twice, I knocked until they opened the door to ask what I wanted. As soon as they heard I needed to make a currency exchange, the doors were closed in my face.

My frustration levels rose as I pounded through the town, looking for some sort of help. My last attempt was at a Thomas Cook's tour/travel agency, where I told them of the pleasant interactions I'd had with their establishment while in Florence, Italy. This warmed them a bit, but they were still reluctant to help. One man, who might've been as close to the top of Saturday's heap as one could find, told me to come back after lunch.

"Okay," I said, looking at my watch. It was a little past 11 a.m. "I'll be here at one o'clock."

"No, two o'clock. After lunch."

The Saturday afternoon, in what was a typically French town, moved lazily before my eyes. Tourists sat near me with coffees of their own, husbands and wives paraded up and down the boulevard with their children, boys and girls were dressed especially for passing one another on the promenade.

My thoughts spun back to another town square where I had seen other such flirtations between the youths. Where did I fit in, where was my place on this dance floor of life's performance? I remembered Rudy, who had mentioned his plans to permanently change his home base from Beirut to California. I also remembered that my sister Anne had spoken of following her fiancee to a teaching position he'd been offered in California. Maybe I could live in that state?

Strange thing is, at that time, I still couldn't clearly envision anything more realistic than marriage to a woman. It's true that everyone wishes to find love, and in fact that's all heterosexuals need to think about it: "I wish I could fall in love." Homosexuals must qualify the remark, for instance, "I wish I could fall in love with somebody I could realistically be with." In my case, the questions were, specifically: 'Can I be with a man, despite my familial and cultural upbringing?' Or, 'Can I be with a woman, despite my inherent predilection?' If the latter were true, she would certainly have to be quite special.

While in my twenties, I imagined I could find that particularly special woman, even expected it would happen one day or another. Until then…. Maybe that's why Rudy seemed a potential choice to me; we knew each other, and each other's bodies, but he wasn't the type to want to settle down for a lifetime. Perhaps I felt that he might be a nice, safe diversion until I could build the family expected of me.

For the moment I had forgotten about Bob, the burly painter I had met in Rome.

Still waiting for the French 'after lunch-time,' I watched the couples, the children, and the young lovers, all those fleshy symbols of a 'normal' life. My imagination led me to 1950s American propaganda-inspired images of a sweet little picket-fence house in upstate New York (or even California). A wife, two children, and a dog. The wife and I would tenderly exude loving care for each other and for our kids, who would attend respectable schools and make us proud. We would barbecue in the summer and celebrate Christmas and/or Hanukkah in the winter, whatever my family's preference might be. I would teach the kids to read and ride bikes and explain they must be polite to everyone they met. Never would I say anything negative about masturbation. No matter what sexual orientation my children chose, I would enthusiastically support the decision.

It could have been a nice life.

Sometimes the memories of that internal dissembling amuses me, other times it saddens me. The thing is, I'm not even sure how much I was lying to myself. In truth, I was simply trying to understand who I was, who I was becoming. I've probably said this before, but I'll say it again: Self-examination was, and is, no less complex for me than it is for any other man or woman on this earth.

At exactly two o'clock, I stepped into the offices of Thomas Cook, and found a new employee who had no problem exchanging my money. I could have kissed him. "I'm finally off," I told him, "to Constantine!"

"You'd better hurry. At this rate, you'll be on the roads long after dark."

I dashed out of town and proceeded through a small city called Philipsville, which was completely devoid of helpful signs. There I lost nearly another hour of driving, unable to find my way out of the cursed road out of there. Once I saw I was, at last, pointed on the continuing highway westward, I parked and examined my map. It didn't take long to throw up my hands and decide to head straight for Algiers, throwing out the idea of Constantine, after all. There was no way I was about to roll into a city like that after midnight, alone.

I could see the best place to stop for the night would be a little town I spelled in my journal as 'Bouji.' On my way there, I passed through green, fertile, mountainous country again. It struck me that most people (at least at the time) had quite a different image of Africa.

Dolly chose this leg of the journey to add to my frustrations by issuing coughs and flutters from her engine. Now I was a man on a mission; it seemed everything was trying to pile up against the closing kilometers of my trip. I stopped in the next mountain town I came to, checked the spark plugs like a professional, and changed one out. Dolly purred, and I laughed at the expression I would see on my friends' faces, when they heard how expertly I had repaired an automobile engine.

I rolled out of the mountains and back to the coastal route, where it began to rain heavily. Dolly's windshield wipers started in with the strange lift-flutter problem they'd had once before, but this time, I refused to stop. It began to grow dark. I set my jaw and drove slowly but determinedly on. Even the thought of the sea to my right did little to lighten my humor, nor did the sight of high rock walls that sometimes surged up around me.

My only grumpy thoughts were, "Why couldn't I have seen this in the daylight? Because of the foolish bureaucracy of banks on Saturday, that's why! Because I had to stop and pretend I know the first thing about auto mechanics! Because I have to putt along at 25 miles per hour in this downpour, since my damn windshield wipers aren't—"

Bang went a tire. It was so sudden, so absurd; *bang* went my dour mood. Now I began to sincerely laugh. Was it a cosmic plot? Had a family of gremlins taken up residence in my car?

It took me all of five minutes to change the tire; I had become an expert at that, if nothing else. Fifteen kilometers later I was in Bouji, but I simply passed through to the opposite edge of the town, parked, and cooked myself a small dinner. Fast and efficient, I rearranged from auto to bed and shooed all the gremlins away. That night I slept soundly through frequent sprints of melancholy, rain drops, bursts of wind, and a distant barking dog.

18

The Last of the Drive

From my journal:

My entry into Algiers was impressive. Everything looked so grand; the highway, the port, the cargo buildings, and finally Algiers itself, sitting on the side of the cliff. Its modern buildings were in complete contrast to their closest neighbors. In such a large city, how was I to find an *auberge*? As luck would have it, there it was, on the main street.

In a city such as this, I would stay in an *auberge* (inn), and the one I found was still under construction. Fine with me, because in that state, it fell within my price range. I settled in, and set off on foot to find some lunch.

Although I had worried about the tense relations between the French and the indigenous people, I found a restaurant where a party of some sort was being held, and was relieved to see some friendly interaction between the two factions.

Perhaps when we're asked, "Where are you from?" we should simply answer, "Earth." We're all human beings, sharing a planet in a lonely galaxy, and it strikes me as extremely neurotic that we must always separate ourselves by borders and politics, by races, classes, and religions.

After lunch I retrieved my car for a larger tour of Algiers. What an incredibly French city it was! The people, buildings, and prosperity were all so European. Until, that is, one visits the Casbah. I saved that for my second day there.

The Casbah was simultaneously everything and nothing I had imagined.

Before I could find the main, steep passage up into its apex, I first had to make my way through the steaming activity of the surrounding streets. Again, as I had experienced before, the mix of smells assaulted my nose, the racket rattled my ears, and the blend of languages baffled my brain. I could pick out French, English, and Arabic, but there was also German, Italian, Dutch, Spanish, and who knows what else being spoken all around me. Walking vendors constantly approached with whatever they could carry by hand, including clothes, toys, and collectibles. Jacks of all trades were on the streets, too, including beggars, couriers, a barber and a scribe.

I stopped at a cafe to catch my breath, but couldn't so much as inhale without suffering the intrusion of tobacco, liquor, bread, spicy meats, and acrid sweat. My eyes followed the main path of the throngs of people, which drew my attention to the entry of The Casbah proper. Everyone ignored the giant sign that read 'Off Limits,' which had become meaningless after the war. (I still don't know why it had been off limits *during* the war.)

The steep walk up is breathtaking in a literal way. As I climbed the endless, narrow, dirty, damp steps, I passed native women who were fully covered but for a slit to see out of. It seemed the worst thing I could possibly do was stare, but found it hard to avert my eyes.

Along the way, I was able to catch glimpses of life on the Casbah stairs through doors left open. Some interiors were little shops, but many were homes, and filled with children. I found these little urchins enchanting. I loved the native children, more than anything else in this strange world of the Casbah.

Otherwise, there were many secrets that would remain such to me, hidden behind the doors of homes I passed. The shops, on the other hand, openly displayed all trades and wares; shoe cobblers, metal-workers, toymakers and their toys, Arab pastries and other edibles.... Not one of these places drew me in, though, because I wouldn't have been able to bear such a dirty, crowded interior.

I'm not positive I definitely reached the top of the route, but I believe I did. After such a climb, the most attractive idea was to turn around and comfortably descend again. Drops of rain followed me back to the bottom, where I settled in a little French cafe and enjoyed a slow, pleasant lunch. I spent the last of that relaxing day at a theater, working on my language skills by watching a French-dubbed Barbara Stanwick movie.

A pleasant surprise awaited me back at my *auberge*; who did I find checking in but Jacques, Jean, and Michel from Tunis! They'd had no luck finding work in that city, so had decided to move on to Algeria, and had seen my car. It was a small world, back then, or maybe it's just that there were fewer people.

The boys were tired and soon went to bed, but in the morning, the four of us shared a breakfast together and toured through the 'downtown' area of Algiers. We returned to the auberge. There the apparently lonesome parents, a French couple, asked us to sit and share some conversation. It seemed like an agreeable diversion; it had begun to rain again outside.

Coffee was poured and cigarettes were passed around. The wife asked me, "What do you think of our city so far, Will?"

"Fascinating."

"And you," the husband said, addressing my friends, "are you young men having any luck finding work?"

Jacques answered for the group; "None so far."

"Have you considered the military? You may be needed there."

This caused the trio to exchange concerned glances. "The war is over, *monsieur*."

"A new one is on its way."

The wife gave her husband a shushing pat on the arm. "Don't concern these boys with gossip."

"It's more than gossip, *cheri*. The Arabs believes this country belongs to them, and wish to be left to govern it themselves."

I asked, "Do you think France should give in to their wishes?"

He responded with an elaborate sort of Frenchman shrug that I thought had been exaggerated for movies.

The wife lightly slapped his arm again. "This is our home, it is where we live." To me, she added, "I was born not 25 kilometers from this very spot. It is my country, too."

Who was I to argue? I'd been born in the United States, but Native Americans were there first. Still, America was and is 'my country.' When I explained as much, the wife, Jacques, Jean, and Michel all began agreeing at once, their words tumbling over each other.

Jacques: "Of course it is your country, because you are the ones who have developed it into what it is now!"

Jean: "If Europeans hadn't traveled there, it would have been someone else. Such rich lands could never have lain dormant."

The wife: "Wherever you are born, that is your place."

Michel: "France didn't *take* Northern Africa as much as she has protected it!"

The husband interrupted everyone with a silently raised hand. Apparently, he saw a broader picture. "When the Vichy, the Italians, and the Nazis tried to win these lands, we Frenchmen fought them. We proudly celebrated our victory. Can't you understand why the people of Algeria wish to fight us now?"

This astute observation was met with a pregnant silence, not broken until Michel asked, "They do want to fight us now, don't they?"

"Mitterand will never stand for it," insisted the wife.

"And that," concluded the husband, "is why there will be a war."

Fortunately for me, they held off until about seven months after I was back in the States. The husband and wife had been right, too. The French Minister of the Interior, Francois Mitterand, had responded to increasing guerilla attacks by saying, in essence, "Algeria is French. Your guerillas will attack the French on their own land? This means war." That terrible, bloody chaos started in November of 1954, and dragged on eight years, until at last, people like the parents of my hostel could then apply for Algerian citizenship.

If, that is, they survived. I have no idea whether any of my friends of the hour lived through it all, and it wouldn't surprise me to learn they hadn't.

The next morning, I said my goodbyes, telling the boys to look for me if they continued on to Oran.

I reached Oran early that evening, and my first impression was that it was 'the Chicago of Algeria.' Indeed it was an industrious, commercial place, with hundreds of railroad tracks leading in and out of the city.

Before I came across a hostel or hotel, I found the offices of the Youth Council in Oran, which turned out to be a club room of the youth movement of Algiers. It was hard to picture those friendly young men gathered in smoky cafes planning a war with France, but I imagine such meetings were going on. In any case, a few of those boys set me up with a room for the night, where I slept comfortably.

The next day I called Kassim, and we met in the afternoon. When I saw him again, it was not so difficult, when compared to the fresh faces where I'd spent the night, to see him as a guerilla. It could be that part of his handsome charm was the danger that simmered beneath the surface of his countenance.

His friendliness toward me was a factor of my attraction, too. He showed me his home town with the respect any tour guide would give a visiting dignitary, then drove me up a nearby mountain for an overall view. From there Oran was distinctly outlined, with its original port on one side and the French Naval port on the other. Kassim pointed out an old church and said, "Before the French were the Spanish. That is the church of Santa Cruz. Where is the state of Islam?"

A nervous shudder shook through me, but I don't think he noticed.

Kassim told me I would be dining on an Arab meal at his house that evening, and at that time I would meet his father. "First," he added, "I must pick up some friends of mine."

Within about five seconds of meeting one of these two friends, I began crossing my fingers that he wouldn't be joining us for dinner. That young man was a communist, trained in Moscow, only recently returned to Algeria. When Kassim introduced us in French, he looked at my outstretched hand and turned away. If only the mysterious man called Jon had been there to see it! It was rude though, of course, and Kassim angrily muttered something to the man in Arabic.

Before we were all in the car, I quietly asked Kassim, "Did I offend him in some way?"

"A newborn child could offend him. Perhaps he does not like western men, or he may be envious of your freedom of travel. He will not be with us long; we are only giving him a lift."

Kassim and I attempted a few conversations in French, but the angry communist continually interrupted in Arabic. He obviously wished I could not only be left out of the conversation, but out of the car, as well. When we reached his destination, I ignored him until after we had driven away.

Kassim's other friend, who had been quiet until that moment, began to speak with us in French. I learned that 'Hadad' was a young jeweler, and when I told him of some of the fine pieces I had seen on my travels, he insisted I visit his shop.

Kassim added, "We will pass it, anyway, on the way to my home."

We parked in front of a jewelry store and Hadad led the way through to the miniature factory at the back of the shop. There, he showed me in detail how gold bracelets were made. It seemed to me a combination of mechanics, science, and of course, art.

Hadad, a budding master of his trade, became involved in a conversation with one of the jewelers, and we said quiet goodbyes to him. Kassim led me to a short, dark hallway, through an inconspicuous doorway, and up a few steps. This strange route brought us to a terrace which had amazing flooring of a tile mosaic. Kassim opened one of the two doors before us and showed me his long, spacious room, which was sparsely but tastefully decorated with an impressive style of comfort.

And by the way, he wasn't kidding when he said we'd pass the jewelry store to get to his home!

The only thing that looked out of place in Kassim's big room was a table that had been set up in the middle of it. Noticing how I eyed it, Kassim told me, "That is specially for you, my friend. Tonight we will dine in western style on Arab food."

I had already learned it was the custom for Arabs to seat themselves on pillows at a low table for dining, and in fact that's what I would have preferred. It makes me wonder, how often do we commit this mistake when entertaining traveling foreigners? An immigrant might miss the ways of his homeland, but travelers often wish to experience the practices of the lands they're visiting. At least with respect to the food that was served, I wasn't let down.

I don't know how many Americans in the 1950s had ever heard the word 'couscous,' but even if they had, I doubt they would have identified it as a type of food. For Arabs, it was as common as (from my journal) 'steak and french fries.' The way it was served during my meal was that a soup plate was filled with a big forkful of a white grain, then a flavorful juice was poured over that, and it was all topped with meat and vegetables. It was filling, although I tried not to eat too much, suspecting there was more to come. Sure enough, I was next served a fresh salad, and a side-dish of mashed carrots spiced with something I might be able to name now, if I tasted it, but at the time, I was baffled.

Before I could wonder if the meal was complete, we were brought a savory pastry, which Kassim's mother had baked especially for the occasion. It was shaped like a figure eight cruller, quite crisp and coated with a sweet syrup. I thought it a perfect dessert, and also thought, with relief, 'One more bite and I would have burst.'

We didn't leave the table, and to my gastronomical concern, plates of fruit were brought out. It's hard to understand how people can eat so much and maintain any sort of waistline. I nibbled as carefully as possible.

Throughout our meal, I never saw any women, although I couldn't help but wonder if they were peeking at us through keyholes. I also wondered about Kassim's father, who I was supposed to meet, but it wasn't until after the table was cleared that the venerated gentleman appeared.

Kassim and I both stood when the tall man entered the room in long, black robes and a huge, white turban. His face was leathery but distinguished, his dark intelligent eyes were framed by thick-rimmed glasses, and he wore a gray mustache and long beard. He spoke no English, but his French was slow and modulated enough that we had no trouble understanding each other.

"*Bonjour*, Will," he said. "It is a pleasure to meet you."

He was balancing his weight with both hands on a thick, heavy cane, so I didn't offer to shake his hand. I gave a polite nod and responded, "The honor is mine."

After he seated himself at the table I offered him a cigarette, as I could see his mustache had that slight, tobacco discoloration. He refused my offer—I imagined he was more of a hookah-smoker. "I would like to thank you," he said, "for helping Kassim to come home. I trust you found him to be a pleasing traveling companion?"

"Very much so." I glanced at Kassim, who was sitting back in his chair with his left arm across his waist, bracing the elbow of his right arm, and his chin resting on the thumb of his raised right hand. With his forefinger he repeatedly stroked his upper lip. He acted calm and contemplative, but it was the most nervous I had ever seen him.

"Will," the Father continued, "I understand you have driven around the entire Mediterranean Sea. I am curious about the American view of the cultures you've seen."

I told him an abbreviated version of what I've written in this book, although it must be obvious which scenes I omitted. Anything sexual, of course (other than to comment on the beauty and charm of some of the women I had seen), and I studiously avoided mentioning my own Jewishness. Although we brushed across the topic of the Israelis, Kassim's father was more intent on the France/Algeria situation.

"Who," he asked, "do you think the Americans would support, in the idea of Algerian independence?"

"I have to admit, I had no real knowledge of the situation between your countries until I came here. The American public might not be very aware of it. If it does become common knowledge, my first thought is that we would support the Algerian people."

"I was referring more to your government, than to your people."

Here was a wise man. I had the feeling he'd never been outside of an Arab country, yet he understood something it had taken me months of foreign travel to figure out. I said, "I'd like to think my government would support it, too."

"But I heard your Indians have been treated poorly."

"That may be so. However, we at least recognize the problem, and even try to make amends. In your situation, it doesn't seem the French feel any inclination to consider this country anything but a protectorate that belongs to them."

Kassim's father nodded sagely and gestured I should continue, if I had anything else to add.

"We did support the forming of Israel," I said, "even though we have no argument with the Arabs. But people need a place to…. Well, to *be*. Americans believe in that."

Kassim cringed at my mention of Israel, almost imperceptibly, but his father had a different reaction. "That is a good observation. I would have enjoyed having a student such as you."

"You were a teacher?"

"Yes, but my health failed me." He held up his hand at the concern that crossed my face. "I am better now, but retired. Still, I enjoy intelligent conversation."

"What did you teach?"

"I was a professor of Arab language. As you can see I also learned French, but I find myself wishing I had spent more time with your English language. America fascinates me."

"It's a country to be proud of."

"I agree. Roosevelt made mistakes, but I believe Eisenhower will do much better." He lifted his huge, wrinkled hands and rested them on the top of his cane. As he gazed silently at his flexing fingers for a long moment, I examined his face again. It was like looking at an ancient philosopher of the Islam world. He lifted his eyes and I could see in them that he was ready to end the discussion. When he began to push himself to his feet, Kassim rushed to his side, but didn't touch him. Once steadied, the gentleman spoke briefly to Kassim in Arabic, then turned to me. "It was an honor to meet you and speak with you, Will. Goodbye."

I responded in kind, and after he was gone, Kassim clapped a comradely hand on my shoulder. "He told me he couldn't have been more proud and pleased than if I'd been entertaining your president."

Wow. This was, of course, very flattering, but now, I wish I would have at least written Kassim after I was safely home, and admitted to being Jewish.

My friend suggested a cordial, which I said sounded nice, but he had no alcohol in his home. (He hadn't touched liquor throughout the entire time we spent together, as a strong follower of his faith.) He did say, "I know of a cafe where we can find you a drink," and we stopped at the jewelry store to ask Hadad if he'd like to join us. He readily agreed, not being such a strong follower of his faith as Kassim.

At the cafe, Hadad asked when I would be returning home.

"Not for a while yet. I'm going to spend another month or two in Europe, see England, visit my uncle in Germany, hopefully do some skiing. I'll be sailing out from France in May."

Hadad tapped the table in front of Kassim and spoke to him. "If you were to go to France in May, you might have a chance to say one last farewell to your friend."

Kassim lifted one shoulder, let it drop.

Hadad said to me, "He has his university degree, but it is hard for him to find work here. I think he should go to France." To Kassim he added, "You're still considering it, aren't you?"

"I am considering it."

This surprised me. The man who despised everyone not Arab, moving to another country? Specifically to France, the country he'd once fought against? I asked Kassim, "What would you do there?"

"I'm sure I could find work as a translator."

He could, too, his French was quite fluent. "Wouldn't you miss your home?"

"Somewhat. However, if this unrest between our nations explodes, which my father thinks will happen, I would rather not be here. I have lived with enough war."

A grin escaped me. How curious! For such a long time, I had been thinking Kassim was a soldier at heart!

"Why are you smiling?"

"Because I'm worried about the people here, and this talk of war. I'd prefer to imagine you're safe rather than here, fighting."

He gave another one-shouldered shrug. "I cannot bear the thought of returning to a life of robes and turbans. We must advance with the rest of the world."

It's good to know my affections for this man weren't misguided. Certainly, he had been raised with prejudices, but sometimes I can't help but wonder if that intelligent man suspected me of all my secrets, and accepted me anyway.

I suppose all we can really do, when dealing with contradictory cultures, is approach each other one at a time. Find our common humanity. Try to understand one another. If we can't form actual friendships, empathy will do.

During my final night in Algiers, in another hostel, I woke at about one in the morning to the recognizable sound of a desert Volkswagon. Jacques, Jean, and Michel again! They came in as quietly as was possible for such spirited young men, and told me they had once again seen my car parked outside.

We sat up late, talking, old friends catching up. When they asked where I would be going next, I said, "Oujda," and they all gave a cheer, albeit quietly, with respect to the household. "That is where we are going too!"

We decided to meet in that town, which is on the border of Morocco, the following night.

Before reaching Oujda, I found a Foreign Legion town called Sidi-Bal-Abbes. There were soldiers, mercenaries, and veterans everywhere, wearing every sort of uniform. I suppose if war is your work, the Mediterranean region is the place to be.

The guards of the main Legion compound allowed me to enter that area, and here is what I wrote about it in my journal:

> I was shown through two separate museums, both rather interesting, but with too little to be seen to make it really worthwhile. They glorified many of their members by keeping their personal belongings under glass, but these strangers were unknown and therefore unimportant to most of the museum visitors.

The overall area was quite extensive, and the faces of the legionnaires showed no similarity of origin. I kept thinking all the while of the glory of this fighting organization and of movies like "Beau Geste." These men had joined the Legion from all over the world, few giving their right names, and many had done things that would not let them again face society as they had before. No questions were asked when they joined, it was enough that they wished to be a part of the Legion.

I pushed on westward, through another wonderful drive. Especially pretty was a waterfall flowing into a gorge, which I crossed on a bridge. The road brought me to Tlemcen, an ancient-looking city, where I stopped for lunch. After Tlemcen the mountains grew fewer and further between, and before nightfall, I was in Morocco.

Because Morocco was another French protectorate, Oujda was as clean and modern as all Northwest African big cities. However, because of its size, it wasn't so easy to find the Oujda hostel. I ended up asking around, eventually approaching a young man who looked like a hosteler himself, and he was more than happy to help. He told me I could pick up the keys from a place in town after a few hours.

I found a sunny cafe across from where I would be retrieving the keys, a perfect spot for some reading, writing, and coffee. (If a U.S. state ever becomes a French protectorate, I'm heading straight for the cafes!)

Barely an hour had passed when I heard the sputtering racket of not just any old car, but the Volkswagon of my French friends. Jean leaned out the passenger window and called to me with a grin, and soon the four of us were exchanging stories again.

There was still a little time to kill, so we went to the local Monoprix and stocked up on some dinner foods. The key to the hostel was available by the time we returned. When we arrived at those lodgings, we found there were only two small rooms, empty but for three mattresses. Fortunately, I had my air mattress, and hauled it inside for our slumber party.

After an enjoyable dinner of French blood sausages, wine, bread, cheese, and fruit, we all tucked in for the night in the strangely abandoned, quiet hostel. When we woke, we couldn't find anybody to pay, but what could it have been worth?

This time, when I told the boys my next destination was Fez, Michel (the beardless, balding one) asked, "Would you mind if I ride with you?"

Yes! Finally, someone new to sing with me along the drive.

We drove past the Fez medina, which was the original city, into the new area, which had once again been modernized by their protectors. It couldn't have been more obvious that it and the original city had been developed by two different worlds.

We found the local hostel, and after a good meal, we headed for the medina. Most enchanting to me was seeing all the ostriches perched in trees, making homes high in the branches. It isn't what I would have imagined an ostrich lifestyle to be like.

I'll show here what more I had to say about the medina of Fez in my journal:

> There were excellent examples of tile work everywhere, especially near some of the public baths with their water fountains, where there was always great activity going on. Our walk took us over many bridges that crossed the little streams running through town. There was much dampness

and mud, which was typical of every medina I had seen. We were stared at as much as we stared. Often we came across food stalls, with meat hanging openly from hooks, covered with flies. There was much fruit to buy, too. Soon we were lost in all of this.

'Lost' was putting it mildly. Everything looked the same to us; the buildings, the people, the high walls, the stalls, and each gate seemed as elaborate and popular as the next. We asked quite a few people where we could find the main gate before we were given what we thought were proper directions. As it turned out, the gate where we had parked wasn't the 'main,' after all. It was, in fact, at the opposite side of the huge medina from where we then stood. Ridiculously, we had to take a bus back to the car.

Near one of those portals I saw a small crowd gathered, and pulled over to see what had caught their interest. A snake charmer! I climbed out of my car to observe this fascinating, distinctly Arab form of entertainment up close. Wait—'entertainment' might be the wrong word. For them, this was more a form of magic, maybe?

Young Arab boys sat in a wide circle, staring intently at the snake charmer who looked rather like a witch, with his brown hairy legs covered in sores, and strings of grimy hair hanging down from his head in braids. He chanted eerily, accompanied by a music I can best describe as 'mysterious,' and which was provided by his three (equally grimy) helpers. One boy played sort of a drum, the other a string instrument, and the third a horn, which almost put *me* into a trance, let alone the snake.

While he chanted, the charmer stepped toward people in the crowd, accepting donations, blessing those who gave. After a few payments, he would step closer and closer to the ominous snake, both teasing it and offering it loving caresses. Whenever there was a lull in contributions, he would chew straw and blow smoke through it from his mouth.

At some point, he must have felt the right weight of coins in his pockets. Curling the big snake around his neck, he entered into an Arab chant so long and entrancing I thought it wise to break free. I had been entertained enough, and didn't want to become bewitched.

I drove slowly along a back route toward the French section, and found dark native women of the evening plying some daytime trade. They stood at the mouths of caves in the rocks, and when they beckoned me I didn't look away, as did most other passing tourists. This was simply one more fascinating aspect of a land I had never seen before. The only men openly responding to the siren songs were locals.

Back at the hostel that night, I shared another home-made dinner with my French friends, and Michel asked to ride with me again in the morning. They'd found no promise of employment in this city, and were determined to continue westward to the end of the line. We all went to sleep early, and Jacques and Jean departed before Michel and me.

Fez left me with a feeling that I had seen some of the truest aspects of Moslem life. As far as I could ascertain, it was a throbbing center of their cultural world.

Because we were a few hours behind Michel's friends, we made our way quickly to Casablanca. Now the waters in sight were the Atlantic Ocean, which reminded me how close I was coming to my trip's end. True, I would be spending more months in Europe, and would have a few more fascinating experiences, but my lovable Dolly wouldn't be with me. I would be a predictable tourist.

The U.S. Air Force had established bases all over the area of Morocco, and Americans were everywhere. I initiated friendly waves until we were in Casablanca proper. There, Michel and I quickly made our way to the hostel we had all agreed upon. (I should mention that there were certain tricks to finding hostels; they were often located in specific sections of cities, or owners would pass on information for us all, across the countries, to help us find our way from one establishment to the next.)

The Casablanca hostel was quite crowded, which was unusual, but it brought hope to my French friends. Upon our arrival, Jacques and Jean informed Michel they believed there was work to be found in this place. They introduced us to a few other young Frenchmen, who said, "If you don't want to work for the Americans, you can take the place of locals who left other jobs to work for them."

My friends went off to research the details, and I took the opportunity to make some purely English-speaking acquaintances.

What a scatter of nationalities I found there! Most entertaining was an Australian, who told me Casablanca was not exactly a city of great tourist interest. "It's worthwhile to see for a day or two, though," he told me in his charming accent. "Come along, I can show you around."

This man, who I'll call Preston, was about thirty years old, and about as average as a man can get. Medium height, build, complexion, hair-color, eye-color… I can't quite remember his face, other than the fact that I found it relaxing. Such a common sort of fellow, except (at least for me) his Aussie accent.

He explained to me that the evidence of the French occupation was as clear as could be. "Look there," he said, as we stepped out of the hostel. "All those tall white buildings, fancy hotels—and look at that shopping center. All French, easy to see, ain't it?"

"It sure is."

"Now come along over here." We stepped around to the other side of the hostel, and he pointed out a native section. The houses were ramshackle, most of the stores were boarded up, and it looked nearly deserted.

I asked, "Where is everybody?"

"Still in their original homes, is my understanding. You see, the French built this neighborhood as an incentive for the natives to relocate. Only the ones who had no other choice moved here, and they've turned it into a shanty-town."

"I heard about such a thing in Thebes. That the natives have no inclination to leave the places they've lived in all their lives, and can't even be bribed by brand new homes."

"Spot on, mate. Sometimes I wonder why people can't just leave each other alone. I guess they'll get moved soon enough, though. They're going to start a war with France any minute, which isn't very bright, because the French have got better weapons, and a better military. A lot of Arabs will die."

"But if it's a question of re-establishing national identity, won't the U.N. become involved?"

"Might. Your country might, too. Everybody likes to hold off as long as they can, though, to see if things can be worked out between the battlers. While the world waits, the natives in Northwest Africa are going to have to build themselves a lot more refugee camps. It'll be another bloody mess."

The foresight of this simple man was extraordinary. The only place his prophecy fell short was in the level of violence of the conflict, which exceeded his prediction.

I suggested we take my car to the original section of Casablanca, which was a ways from the hostel. Once there, Preston pointed to a restaurant and said, "You might like a bit to eat there. You're Jewish, ain't you?"

To have that secret so boldly (and blandly) spoken aloud startled me, but I only responded by asking, "That's a Jewish restaurant?"

"This whole area is the Jewish quarter. Come on, I could eat a kangaroo."

We parked and my eyes darted around the restaurant as we entered. Here I was, among what could be considered my ancestral people, but I felt entirely separate from them. They looked, dressed, talked, even ate differently than I did. Preston and I shared a simple meal of bread and eggs, and headed back out into the town. The rest of old Casablanca didn't seem in much better shape than the shanty-town I'd seen, but it was much livelier. It fascinated me to see Arabs and Jews living so calmly alongside one another.

That night, Preston joined me and my French friends for another improvised dinner. During that meal, Jacques said, "We've committed to some lodgings in the city, and we'll be moving there tomorrow."

"You've already found jobs?"

"No," said Jean, whose English was the rockiest of the three. We were avoiding French, because Preston couldn't understand it. "But she is better-looking here than is any different place we see."

Preston lifted both hands in a sort of mock surrender. "You've done better than I 'ave, and I've been here a month! I *knew* I should have learned the bloody language!"

I laughingly asked, "Which one?"

"French or Arabic—they're both here for the duration."

"So, we will try to settle here for a time," said Michel, giving me a smile of endeared friendship. "It is time for us to be parting ways,

Will."

"I'll miss you all."

The three lifted their glasses of wine to mine. Preston joined in the toast, then asked, "Tell me again how you all met up?"

We explained the nature of our separate journeys, and Preston grasped me by the shoulder and gave me a friendly shake. "Sounds like you'll need a new traveling companion, now. I know it would be an improvement on my bank account if I could get across the Strait with shared expenses."

"You're going to Spain?"

"As good a place as any. Should have learned bloody Spanish, though."

Our deal was made, and that night, I said my final goodbyes to Jacques, Jean, and Michel. It worried me that they stayed entrenched in the unrest of that region, and I'd be surprised to learn that any of them lived past their 30th birthdays. It truly was a nasty war between North Africa and the French. What war isn't so?

Preston and I spent the following day at the beach area of Casablanca. Because the sea and coast were too rough for swimming, the city had decided to build pools along the shore. That was disconcerting enough, but that they were filled with seawater was stranger still. However, at the time I was there, the real claim to fame was that one of the swimming pools was the largest in the world, extending quite a distance along the beach. To date, I can't imagine a larger pool has been built.

By midday, I was ready to head back to town, and told Preston my car needed another once-over by the local Renault agency.

With fresh funds in my pocket, I took another walk through the shops, wondering what memento I might find for this near-end of my journey. Unfortunately, the prices were the highest I had seen yet in Northern Africa, so I held off. In retrospect, I wish I would have bought a strange-but-cute carved phallus I found. It was life-sized (for an average man), and highly polished, but where would I have displayed it in any home I might find? Decades would pass before the world would catch up to the propriety of a man exhibiting such artwork.

Preston and I set out in the morning for Marrakech, taking a slow drive, because the mechanic at Renault had installed new pistons in my car. Preston said he missed driving, so I let him take over for a while. It was refreshing for me to watch the pretty landscape passing by, musing about what the legendary Marrakech would be like.

Our first view of it from the road was of the snow-covered Atlas, the mountains of which rose like a giant wall blocking the rest of Africa, or dividing it. I couldn't see where it began or ended, but felt it extended beyond my imagination. The white snow was like a cake frosting, separating the peaks from the sky, which was a brilliant blue when we arrived.

It had struck me that it was always sunny in Morocco, but the sun really jumped out at me in Marrakech. Bright rays brought the mountains of snow to life, made the greens of the palm trees more vivid, and gave a special individuality to the colorful buildings.

That the place had been Frenchified like the other Northwest Africa cities I had seen was a bit of a let-down. From the stories I had heard, I half-expected to be the only motorized vehicle on the road. But no, a wide boulevard brought us into the city, busy with many giant 1940s and '50s cars. The street was lined with modern buildings, cafes, and French women wheeled their babies in carriages through parks.

The segregation between this area and the native section wasn't as distinct as it had been in Fez, but it was still clear. In the older part of town, searching for the youth hostel, we wandered past hookah-cafes, Arab restaurants, and dilapidated houses. Preston's sense of direction was even worse than mine, and it took us a few hours to find the hostel. Fortunately, when we did find it, (right in the middle of the medina), it was exotically Arabian, the expanded residence of a native family.

The little girl who answered the door, with a shy smile radiating out from her sweet face, looked like anything but a hostel 'parent.' She led us through the main courtyard to one of five surrounding doors, and showed us a room with two beds, and cushions on the floor for seating at a low table.

Preston and I settled in, then returned to the medina for an excellent Arab dinner (couscous and all) at a local cafe. On our way back to the hostel, near its main door, I saw a disreputable-looking bum noticing my packed, parked car. I approached, and he asked in poor, French-accented English, "You car?"

"Yes."

"I watch, tonight?" He pointed to his eyes, then to the car, then held up his fists to make sure I understood he meant to guard it. Another poorly-dressed fellow passed by and muttered a greeting to the bum, who smiled and responded with a friendly 'hello.' He turned back to me and intimated, "He, no good. He take car, all things. I watch, stop him."

Hmm. Extortion? I unlocked the door, retrieved a bottle of wine that sat too conspicuously on the rear seat, and handed it to Preston. "I'll meet you back at the room."

"You sure?"

"No problem." I faced the bum again, who had watched the departing bottle of wine with greedy eyes. "Sir," I said in French, "what would it cost me for you to guard my car?"

"Very little. Thirty francs."

"I'll pay you twenty."

"I accept. I will guard your car." He then proceeded to open the door, climb inside, and shut the door behind him.

I was so surprised that I could only stand there at first, gaping, while he made himself comfortable. When I abruptly pulled the door open again he started as though he had actually begun to doze off.

"Our agreement," I explained in French, "is that you *watch* the car, not inhabit it!"

This didn't faze him in the slightest. He stepped out, walked a few paces to a doorway, and sat down with his eyes fixed on Dolly. I relocked the car and backed away slowly, wondering if I had made an intelligent decision, but could think of no better option.

While Preston and I shared the wine in our room, he asked me, "Have you ever wondered what it might be like, you know, to have a dalliance with another bloke?"

An obvious proposition, bless his heart. Unfortunately, if I added up every ounce of sexual attraction I felt for him, the sum total would be zero. "Yes," I answered. "I've wondered, but I don't anymore."

"Right, then." He'd had his answer, and was gentleman enough to abandon the question for the remainder of the time we spent together. I've heard that some heterosexual people are concerned that Gays might be pushy, or manipulative, or try to 'convert' others into same-sex experiences. Never in my life have I witnessed such behavior.

Preston and I finished our wine, then departed for the *Djamaa Al Fna*, famous for the way its picture of native life was displayed so openly to all passersby. It was a sight which Hollywood, in its better moments, would have had difficulty in equaling. I wrote about it in my journal:

> In one small square was gathered all the fascination of the Moslem world, including snake charmers, sword eaters, story tellers, native medicine men, dancers, and barbers. The waterboys were the most colorful sight, with their bells sounding off in the bright sunlight and their brim hats covering their smiling, sunburned faces. We could not wander very far before we were approached by people eager to be paid for having their photograph taken. Occasionally, we stopped to watch one performance or another, but if the performer's eyes caught ours, we would instantly be approached for coins. The dancing was worth a small fee; it was quite primitive, and more African than Arabic. The performers were mountain people, Berbers, who were the original inhabitants of this area even before the Arabs came to conquer. Such a strong-looking people, with eyes more still and content than those of the Arabs I have seen.

Here is where the Moslem world came—as much as tourists—for entertainment, business, relaxation, and adventure. There were numerous brothels of all types located in and around the square. The faces of Arabs and tourists alike expressed happiness, interest, concern, and deep fascination.

When we'd had our fill, Preston and I both made a purchase from one of the popular peanut stands, and headed back to the hostel. As we passed my hired bum and his charge, he gave me a loose, but aware, salute.

I found Dolly's guardian still seated in the doorway the next morning, looking as though he had barely changed position for sleeping. Wondering why such a reliable man couldn't find a regular job, I paid him the original price he had requested.

Preston and I checked out of the hostel and packed up the car, but I wanted to return to the *Djamaa Al Fna* for one more peek. It was my intention to see how it looked with fewer people, but there was already much activity, including performers surrounded by admirers.

However, during this visit, I was struck by a different faction of the square:

> The blind were pathetic to watch as each were led around by a poor child who would beg for change. These people were accustomed to tourists, and it seemed they only saw us in a capacity of what we could give them. This was their Times Square, and the pulse of human activity was just as strong.

I had passed through Rabat on my way down to Casablanca but hadn't stopped. (At the time, Michel and I had been on a mission to meet up with his regular traveling companions.) Now, I would stay a few days, see what the city had to offer.

What first enchanted me was the beach, where the Atlantic struck the ragged rocks of the coastline with a mighty force. Preston and I spent our entire first day watching those waves, sunbathing, and snacking on food I purchased at the local PX.

The following day was even more glorious, especially once we found a magnificent tropical garden. Dolly had been giving me trouble starting, and I brought her to a garage to have the battery charged. The mechanic recommended we wait at the nearby garden, and I can't imagine time better spent. The place struck me as very old, but Preston told me it had been built by the French colonials not so long ago. It was thickly lush, with dozens of trees, plants, and flowers, many I couldn't identify. What stands out most in my memory were palm trees with trunks thickened by richly lavish layers of climbing vines.

While we lounged on a bench, which had been placed on a neatly combed gravel path, I said, "Preston."

"What's on your mind, mate?"

"Tomorrow, we'll be in Tangier, boarding a ferry to cross the Strait of Gibraltar."

"Spot on."

I lowered my head, closed my eyes, and ran through the journey in my mind. First it came to me like scenes in a play, then like a chapbook of stories, and finally I captured it all, as best as I could, like the unbroken stream of a movie.

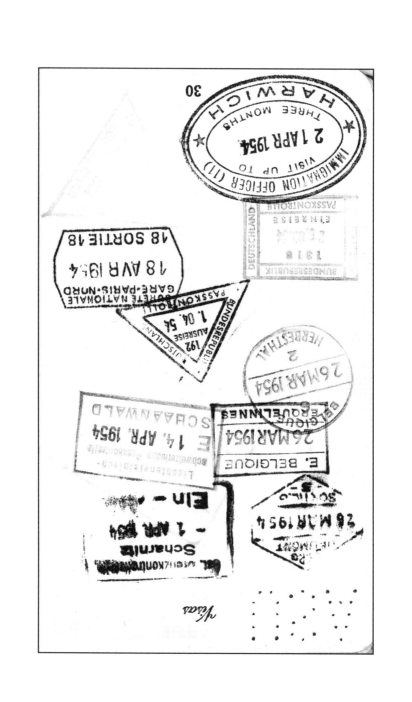

19

The Trip's End

Aside from a few passing comments about Tangier (I was not impressed), my journal ended with that garden. The rest is left to my most significant memories.

The prescient Preston and I fondly parted ways in Spain, but we never corresponded after that. European Spain seemed positively tame after my North African adventure, and I was only in that country for a day or two. I was in a hurry to return to France where I would offer my overall advertising package to the main Renault agency.

Throughout my travels I had been building the presentation. I had gathered it in a scrapbook, and it consisted of photos and clippings of text, which I was able to type (or have typed) in one way or another. Once I was back in France, I spent a few days with a man in upper Renault management, who was obviously reluctant to part with many francs, but willing to consider some of the notoriety I offered. "Of course," he first said, "we will speak with the local newspaper, and they will probably like to write an article about your trip."

"That would be terrific. How much do you think it will pay?"

"Not very much."

Too bad. I intended to see a few more countries in Europe, and do some skiing. A pair of custom-made ski boots still awaited me in Innsbruck! Funding would be imperative.

"Next," the manager continued, "we will consider your advertising campaign, but at this time I do not think it is something we would like to purchase from you."

"That's your decision," I responded politely. Inside, frustration tied a sad knot in my stomach.

"However, I am wondering what you now intend to do with your Renault?"

Hmm. Could this be a bargaining position? I had planned to have the car shipped back to the States with the money Renault should have paid me for advertising.

I began in a roundabout way; "Well, I'm going to approach the newspapers back home, and one day I might even write a book about my adventures. It would be nice to have the car to display. As far as I've been able to ascertain, this is the first time anyone has ever driven an automobile around the Mediterranean Sea. The car itself could become quite a collector's item."

"Ah, yes, I can see what you are saying." He stroked his inevitable goatee while his thoughts seemed to spin with possibilities of what to do with the car—ideas he must have already considered, because he was the first one who had broached the subject.

"If you would be interested," said Monsieur de Renault, "you may leave the car here, and we would consider shipping a replacement to your home in—" he scanned the papers in front of him—"New York."

Meeting his calm demeanor with an admirable composure of my own, I sat back in my chair and silently contemplated this offer. He began to shift nervously behind his desk. While I thought, it occurred to me that he had probably outright lied when he said they would ever consider using my advertising campaign. I'd been giving them the opportunity for nearly seven months, as it was now March. I responded with a lie of my own, told in the hopes of urging him toward some sort of financial compensation.

"*Monsieur*, I already have a car in New York. Would you consider re-purchasing the Renault from me? If you do, I would make no further claims on it, even if it becomes famous for its journey."

Four days later I was on a train to Innsbruck, ready to retrieve my boots and use them for skiing, with the equivalent of $8,000.00 USD in my bank account. It would be more than enough for high times during the remainder of my trip across the Atlantic, and leave plenty of change for setting up a new life back in the States.

*   *   *

At the time of the writing of this book, I am eighty years-old. Although my senses are as sharp as they've ever been, my memory has certainly been in better condition. For this reason, I can't say exactly what Renault did with my dear Dolly. They might have displayed her as some sort of 'Renault Wonder' at a dealership. Yes, that would have been a shameless theft of my advertising idea, but then again, they had given me $8,000.00 for a car that had gathered approximately 15,500 rough miles in about seven months. I was satisfied with the bargain.

The bootmaker in Innsbruck remembered me well, and my boots were ready for the slopes. After my less-than-satisfying experience of skiing at the Cedars, I spent two glorious weeks gliding down the Alps of Austria, in my element. It was hard to match that experience throughout the following decades, and I was an enthusiastic skier well into my sixties.

After Austria I stopped for a visit with my aunt and uncle in Western Germany. After my low-budget trip, this was five days of grandeur, because Aunt Eva's husband Mario was the Brazilian ambassador to Western Germany. While I was there, they had various functions and duties to attend, but Uncle Mario told me, "Whenever you want to travel about the town, call my chauffeur."

The visit was an opulent blur, but for one particular evening. Uncle Mario invited me to a dinner that would involve politics; perhaps it was an attempted meeting of the minds between the upper-echelons of West Germany and the still-communist East Germans.

It was now well into May of 1954. Less than two months before, President Eisenhower had told Richard Nixon, his Vice President, to go for McCarthy's throat. Nixon proceeded to make a politically correct speech in which he didn't use McCarthy's name, but everybody knew exactly who he was talking about. I've even found the quote: "Men who have in the past done effective work exposing communists in this country have, by reckless talk and questionable methods, made themselves the issue rather than the cause they believe in so deeply."

Now McCarthy, and the possibility of a communist under every American rock, had become a joke.

At the political banquet we were escorted to tables with arranged seating, which put me with my ambassador relation near the head of the heap. What I saw on the other end of the spectrum was a scene that can make me laugh out loud, to this day.

Some lowly tables had been set up in a darker corner of the massive dining room, near the bathrooms. I'd been forced by convention to wait for the proper moment at the end of the festivities to relieve myself, and the urge had become quite strong. As I hurried toward the bathroom with as much propriety as possible, I saw two men seated at one of the back tables. One I would have referred to as a boy, because he couldn't have been more than about 21. His hair was longer than was generally accepted, and conspicuously styled, and he was speaking to his companion with such a pronounced lisp that it drew my eyes in their direction. He was telling some sort of amusing story to the man whose back was to me. When he reached his own punchline, the boy literally flapped both wrists and trilled out laughter.

That behavior, those actions, even the laughter, was so patently obvious that his tablemate glanced nervously around, embarrassed.

I couldn't believe it. Jon.

Now, I must admit I only had a passing glance, because the need of my bladder was quite pronounced. I didn't think Jon had seen me, so I darted into the bathroom and dealt with my business as quickly as possible. While I washed my hands, I had a images of strolling up to the table and saying, "Why, if it isn't my old friend Jon! Are you here to support the Germans from the west, or the east? Oh, and who's your handsome companion, please introduce us!"

Sadly, when I left the bathroom, their table was empty. I guess the only certainty I'll ever have is in my funny-bone.

After Germany I had another European adventure I would like to relate. Although it wasn't in any of the countries I've mentioned so far, I can't leave it out, because I did allude to it earlier in this writing.

Amsterdam had always struck me as a place that would be fascinating to visit. I'd heard it was freer and more relaxed than any other city in the world, and I'll say right now that indeed it was (and reportedly is).

I bid my aunt and uncle farewell, boarded a train, and made my way to the northern peninsula of Europe. While the tracks rolled away beneath me, I met my first Dutch nationals. Three boys (mid-twenties) were returning home from a visit to southern Europe, and in the spirit of their country, they were on their way to becoming quite inebriated. They insisted I join them in some beers.

In about a week, I would be leaving this continent to return to my relatively sober, normal life. Drinking too much beer with these affable strangers was just the diversion I was looking for.

By the time we arrived in Amsterdam, we were no longer strangers. As is the way with alcohol, we now knew each other well, and we entered the city as old friends.

"Will!" shouted one companion, a short, stocky boy of about twenty-four. He threw his arm out to the streets before us. "This is Amsterdam! The only thing better than the booze and grass is the women!"

"Or," said his taller, more sinewy companion, "the men!"

They all laughed as though this was nothing more than a passing amusement, but my ears had pricked. I hadn't noticed whether any of the them had been making advances toward me, but I was aware that they were quite physically affectionate with each other.

With little ado we made our way to a club the boys knew well, and in fact it was a place where they seemed to be well known. We chose a large table and sat around it, and while we continued our drinking binge, people often stopped by to greet them. "How was your trip to Cannes?" my friends were asked. "How long have you been back, have you seen (insert names of other acquaintances) yet?" and "Let us buy the next round!"

Our table was never quiet, except for one moment, and that I believe was only in my mind. my thoughts when a particular woman, probably about my age, floated gracefully into the club. She headed right for us as my friends called out, "Hettie!"

Hettie walked like a dancer, and as it turns out, that's exactly what she did for a living. She bent fluidly at the waist and spoke to one of my companions in affectionate, accentless English. "You've come back!" Before I could think *Is he her lover?* she turned to another and said much the same thing. "You're home."

My friends begged her to join us, and when she accepted, she stepped—glided?—to a gap next to me. A chair was moved to my side, and she sat as gracefully as if she had practiced the move her entire life.

Although it's possible there's no such thing as 'perfect' posture, I couldn't imagine the line of her neck, back, and shoulders as anything less than that. She wore a minimum of makeup, which wouldn't have been necessary, anyway. Her nose, cheekbones, and chin were an artist's rendition of beauty, and her long hair was pulled back to accentuate the classic lines of her face. Grayish blue eyes looked out at me   from under eyebrows plucked by God, but she only held my gaze for a moment at a time.

"What is your name?" she asked me, her voice a smoky octave below the youthful hubbub around us.

"William B. Carr."

She laughed demurely. "You're not going to tell me what the 'B' stands for? Your date of birth, rank, serial number?"

I'm not exactly the blushing type, but it happened to me then. "You can call me Will."

"And you can call me Hettie." She lifted a cigarette and held it distractedly, looking at her friends, and I produced a flame post-haste. When she had blown away her first draw of smoke, she asked, "How long have you known my friends?"

"I met them on the train, and they invited me to join them. Do you live here in Amsterdam?"

"At the moment, yes. I am presently working here."

"What is your work?"

One of my friends overheard this part of the conversation and leaned against me from behind, resting his chin on my shoulder. "She's a ballerina, chum. We Dutch love our ballerinas, don't we, Hettie?"

She smiled tolerantly at him, but nodded an affirmative to me.

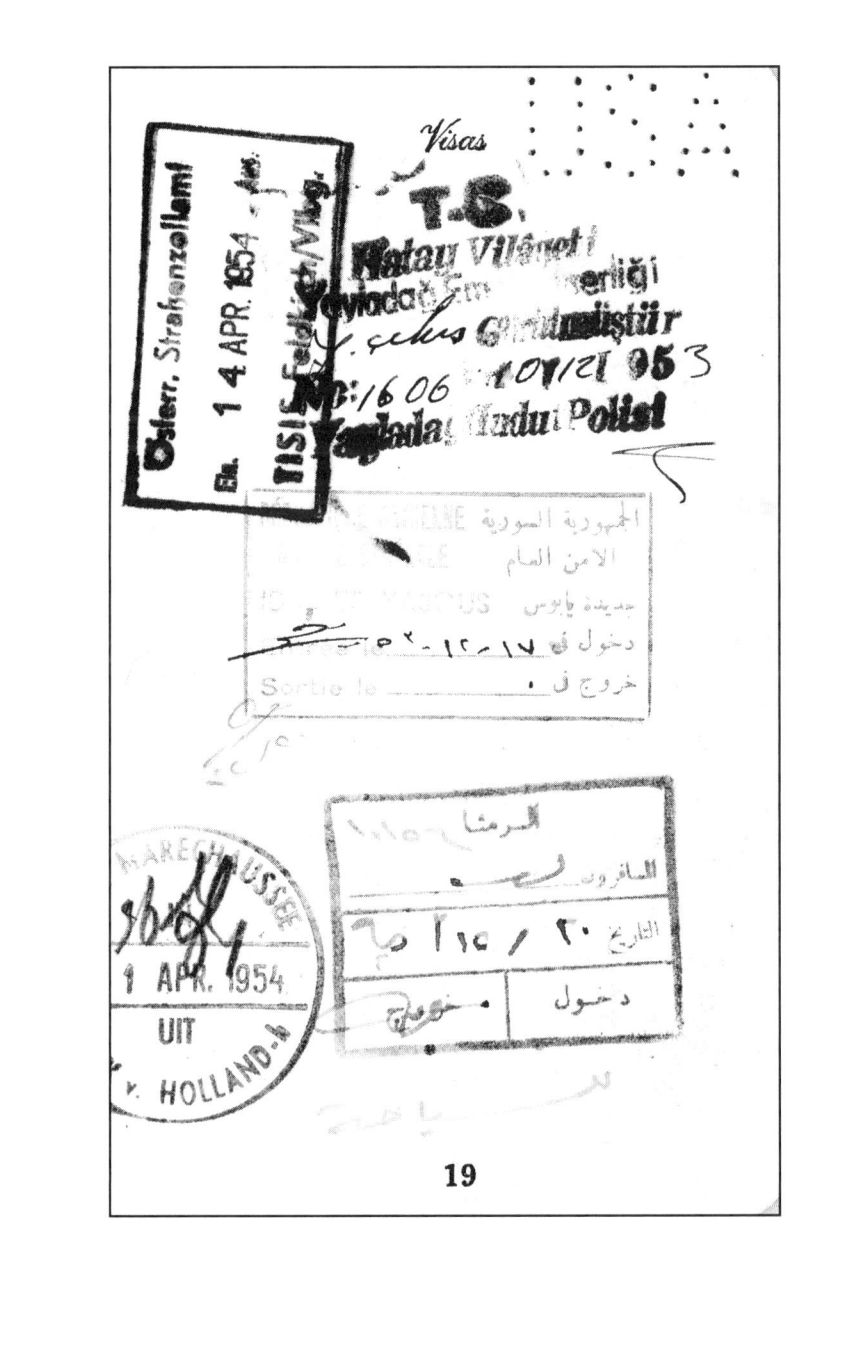

Visas

Österr. Straßenzollamt
Ek. 1 4 APR. 1954
TISIS Feldkirch/Vbg.

T.C.
Hatay Vilâyeti
Yayladağı... ...erliği
...çıkış Görülmüştür
No: 16 06 ...101/21 953
Yayladağı Hudut Polisi

الجمهورية السورية
الأمن العام
جديدة يابوس
دخول في ٢٠١٢/١٧
خروج في

RÉPUBLIQUE SYRIENNE
...
...T YABOUS
Entrée le
Sortie le

المرشا
الناقوت
التاريخ ٢٠ / ١٥ / ٢
دخول   خروج

MARECHAUSSEE
1 APR. 1954
UIT
V. HOLLAND-Ö

19

When the interrupter turned back to his own conversation, Hettie said to me, "I'm hungry. Are you hungry?"

"Yes!" Was I? Who cared! I asked, "Do you know of a good restaurant?"

"Do you have a car?"

I couldn't help but laugh. "Not just now."

"That is not a problem. I know of a place nearby."

When we walked out into the night she took my arm, and we cozily passed through the lights of the city and its canals. By the time we found the restaurant (I don't remember the meal at all) she had heard about my adventure, and seemed impressed. "What are your plans," she asked, "when you return to America?" Even the act of stirring her coffee seemed possessed by a ballerina's grace.

I answered her question, "It's open just now. My dream is to be an artist, but I suppose I'll get back into the advertising game, if I must."

"Hmm." She was holding my eyes for longer stretches, now, and gazed at me through the smoke rising from her cigarette. "A true artist who must work at something else for a living doesn't stop being a true artist."

Looking back at her with no shyness, I sat quietly for a long time, thinking about what she'd said. My eventual response was simply, "Thank you for that."

I paid for our meal and we left the restaurant. With intentions that only confused me, I meant to ask, 'Where to now?' but Hettie spoke first. "That group you're with, they'll take it as the highest insult if we don't return to them."

This woman's wish was my command. What I would have given for a video recording of my walk down the Amsterdam boulevard with such a classy, luminous lady! To have her at my side was fulfillment of a fantasy.

Back at the club, the boys were still deep in their cups, and some girls had joined them. When they saw us, one of them leapt to his feet and said, "You're right on time! The party's moving to my house!"

One of the girls asked him, "Will your mummy and daddy be expecting us?"

"They're off on a trip of their own. We'll have the place to ourselves."

I waited for Hettie's reaction, and she sensed that. She leaned close to my ear and whispered with hot breath, "Come along."

I followed like a cartoon character whose feet leave the ground, and he floats behind the girl who guides him with a finger under his chin.

The boy's house, or rather, his family home, was magnificent. In an Amsterdam suburb, two stories, huge. His bed was proportionately large.

Yes, the group of us, four men and four women, headed straight to his bedroom. There he had a bed the size of some of the rooms I'd stayed in while at youth hostels. All the flirting and foreplay must have occurred at the club; everyone fell across the bed and began undressing one another.

My exact thoughts of the moment are lost to me now, but I do remember a few symbols, including "??" and "!!"

As I've mentioned before, amorous tastes haven't changed much over the millennia. Throughout time, human beings have been heterosexual, homosexual, bisexual, and try-anything-sexual.

Well, I should say many human beings are that way—not all. Hettie intuited my hesitation, but gently pulled me down next to her and rid me of my pants and shirt. I kept my eyes on her as she then undressed herself, because she was the only person in that bed who attracted me. Somebody slid his/her hand into my underpants, but I felt no reaction, even holding Hettie's eyes with my own. That might have been the moment she stood and took my hand. "Let's go somewhere else."

Her body undressed was as superb as one might imagine. She was easily twenty-six years-old, but not a mar or mole on her skin, and the only fat was perfected in her breasts. Apparently she didn't want to take the time to find another bed; she headed for the nearest room that had a door, which happened to be our host's private bathroom. She closed the door behind us, locked it, and stared at the large, elaborate tub. With a seductive smile for me, she said, "This will have to do."

'Do' it did, and I did, too. For the first time in my life, at the age of twenty-seven, I lost my opposite-sex virginity. Was it lust? I don't think so; I believe it was the elusive, unusual, brief sort of love I've been trying to describe all along. Or, maybe I'm wrong. It could be that even the most devout homosexual can be seduced by a strikingly attractive member of the opposite sex. That can be mixed and applied to heterosexuals, as well, I'd guess.

In any case, I was as proud as an Arabian horse. Throughout the following days of my visit, which were spent in a blur of parties, drinks, and hash-pipes, I strutted around Amsterdam like I'd won the Kentucky Derby.

It felt surreal, when it came time for me to leave, to say goodbye to Hettie. We promised to write, but never did. Here's why: She had said, "I will wait for your letter, and as soon as I receive it, I will respond."

I'm the one who never did write to her.

These days, many of us have heard the term 'LTR,' for 'Long Term Relationship.' The numerous family members of the homosexual world needed a reference other than 'marriage,' because even at the time I'm writing this, for us to marry is only a barely acceptable concept. I guess it also helped that so many heterosexual couples also stopped leaping into that special commitment 'in the eyes of God,' so we have our new, appropriate label.

Hettie, like Rudy, was for me an 'STR.' Short-term, but a relationship nevertheless. I even had another of those, after I left Amsterdam. My ship would be sailing at the end of May, and as is true with Hettie, I can't know what more would have come from the enchanting days spent with Brian, had I been able to stay. I met him in London, and still remember him fondly. I imagine I might have settled with him, except that I never once entertained the possibility of living full-time outside the United States.

Also, ultimately, I still hadn't come to terms with the idea that a person might be able to call me a 'fag' and get away with it.

After a tearful goodbye to Brian on the British Isle, I had to return to Paris to make sure all my papers were in order for my ship's departure. From there, I would take a train to Le Havre, where I would board.

When I arrived at the ship's offices in Paris, I was informed the vessel had been experiencing difficulties with its motor, an was canceled. "We will find another ship to get you home, *Monsieur*, do not be concerned. One, perhaps two days."

They even put me up at a decent hotel, but I didn't spend much time in the room. All I could do was wander through the streets of Paris, a city I now saw through different eyes. With an inner voice, I said goodbye to the Seine, the parks, the great monuments…all the history and grandeur of the place.

The farewell extended to every land I had visited, but in Paris, which was where I'd had my first true experience of what lay 'overseas,' I sought some sort of closure. A final climax in the city of love. That craving created a disconcerting mix of loneliness, regret, elation, and hope.

Sitting in cafes, I watched the passersby, sipping wine or coffee and smoking cigarettes (the last being a habit I have long since abandoned). My mind had become my journal, because my musings at the time weren't the type meant to be openly shared. Although my odd mix of thoughts captivated me and moved me, they didn't exactly leave me feeling conflicted. Only curious and mildly distracted by that complex sense of loneliness.

One question I asked myself: "What sort of woman will I marry?" Another question: "Where will I find the right kind of man to satisfy my needs?" Watching the animated couples and friends flowing through their lives in the Parisian sunshine, I wished my wife or lover could be with me at that moment. "Whoever you are," I thought, "I'm ready. I'm here. Waiting. Wishing you were here too." It didn't matter whether it was the male or the female aspect of my desires. But how could that fact not have mattered?

As I write this now, a powerful epiphany strikes me.

I cared about my sexual orientation; of course it gave me pause, even cause for concern. But those concerns were never truly based on my sense of Self. It was always outside influences that created my opinion of who I should be, who I was expected to be, how it was determined I should behave. As a loving man, I cared about the feelings of those close to me, and would often respond to what I could see were their needs for me. However, please note I used the word 'often' in that sentence. Not always, not even usually. Just often.

Early in this writing I talked about asking, essentially, "Who am I?" It pleases me to have found the answer: "I am my own man."

Intriguing…. That statement gives me a powerful sense of closure with not only my father, but with my mother, too.

The question now is, "Am I Gay or straight?" If a label must be applied, and if forced to choose, I would say "Gay" because that's the term of the day, and my overall preference is for men. However, whenever the right woman came along at different times in my life, which did happen once or twice, I didn't hesitate to pursue my feelings for her. Therefore, I say again, "I am my own man."

Now to finish describing my last day in Paris. I heard from the ship service that a berth on an American line had been secured for me, and we would be departing early the following morning. I checked out of my hotel and left my bags at the station. My destination was a café—any café—on the famous *Saint Germaine de Pres*. There, I would while away my final hours in Paris.

Slowly, I walked the St. Germaine, that street where locals and visitors alike congregated at the famous cafes. I gave great attention to absorbing every detail. Many of the cafes tempted me, but something kept my feet moving until a guttural, strange-sounding bark of a call reached my ears. "Will!"

In those sharp-witted years of my twenties, my mind spoke before my eyes saw the source of the shout: "Bob!"

I peered forward and saw the burly, deaf artist from Rome, half-risen from his seat at a cafe. Again he growled out, "Will!", waving his arm for me to come to him.

The surge of emotion that washed over me caught me by surprise and spurred me to a fast approach. But I stopped, fifteen feet away from him, stunned by the look in his eyes. Desire. Need. Focus. Here was a man who gave me the impression that he more than saw me, he *noticed* me. He was fully standing now, and my intuition was flooded by a sense that I had read his expression correctly. He wanted me, very much.

The destiny of this meeting captivated me. Had Bob drawn me to this street, this cafe, by sheer strength of will? Might the fact of this man have been the deepest, fate-driven reason for my entire trip?

It seemed anything else I had experienced would suffer by comparison to this chance meeting.

There was no doubt my own magnetic interest was reflected on my face. Worried that I might behave foolishly, I tried to gather my thoughts, but those thoughts chose their own route and began undressing him, removing his clothes piece by piece. When he stood naked before me, his body appeared sculpted like Michelangelo's "David," only aged some fifteen years older than the model.

Surprisingly, none of this gave me an erection, but a small, significant spot had moistened my underwear. It was similar to the reactions I'd once had to fantasies of undressing my Father, having him hold me and hug me as close to him as two human beings can be, both naked and hard.

Strangely, although Bob's body was the focus of my fantasy, I never took notice of his large and growing penis. It was as if he was complete with nothing but his general masculine essence and his desire for me. My attention moved to the Mediterranean coloring of his strong, square, ruddy face and smooth, artist's hands. The wide, light-colored, striking, dancing eyes. A whole, enticing man, so much more than the brute physicality of his erectile tissues. It was all of Bob, the human being, that entranced me. Is this the difference between love and sex?

When I resurfaced into the moment of reality, I could see Bob had been contemplatively examining me, in return, while I paused frozen. When we both reawakened, he moved one of the chairs closer to him, energetically waving. I stepped closer, and both his arms lifted; *Come embrace me!*

Our chests met in a powerful hug, strong and fast, then we were seated and looking at each other. My intense happiness was reflected in his eyes. Bob moved with a physical desperation to communicate, speaking with his body instead of using the voice most of us take for granted. His thoughts came through his eyes, and from deep within his throat as he tried to force speech.

The sounds he made were the antithesis of anything musical, rather unpleasant on the ear, to be honest. But when he did speak aloud, it conveyed a song-like urgency of his attraction to me. I found it endearing, then sad, as it was necessary to tell him I would be rolling away on a train in a matter of hours.

He snatched up the tablet that lay next to him on the table and drew a line through the words that had informed the waiter of his order. Patiently, I waited for him to write what he had to say, and it was this: "I have a room nearby. Come with me?"

It couldn't have been more evident; both his meaning and my response. As we walked, without further communication, to his room, the click of destiny tickled my thoughts. Here would be my final climax. The coincidence of meeting him on this last day in Paris, and that we would make love, was the culmination of the ultimate adventure. There had been enough lonely nights throughout my trip, but they would all be minimized by this definitive closeness.

We mounted the stairs to his room, he pushed through the door, and turned to me. I could see he already had an erection, and with tender, loving care, I set it free.

Before Bob and I parted, he wrote me a note: "I will be in New York next week. When will you?"

He read my lips as I told him it would be about a week before my ship made it back.

He wrote, "Do you still have my address? My number?"

My grin answered that question, and forestalled the next; would I use it? I told him, "You'll be the second call I make. First, I'll need to tell my family I'm home."

Bob dropped his implements of speech and grasped my forearm in both his thick, paint-stained hands. "Don't forget," he said aloud.

I didn't.

Ahmed, Kassim, and I in Benghazi, Libya

Above Fez. I always gravitated to children.

Leptis Magna, ancient Roman city on the
Mediterranean. By this time, Anne's sweater
was getting pretty dirty and so was I.

The barber shop, Marrakech, Morocco.

After completing my trip, I visited my aunt and uncle in Bonn, West Germany. My Uncle Mario, His Excellency Mario de Pimental Brandäo was the Brazilian ambassador to West Germany.

20

The Final Chapter, So Far

Bob became my first LTR.

Our first meeting in the States was at a dinner with his parents. As soon as I was welcomed home by my family, I called as promised, and caught Bob and his family about to sit down to Sabbath dinner. "Come join us," his mother said on the phone. "Bob has already told us all about you."

I couldn't imagine what he might have said. We weren't able to interact much in Rome, and we'd only had a few hours in Paris. Yet when I arrived, Bob's mother greeted me fondly. I'll call her Mara, because in Hebrew that means 'bitter, sorrowful,' and oy, was she that, at least eventually. She sat me next to Bob, which placed me directly across from her chair, and proceeded to verify everything he'd told her. It seemed he'd memorized our two short conversations to the letter. Bob's father barely said six words throughout the entire meal.

Halfway through the dinner, Mara changed tactics. "Robert tells me you're an aspiring artist."

"It's something I aspire to, yes, but I'm also a realist. I'm going to have to find a job to support my art."

"So you're looking for work now?"

Bob gave me a nudge and when I turned to him, a wink. Smiling with him, but in confusion, I said, "I've only been back a little while, but I will be looking, yes."

Bob squeezed my leg under the table, then stroked it. I struggled to control both my expression and a potential physical reaction. Taking no apparent notice of this, Mara said, "Robert could use an assistant, and in our opinion, a young artist would be perfect."

Another squeeze, a more provocative stroke.

"He has," Mara continued, "his own apartment, and we've arranged things with regard to his inability to hear. Lights flash when the doorbell is pressed, that sort of thing. However, there's room for another, and it would help him so much if his assistant lived with him."

"What would be expected of his assistant?" I could have added,

'Aside from the occasional orgasm?'

"His assistant would handle telephone communication, of course, also arrange his appointments, keep track of his schedule, and whatnot. He does have a very nice apartment, on West 57th Street, and you wouldn't be expected to pay rent. He also has a maid. Are you interested in the job?"

I couldn't resist a glance at the sweetly-smiling Bob. "Definitely. I'm definitely interested."

A week later, we were living together.

Here I had found a man built like my father, but as affectionate as my mother. Unfortunately, he was also almost as crazy an artist as Van Gogh.

No, that's too rough. He was neurotic, true, but not crazy. Also, it's possible that most of his neurosis manifested through his disability, and remember in those days, it was even harder to live with being disabled than it is now.

Bob and I would go to movies, but if the actor's lips weren't visible while speaking, it was my job to let Bob know what was being said. It wasn't hard to do, at least not physically; I could simply mouth the words in the half-dark and Bob would read my lips. However, mentally, it was a challenge to stay abreast of the conversations and move my lips to them at the same time. Whenever I slipped in my duty, Bob would speak in that voice which he couldn't hear at all, but which was loud enough to transmit to the street outside the theater. "Will!" he would shout thickly, "You didn't finish telling me!" We'd be shushed all around, but of course Bob had no knowledge of this. "You don't even care if I know!" he would moan. "You're just watching it yourself!" It became trying, to say the least, and soon I began to beg off going to the movies with him.

My friends would invite us to parties, and everyone made a jovial effort to communicate with him, but he couldn't express his remarks as quickly as others. Always, he would end up sitting alone, in a corner, moping. More often than not, after a few hours of this, he would call out to me (whether I stood near or far from him), "Will, I want to go hoooome!"

I would like to qualify the problems in this mixed-ability relationship by saying perhaps a man not as naturally social as myself would be better suited for someone like Bob. I love nurturing, but

I do believe there's a difference between being needed and being suffocated. When my friends began avoiding contact with me, specifically because of Bob, I decided it was time for a talk.

How do such talks begin? They vary, of course, but the subject stays the same. I first said something like, "I'm not sure if I can continue living with you in this apartment."

The voice, mournful and plaintive, "Why not? What's wrong? Don't you love me?"

"I do!" I really did, too. I simply couldn't live with him anymore. That fact didn't make my love for him simply disappear, although it soon followed that I couldn't continue to be his lover anymore, either.

"But you *don't* love me!" he countered. He stormed out of the apartment, and a half hour later, the phone rang. It was his mother, Mara.

"Robert tells me you want to move out of the apartment. That you don't want to work for him anymore. That you no longer want"—(I swear, there was no hesitation when she said the next)—"to be his lover."

When I regained my equilibrium I replied, "I'm so sorry, but it's true. Bob and I have enough natural difficulties in our relationship that we need to try harder, but he doesn't seem to be making any effort at all."

"You have no idea. No idea whatsoever how difficult it is to be deaf. I do know, because I have gone through it with my son throughout his entire life, every step of the way."

I couldn't disagree, but her point wasn't clear to me. "Mara, if our relationship isn't working, I can't be with him anymore."

As if she hadn't heard me, she continued, "What more effort does he need to make than paying all your bills for you? Keeping a roof over your head, and food in your stomach?"

"Kindness and decency are as important to me as food and shelter."

"What about respect? Is that important to you?"

"Excuse me? I have never treated Bob with anything less than complete respect!" It was not something I could say so easily about his behavior toward me.

Bless his heart; I could hear Bob in the background expressing much of my voiced sentiment to his mother. His harsh voice growled out, "Respects me!"

A moment of silence, during which Mara must have been signing or mouthing something to her son. Then, "I'm speaking of the respect your family has for you."

"Why would my finding a different job have any impact on my family's respect for me?"

"Because if you *do* dare to leave Robert, they will be the first to learn exactly why."

In a moment of absolute confusion, I asked, "What do you mean?"

"The only reason you're leaving is because you've fallen out of love with him."

Here I should mention that in the beginning of my relationship with Bob, our parents had met, and had developed a type of friendship that was popular in the fifties: bridge buddies. Bob's parents had gotten together with mine, fairly regularly, for games of bridge, and Bob's mother had become quite chummy with mine.

Now Mara burst through my stunned silence by continuing, "Your mother would be quite interested to learn the details about your relationship with my son." A wicked little laugh crept from her as she added, "Oh, and what will your father think?"

Mother would be enough of a challenge, but I knew she loved me. I assumed she would always love me, through best or worst, rough and easy times. But Father? Because I always suspected he never actually loved me, all I'd ever had left to hope for was his respect.

Mara knew me too well. The reason could have been because Bob had been reporting to her every nuance of every conversation he and I ever had.

"Mara," I finally managed to whisper, "please don't."

"That's all Robert is asking of you, Will. Please don't. Don't leave him."

The line went dead.

That night I roamed the streets and coffee shops of New York, thinking. The situation with Bob had become intolerable, but wouldn't it be worse to become an outcast from my own family?

Would I become an outcast? Was it possible they could accept me as I was?

Should I allow the behaviors and expectations of others to define me?

When I returned to the apartment, I found Bob seated in his chair beneath a portrait of me. He had painted the portrait during our first month together, and had captured the love I had for him in my eyes. He really was a talented artist.

I sat across from him. "Bob, you must know I love you."

He turned his head away, at that moment pouting more as communication than as reaction. When he faced me again to watch my lips, I continued.

"It's true, and you know it. You can feel it in your heart. You must also be able to feel how impossible it is for me to stay here with you. To be with you."

"You don't want to be with me!"

"To tell you the truth, there's nothing that gives me more pleasure than making love to you. But to be with you, in this relationship, it's tearing me apart. None of my friends want to spend time with me anymore. And the studio is yours; my little corner of it is meaningless."

"Can't work with you!"

"Exactly. Since you can't work while I'm in there, and you work so much, when can I find time to paint?" I slid from my chair and knelt in front of him. "We as a couple means all your needs are met, while all of mine are ignored."

In the way of those bizarre passions that erupt during a break-up, my last statement infuriated Bob. He leapt to his feet, pushed me back roughly, and began to stomp around the room. With his solid, angry bulk, it seemed he could have walked through a wall, if one happened to be in his path. "You don't love meee! Why don't you love meee?"

"I *do*, that's what I'm trying to tell you! But I love myself, too! Can't you understand?"

"NO!" He stormed out again, I assumed to return to his mother, slamming the door hard enough to crack the frame.

Quietly, tearfully, I gathered my things, and left to return to my own parents. By the time I arrived, my mother was waiting for me. She said, "I've just had the strangest telephone call from Mara."

Yes, the bitter mother who'd spent thirty-some years of her son's life suffering with him, and for him…. She had followed through on her threat. Either she had no idea how that action would cement my decision, or she sensed the finality of the break-up, and this was her revenge.

Tough luck for Mara; Mother was understanding. She and I spent a long evening that night, first over tea, then over cocktails, discussing my predilection. I don't know where Father was at the moment, but Mother said, "As far as I'm concerned, he'll never know."

"The four of you won't be able to play bridge anymore. Won't he wonder why?"

Mother waved this away with a flutter of her fingers. "I was polite to Mara on the phone, but seething inside. This felt to be exactly as you've described it. An attempt to sabotage your character, even though it is true."

"It didn't work, did it? I mean, do you still respect me, despite who I am?"

Maybe I had become accustomed to reading eyes as well as Bob read lips; Mother didn't need to answer, but she did. "I'll always love you, and I respect you, too. Come here." She patted the couch next to her, and I sat there. With her elegant fingers, she brushed my hair back from my forehead. "You're my son, and I will love you forever. Nothing can change that." She dropped her hand and gazed into her glass, now empty of liquor, but still misty from ice. "However, if your father finds out about this, you and I would have to meet in secret." Some inner witticism caused her to laugh softly, and she hid it with the back of her hand.

I asked her, "Do you really think he'd disown me?"

"To be honest, I can't say for certain. He'd probably be more inclined to embarrassment than any kind of…disgust." I guessed her following explanation was what had caused her soft laugh; this is the time she told me about his college days, and the artistic roommate he'd had.

Leaning back on the couch, I stared up at the ceiling and said,

"I'll be looking for work again, now."

"You know you can stay here as long as you like."

"Yes, and thank you. But I have enough savings that I can take another apartment in the Village, and there are plenty of jobs in the city."

A long, deep sigh from my mother caused me to look at her again. She was staring at me with eyes that were wet, but still loving. "You've always been such a sensitive boy. Did I mother you too much?"

"I don't think that has anything to do with it."

"I'd like to find out." She handed me her glass, and as I went to pour her another drink, she said, "I'm going to learn as much as I can about this 'homosexuality.'"

I brought back her fresh cocktail, but set it on the table next to her, took her in my arms, and hugged her for a long time.

It was just as well I didn't stay long in my parents' house. Bob called there constantly, grunting out monologues until he guessed either I had answered, or my mother must have passed the phone to me. Then he would begin his litany of, "Why don't you love me? Why did you leave me?" It was fortunate for me that Father was usually working or cavorting, and not often inclined to answer the phone while at home, anyway.

It only took me a few days to find another apartment, and as I'd planned, I was in Greenwich Village again. In his sadness over our parting, Bob was able to find me, and I'm somewhat ashamed to admit I ran away—off to the slopes. I needed free gliding down a mountain, the closed-off but wide-open feeling of wearing thick clothes and a hat and heavy boots while moving at dangerously fast speeds.

When I returned from my ski trip, I pulled up in front of my apartment and saw the nose of Bob's car parked around the corner. A quick look at my apartment window showed a light I hadn't left on. I ran to the stoop and up the steps, flung open my door, and found Bob rushing toward me with a sharp letter-opener in his hand.

When my life flashed before my eyes, it must be clear by now that even at my tender young age, I had plenty to see.

A shout burst from me. I don't know what it sounded like, perhaps a composite of shock and angst. I didn't feel angry—as I've said, my love for him hadn't simply disappeared. I believe it was that love he saw in my eyes, rather than fear or anger, and that's what stopped him before he reached me.

Spreading my arms, I said, "You know I love you."

Was it really love that stopped him from stabbing me? There is another aspect: Bob, though emotionally battered by the harsh realities of his handicap (and possibly spiritually tattered by his mother's domineering devotion), was not the murderous type. But he loved me too, so I prefer to think love is what saved my life.

Nevertheless, the rage of the moment hadn't left him. He spun around and strode to a fabulous oil painting he had created of me, a second one, done later in our relationship.

At the top of his formidable lungs, Bob hollered, "You DON'T love meee!" and began to slash. I sidled to the phone and called the police, thinking as much in terms of help for Bob as for myself. The officer I spoke with told me my neighbors had already called, and a squad car was on the way.

They arrived quickly, but the portrait—Bob's catharsis—hung in ribbons. While he was being handcuffed, he cried to me again and again, "Why did you leeeave meee? You don't love meee!"

Of the two policemen, only one of them acted disgusted by this spectacle of a homosexual relationship. That officer gave a rough jerk to Bob's arm. "I said come *on*. Let's go!"

I told him, "He's deaf! Could you be a little more gentle?"

Bob began to hurl out his pitiful laments again. The angry officer snarled to me, "You sure he's not blind, too? Doesn't he know you're another fellow?"

Pointing to the sliced painting, I said, "He can't be blind. He's an artist." When I spoke that last, my voice broke.

Angry Officer's lip curled up in a stronger grimace of contempt. "Oh, one of *those* types. And what are you, a ballerina?"

The more polite officer said to his partner, referring to me, "Leave that boy alone. He's been through enough tonight." Then he took Bob's arm in a firm but less aggressive grip.

I watched them pull my ex-lover away, wondering which style

of attitude would win out in the approaching decades. Looks like the good guys are ahead by a nose. For myself and possibly many others, I would like to thank all the thoroughly heterosexuals on the planet who have allowed us to be as we are, which is only human.

Mara had her son out on bail in no time, of course. She called me and although her tone was not civil, mine was. I answered her abrupt question; "No. I definitely do not want to press charges against him. But I will." Before she could unleash her venomous tongue I added, "I will, but only if it ever happens again."

The experience worked some sort of necessary magic on Bob; when I saw him next, months later, I invited him to join me for coffee. We sat and talked, and he told me all he wanted from me anymore was friendship. We remained friends until I moved to the west coast.

One final incident, with regard to my Mediterranean trip, occurred before I left for California. I came home from work (a new job, back in advertising) and found an adorable young man sitting on my stoop. He stood and said, "I promised you, didn't I? You didn't believe me."

"Thomas!" The sweet Greek, Thomas Erasmus, the boy who had fallen in love with me in Athens. "You're really, truly here!" We embraced, and I led him into my apartment.

All smiles, Thomas said again, "You didn't believe me, did you?"

He sat at my kitchen table while I busied myself with coffee. "You have a strong character," I told him, "and although I wasn't certain, I can't say I'm quite surprised."

"I still love you, you know."

I turned from where I stood at the counter and smiled at him. "There's love in my heart for you, too." It wasn't the same sort of love, and I hoped he could read that in my voice. "How long are you in town? Where are you staying?" I didn't come out and ask, but I couldn't stop wondering, *What do you expect from this visit?*

Thomas, ever the young gentleman, said, "What is sad is that I can only see you this afternoon, then I must return to my lover."

Aha. "You've found a lover! That's terrific!"

"Yes, he is a wealthy shipping magnate, he takes good care of me. When he said he was coming to New York, I told him I have always wanted to see this place."

"How did you find me?"

"The phone book."

"Of course." I sat down with our coffee. "Thomas, tell me about your life since 1953."

We spent the following hours sharing the details of the lives we'd led since our last meeting, and the lives we were moving toward. He thought California sounded like a charming place to live, but sadly noted that his benefactor only worked with east coast shipping in the States. When he asked what I would be doing in the west, and I replied that I planned to teach, I caught a hint of regret in his eyes. Even if I returned the style of love he felt for me, I could never afford to take care of him as well as the shipping magnate could.

When we parted, we didn't bother to exchange addresses. We knew we had seen the last of one another. However, here's one more message to Thomas: Thank you for your steady love. It enriched my life.

My sister Anne was living in California with her husband by the time I moved there in the sixties. California in the sixties, such a nice, open-minded land.

The man Anne had married was the man my parents had sent her to Europe to avoid, back in late 1952. Although David was from a perfectly acceptable family, and was a fine, intelligent, and eventually successful man in his own right, remember that he was Catholic. Because Anne had successfully married him (they remain married today) despite my parents' protests, and had moved with him to what was then called 'the land of fruits and nuts,' I felt that I would prefer to be near her rather than my parents. David was teaching at a university by the time I moved there, and Anne was raising their children. I found my own niche as a high school guidance counselor and teacher, and spent decades in those endlessly valuable professions.

At one point during those decades, I married. Really. A Rabbi, a woman, everything.

Here's how that happened: First, I was sitting with Anne one evening in the early 1970s, wondering if I could ever come out of the closet to her. She lived in the Gay mecca of the Bay Area, after all, and I know she had even occasionally gone to Gay bars with her husband and their acquaintances. She had never seemed to take notice, certainly not in any sort of negative way, of any male 'friends' I had introduced her to. Not once did I ever feel that vibe or energy Gay people can sense, when heterosexuals are uncomfortable or disapproving of them. She and her husband were both, to use the terms of the day, groovy and laid back.

I began our conversation by asking my sister, "Do you remember Antonio, from Rome?"

"Of course I do. How could I forget him?"

Laughing, I said, "Yes, the one man on the planet who actually refused your advances."

"Why do you bring him up, Will?"

"I've been thinking of him, that's all."

"You two really enjoyed your time together, didn't you?"

One of my rare blushes appeared, and Anne peered at me closely. She had noticed that although I had occasionally spoken of women while in California, she hadn't ever seen me enter into a relationship with any of them. She hadn't ever questioned it, though—she's another of the people I can thank for allowing a Gay person to be who he is. No problem, no bad attitude about it; if it wasn't her husband it wasn't her business.

Now she said, as if out of the blue, "Father has been wondering why you never date anyone." I knew she was referring specifically to females.

"I'm thousands of miles away from Father. How would he know who I date?"

"Mother gossips to him about everything I write to her. Father wonders why you never think of getting married. The fact that you're not settling down is killing him."

She spoke with authority, and she would know. It wouldn't have surprised me to learn he often confided in her. I asked Anne, "Have you and he talked about me?"

"Not directly, but I know what he meant. Will, do you think you'd prefer to never marry…a woman?"

The answer I could have automatically blurted didn't emerge. Even in the 1970s, I didn't think I'd prefer to *never* marry a woman.

I came to learn that my continually single status had become quite an issue for Father. If I'd given it much thought I would have known already. Because it never seemed particularly relevant, I haven't mentioned this yet, but before my own trip to Europe my parents had been trying to arrange a marriage for me. The girl and I dutifully dated, and she did fall in love with me, but I had felt no similar feelings for her. After my return from the Mediterranean, I had introduced her to Bob, and could tell she understood what had happened. Obviously Mother understood soon enough, too, but Father had always been in the dark.

After my conversation with Anne in 1970, Mother began writing to me about how worried Father had become. She even mentioned his regrets that although he'd believed throughout my childhood that I would become a doctor, I had let him down on that. Now this? Would his only son, who had decidedly *not* become a doctor, not even give him grandchildren?

Around the time when that pressure began getting heavy, I met Naomi.

Naomi, a few years younger than I, was a nice, cultured Jewish woman. As soon as we met I could tell she was attracted to me, and I knew my father would love her. I think the part of me that honored him is what gave in and asked her on a date, but it might have been more than that. There's an aspect of the Jewish faith that isn't unlike other religions, or even like royalty: A man with a name but no wealth must marry a woman with wealth who seeks a special name. Or, a man with wealth but no specialness connected to his name must be captured by a woman with a name who sought wealth for her family. In cases like mine, where I wasn't wealthy and didn't have a particularly important name, a woman like Naomi would be, well, priceless.

Anne couldn't wait to write to Mother and Father about her. Mother called me right away and said, "The lady you're seeing is from a very well-to-do, respectable family. They own one of the largest department stores in New York! Naomi herself, she graduated from Radcliffe!"

She knew more about my girlfriend than I did. I asked, "Where did you get all this information?"

"A mother has her ways." She lowered her voice to a conspiratorial whisper, although I was certain my father wasn't anywhere near the house. "Will, you once told me that your love is for other men. I don't want to know how many you've…seen in your life, but it seems to me you're always single. Are you sure your life would be best spent with a man? It wasn't exactly a walk in the park while you were with Bob, remember."

Something in her tone made me wonder if the reading she'd done on homosexuality, after our conversation nearly twenty years before, had led her to nothing but psychiatry books.

She was right, though; in twenty years I might have dated about ten men, none longer than a few months. Aside from them, I might have had three especially brief flings. I was feeling as lonely as I often had during my distant travels.

Mother asked, "Could this woman Naomi fall in love with you?"

It didn't take me long to think that one over. "You know, I think she could."

Mother tossed out the big guns and went for the cannon: "Son, this would make your father the happiest man alive."

What can I say? I don't think Father ever forgave me for bowing out of the marriage he had hoped for me all those years ago, before my trip. That I preferred art over medicine never stopped rankling him. And my mother, she had counterbalanced all that and made up for his never-changing non-affection with an endless, doubtless love. This was something they both wanted, and in their own ways, they deserved it.

Naomi and I married. She loved me well, I knew that, because her strong personality was what had led the way to my proposal. And I loved her, not only because she was a fine woman deserving of my love, but because she had helped me provide something my father had always desired of me.

But didn't I still prefer men, despite everything? How could that be if I had become a husband to a woman? She had two children from a previous marriage, a son and daughter, which meant I suddenly had a complete family. How could I be fully homosexual if I could make love to my wife? All of that is what I continued telling myself while in my forties.

Naomi and I did indeed make love. Although the love was there, our relationship lacked the romance I've always craved in my life.

Ultimately the marriage was, for Naomi, physically unfulfilling. The same was true for me, on a more emotional level. We only lasted five years. However it was during that time that I gained my architectural experience: I designed a home. With Naomi's financing, it was built, too, and can still be seen on the coast of California.

Am I fully a member of the Gay culture, even at this time? That's hard to answer. Labels, these labels are disconcerting. A couple of times in this book, I talked about what psychiatrists might have said to me, yet when I think about it, it seems the biggest issue that would cause a person to seek a shrink would be self-ignorance. Although I do know myself, it's still too difficult to apply something as shallow as a label to something as complex as a human being. What I know about myself is that my preference may be for men, but I have been truly passionate about certain women. I am a loving lover. If I had ever found the woman who balanced my personality just so, and if she'd had no issues with my occasional need for male-with-male sexuality, I believe I could have lived comfortably within society's demands. I never found such a woman.

Besides, did I ever *want* to live within society's demands? Would that have been best for the man I am?

What feels best right now is the discovery that I am my own man, and I am content with that.

*   *   *

The following thirty-some years of my life could fill another volume, but it feels unnecessary to speak of it all; it could be a life that many homosexual men would be too familiar with. I did finally share a 17-year relationship with a man, and we remain close to this day. Once, I made love to a man who was HIV positive, and yes, I contracted the disease. (Although it's sometimes like existing beneath a sky of endlessly overcast weather, I'm living well with it.)

I've had a few pets, adored and adoring, and currently, my four-legged companion and lover is AJ, a fifteen-pound bundle of energy. He came to the United States from a puppy farm in Mexico. Yes, he is an illegal immigrant, but please don't tell the Immigration Service. The vet believes he is part long-haired chihuahua, part cocker spaniel, and part dachshund. His front legs are double jointed and when he is still, his feet point out like a ballerina. Like me, he loves Chinese food, particularly the fortune cookies.

One day I presented him with three fortune cookies, asking him to tell my fortune by picking one. Of course he wanted them all at first, but I insisted he choose. Inside the cookie he chose was the following message: "Stop searching forever. Happiness is right next to you." To make sure I understood, he pressed his head against my thigh. From that day on, I began to understand that there is a point in one's life when one has to stop searching forever for what it is that fulfills one's ultimate happiness. Take notice of what one has and be content with that. I have so much. Besides AJ, I have a loving family close by, many accepting and close friends, a great team of health providers, good health, enough money to eat well and pay my bills, and a sustaining, positive attitude towards aging, recognizing its rewards after living a rich life.

Despite my inherent sociable personality, I've been pleased to discover I'm quite comfortable living alone with AJ. Over the decades, I have learned that it is possible to live a full life while predominantly single. The trick is to discover the true pleasure of it, its beauty and its benefits. Yes, a loving life partner could have enhanced these pleasures if I had been fortunate to find one, but it could also destroy the pleasures of self-discovery. A mate could have expanded my life, but I am the only one who can expand myself.

I do still date, although age and being HIV-positive discourages any interest in seeking me out. There is a site on the Internet called SilverDaddies that describes itself as "a meeting place for mature men and other men (both daddies and younger) who are interested in keeping their daddy happy and/or sexually satisfied. The site offers the possibility of having a personal ad and also features galleries (changes daily) and a chat—and it's free." I enjoy and use it more for entertainment and to satisfy my curiosity as to what is out there in the gay world rather than any expectation that I might find a suitable partner.

I have an occasional date but I am very selective and cautious and very up-front about being HIV-positive to anyone who shows interest. As I've learned, my age and HIV status discourages most men who might otherwise be interested. I do have a long term special relationship with someone I met on the Internet. Unfortunately he lives in Mexico. Our visits are too infrequent, but sweeter because of the distance between us. I will shamelessly admit that I never needed to use any enhancement drugs. He refers to me as Tarzan and Superman when it comes to sex. Since he is thirty-nine I take that as a rare compliment for someone my age.

Now that I have reached my eighty-first birthday, still well put-together, enjoying the blessings that come my way, how am I different from the young man who had fire in his eyes and ready to undertake the challenges that took place so many years ago? No longer do I feel I have to participate in the madness that surrounds me. "I've seen that, I've done that," I hear myself saying many times. Now it's the little things that make life a happy and worthwhile adventure, nothing earth shattering. Life is indeed rushing by, but at a slower pace, if that's possible. There is time for observation rather than activism.

Just the other day, AJ, my dog, was resting his head on my thigh while I was watching TV. Suddenly he started whimpering and making strange noises and going to the door to be let out to my small garden in back of the house. Reluctantly I followed him to my fig tree where a small bird was caught in the net protecting the ripe figs from being eaten by the bird. AJ pointed with his nose at the bird, struggling in pain, and looked at me, pleading with me to do something. I, of course, could not hear the bird crying in pain, but he could. I cut the bird loose, and it flew away. It's a small happening, but it is big in my life now. I saved a life, thanks to my best friend. That's worth a lot.

Reading in the morning papers that Peet's Coffee House is opening a branch within a short walk from where I live, is a small happening, but big in my life now. So if you are passing by and see a rather handsome, elderly, mustached gentleman reading his morning paper while sipping coffee with a small beige dog at his feet, waiting to be fussed over and eager to say hello, join me for a cup and we'll talk about growing older gracefully.

So now, it feels that I've *truly* done it all. Oh, except for having children. Sorry, Father (may your soul rest in peace). I really did try my best. But, while I have your attention, there's something I've been meaning to say: Thank you. Your treatment of me gave me a sharp awareness that loving affection is not commonplace. That understanding is probably what originally spurred me to take my trip so many years ago, and in fact it has sweetened all my life's journeys.

Looks like I've found a point to all this, a reason for officially describing the awakenings I experienced fifty-plus years ago: Never ignore an urge to cross boundaries in your life, because after all, they're everywhere.

END

NOTE: This book is a blend of an artist's vision and an author's dexterity. Words supplied by Will Carr through journals, emails, interviews, and conversations have sometimes been directly inserted, other times extrapolated and arranged by Rebecca George. The result is a true account.

TITLE	AUTHOR	Type of Literature	
9th Man, The	Dorien Grey	Novel (Detective)	Also e-book
A Time To Live	Jim Brogan	Novel	Also e-book
Bar Watcher, The	Dorien Grey	Novel (Detective)	Also e-book
Between Trash and Tramp	Byrd Roberts	Novel	Also e-book
Bi Ranchers Bi Mates	Bill Lee	Novel (Bisexual)	Also e-book
Blasphemy	Roger N. Taber	Novel	Also e-book
Bless the Thugz and Lil' Chil'runs	Fredryk Traynor	Novel	Also e-book
Blood Warm	Robert Burdette Sweet	Novel	Also e-book
Bottle Ghosts, The	Dorien Grey	Novel (Detective)	Also e-book
Boys In Shorts	Chris Kent	Short Stories	Also e-book
Boys of Swithins Hall	Chris Kent	Novel	Also e-book
Boys Will Be Boys: Two Novellas	Chris Kent	Two Novellas	Also e-book
Brass Pony: Two Novellas	Marsh Cassady	Two Novellas	Also e-book
Bravehearts and Memories: Two Novellas	Chris Kent	Two Novellas	Also e-book
Breviary of Torment, A	Thomas Cashet	Poetry	Also e-book
Bunny Book, The	John D'Hondt	Novel	Also e-book
Butcher's Son, The	Dorien Grey	Novel (Detective)	Also e-book
Commonwealth Chronicles	Byrd Roberts	Short Stories	Also e-book
Country Rogues	Bill Lee, Ed.	Short Stories	Also e-book
Crossing Borders	Will Carr	Non-fiction historical travelogue	Also e-book
Dancing on the Barricades	John Coriolan	Novel	Also e-book
Devil in Men's Dreams	Tom Scott	Short Stories	Also e-book
Different Slopes	Bill Lee	Bisexual Novel	Also e-book
Different Voices: Novella and Short Stories	Walter Febick	Novella and Short Stories	SS e-book Nov e-book
Dirt Peddler, The	Dorien Grey	Novel (Detective)	Also e-book
Duskouri Tales, The	Byrd Roberts	Short Stories	Also e-book
Familia Affair	Rod Palmer	Novel	Also e-book
Gay Warrior	Jim Fickey, Gary Grimm	Non-fiction (Psych)	Also e-book
Good Cop, The	Dorien Grey	Novel (Detective)	Also e-book
Good Night, Paul	Robert Peters	Poetry	Also e-book
Guilty As Charged	Jay Hatheway	Non-fiction	Also e-book

TITLE	AUTHOR	Type of Literature	
Hardball for Billy Budd	Richard Gann	Novel	Also e-book
Hired Man, The	Dorien Grey	Novel (Detective)	Also e-book
Homo Erectus	Edward Proffitt	Poetry	Also e-book
Homoaffectionalism: From Gilgamesh to the Present	Paul D. Hardman	Non-fiction (History)	Also e-book
Homonym	Edward DeBonis	Poetry	Also e-book
Homophile Studies in Theory and Practice	W. Dorr Legg, Ed.	Non-fiction (History)	Also e-book
House of Broken Dreams	Byrd Roberts	Novel	Also e-book
In the Steps of Mister Proust	Stanley E. Ely	Novel	Also e-book
Island Mambo	Robert Burdette Sweet	Novel	Also e-book
The King's Assassin	Robert Burdette Sweet	Historical Novel	Also e-book
Kings and Beggars	Paul Genega	Poetry	Also e-book
Man In Shadow	Russell Thomas	Novel	Also e-book
(Ninth Man, The) The 9th Man	Dorien Grey	Novel (Detective)	Also e-book
North American Lexicon of Transgender Terms	Raven Usher	Dictionary	
Paper Mirror, The	Dorien Grey	Novel (Detective)	Also e-book
Popsicle Tree, The	Dorien Grey	Novel (Detective)	Also e-book
Rabbit's Leap	James Hagerty	Novel	Also e-book
Ram Stam Boys, The	Chris Kent	Novel	Also e-book
Real Tom Brown's School Days, The	Chris Kent	Novel	Also e-book
Rogues of San Francisco	Bill Lee, Ed.	Short Stories	Also e-book
Rogues To Remember	Bill Lee	Short Stories	Also e-book
Role Players, The	Dorien Grey	Novel (Detective)	Also e-book
Saint of Sodomy, The	William Tarvin	Fiction and Verse	Also e-book Also e-book
Sea and Stones	T. R. McKague	Novel	Also e-book
Secret Buddies	Mike Newman	Novel	Also e-book
Sensuous Mates: Two Novellas	Bill Lee	Two Novellas	Also e-book
Sex and the Single Camel	Phil Clendenen	Novel	Also e-book
Snapshots for a Serial Killer (Fiction)	Robert Peters	Novella	Also e-book
Snapshots for a Serial Killer (Play)	Robert Peters	Play	Also e-book
Soft Slow Motion	Dixie Schnell	Poetry	Also e-book
Subway Stops	Abnorman	Poetry	Also e-book
Summer Club and the Creatures	James A. Richards	Novel	Also e-book
Tales From C.A.M.P.: Jackie's Back!	Victor J. Banis	3 Novels	Also e-book
Toward the Beginning	Veronica Cas	Lesbian Novel	Also e-book
Unruly Angels	Ronald Nevans	Novel	Also e-book
Weigh-In, The	Winthrop Smith	Poetry	Also e-book